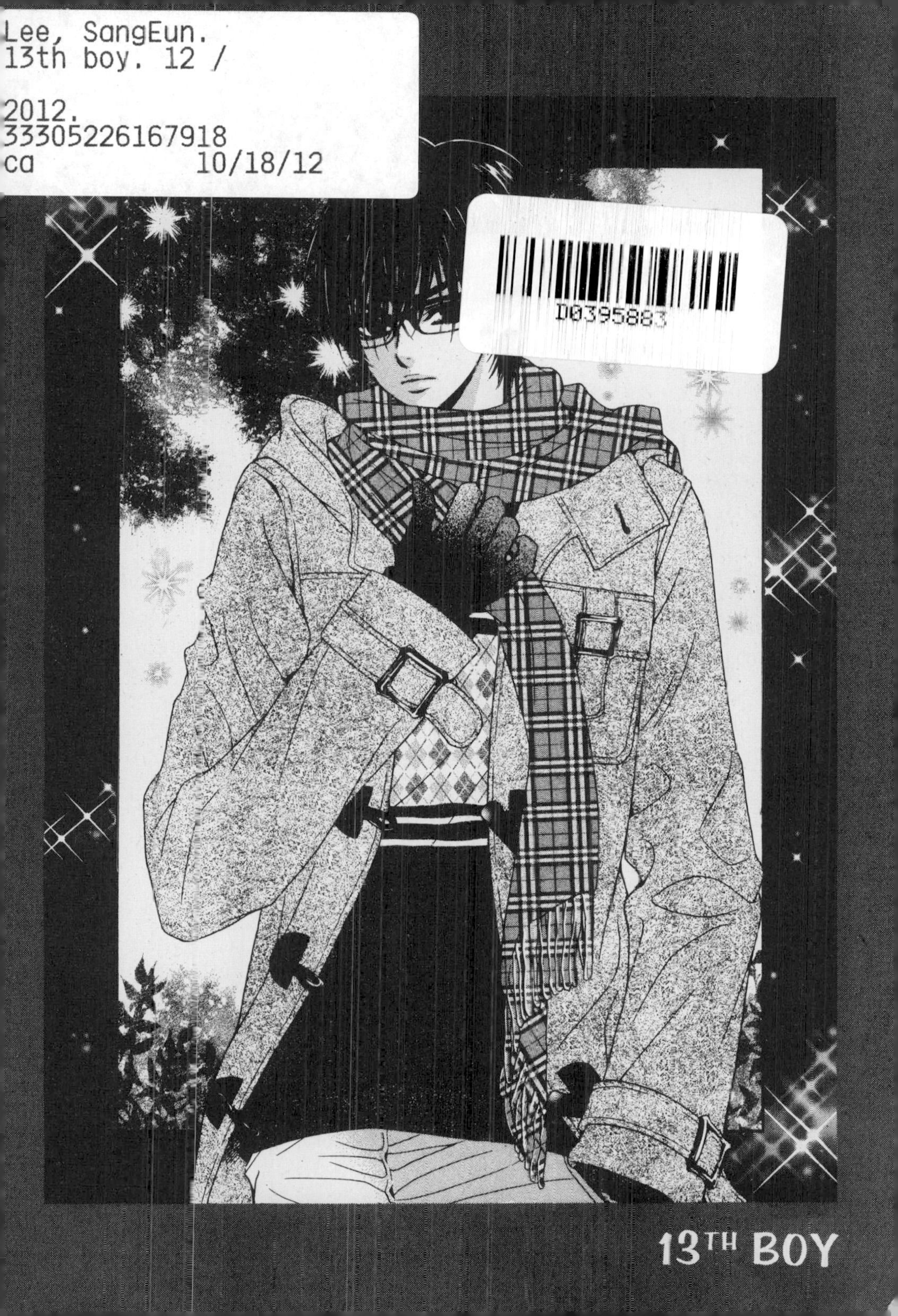

13TH BOY

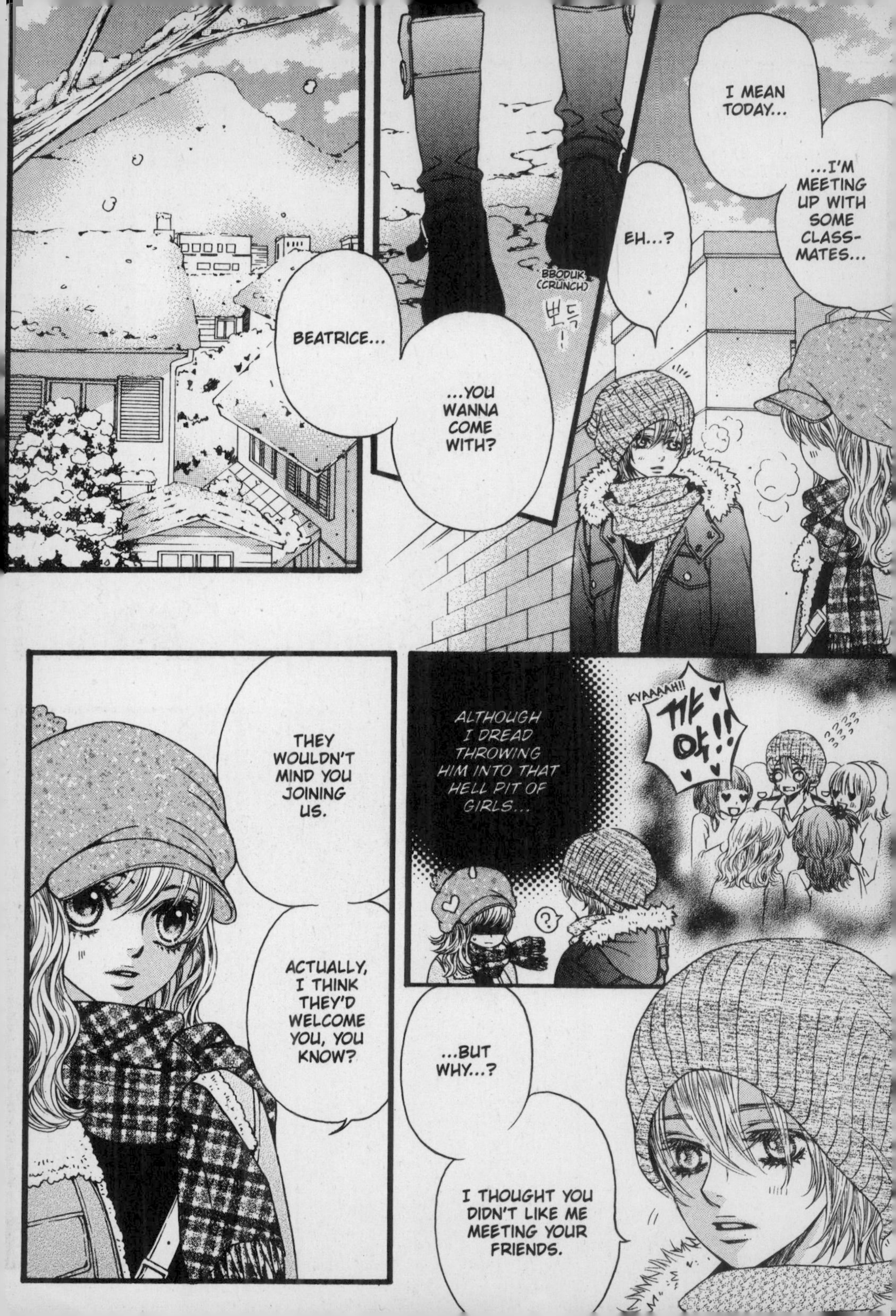
BEATRICE...
...YOU WANNA COME WITH?
BBODUK (CRUNCH)
뽀득
EH...?
I MEAN TODAY...
...I'M MEETING UP WITH SOME CLASSMATES...
THEY WOULDN'T MIND YOU JOINING US.
ACTUALLY, I THINK THEY'D WELCOME YOU, YOU KNOW?
ALTHOUGH I DREAD THROWING HIM INTO THAT HELL PIT OF GIRLS...
KYAAAAH!!
꺄아!!
...BUT WHY...?
I THOUGHT YOU DIDN'T LIKE ME MEETING YOUR FRIENDS.

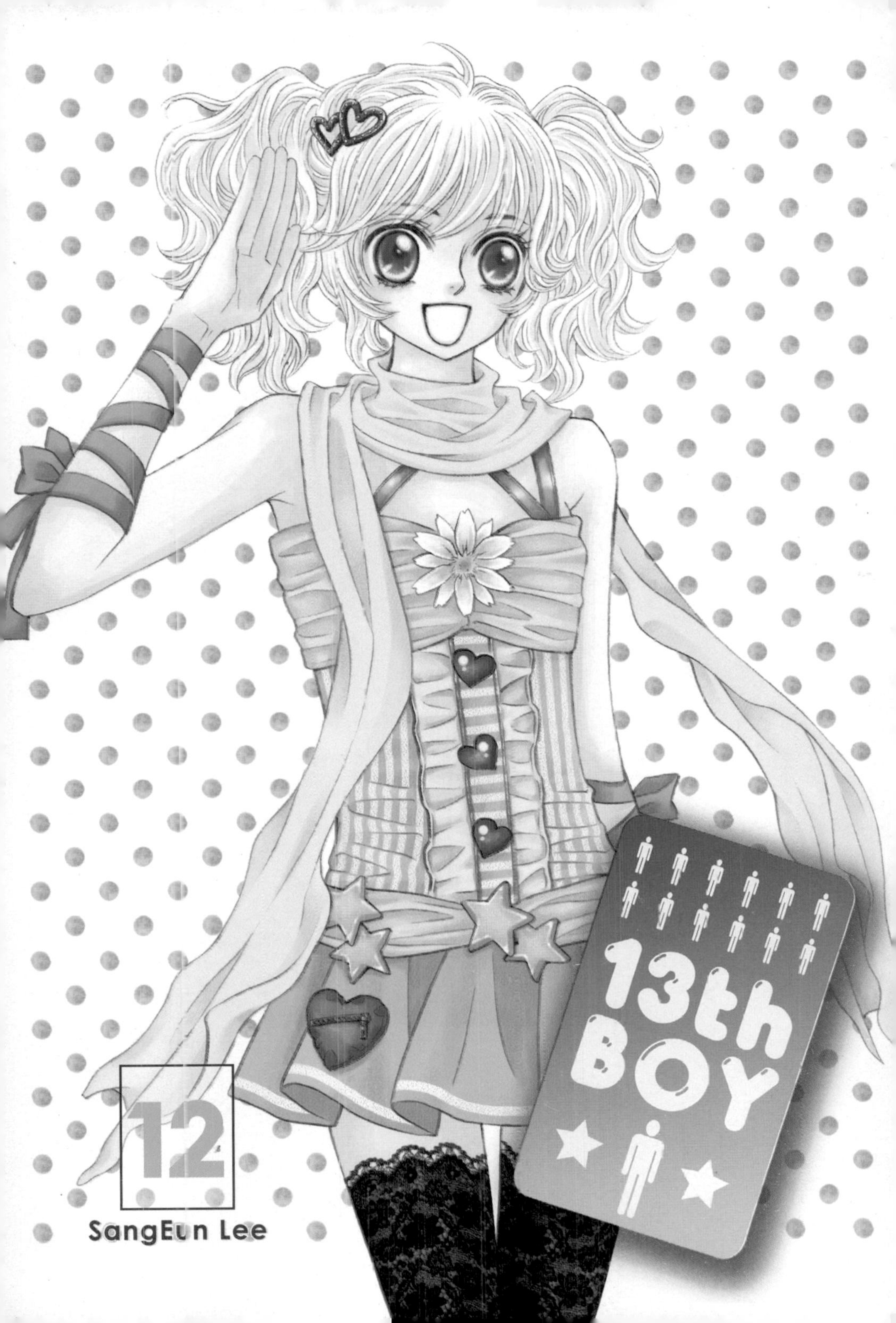
12
SangEun Lee
13th BOY

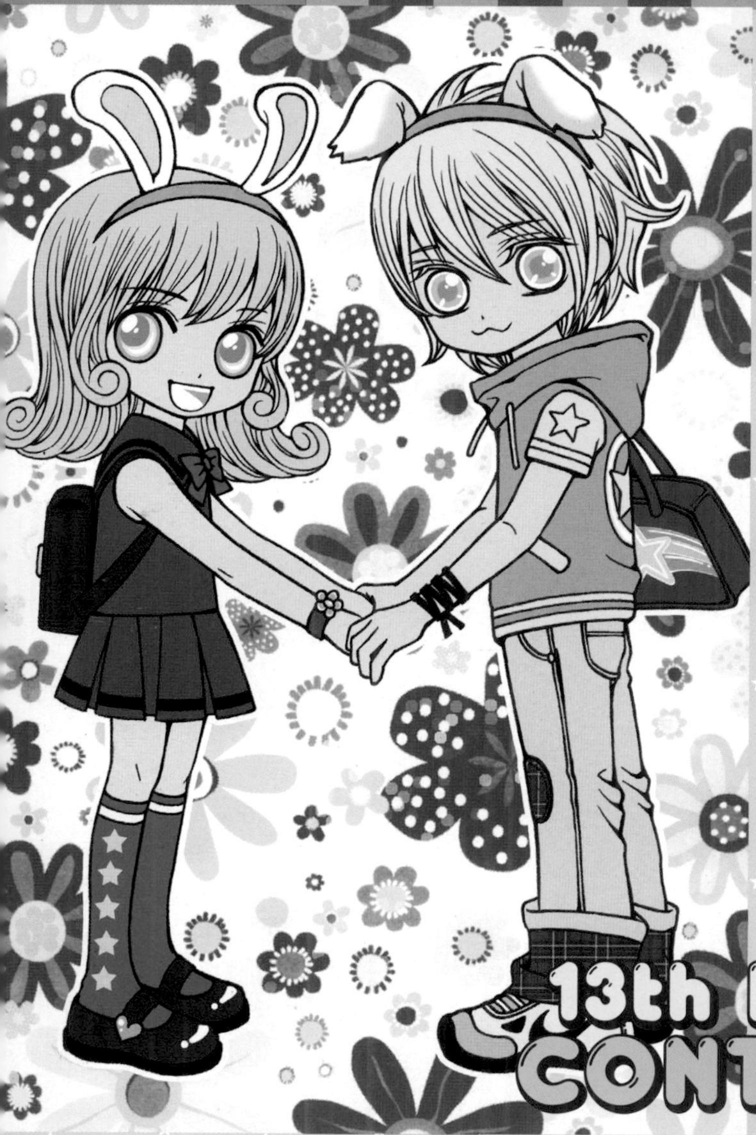

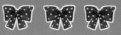

13th BOY♥ CONTENTS

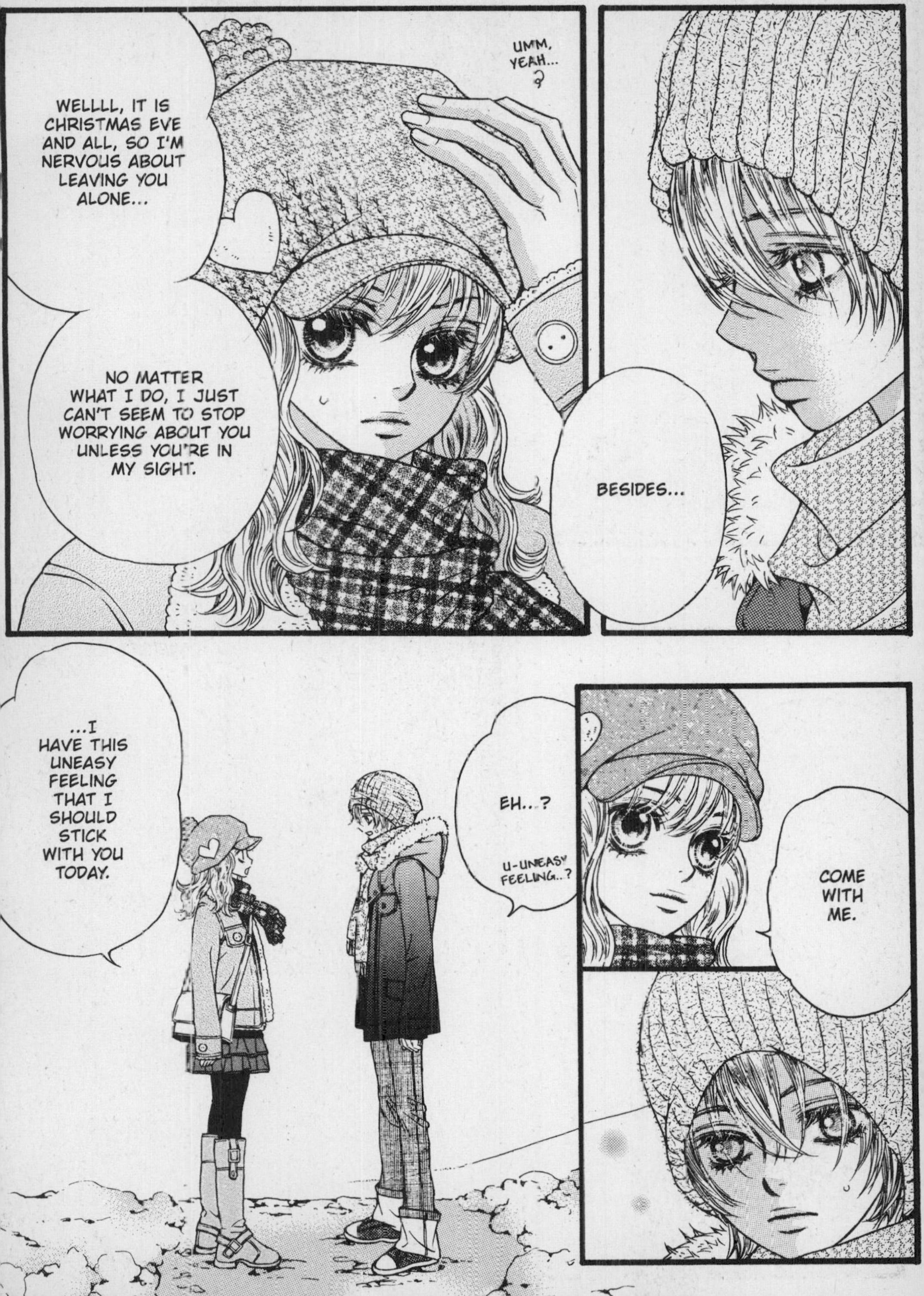
WELLLL, IT IS CHRISTMAS EVE AND ALL, SO I'M NERVOUS ABOUT LEAVING YOU ALONE...
UMM, YEAH...?
NO MATTER WHAT I DO, I JUST CAN'T SEEM TO STOP WORRYING ABOUT YOU UNLESS YOU'RE IN MY SIGHT.
BESIDES...
...I HAVE THIS UNEASY FEELING THAT I SHOULD STICK WITH YOU TODAY.
EH...?
U-UNEASY FEELING...?
COME WITH ME.

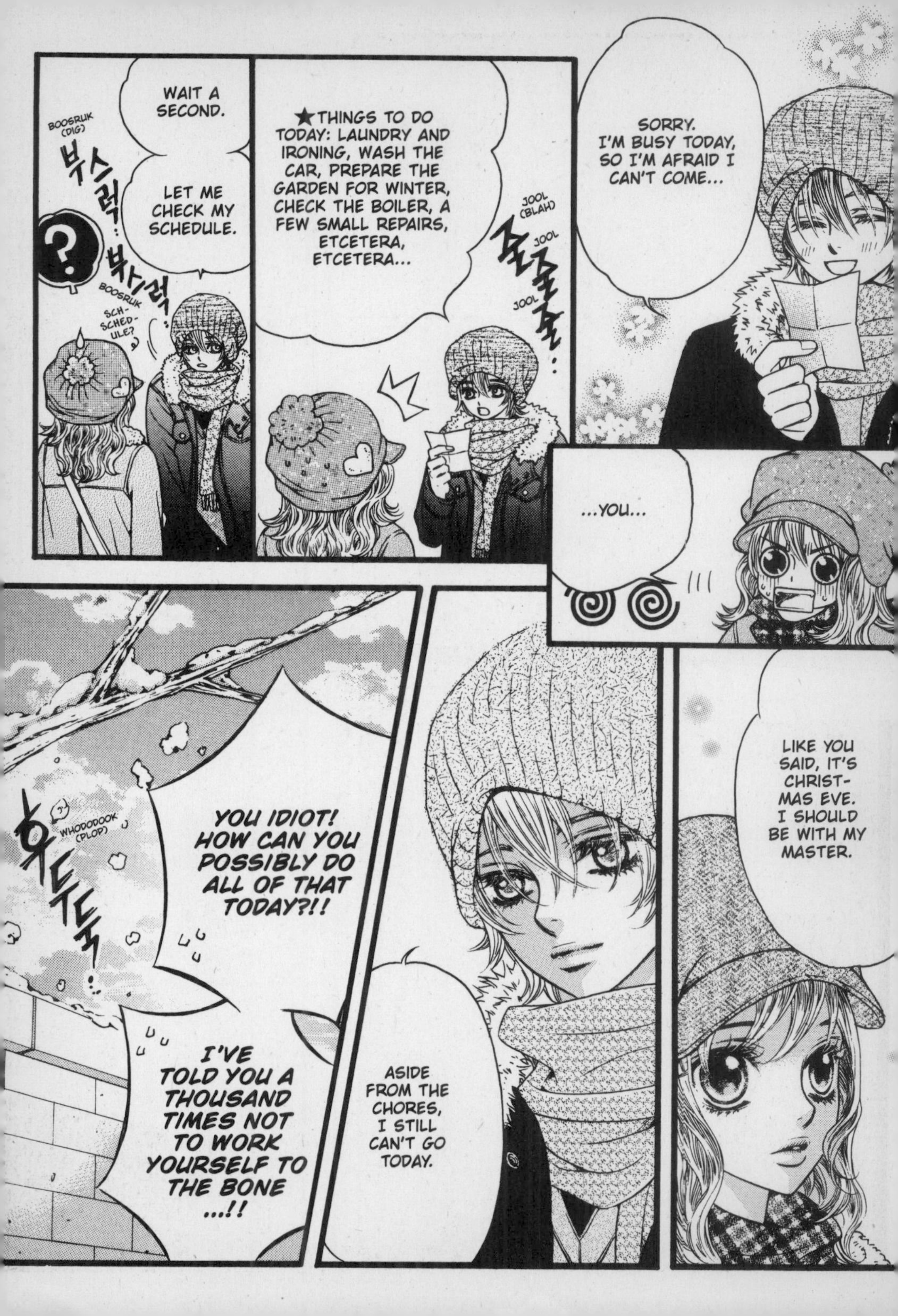
WAIT A SECOND.
LET ME CHECK MY SCHEDULE.
BOOSRUK (DIG)
부스럭
BOOSRUK
SCH-SCHED-ULE?
★THINGS TO DO TODAY: LAUNDRY AND IRONING, WASH THE CAR, PREPARE THE GARDEN FOR WINTER, CHECK THE BOILER, A FEW SMALL REPAIRS, ETCETERA, ETCETERA...
JOOL (BLAH)
JOOL
JOOL
줄줄줄
SORRY. I'M BUSY TODAY, SO I'M AFRAID I CAN'T COME...
...YOU...
WHODODOOK (PLOP)
후두둑
YOU IDIOT! HOW CAN YOU POSSIBLY DO ALL OF THAT TODAY?!!
I'VE TOLD YOU A THOUSAND TIMES NOT TO WORK YOURSELF TO THE BONE ...!!
ASIDE FROM THE CHORES, I STILL CAN'T GO TODAY.
LIKE YOU SAID, IT'S CHRIST-MAS EVE. I SHOULD BE WITH MY MASTER.

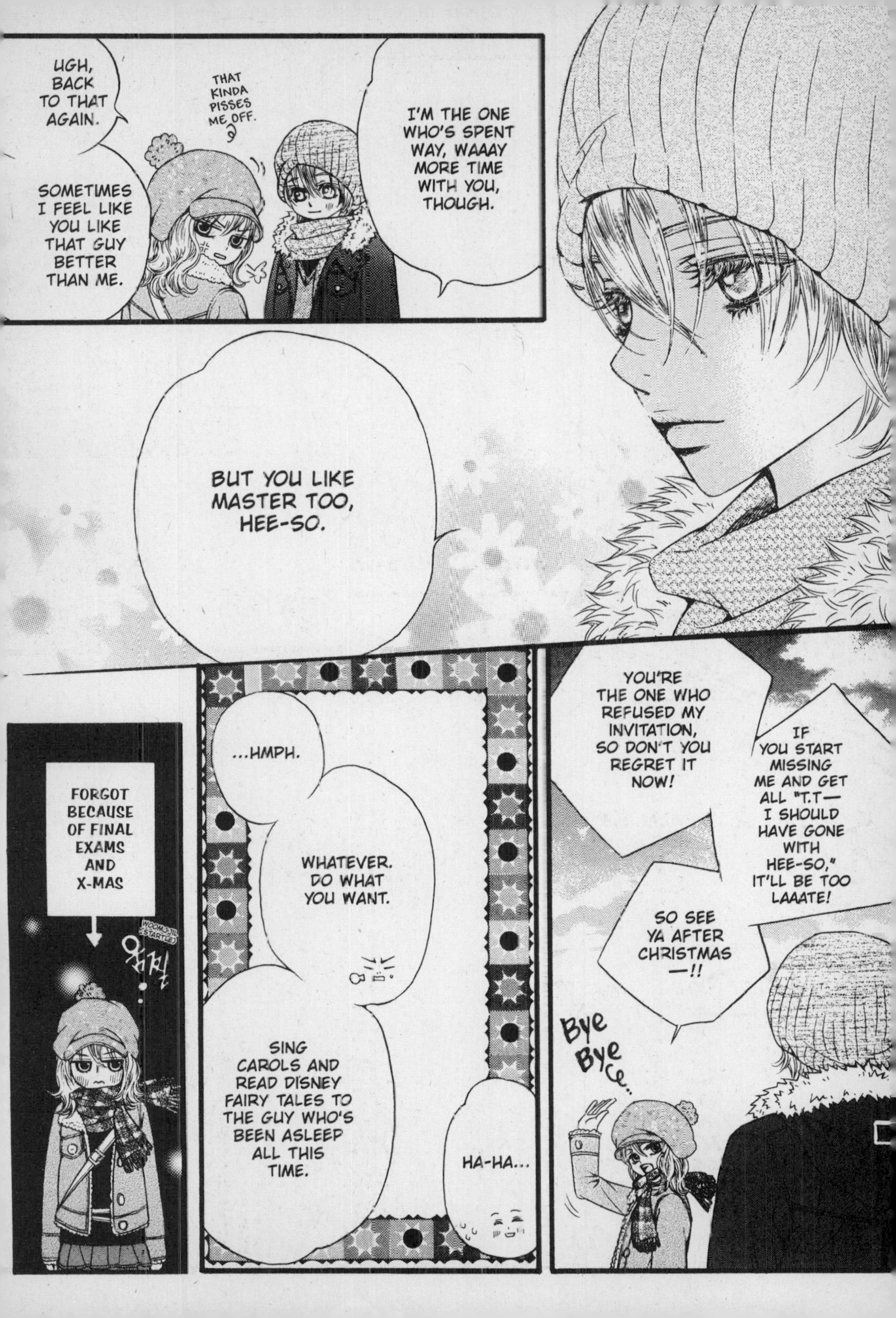
UGH, BACK TO THAT AGAIN.
THAT KINDA PISSES ME OFF.
SOMETIMES I FEEL LIKE YOU LIKE THAT GUY BETTER THAN ME.
I'M THE ONE WHO'S SPENT WAY, WAAAY MORE TIME WITH YOU, THOUGH.
BUT YOU LIKE MASTER TOO, HEE-SO.
FORGOT BECAUSE OF FINAL EXAMS AND X-MAS
WOOMSJIL (STARTLE)
...HMPH.
WHATEVER. DO WHAT YOU WANT.
SING CAROLS AND READ DISNEY FAIRY TALES TO THE GUY WHO'S BEEN ASLEEP ALL THIS TIME.
HA-HA...
YOU'RE THE ONE WHO REFUSED MY INVITATION, SO DON'T YOU REGRET IT NOW!
IF YOU START MISSING ME AND GET ALL "T.T— I SHOULD HAVE GONE WITH HEE-SO," IT'LL BE TOO LAAATE!
SO SEE YA AFTER CHRISTMAS—!!
Bye Bye...

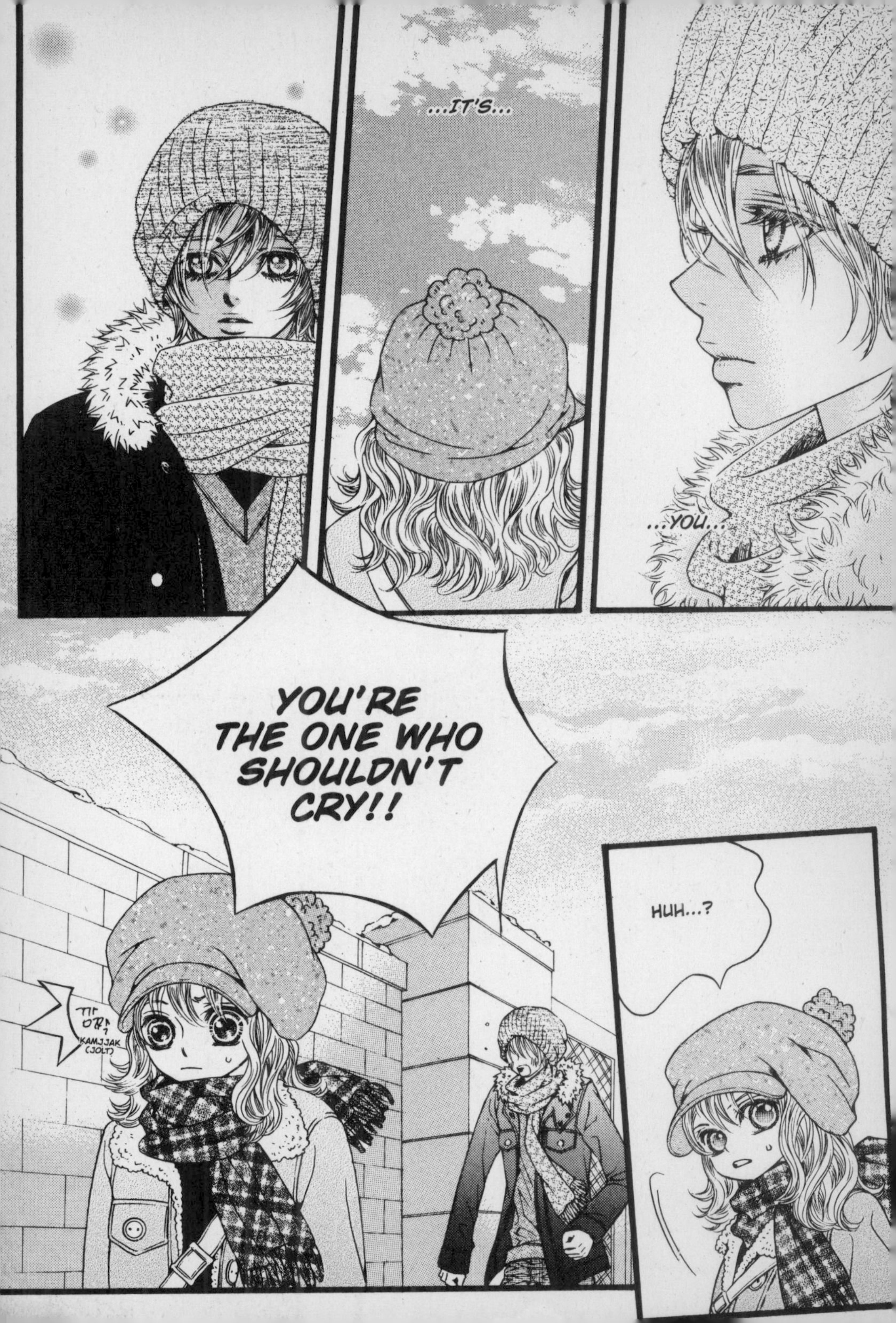
...IT'S...
...YOU...
YOU'RE THE ONE WHO SHOULDN'T CRY!!
KAMJJAK (JOLT)
HUH...?

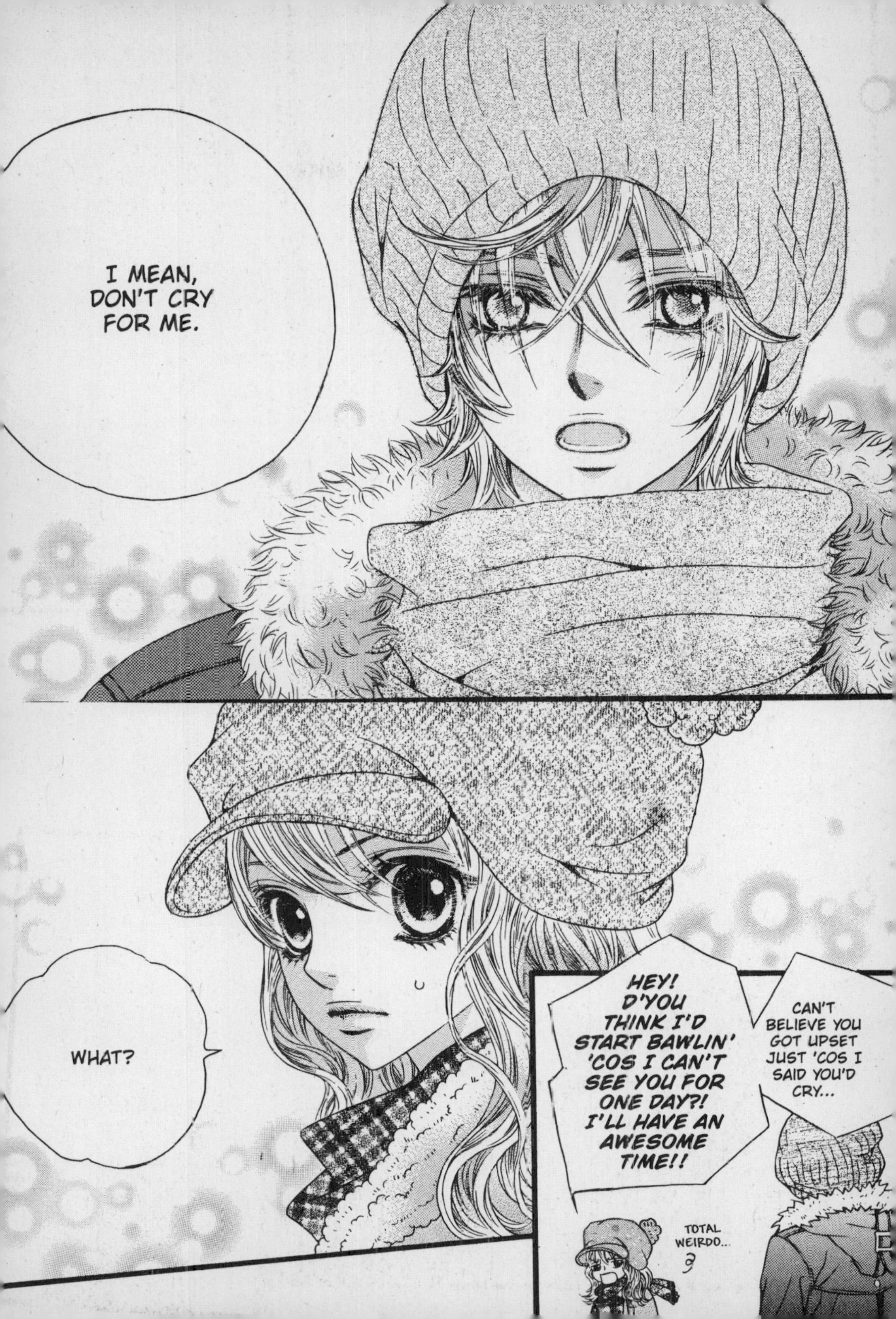
I MEAN, DON'T CRY FOR ME.
WHAT?
HEY! D'YOU THINK I'D START BAWLIN' 'COS I CAN'T SEE YOU FOR ONE DAY?! I'LL HAVE AN AWESOME TIME!!
CAN'T BELIEVE YOU GOT UPSET JUST 'COS I SAID YOU'D CRY...
TOTAL WEIRDO...

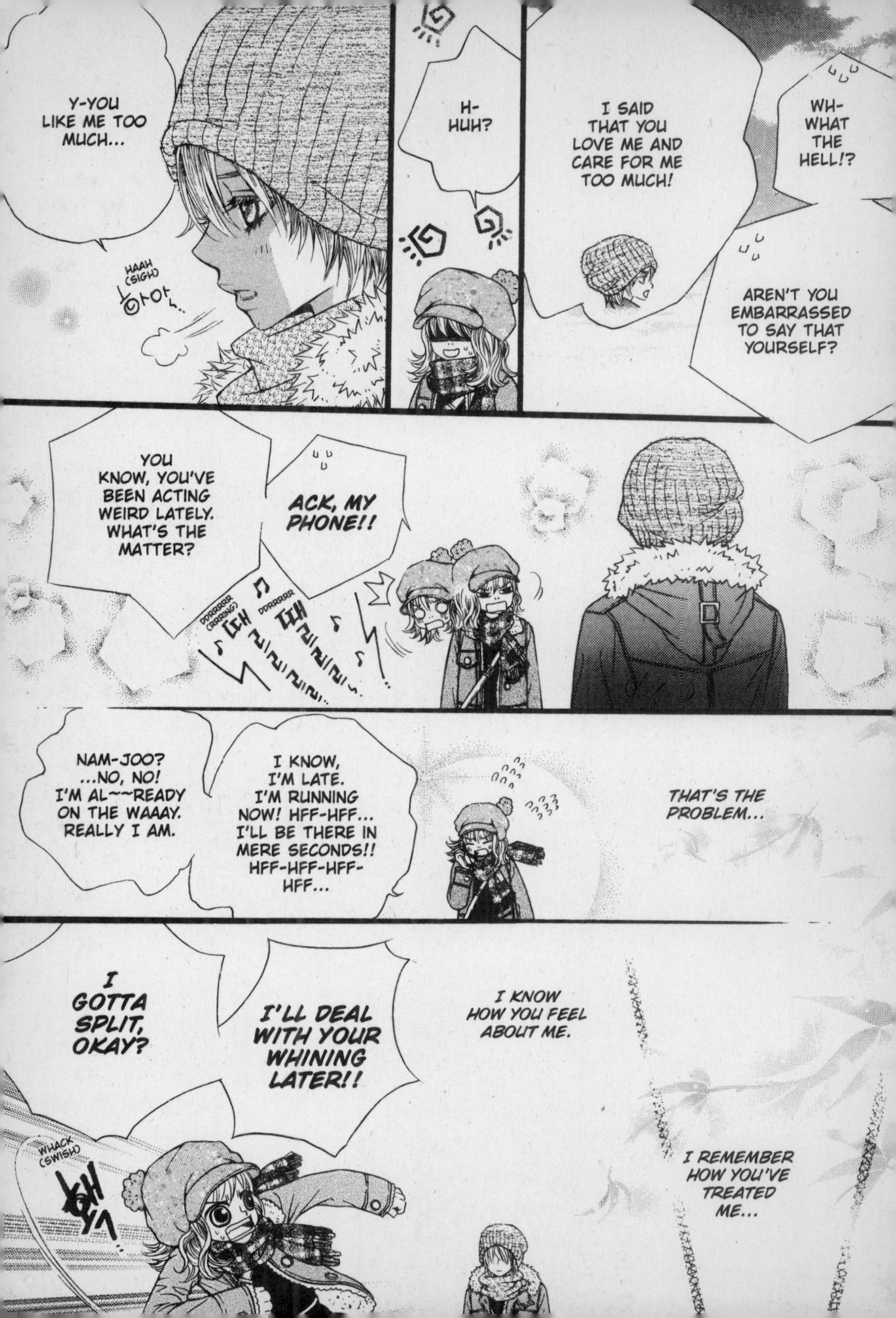

Y-YOU LIKE ME TOO MUCH...
HAAH (SIGH)
H-HUH?
I SAID THAT YOU LOVE ME AND CARE FOR ME TOO MUCH!
WH-WHAT THE HELL!?
AREN'T YOU EMBARRASSED TO SAY THAT YOURSELF?
YOU KNOW, YOU'VE BEEN ACTING WEIRD LATELY. WHAT'S THE MATTER?
ACK, MY PHONE!!
DDRRRRR (RRRING)
DDRRRRR
NAM-JOO? ...NO, NO! I'M AL~~READY ON THE WAAAY. REALLY I AM.
I KNOW, I'M LATE. I'M RUNNING NOW! HFF-HFF... I'LL BE THERE IN MERE SECONDS!! HFF-HFF-HFF-HFF...
THAT'S THE PROBLEM...
I GOTTA SPLIT, OKAY?
I'LL DEAL WITH YOUR WHINING LATER!!
I KNOW HOW YOU FEEL ABOUT ME.
WHACK (SWISH)
I REMEMBER HOW YOU'VE TREATED ME...

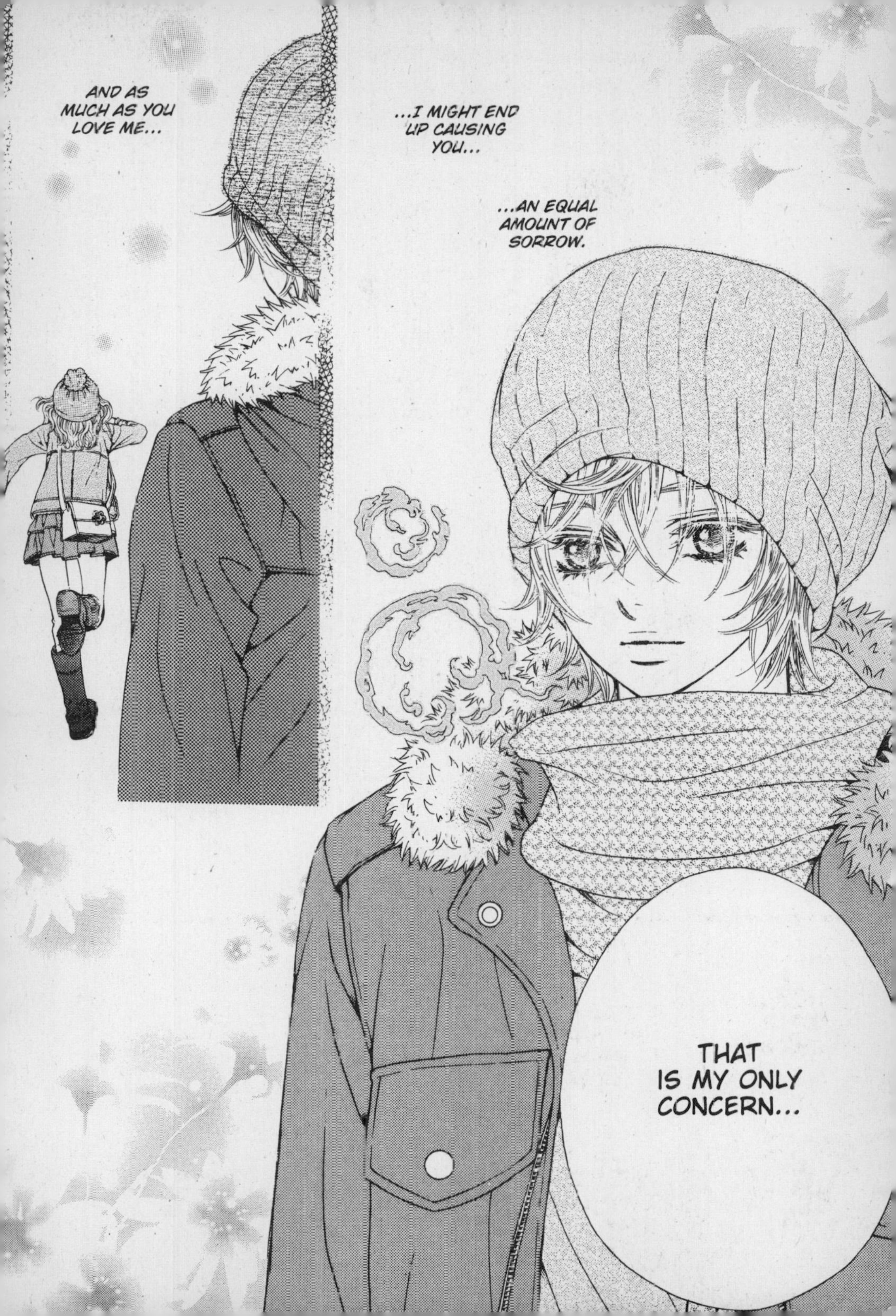
AND AS MUCH AS YOU LOVE ME...
...I MIGHT END UP CAUSING YOU...
...AN EQUAL AMOUNT OF SORROW.
THAT IS MY ONLY CONCERN...

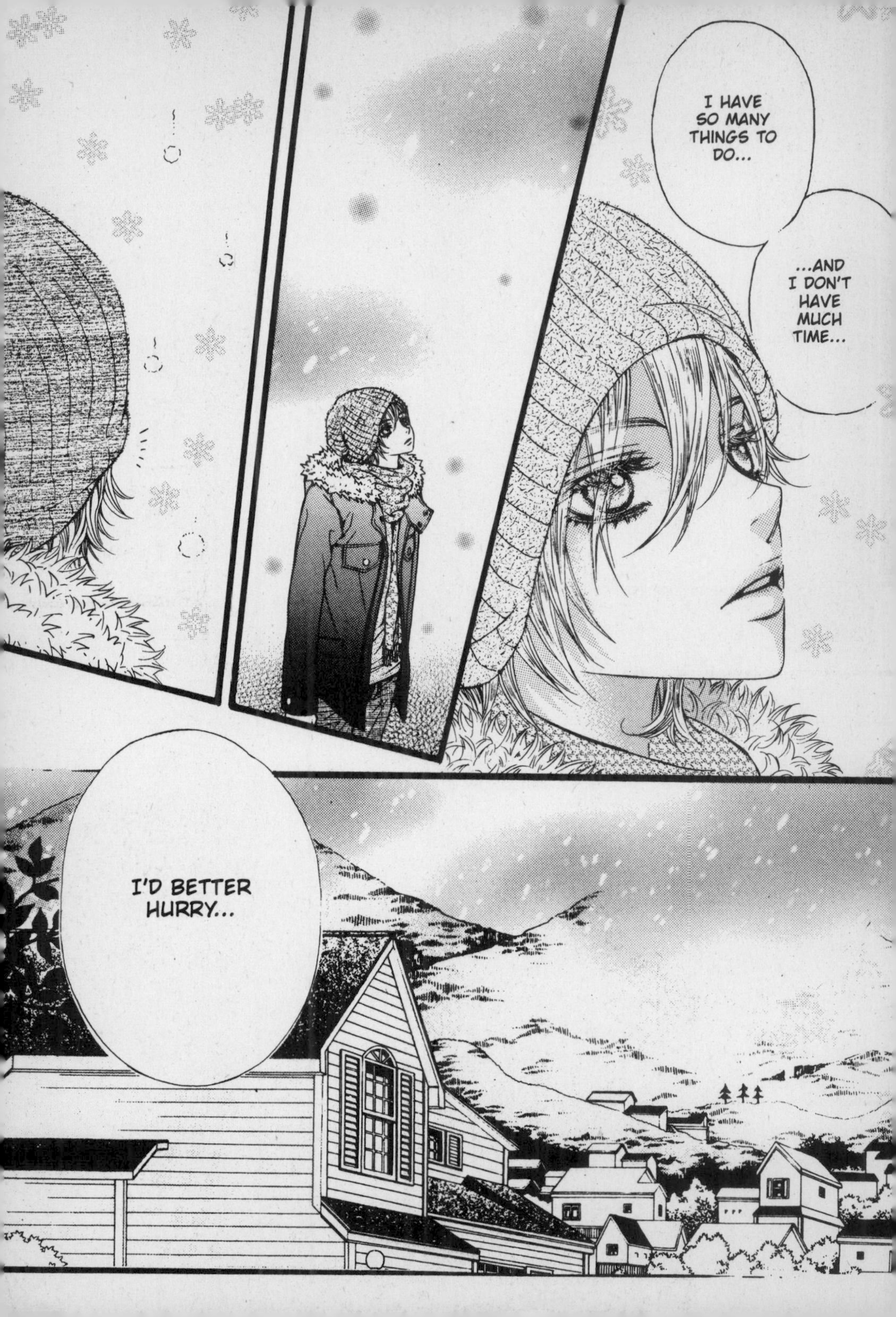
I HAVE SO MANY THINGS TO DO...
...AND I DON'T HAVE MUCH TIME...
I'D BETTER HURRY...

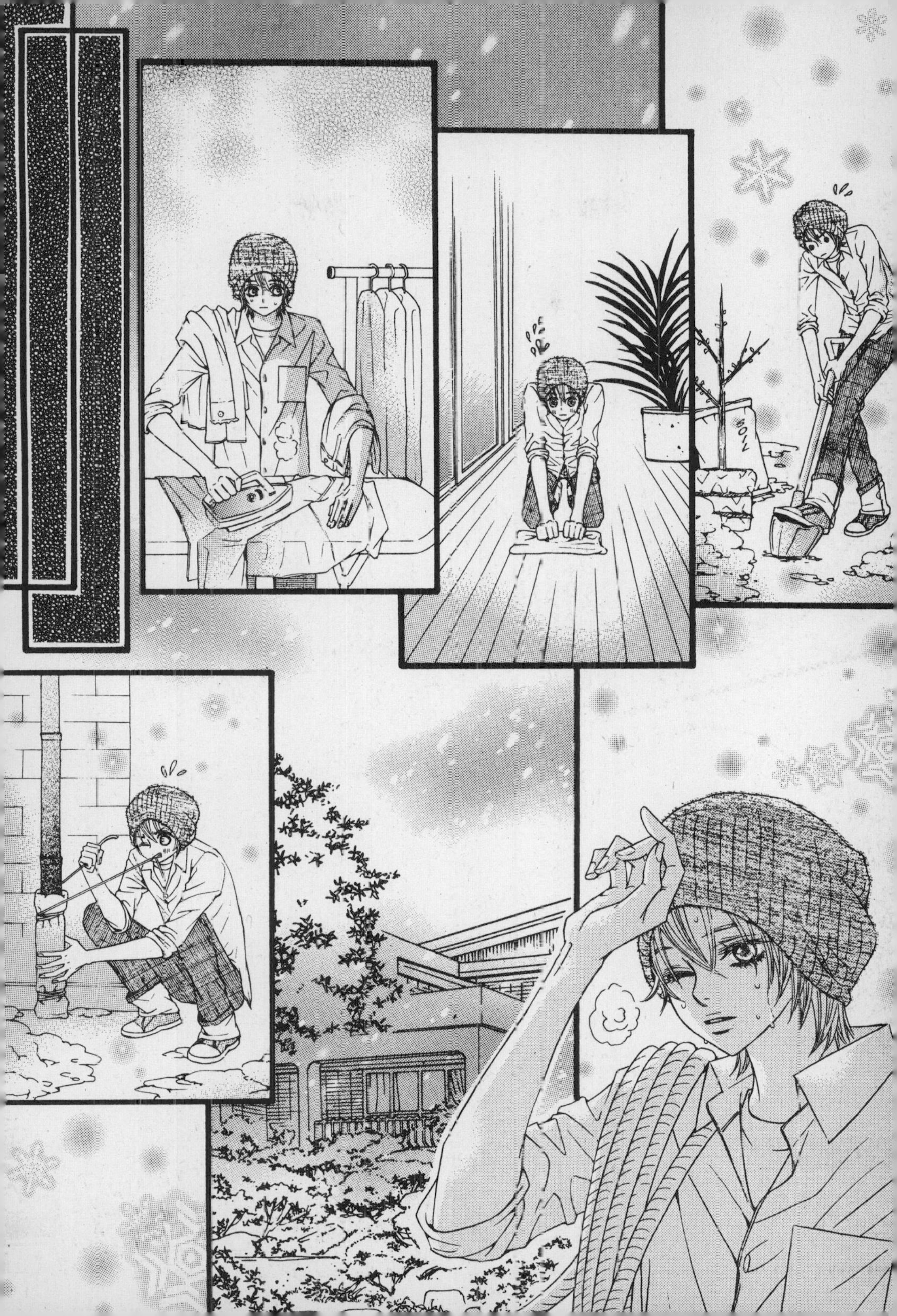

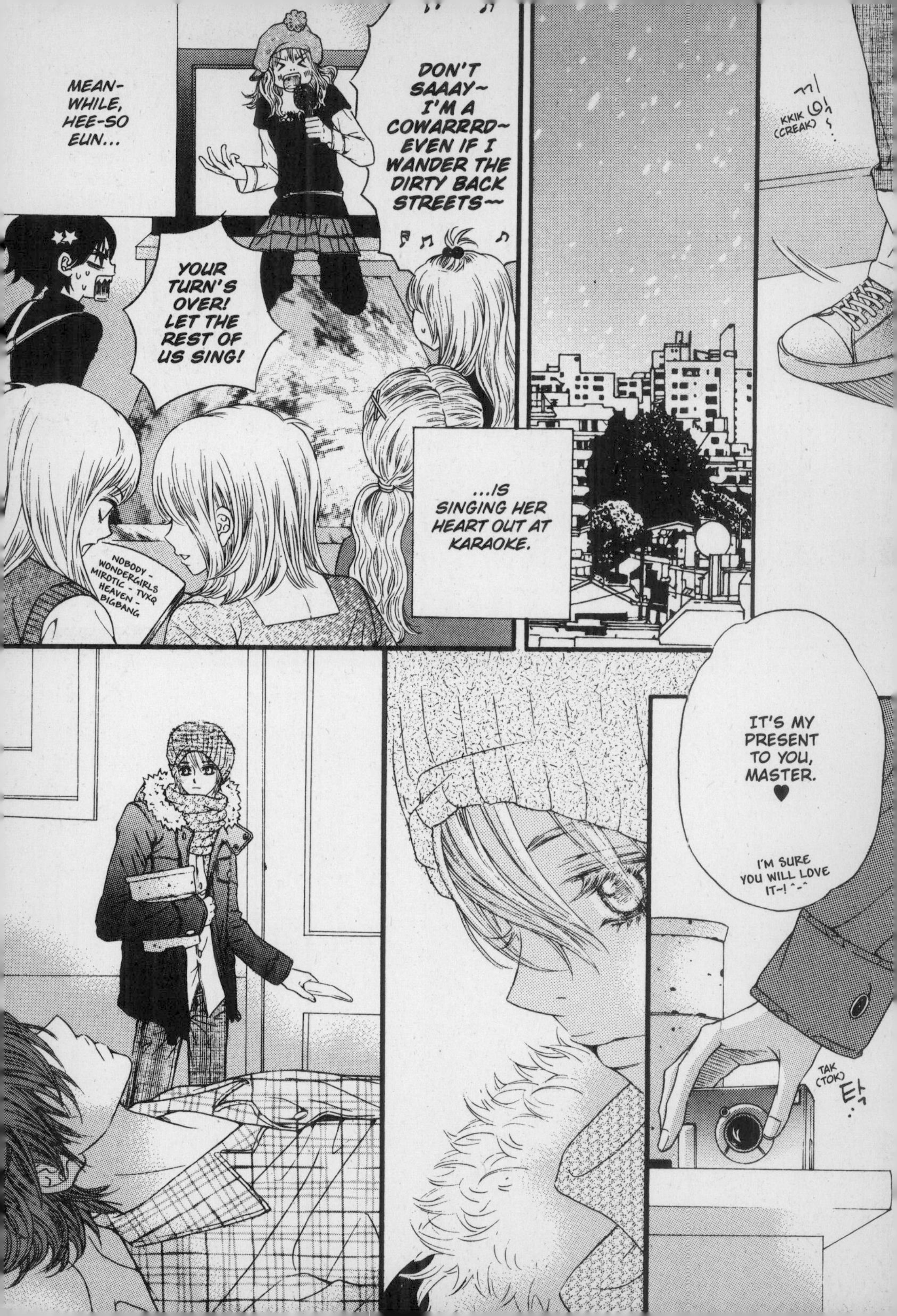
MEAN-WHILE, HEE-SO EUN...
DON'T SAAAY~ I'M A COWARRRD~ EVEN IF I WANDER THE DIRTY BACK STREETS~~
YOUR TURN'S OVER! LET THE REST OF US SING!
NOBODY - WONDERGIRLS
MIROTIC - TVXQ
HEAVEN - BIGBANG
...IS SINGING HER HEART OUT AT KARAOKE.
KKIK (CREAK)
IT'S MY PRESENT TO YOU, MASTER. ♥
I'M SURE YOU WILL LOVE IT~! ^-^
TAK (TOK)

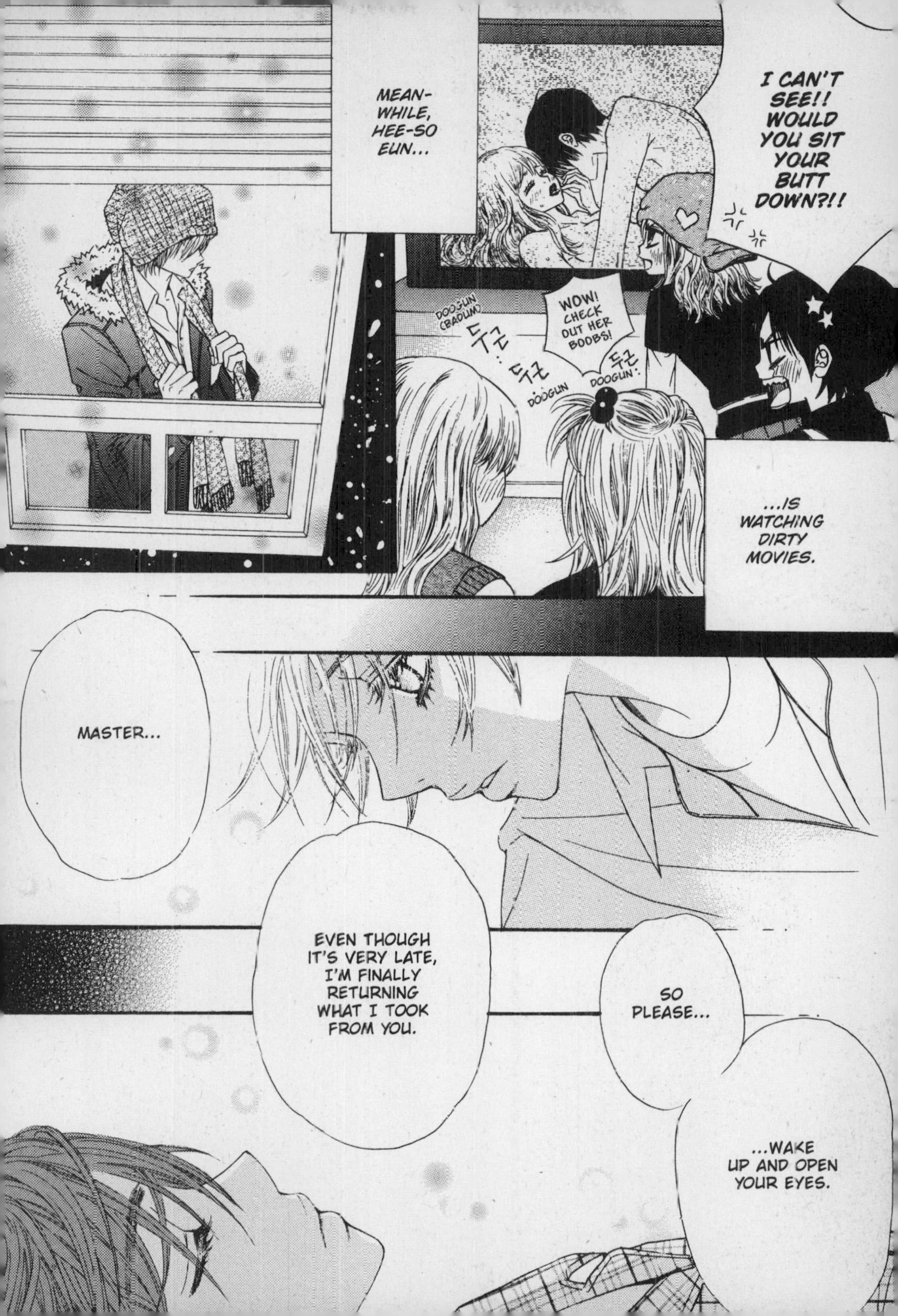
MEAN-WHILE, HEE-SO EUN...
I CAN'T SEE!! WOULD YOU SIT YOUR BUTT DOWN?!!
두근 DOOGUN (BADUM)
WOW! CHECK OUT HER BOOBS!
두근 DOOGUN
두근 DOOGUN
...IS WATCHING DIRTY MOVIES.
MASTER...
EVEN THOUGH IT'S VERY LATE, I'M FINALLY RETURNING WHAT I TOOK FROM YOU.
SO PLEASE...
...WAKE UP AND OPEN YOUR EYES.

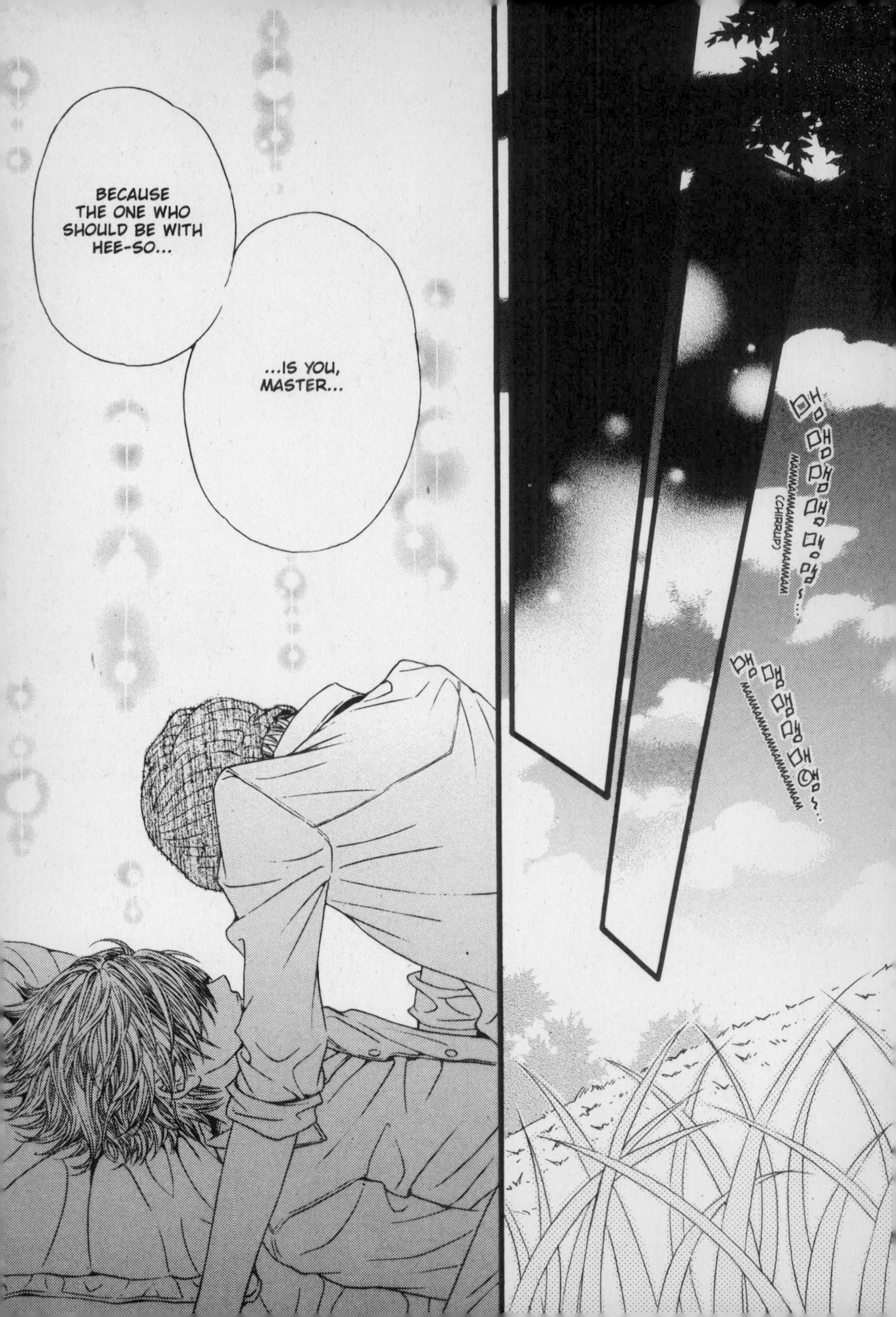
BECAUSE THE ONE WHO SHOULD BE WITH HEE-SO...
...IS YOU, MASTER...
MAMMAMMAMMAMMAMMAM (CHIRRUP)
MAMMAMMAMMAMMAMMAM

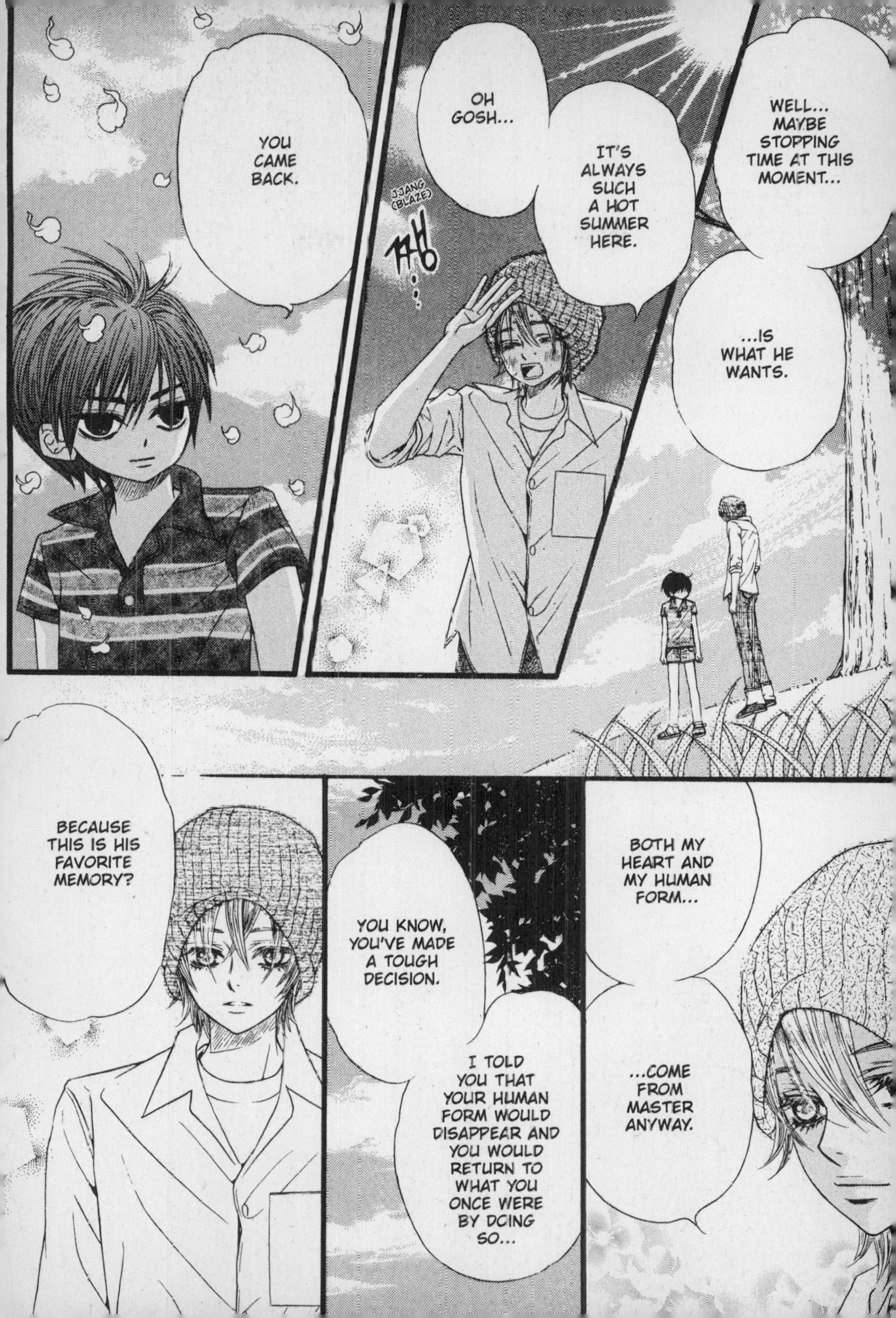
YOU CAME BACK.
OH GOSH...
JJANG (BLAZE)
IT'S ALWAYS SUCH A HOT SUMMER HERE.
WELL... MAYBE STOPPING TIME AT THIS MOMENT...
...IS WHAT HE WANTS.
BECAUSE THIS IS HIS FAVORITE MEMORY?
YOU KNOW, YOU'VE MADE A TOUGH DECISION.
I TOLD YOU THAT YOUR HUMAN FORM WOULD DISAPPEAR AND YOU WOULD RETURN TO WHAT YOU ONCE WERE BY DCING SO...
BOTH MY HEART AND MY HUMAN FORM...
...COME FROM MASTER ANYWAY.

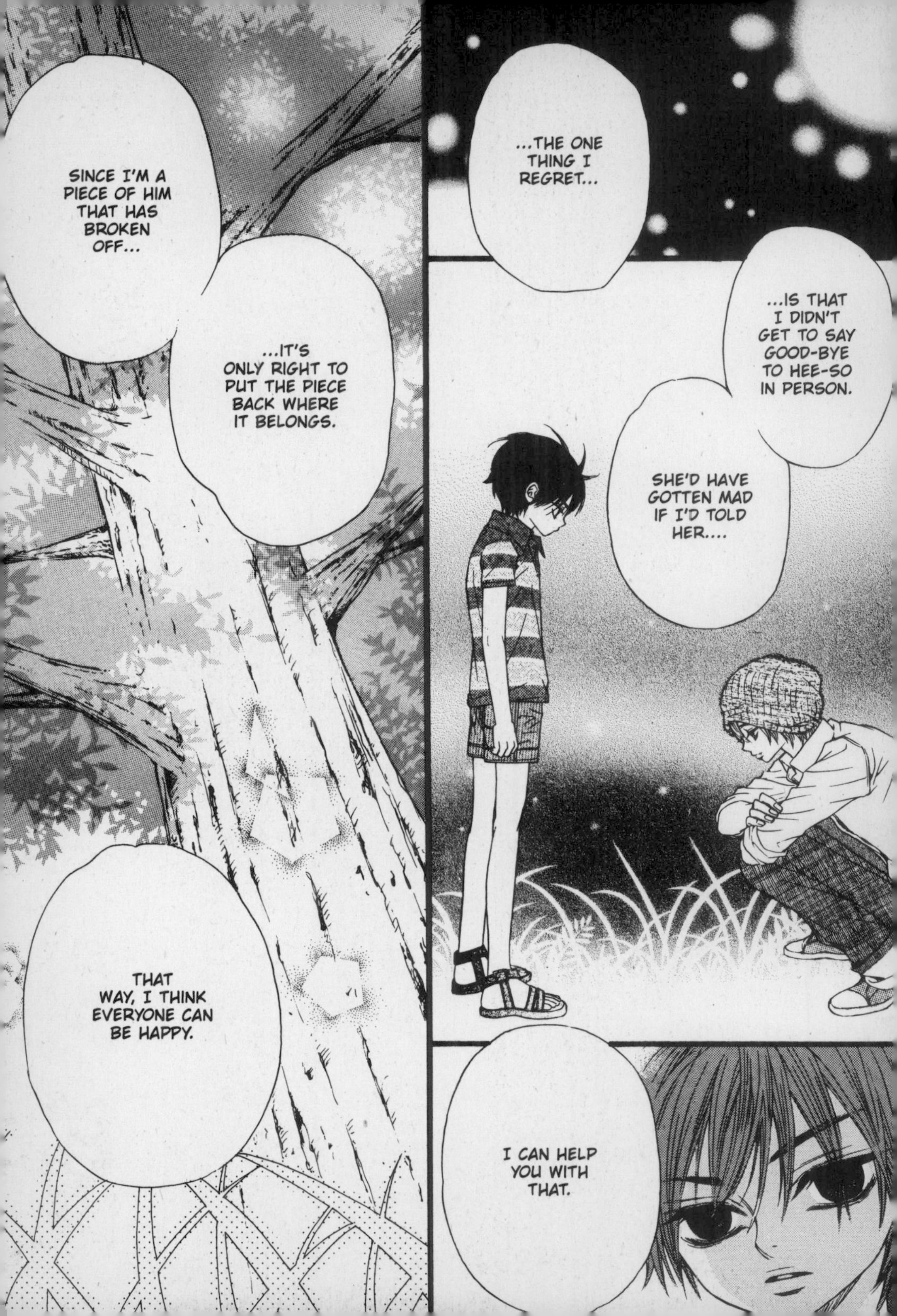
SINCE I'M A PIECE OF HIM THAT HAS BROKEN OFF...
...IT'S ONLY RIGHT TO PUT THE PIECE BACK WHERE IT BELONGS.
THAT WAY, I THINK EVERYONE CAN BE HAPPY.
...THE ONE THING I REGRET...
...IS THAT I DIDN'T GET TO SAY GOOD-BYE TO HEE-SO IN PERSON.
SHE'D HAVE GOTTEN MAD IF I'D TOLD HER....
I CAN HELP YOU WITH THAT.

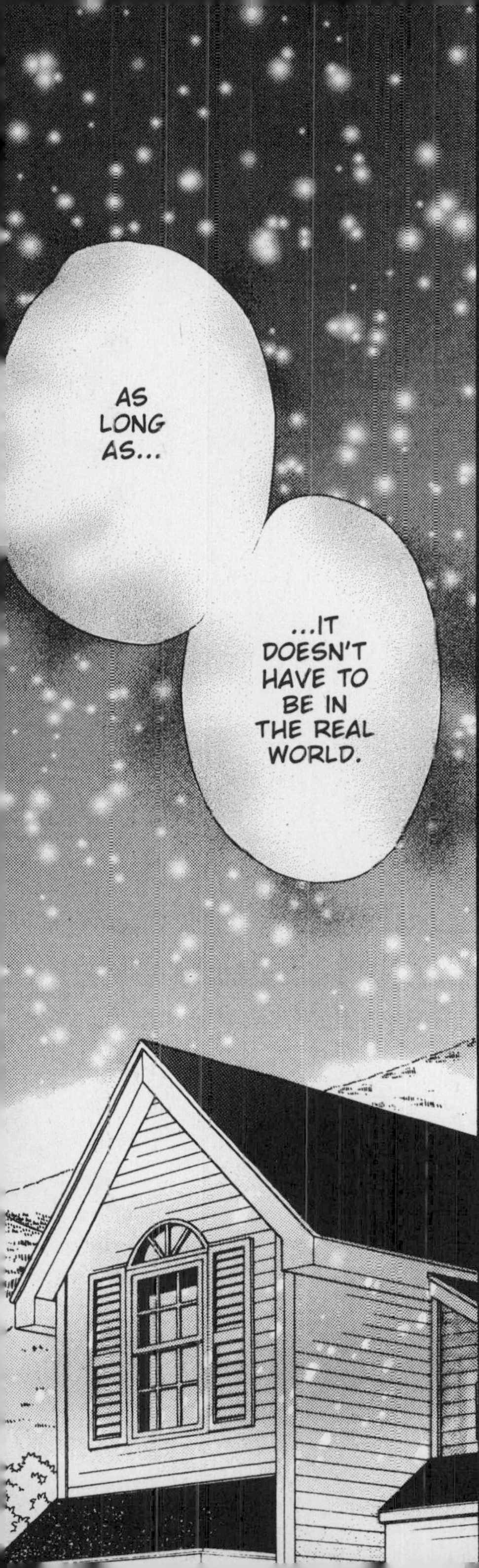
AS LONG AS...
...IT DOESN'T HAVE TO BE IN THE REAL WORLD.

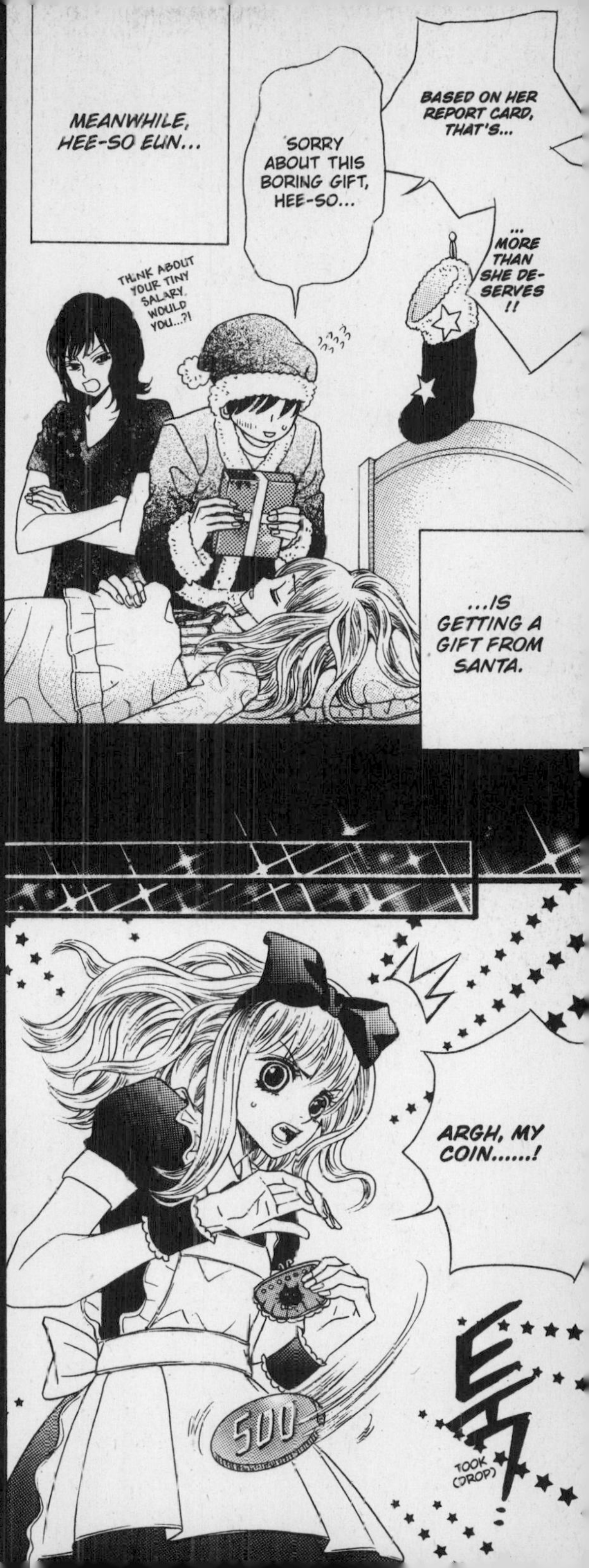
MEANWHILE, HEE-SO EUN...
SORRY ABOUT THIS BORING GIFT, HEE-SO...
BASED ON HER REPORT CARD, THAT'S...
...MORE THAN SHE DE-SERVES!!
THINK ABOUT YOUR TINY SALARY, WOULD YOU...?!
...IS GETTING A GIFT FROM SANTA.
ARGH, MY COIN......!
500
TOOK (DROP)

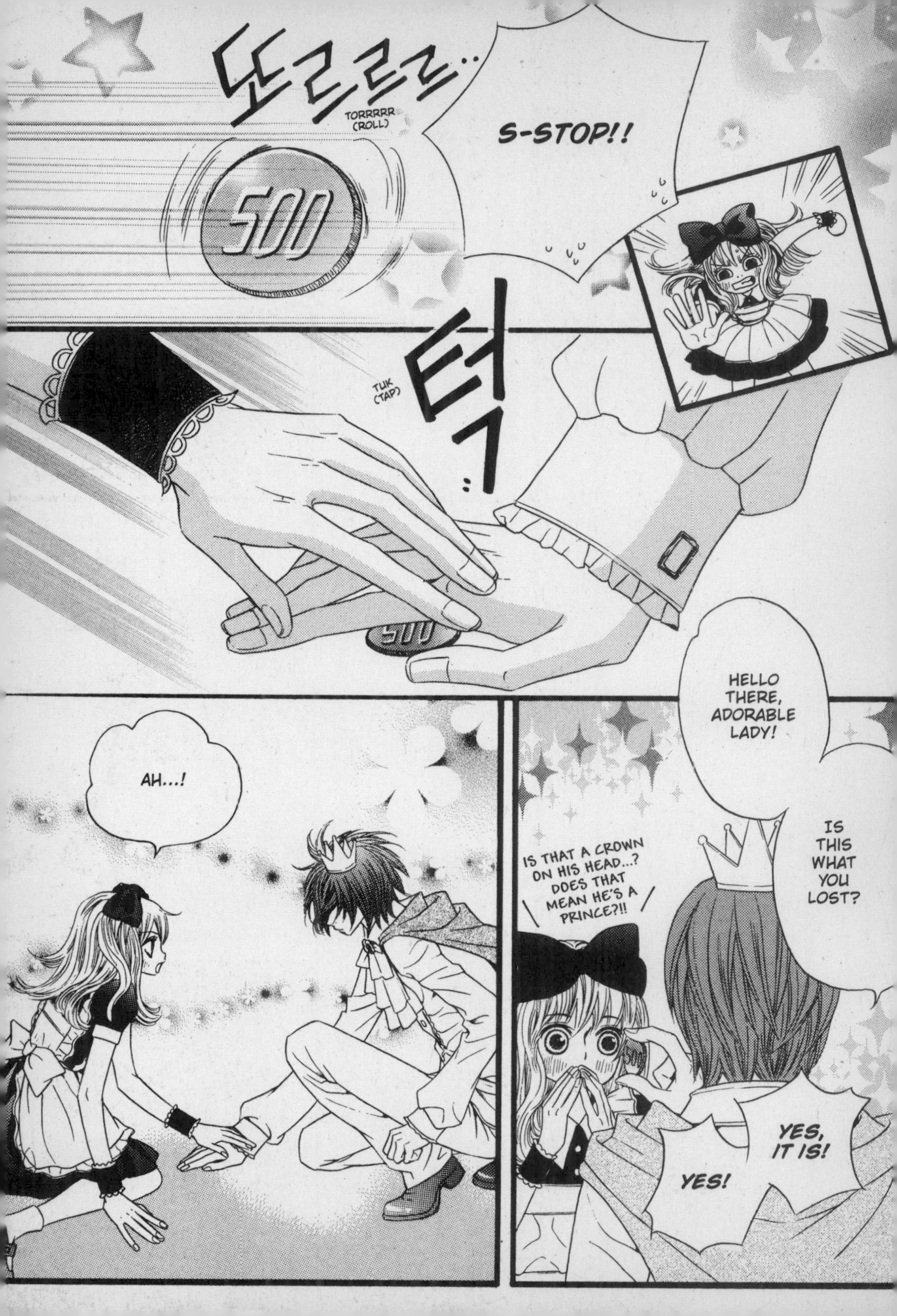
또르르르..
TORRRRR (ROLL)
S-STOP!!
턱..!
TUK (TAP)
AH...!
HELLO THERE, ADORABLE LADY!
IS THAT A CROWN ON HIS HEAD...? DOES THAT MEAN HE'S A PRINCE?!!
IS THIS WHAT YOU LOST?
YES, IT IS!
YES!

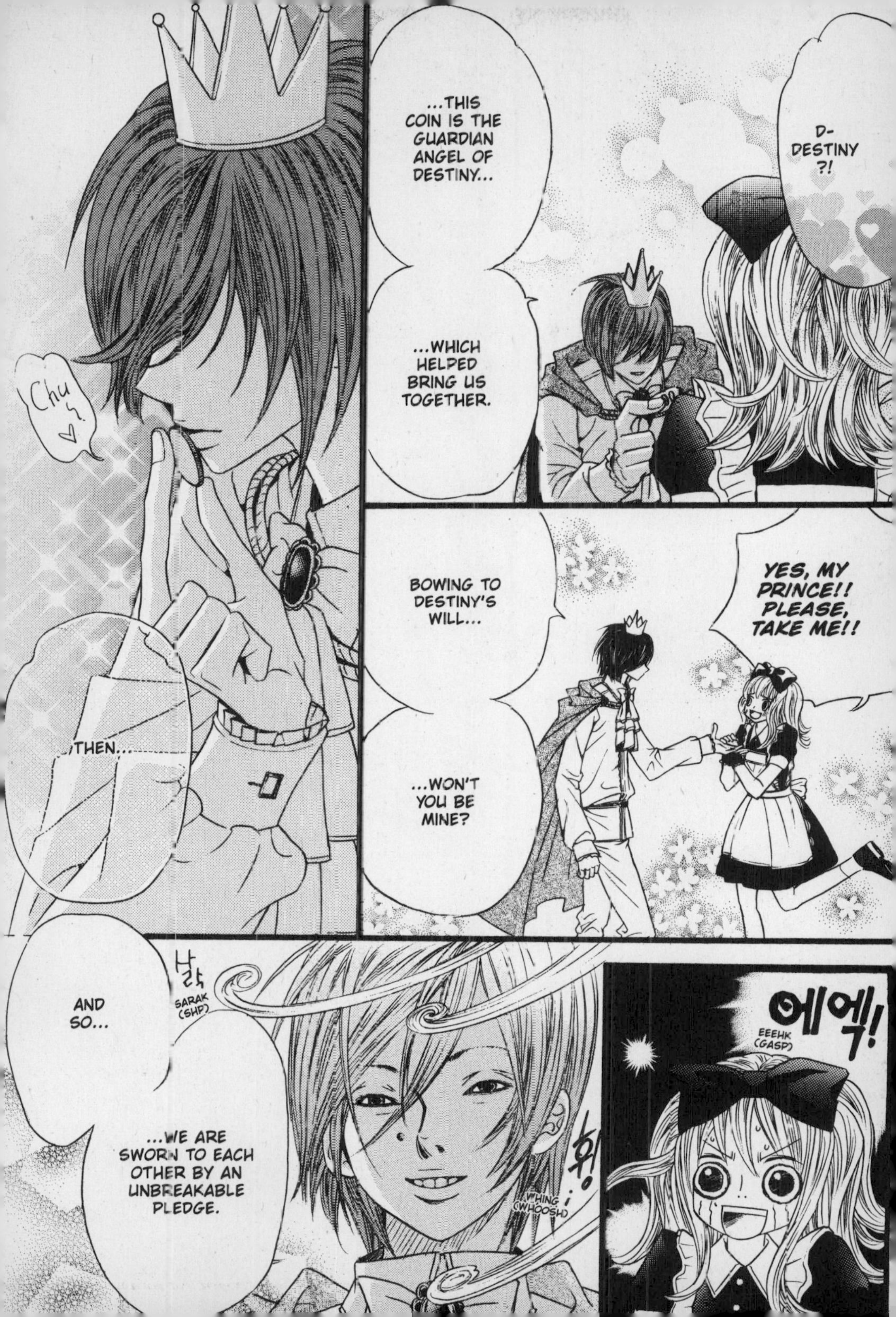
Chu ♪ ♥
THEN...
...THIS COIN IS THE GUARDIAN ANGEL OF DESTINY...
...WHICH HELPED BRING US TOGETHER.
D-DESTINY ?!
BOWING TO DESTINY'S WILL...
...WON'T YOU BE MINE?
YES, MY PRINCE!! PLEASE, TAKE ME!!
AND SO...
사락
SARAK (SHP)
...WE ARE SWORN TO EACH OTHER BY AN UNBREAKABLE PLEDGE.
휙!
WHING (WHOOSH)
에엑!
EEEHK (GASP)

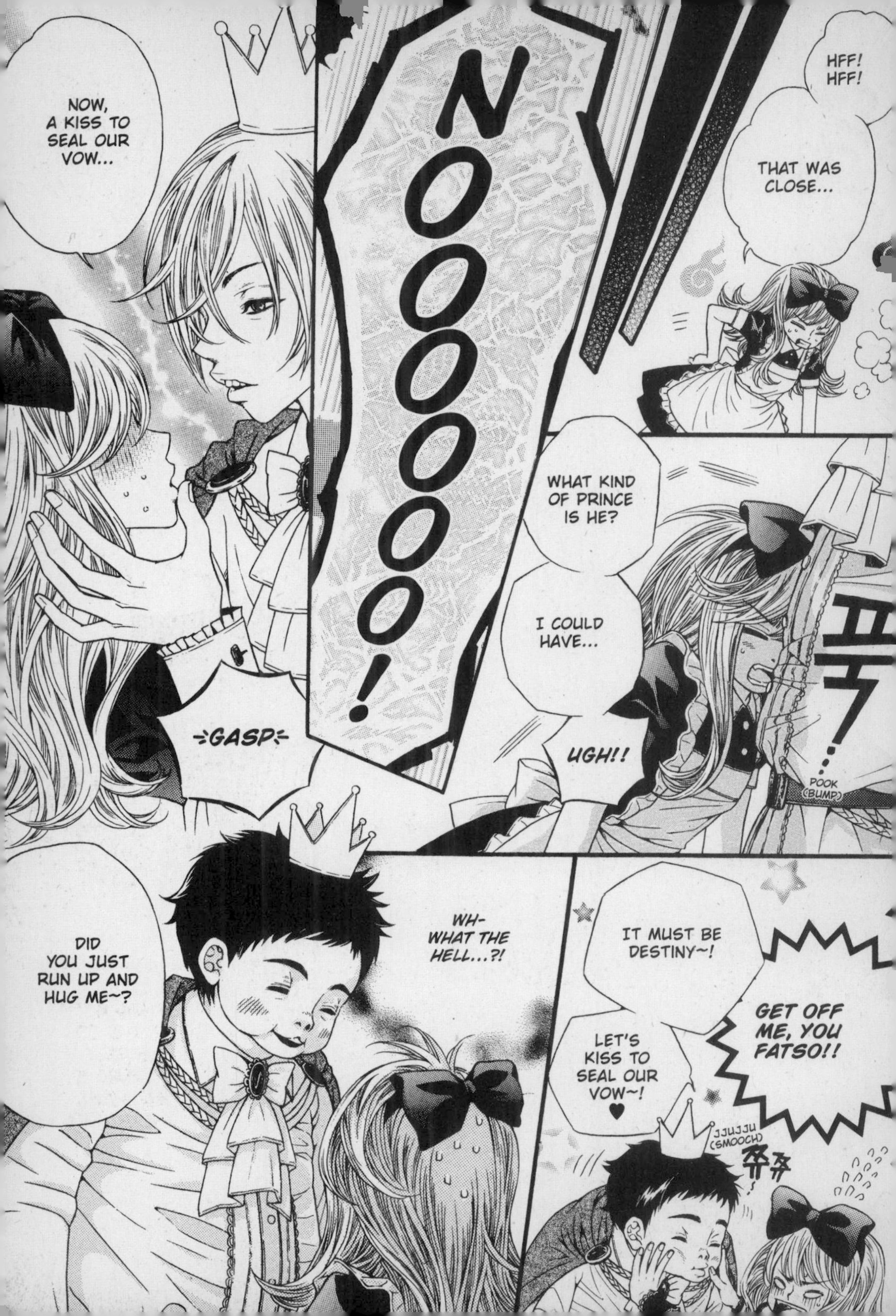
NOW, A KISS TO SEAL OUR VOW...
GASP
NOOOOOO!
HFF! HFF!
THAT WAS CLOSE...
WHAT KIND OF PRINCE IS HE?
I COULD HAVE...
UGH!!
POOK (BUMP)
DID YOU JUST RUN UP AND HUG ME~?
WH- WHAT THE HELL...?!
IT MUST BE DESTINY~!
LET'S KISS TO SEAL OUR VOW~! ♥
GET OFF ME, YOU FATSO!!
JJUJJU (SMOOCH)
쭈쭈

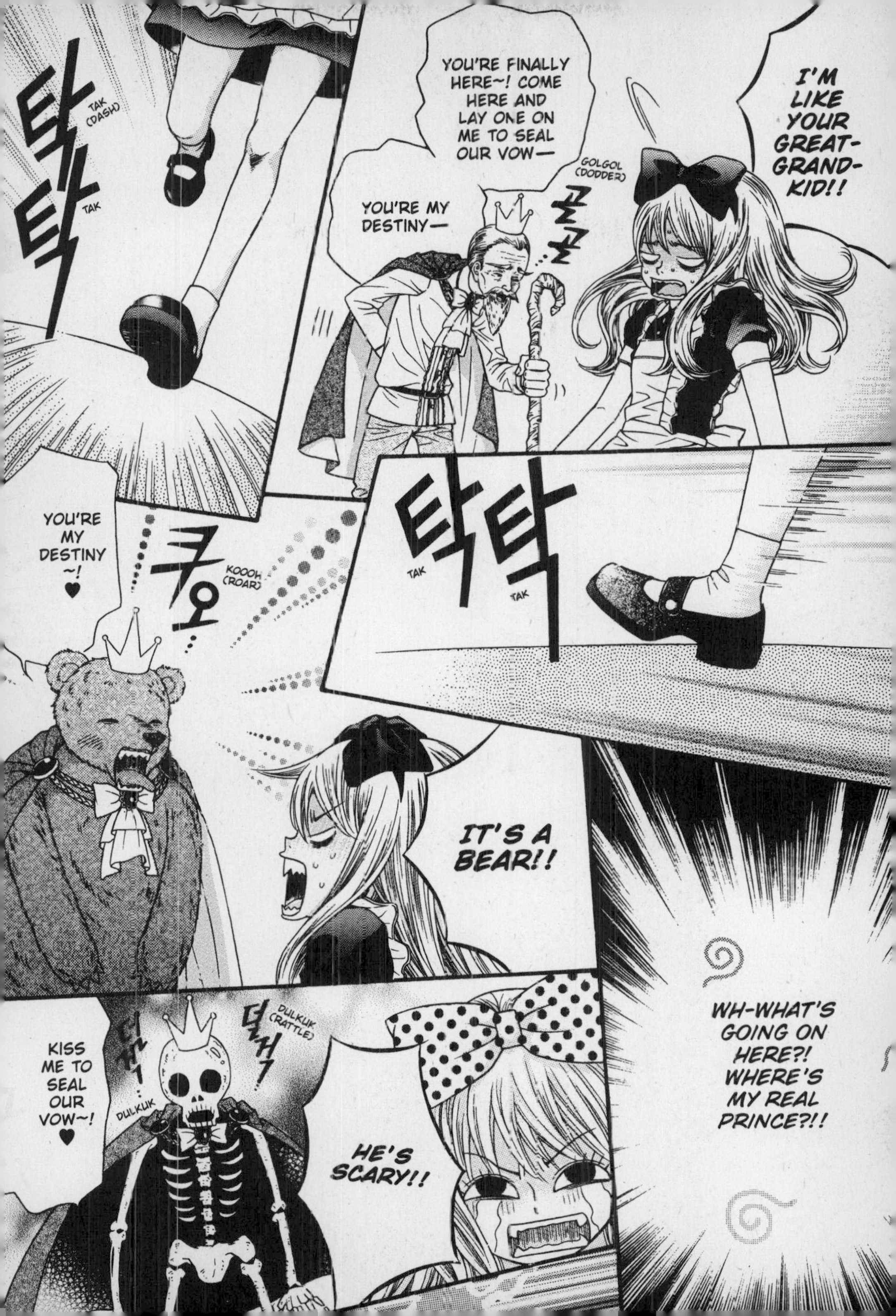

탁 탁 탁
TAK (DASH)
TAK
YOU'RE FINALLY HERE~! COME HERE AND LAY ONE ON ME TO SEAL OUR VOW—
YOU'RE MY DESTINY—
골골
GOLGOL (DODDER)
I'M LIKE YOUR GREAT-GRAND-KID!!
YOU'RE MY DESTINY ~! ♥
쿠오
KOOOH (ROAR)
IT'S A BEAR!!
탁탁
TAK
TAK
KISS ME TO SEAL OUR VOW~! ♥
덜컥 덜컥
DULKUK (RATTLE)
DULKUK
HE'S SCARY!!
WH-WHAT'S GOING ON HERE?! WHERE'S MY REAL PRINCE?!!

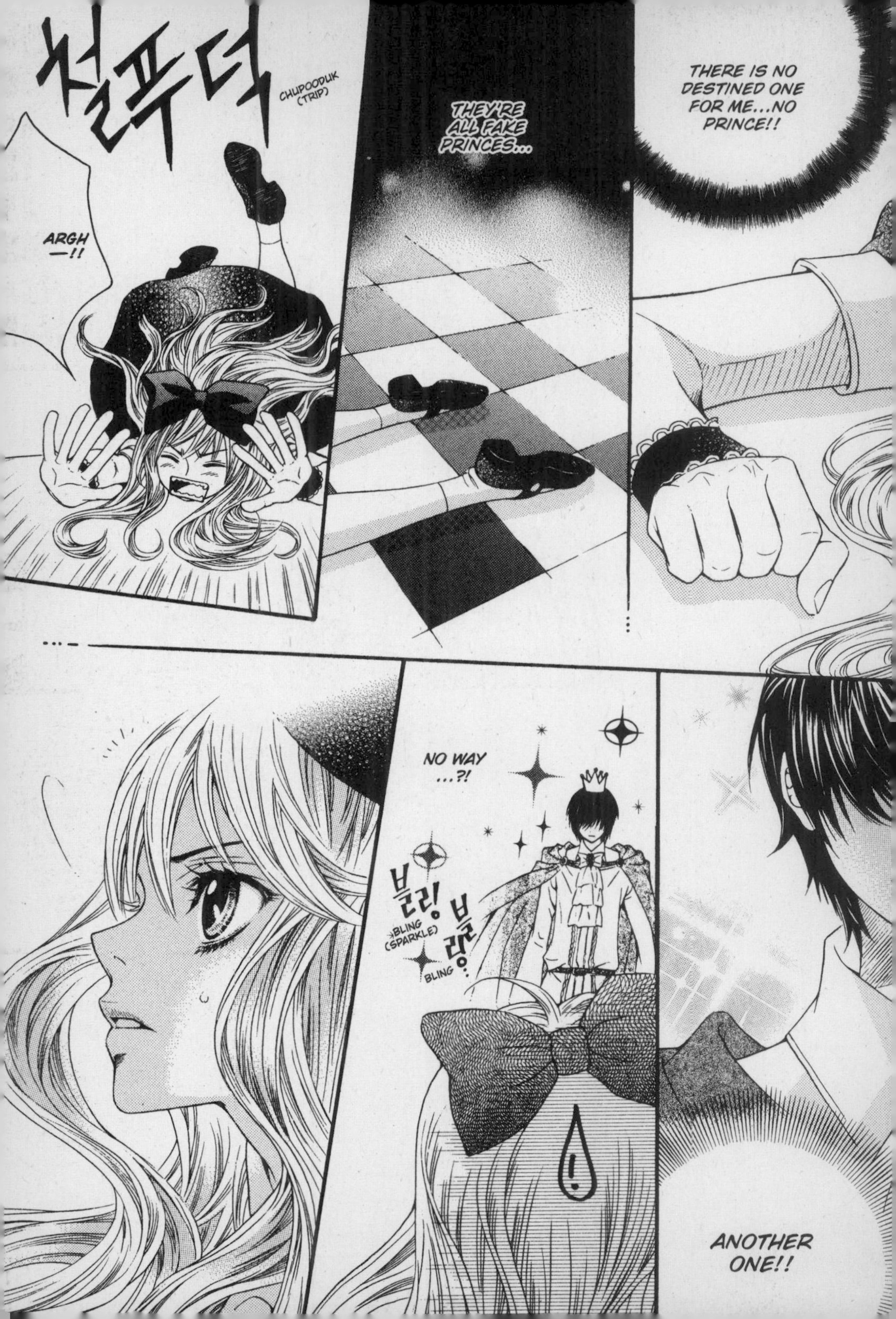
철푸덕
CHUPOODUK (TRIP)
ARGH—!!
THEY'RE ALL FAKE PRINCES...
THERE IS NO DESTINED ONE FOR ME...NO PRINCE!!
...—
NO WAY ...?!
블링 블링
BLING (SPARKLE)
BLING
ANOTHER ONE!!

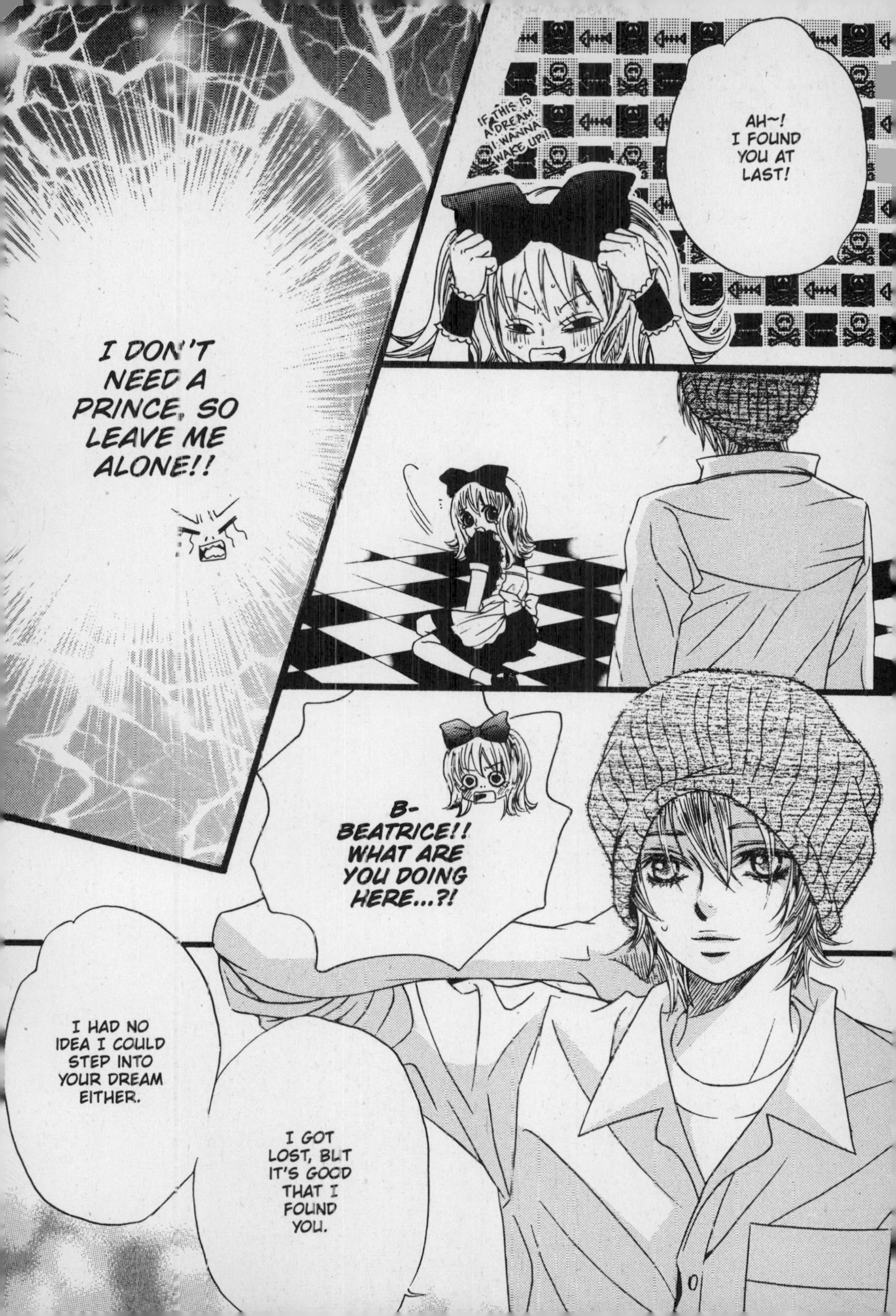
I DON'T NEED A PRINCE, SO LEAVE ME ALONE!!
IF THIS IS A DREAM, I WANNA WAKE UP!!
AH~! I FOUND YOU AT LAST!
B-BEATRICE!! WHAT ARE YOU DOING HERE...?!
I HAD NO IDEA I COULD STEP INTO YOUR DREAM EITHER.
I GOT LOST, BUT IT'S GOOD THAT I FOUND YOU.

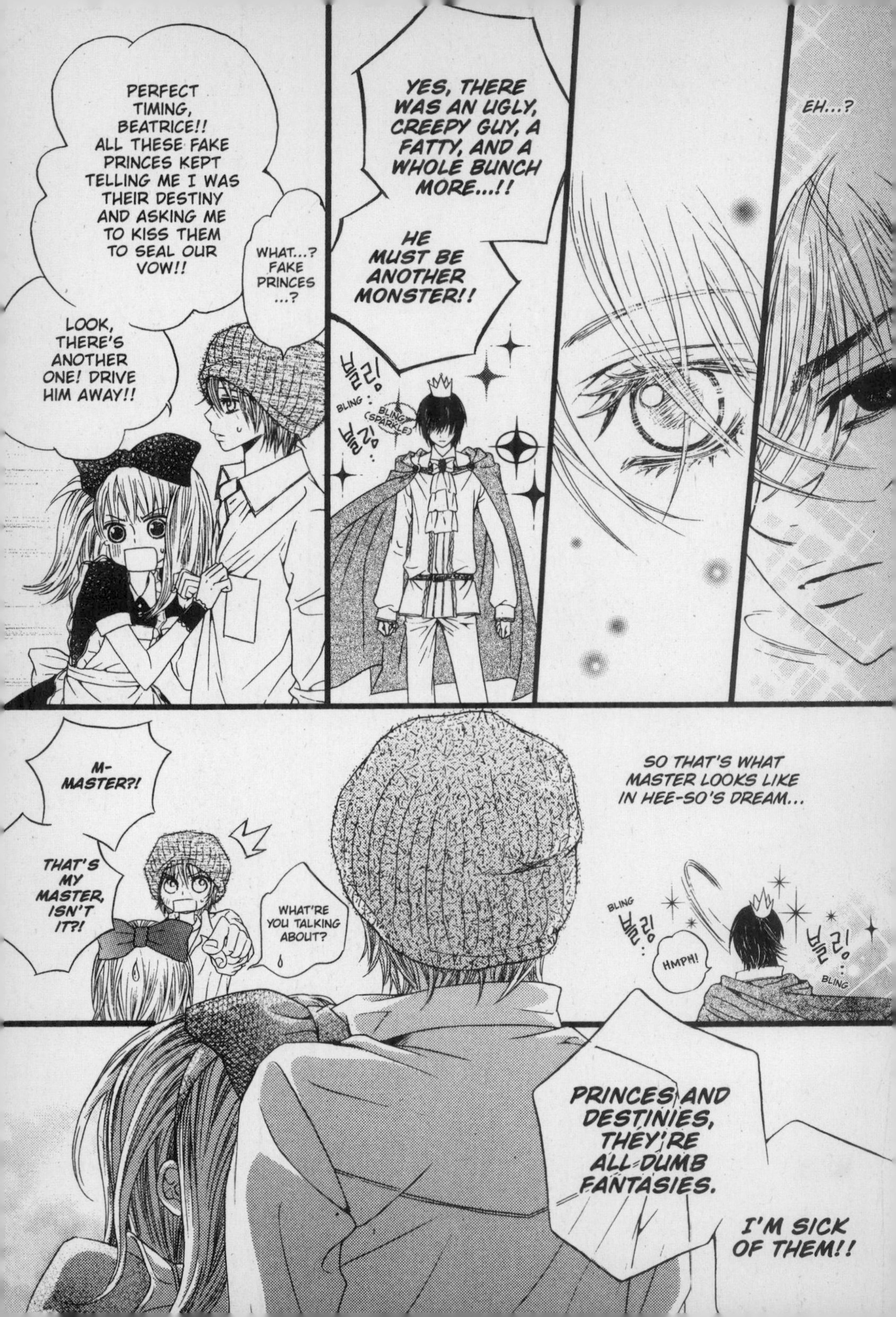
PERFECT TIMING, BEATRICE!! ALL THESE FAKE PRINCES KEPT TELLING ME I WAS THEIR DESTINY AND ASKING ME TO KISS THEM TO SEAL OUR VOW!!
WHAT...? FAKE PRINCES ...?
LOOK, THERE'S ANOTHER ONE! DRIVE HIM AWAY!!
YES, THERE WAS AN UGLY, CREEPY GUY, A FATTY, AND A WHOLE BUNCH MORE...!!
HE MUST BE ANOTHER MONSTER!!
블링
BLING
BLING (SPARKLE)
블링
EH...?
M-MASTER?!
THAT'S MY MASTER, ISN'T IT?!
WHAT'RE YOU TALKING ABOUT?
SO THAT'S WHAT MASTER LOOKS LIKE IN HEE-SO'S DREAM...
BLING
블링
HMPH!
블링
BLING
PRINCES AND DESTINIES, THEY'RE ALL DUMB FANTASIES.
I'M SICK OF THEM!!

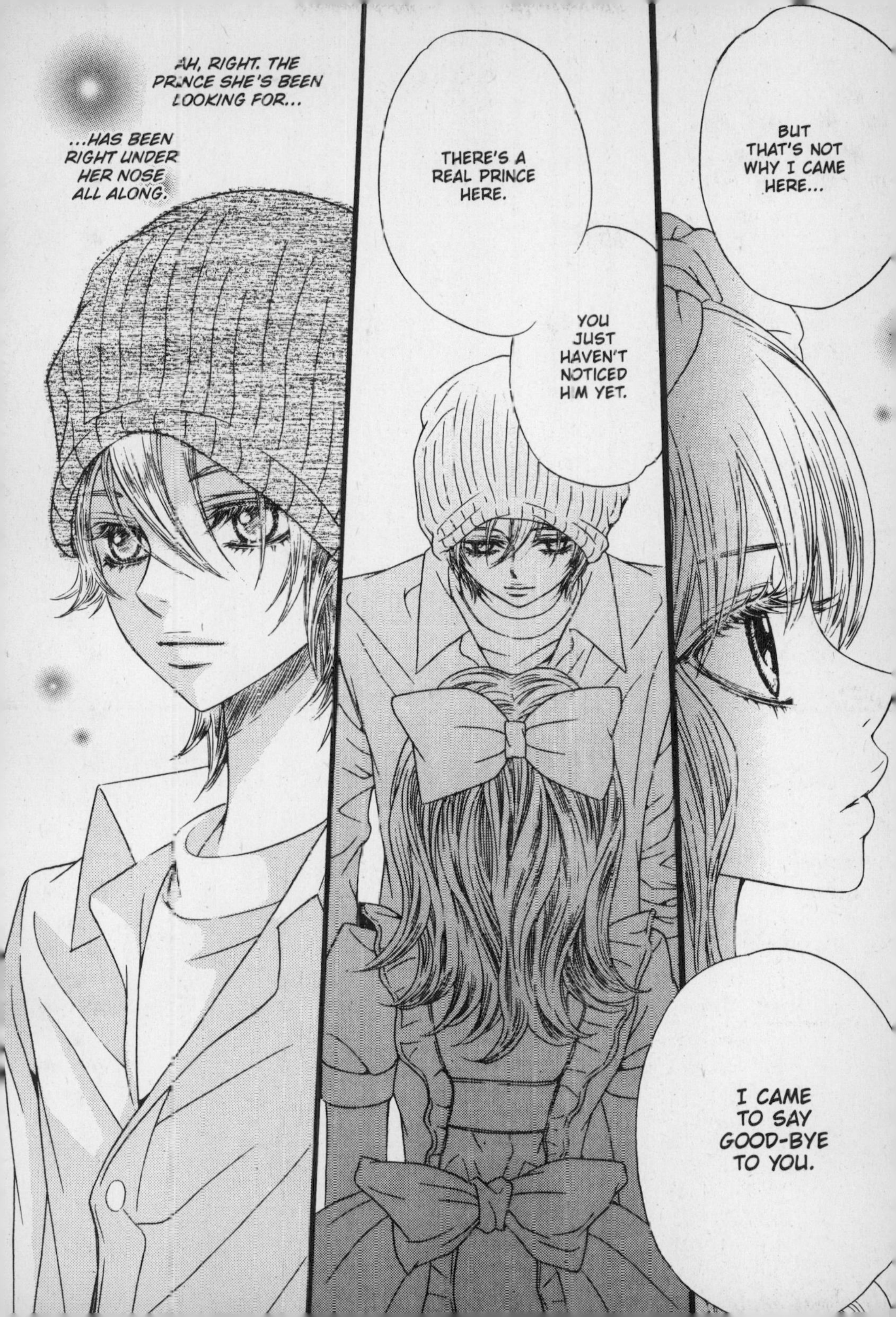
AH, RIGHT. THE PRINCE SHE'S BEEN LOOKING FOR...
...HAS BEEN RIGHT UNDER HER NOSE ALL ALONG.
THERE'S A REAL PRINCE HERE.
YOU JUST HAVEN'T NOTICED HIM YET.
BUT THAT'S NOT WHY I CAME HERE...
I CAME TO SAY GOOD-BYE TO YOU.

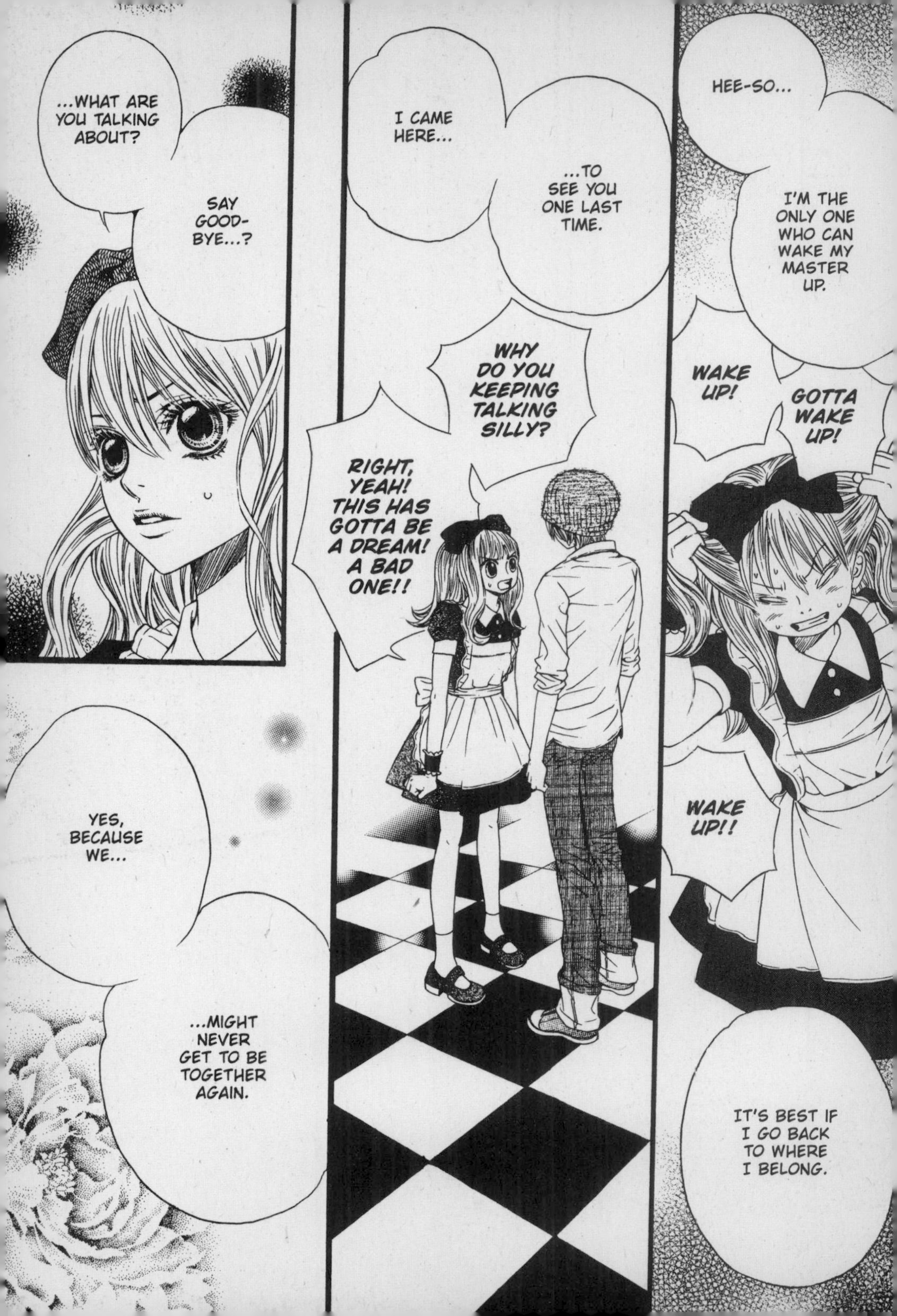
...WHAT ARE YOU TALKING ABOUT?
SAY GOOD-BYE...?
YES, BECAUSE WE...
...MIGHT NEVER GET TO BE TOGETHER AGAIN.
I CAME HERE...
...TO SEE YOU ONE LAST TIME.
WHY DO YOU KEEPING TALKING SILLY?
RIGHT, YEAH! THIS HAS GOTTA BE A DREAM! A BAD ONE!!
HEE-SO...
I'M THE ONLY ONE WHO CAN WAKE MY MASTER UP.
WAKE UP!
GOTTA WAKE UP!
WAKE UP!!
IT'S BEST IF I GO BACK TO WHERE I BELONG.

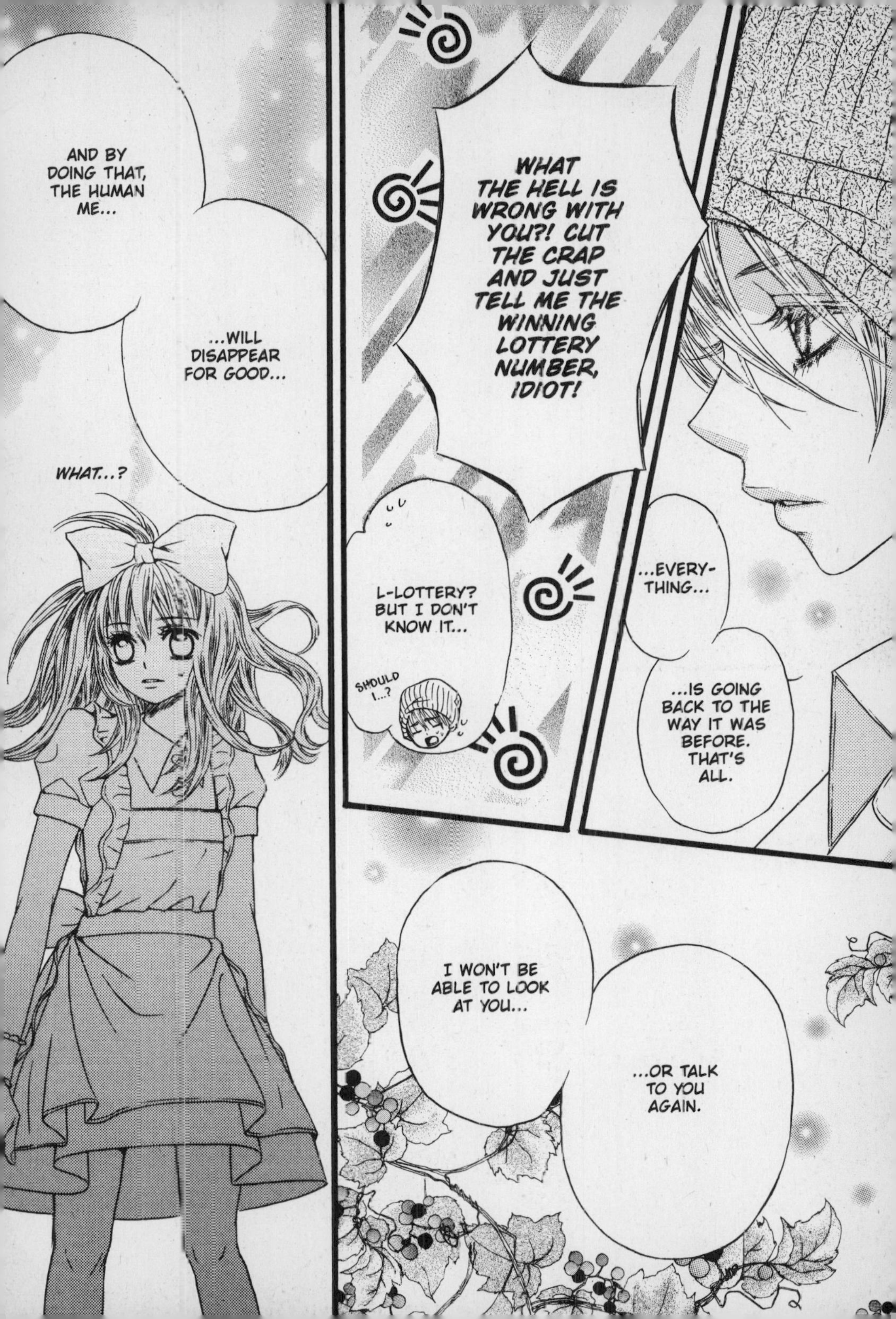
AND BY DOING THAT, THE HUMAN ME...
...WILL DISAPPEAR FOR GOOD...
WHAT...?
WHAT THE HELL IS WRONG WITH YOU?! CUT THE CRAP AND JUST TELL ME THE WINNING LOTTERY NUMBER, IDIOT!
L-LOTTERY? BUT I DON'T KNOW IT...
SHOULD I...?
...EVERYTHING...
...IS GOING BACK TO THE WAY IT WAS BEFORE. THAT'S ALL.
I WON'T BE ABLE TO LOOK AT YOU...
...OR TALK TO YOU AGAIN.

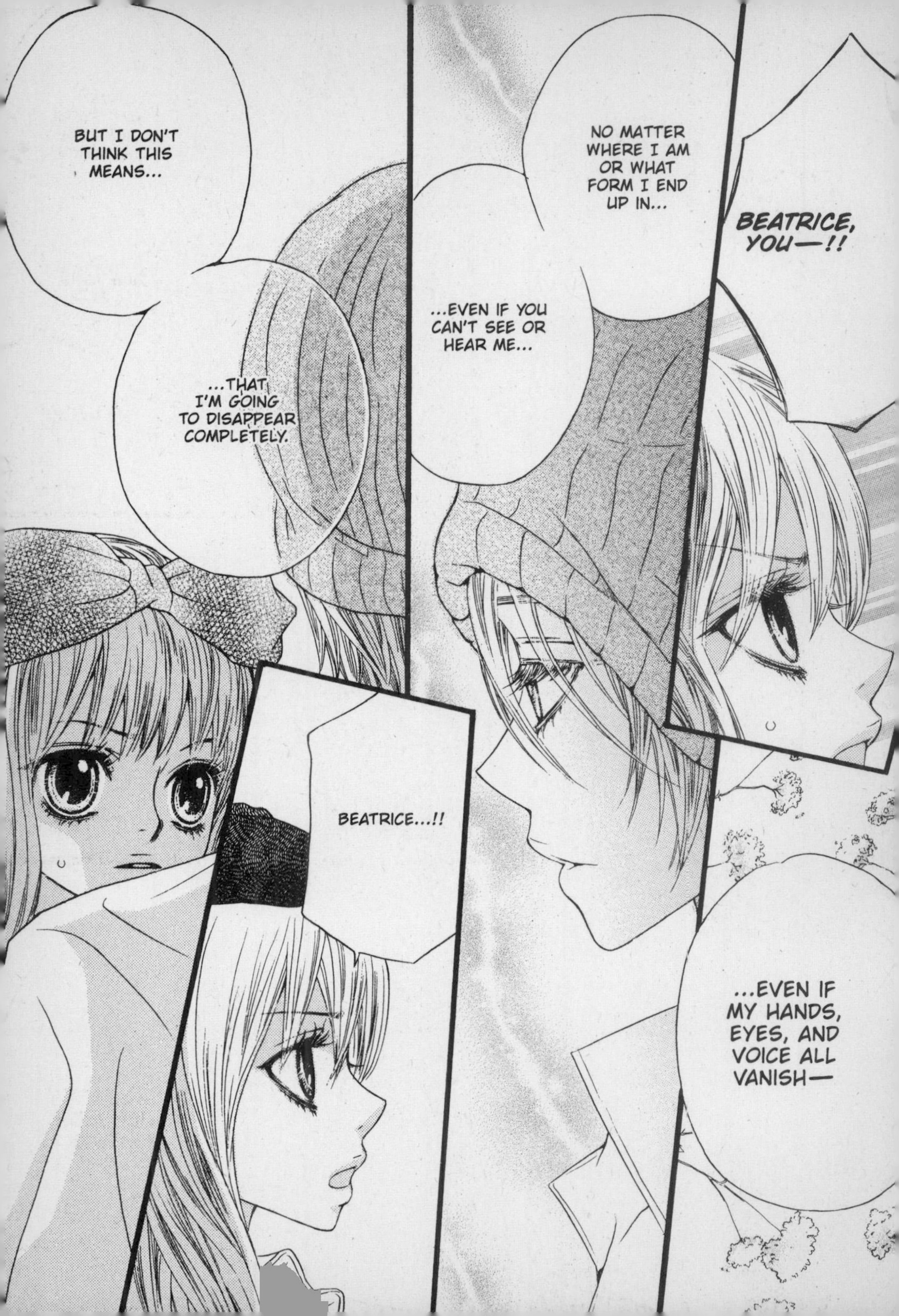
BUT I DON'T THINK THIS MEANS...
...THAT I'M GOING TO DISAPPEAR COMPLETELY.
NO MATTER WHERE I AM OR WHAT FORM I END UP IN...
...EVEN IF YOU CAN'T SEE OR HEAR ME...
BEATRICE, YOU—!!
BEATRICE...!!
...EVEN IF MY HANDS, EYES, AND VOICE ALL VANISH—

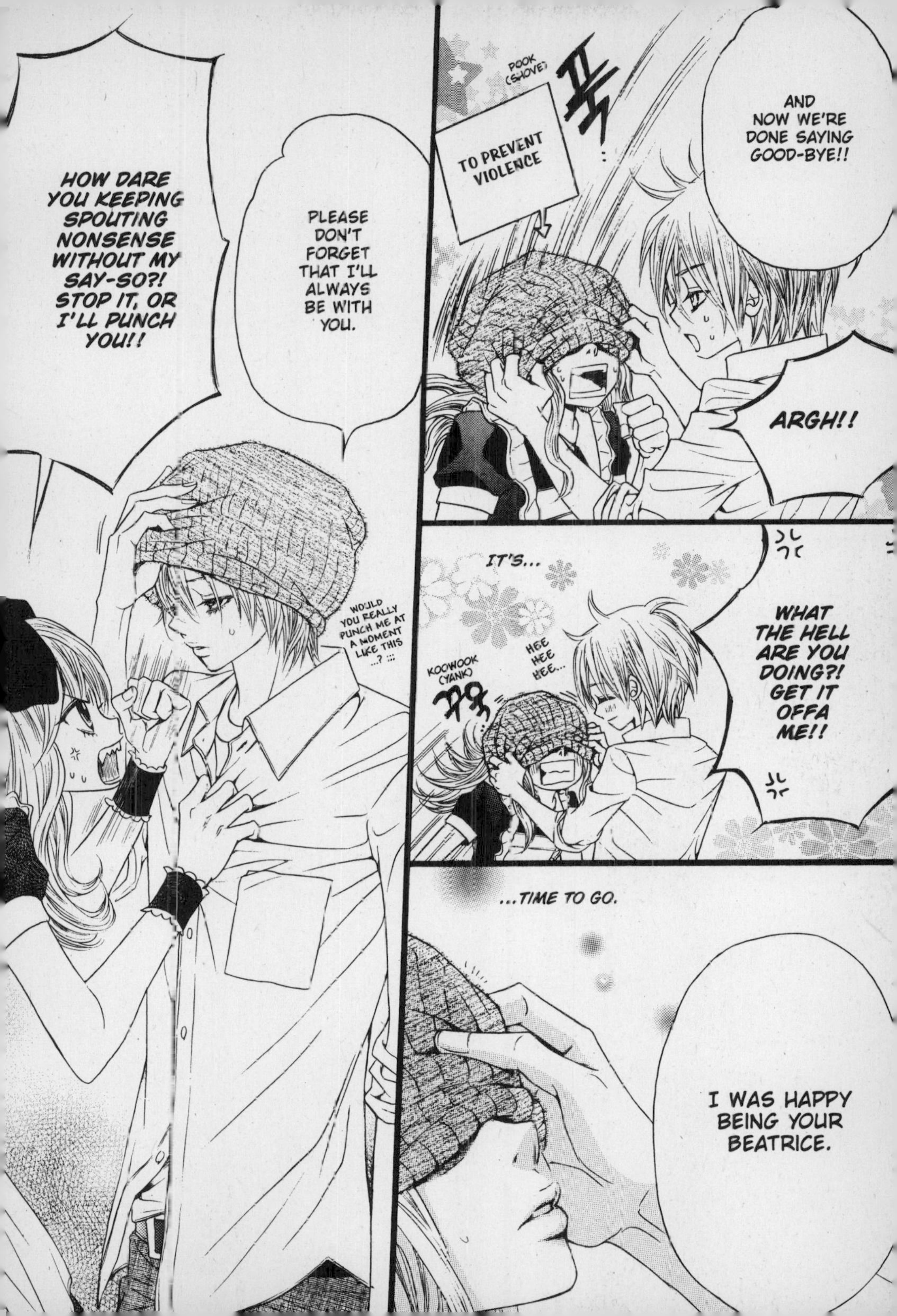
HOW DARE YOU KEEPING SPOUTING NONSENSE WITHOUT MY SAY-SO?! STOP IT, OR I'LL PUNCH YOU!!
PLEASE DON'T FORGET THAT I'LL ALWAYS BE WITH YOU.
WOULD YOU REALLY PUNCH ME AT A MOMENT LIKE THIS ...?
POOK (SHOVE)
TO PREVENT VIOLENCE
AND NOW WE'RE DONE SAYING GOOD-BYE!!
ARGH!!
IT'S...
KOOWOOK (YANK)
HEE HEE HEE...
WHAT THE HELL ARE YOU DOING?! GET IT OFFA ME!!
...TIME TO GO.
I WAS HAPPY BEING YOUR BEATRICE.

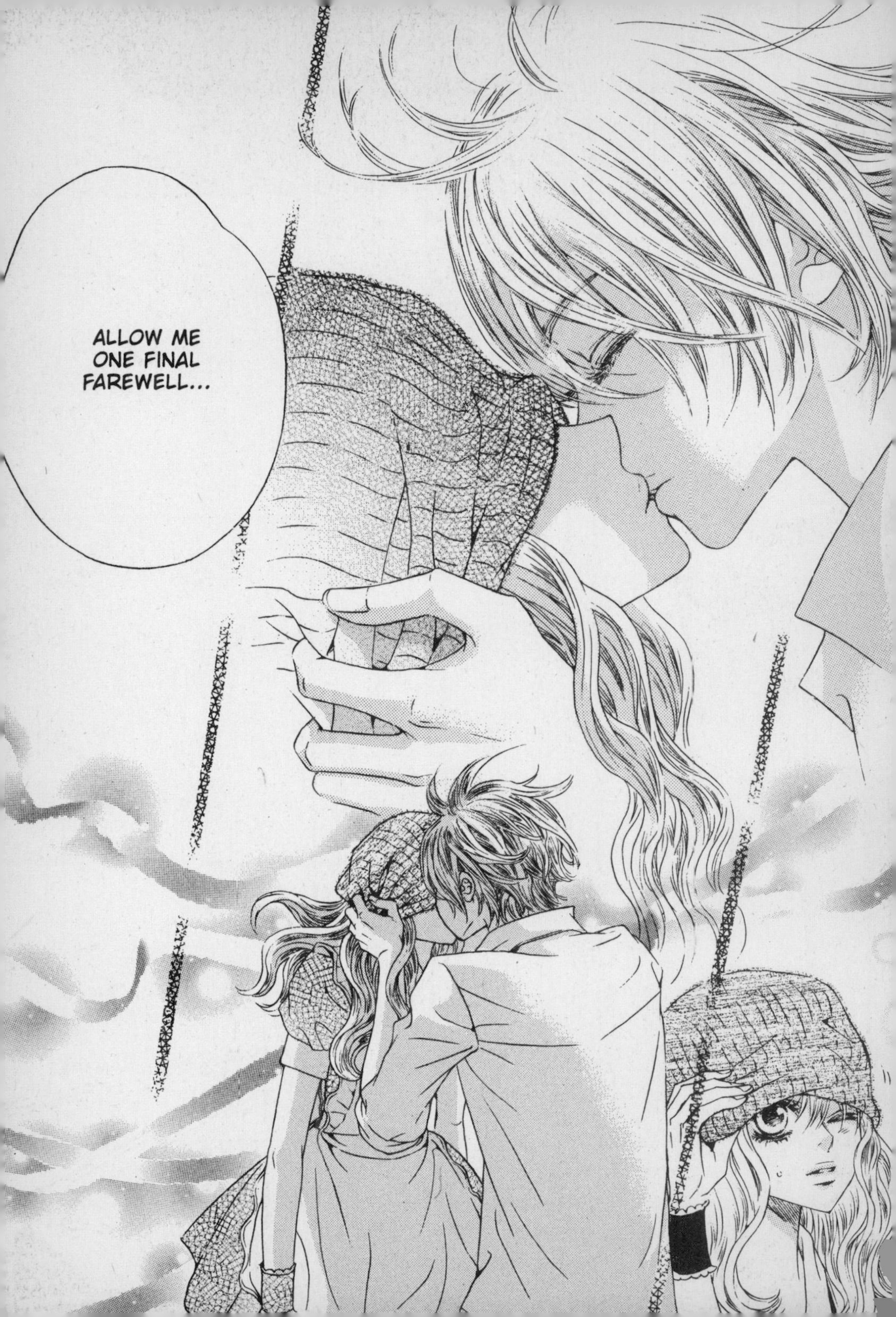
ALLOW ME ONE FINAL FAREWELL...

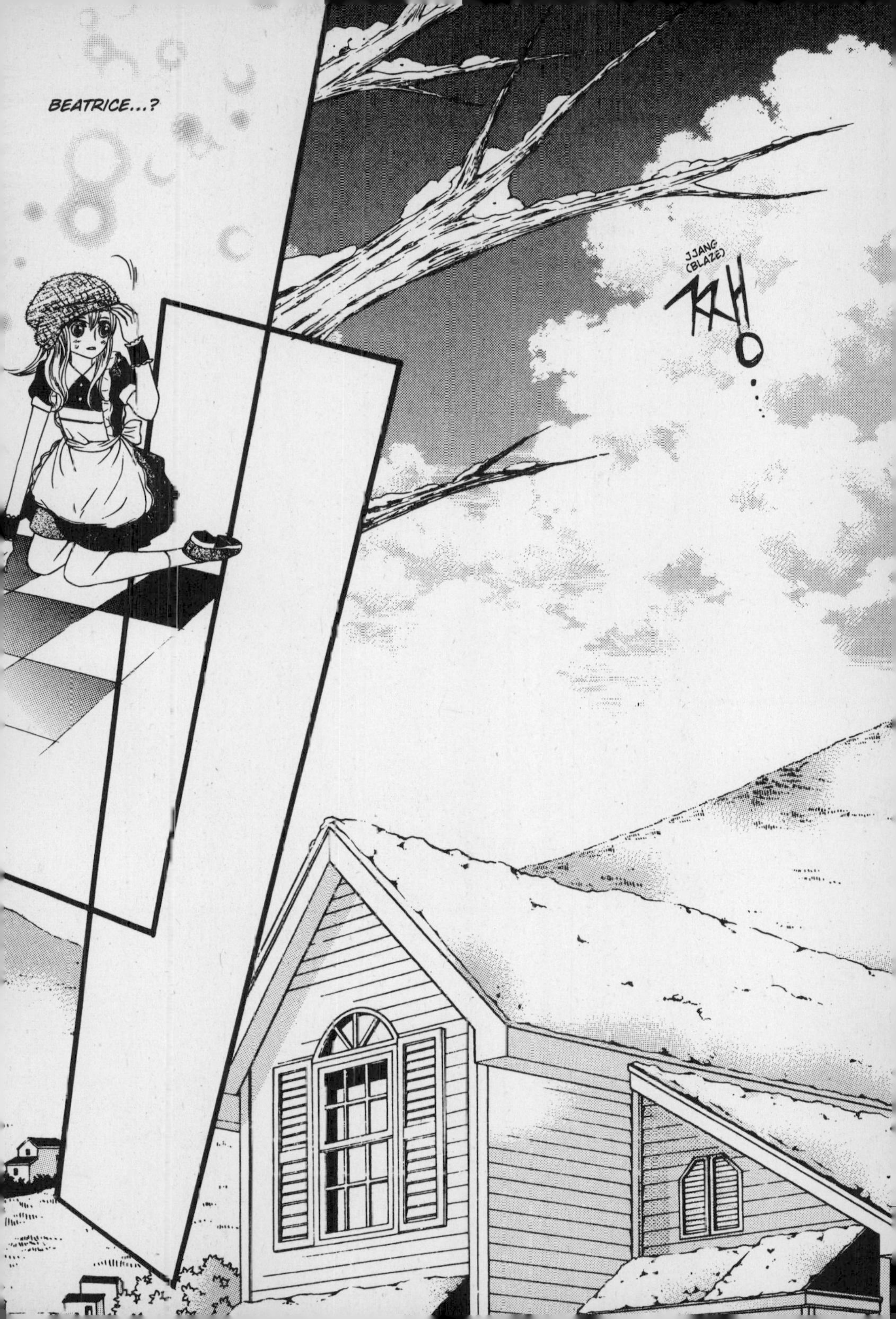
BEATRICE...?
JJANG (BLAZE)

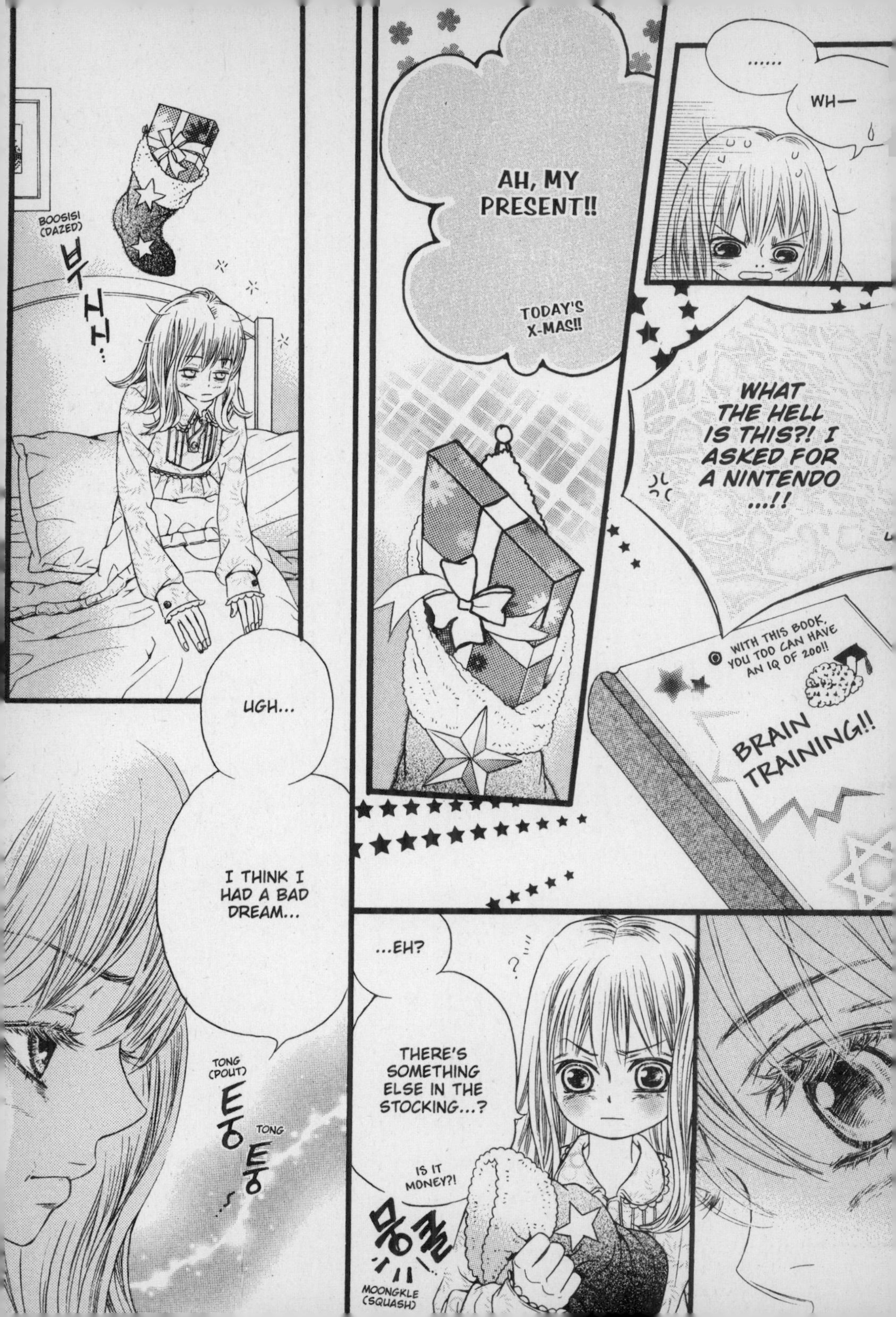
BOOSISI (DAZED)
부스스...
AH, MY PRESENT!!
TODAY'S X-MAS!!
......
WH—
WHAT THE HELL IS THIS?! I ASKED FOR A NINTENDO ...!!
WITH THIS BOOK, YOU TOO CAN HAVE AN IQ OF 200!!
BRAIN TRAINING!!
UGH...
I THINK I HAD A BAD DREAM...
TONG (POUT)
통
TONG
통
...EH?
THERE'S SOMETHING ELSE IN THE STOCKING...?
IS IT MONEY?!
뭉클
MOONGKLE (SQUASH)

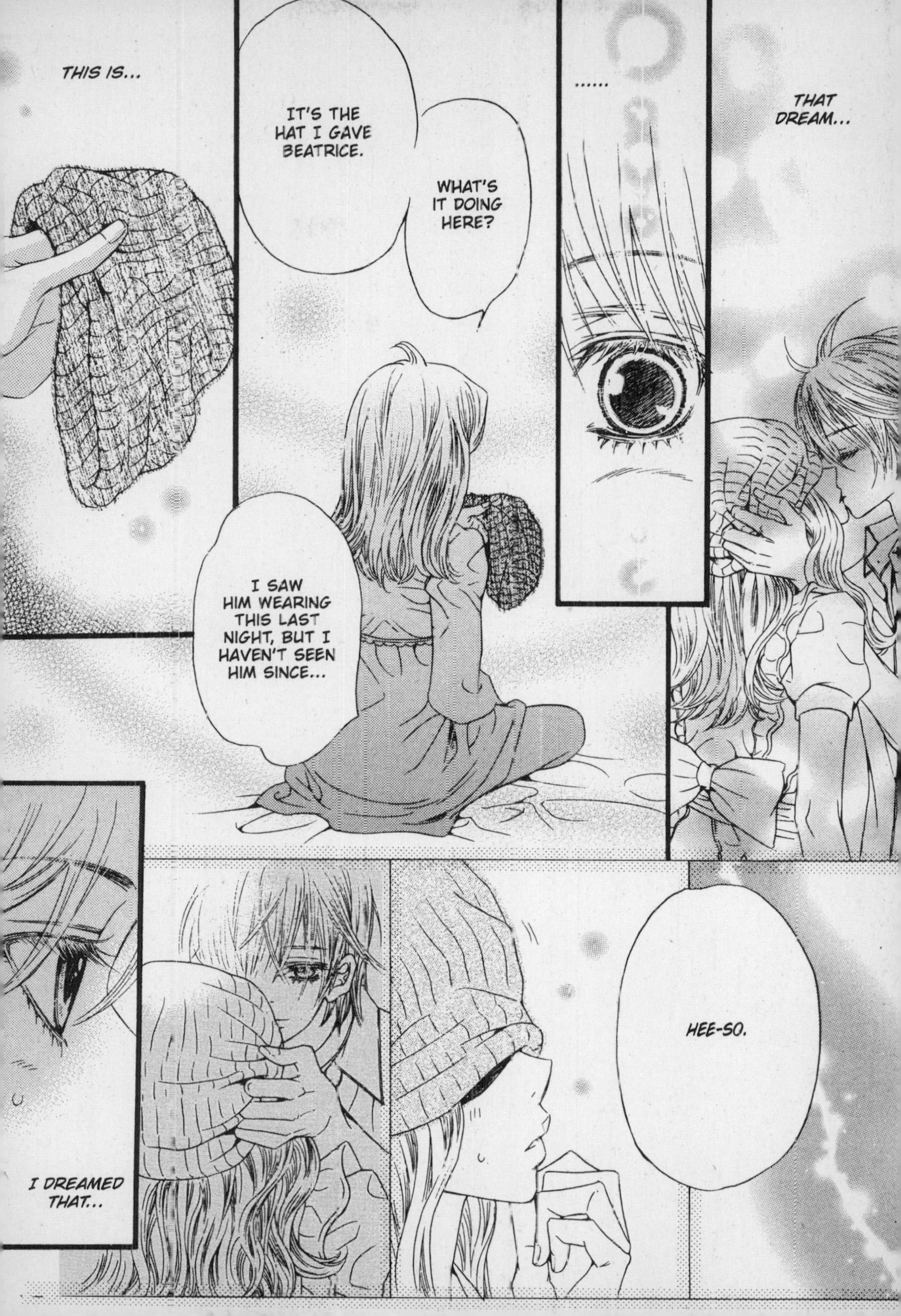
THIS IS...
IT'S THE HAT I GAVE BEATRICE.
WHAT'S IT DOING HERE?
I SAW HIM WEARING THIS LAST NIGHT, BUT I HAVEN'T SEEN HIM SINCE...
......
THAT DREAM...
I DREAMED THAT...
HEE-SO.

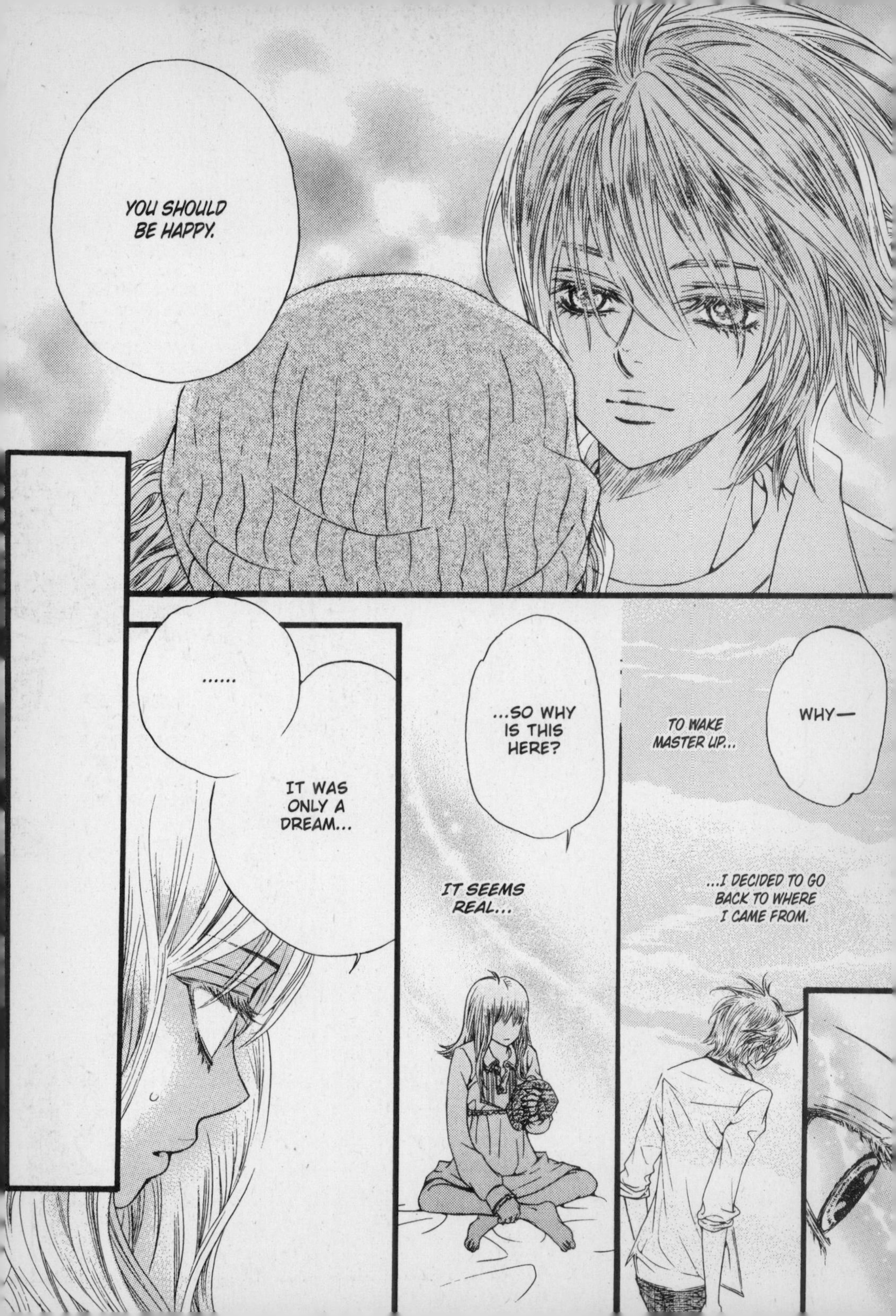
YOU SHOULD BE HAPPY.
......
IT WAS ONLY A DREAM...
...SO WHY IS THIS HERE?
IT SEEMS REAL...
WHY—
TO WAKE MASTER UP...
...I DECIDED TO GO BACK TO WHERE I CAME FROM.

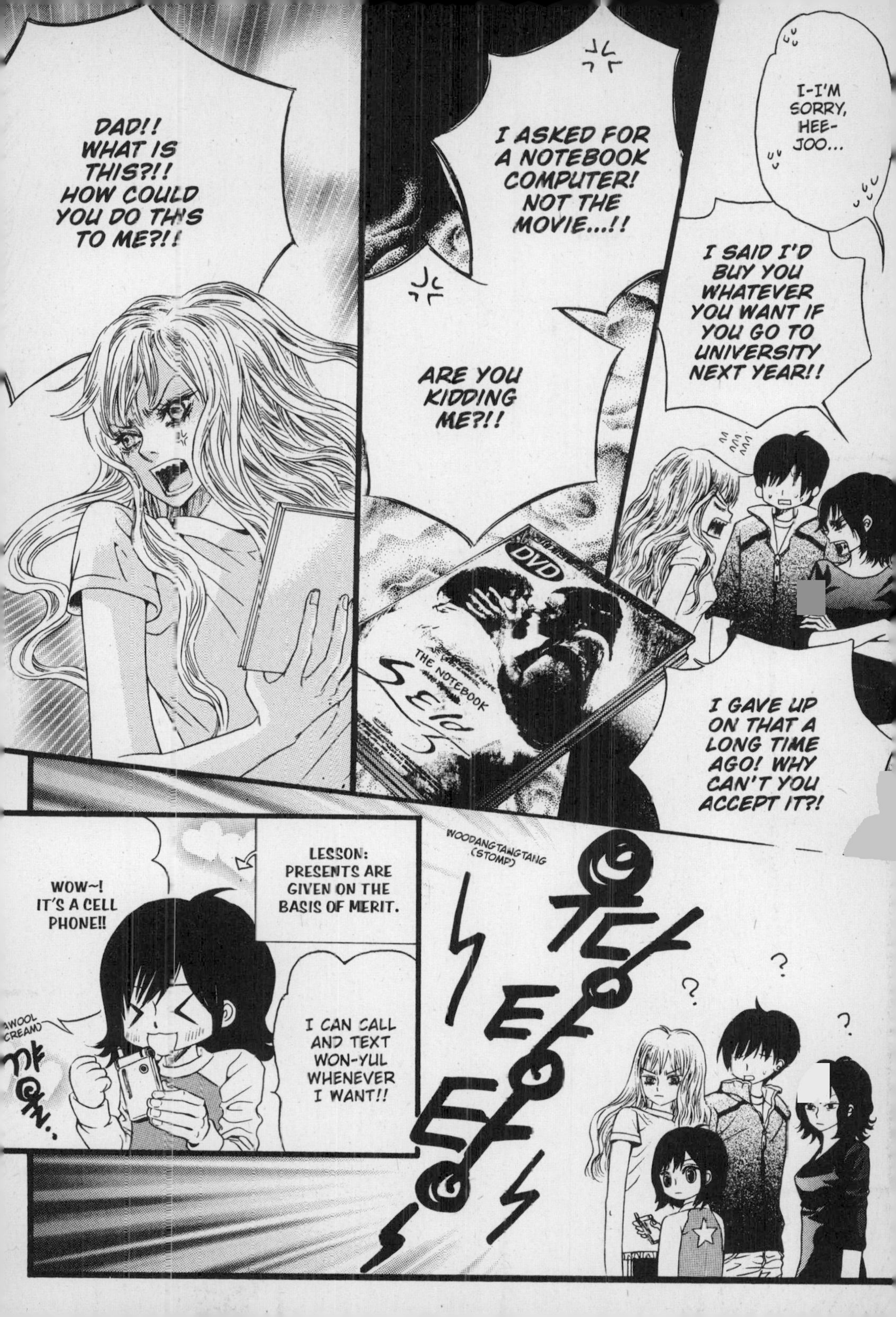
DAD!! WHAT IS THIS?!! HOW COULD YOU DO THIS TO ME?!!
I ASKED FOR A NOTEBOOK COMPUTER! NOT THE MOVIE...!!
ARE YOU KIDDING ME?!!
DVD
THE NOTEBOOK
I-I'M SORRY, HEE-JOO...
I SAID I'D BUY YOU WHATEVER YOU WANT IF YOU GO TO UNIVERSITY NEXT YEAR!!
I GAVE UP ON THAT A LONG TIME AGO! WHY CAN'T YOU ACCEPT IT?!
WOW~! IT'S A CELL PHONE!!
LESSON: PRESENTS ARE GIVEN ON THE BASIS OF MERIT.
I CAN CALL AND TEXT WON-YUL WHENEVER I WANT!!
WOODANGTANGTANG (STOMP)

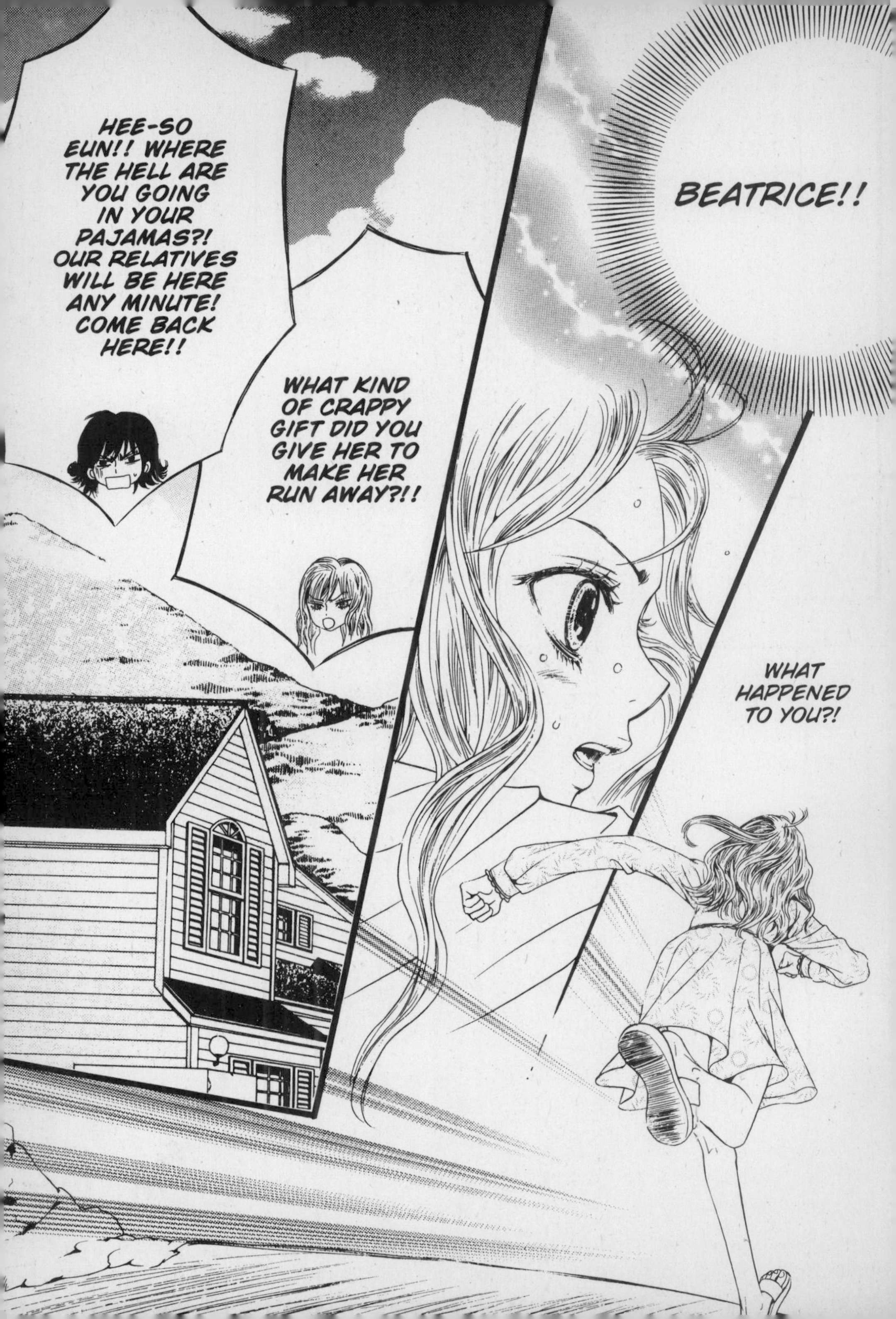
HEE-SO EUN!! WHERE THE HELL ARE YOU GOING IN YOUR PAJAMAS?! OUR RELATIVES WILL BE HERE ANY MINUTE! COME BACK HERE!!
WHAT KIND OF CRAPPY GIFT DID YOU GIVE HER TO MAKE HER RUN AWAY?!!
BEATRICE!!
WHAT HAPPENED TO YOU?!

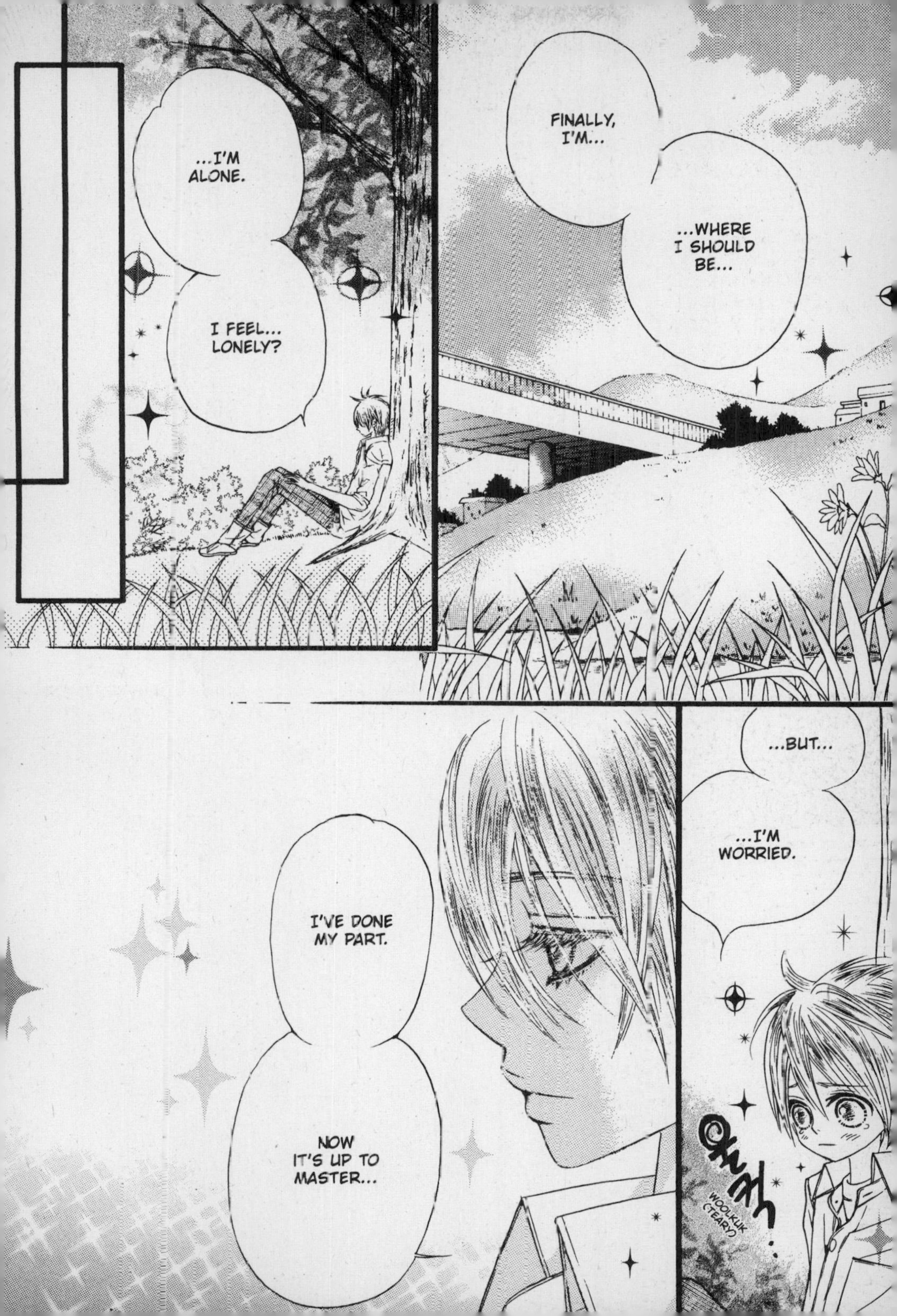
...I'M ALONE.
I FEEL... LONELY?
FINALLY, I'M...
...WHERE I SHOULD BE...
I'VE DONE MY PART.
NOW IT'S UP TO MASTER...
...BUT...
...I'M WORRIED.
WOOLKUK (TEARY)

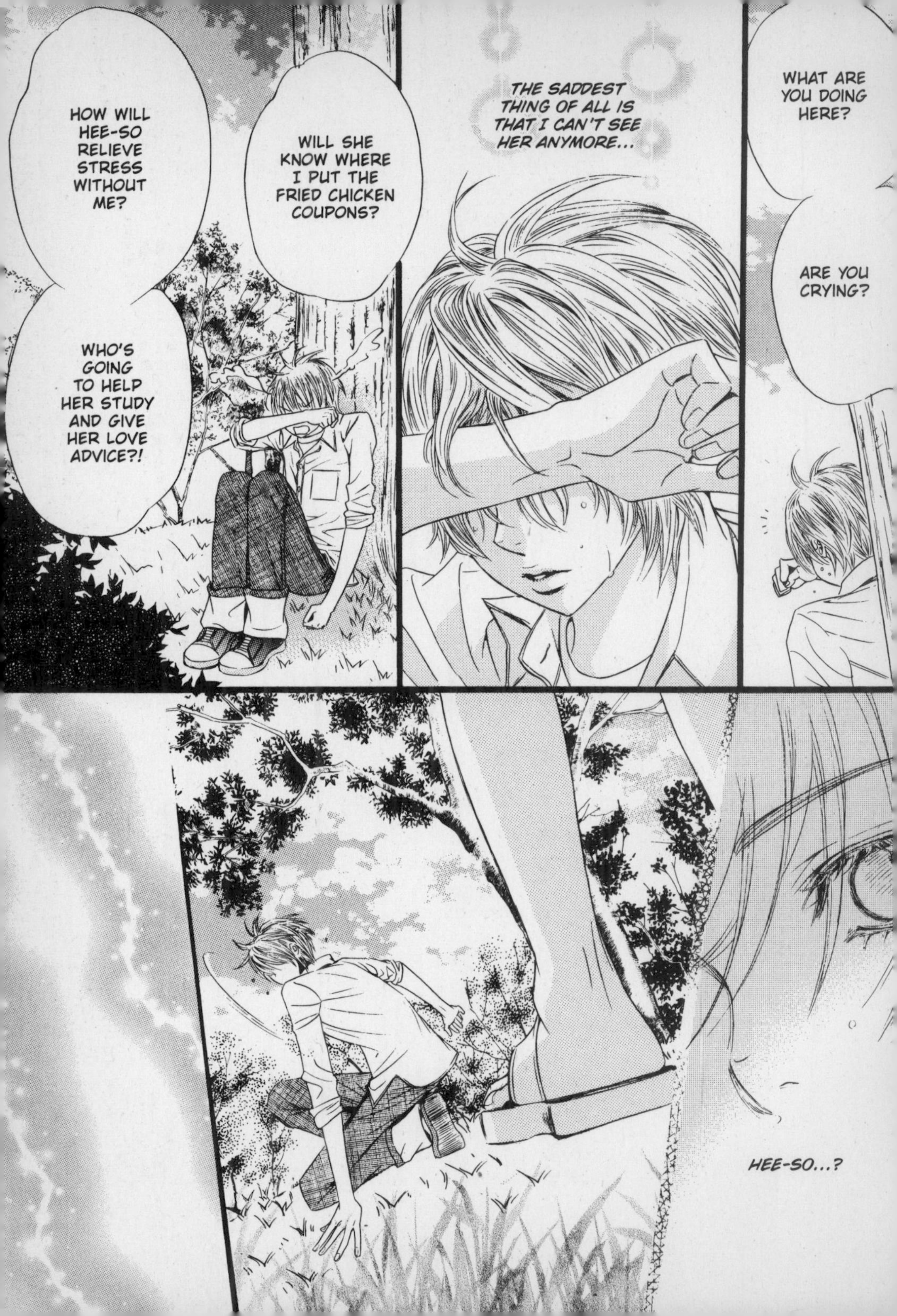
HOW WILL HEE-SO RELIEVE STRESS WITHOUT ME?
WHO'S GOING TO HELP HER STUDY AND GIVE HER LOVE ADVICE?!
WILL SHE KNOW WHERE I PUT THE FRIED CHICKEN COUPONS?
THE SADDEST THING OF ALL IS THAT I CAN'T SEE HER ANYMORE...
WHAT ARE YOU DOING HERE?
ARE YOU CRYING?
HEE-SO...?

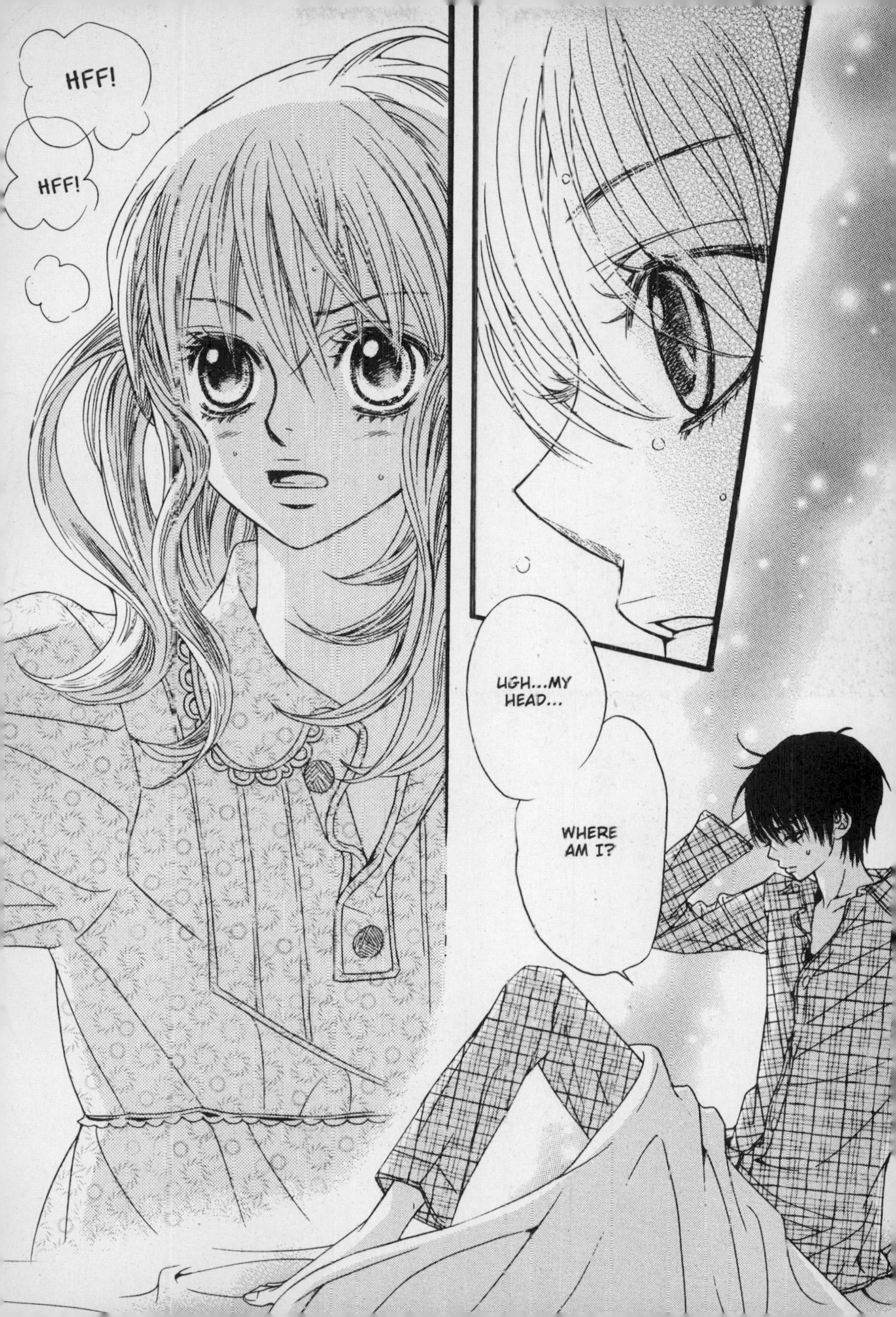
HFF!
HFF!
UGH...MY HEAD...
WHERE AM I?

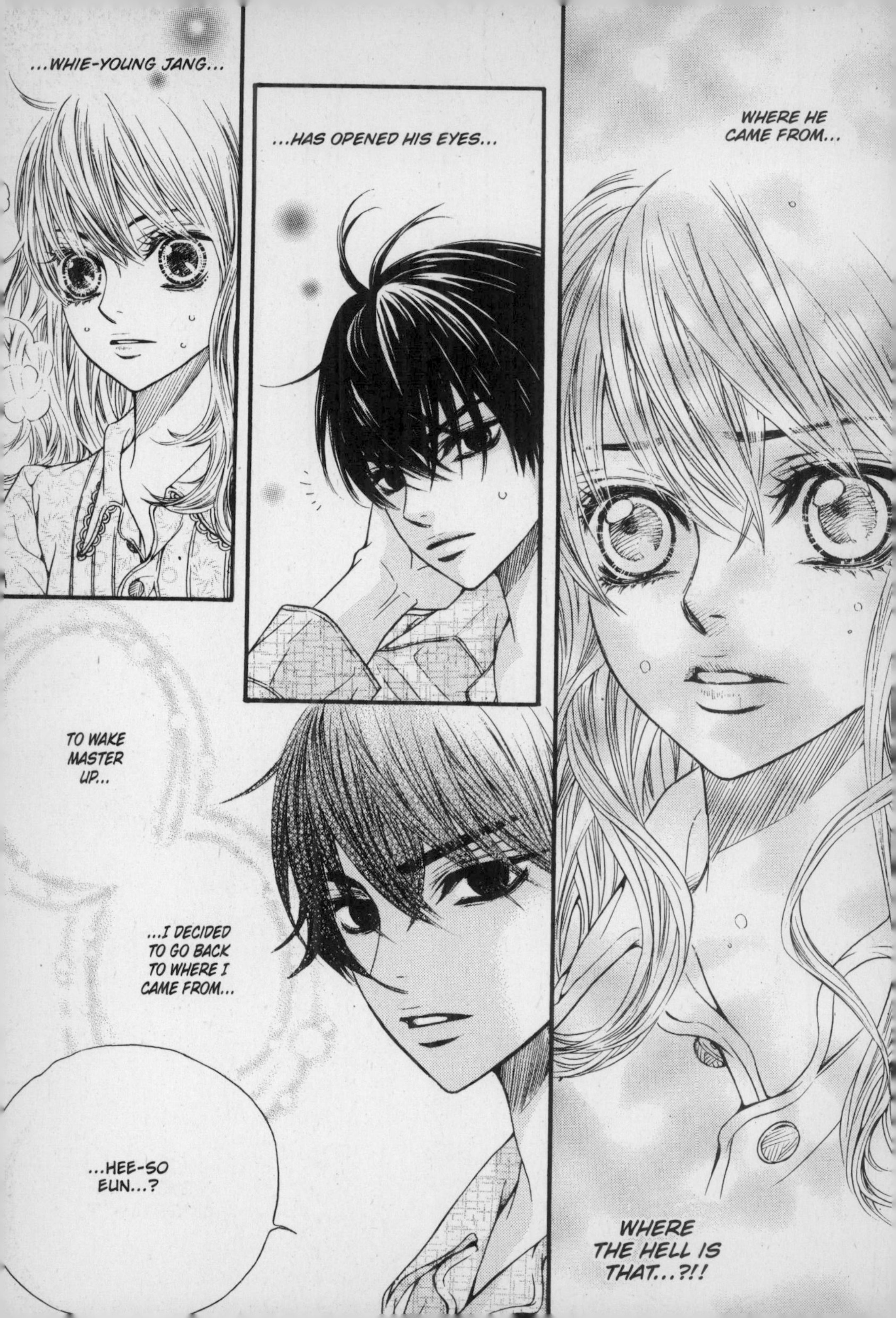
...WHIE-YOUNG JANG...
...HAS OPENED HIS EYES...
TO WAKE MASTER UP...
...I DECIDED TO GO BACK TO WHERE I CAME FROM...
...HEE-SO EUN...?
WHERE HE CAME FROM...
WHERE THE HELL IS THAT...?!!

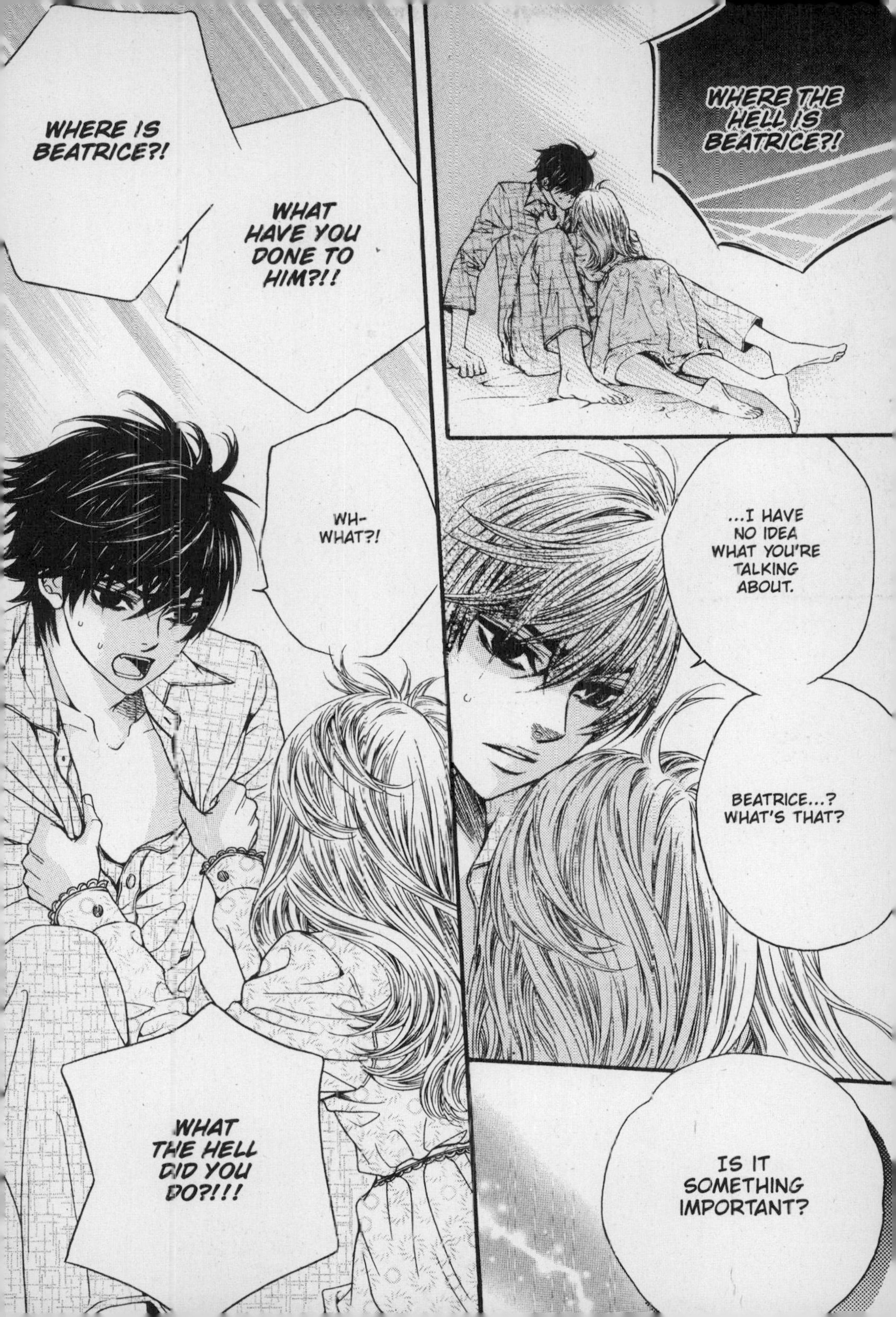
WHERE IS BEATRICE?!
WHAT HAVE YOU DONE TO HIM?!!
WH- WHAT?!
WHAT THE HELL DID YOU DO?!!!
WHERE THE HELL IS BEATRICE?!
...I HAVE NO IDEA WHAT YOU'RE TALKING ABOUT.
BEATRICE...? WHAT'S THAT?
IS IT SOMETHING IMPORTANT?

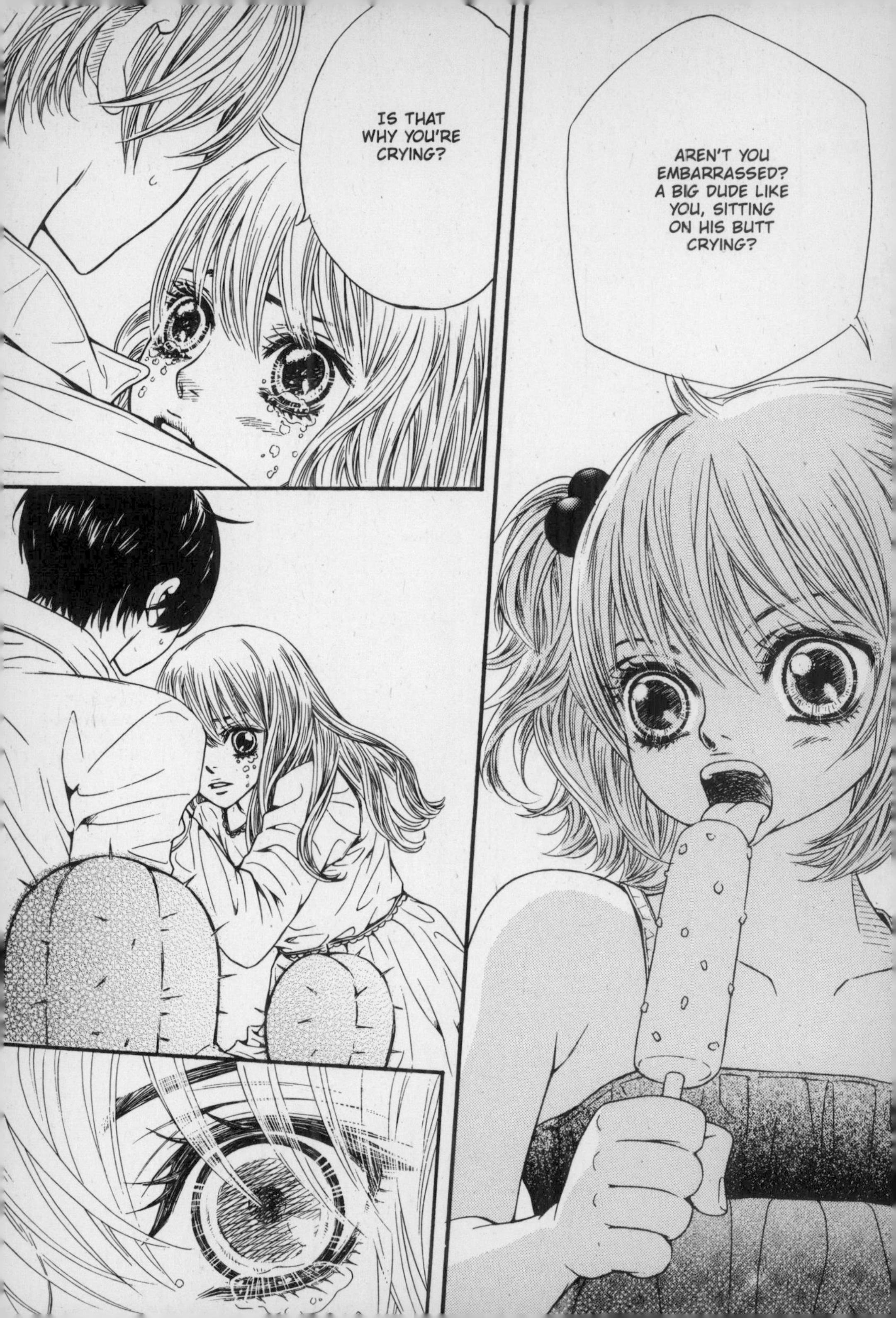
IS THAT WHY YOU'RE CRYING?
AREN'T YOU EMBARRASSED? A BIG DUDE LIKE YOU, SITTING ON HIS BUTT CRYING?

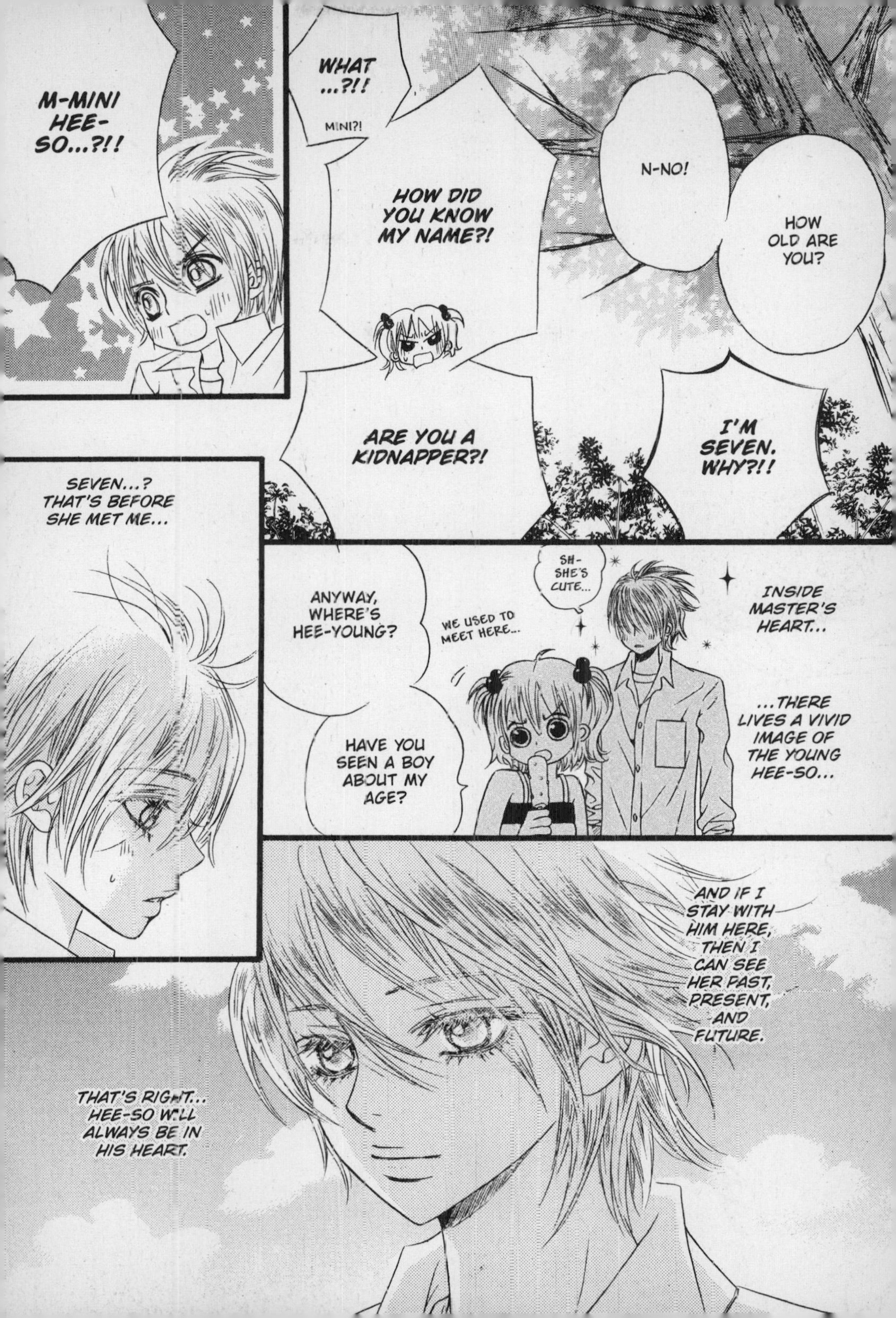
M-MINI HEE-SO...?!!
WHAT ...?!!
MINI?!
HOW DID YOU KNOW MY NAME?!
ARE YOU A KIDNAPPER?!
N-NO!
HOW OLD ARE YOU?
I'M SEVEN. WHY?!!
SEVEN...? THAT'S BEFORE SHE MET ME...
ANYWAY, WHERE'S HEE-YOUNG?
HAVE YOU SEEN A BOY ABOUT MY AGE?
WE USED TO MEET HERE...
SH-SHE'S CUTE...
INSIDE MASTER'S HEART...
...THERE LIVES A VIVID IMAGE OF THE YOUNG HEE-SO...
AND IF I STAY WITH HIM HERE, THEN I CAN SEE HER PAST, PRESENT, AND FUTURE.
THAT'S RIGHT... HEE-SO WILL ALWAYS BE IN HIS HEART.

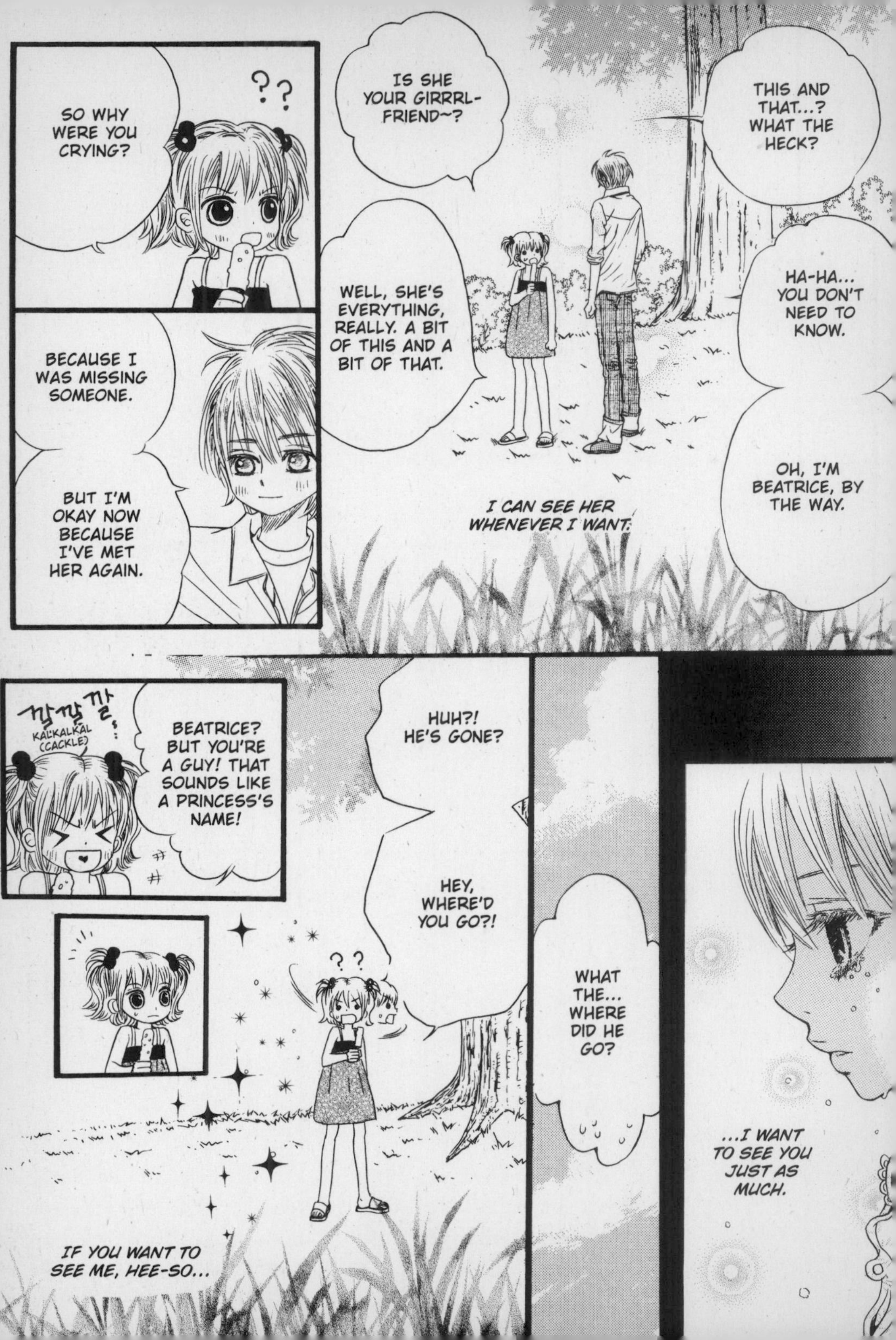
SO WHY WERE YOU CRYING?
??
BECAUSE I WAS MISSING SOMEONE.
BUT I'M OKAY NOW BECAUSE I'VE MET HER AGAIN.
IS SHE YOUR GIRRRL-FRIEND~?
WELL, SHE'S EVERYTHING, REALLY. A BIT OF THIS AND A BIT OF THAT.
THIS AND THAT...? WHAT THE HECK?
HA-HA... YOU DON'T NEED TO KNOW.
OH, I'M BEATRICE, BY THE WAY.
I CAN SEE HER WHENEVER I WANT.
깔깔깔
KALKALKAL (CACKLE)
BEATRICE? BUT YOU'RE A GUY! THAT SOUNDS LIKE A PRINCESS'S NAME!
HUH?! HE'S GONE?
HEY, WHERE'D YOU GO?!
??
IF YOU WANT TO SEE ME, HEE-SO...
WHAT THE... WHERE DID HE GO?
...I WANT TO SEE YOU JUST AS MUCH.

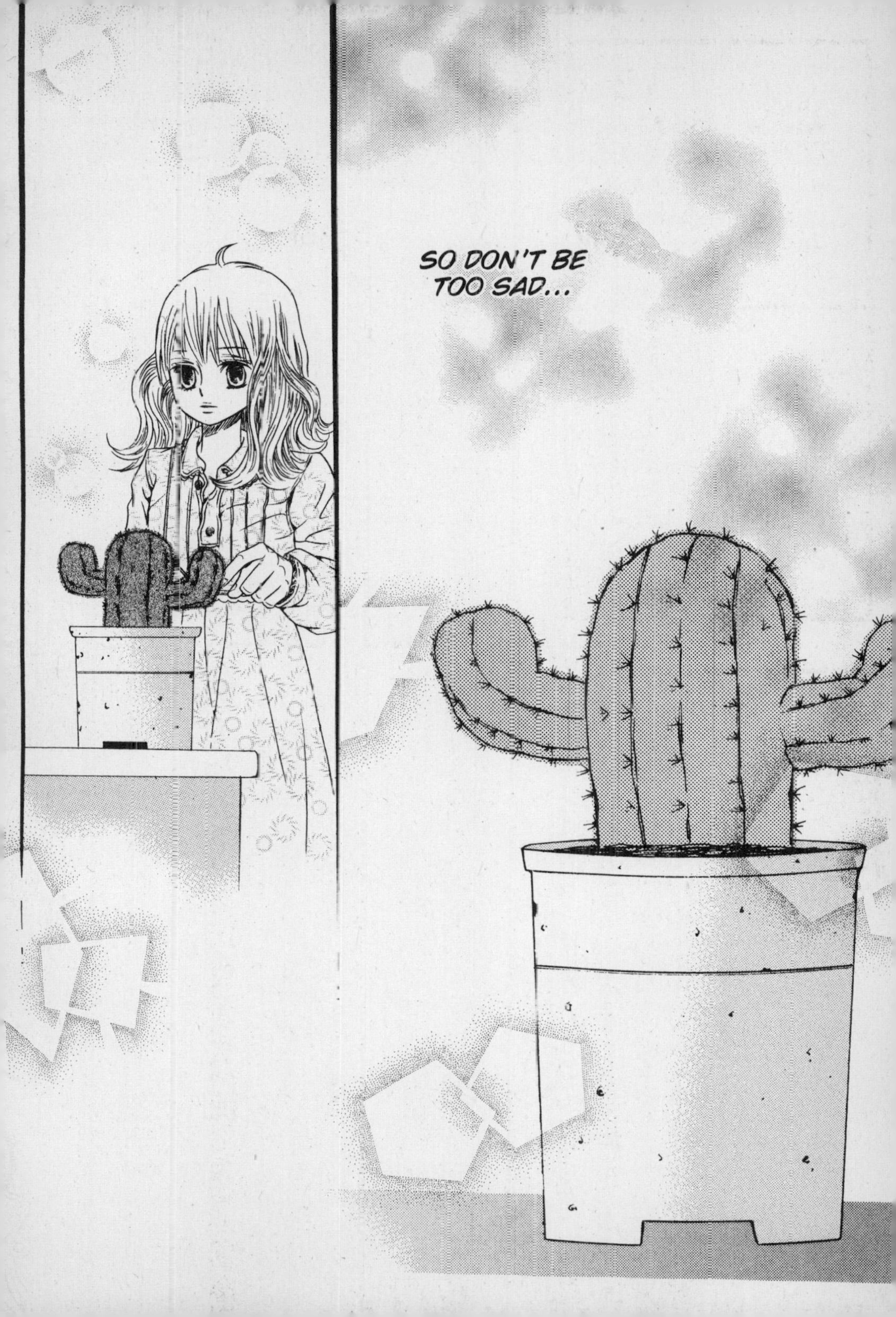
SO DON'T BE TOO SAD...

13th Boy

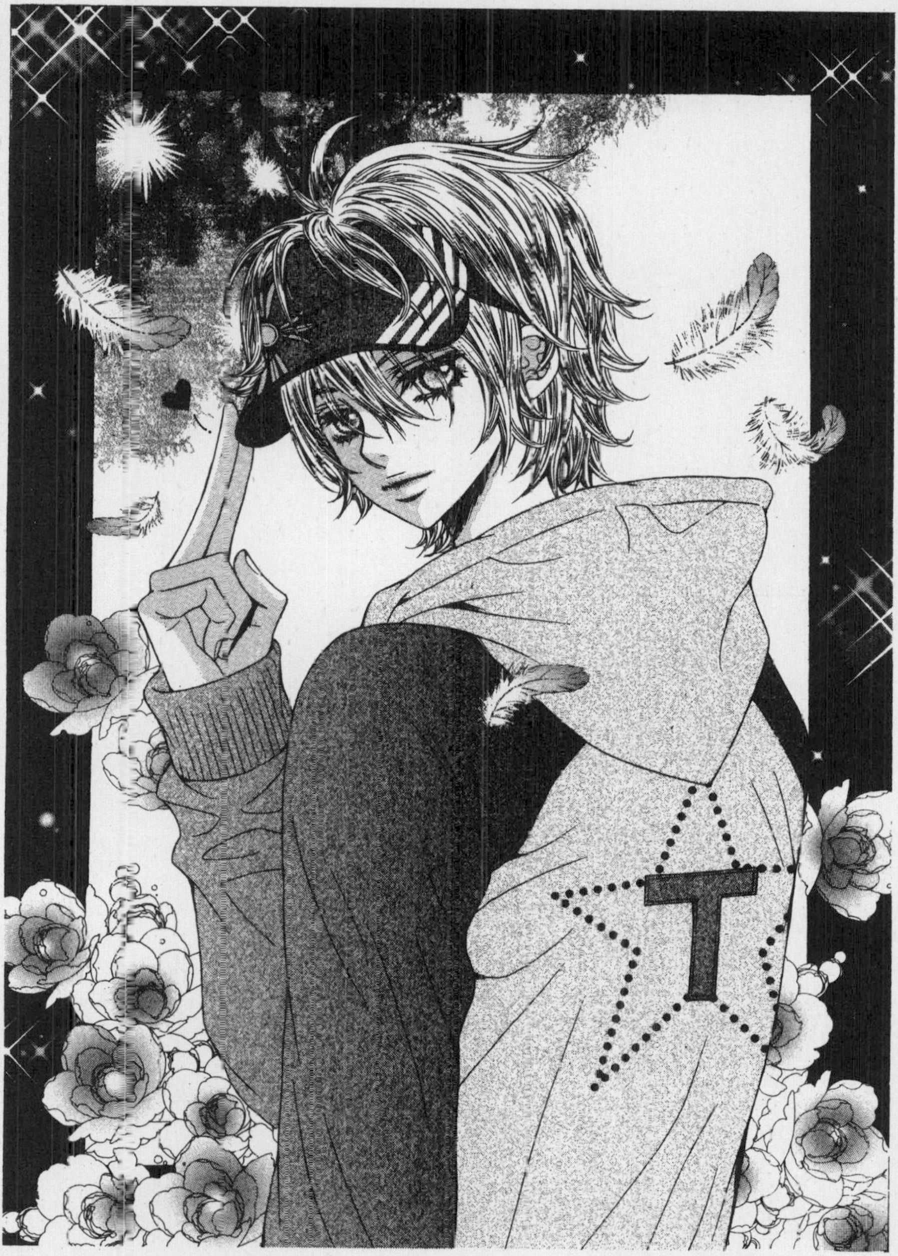

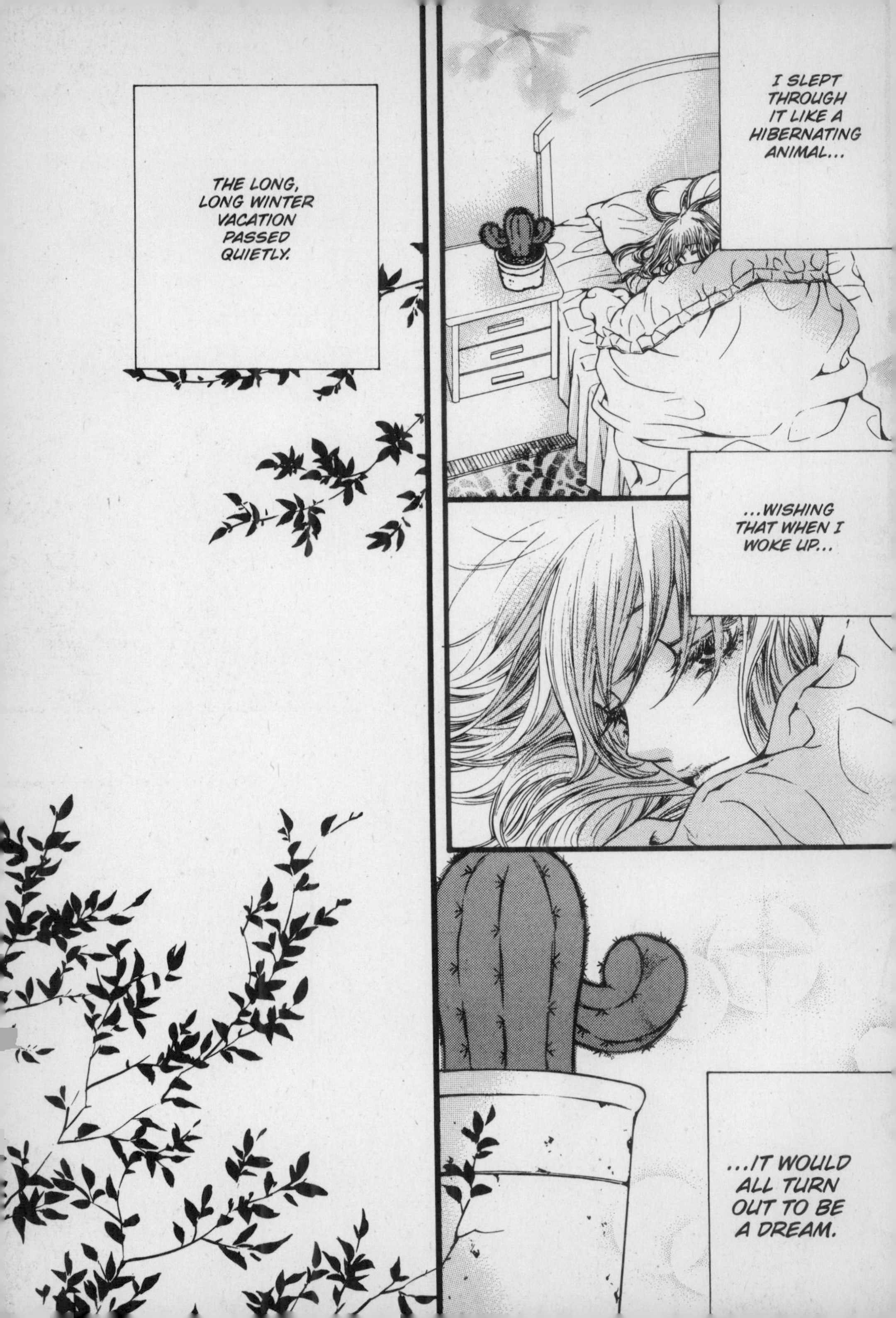
THE LONG, LONG WINTER VACATION PASSED QUIETLY.
I SLEPT THROUGH IT LIKE A HIBERNATING ANIMAL...
...WISHING THAT WHEN I WOKE UP...
...IT WOULD ALL TURN OUT TO BE A DREAM.

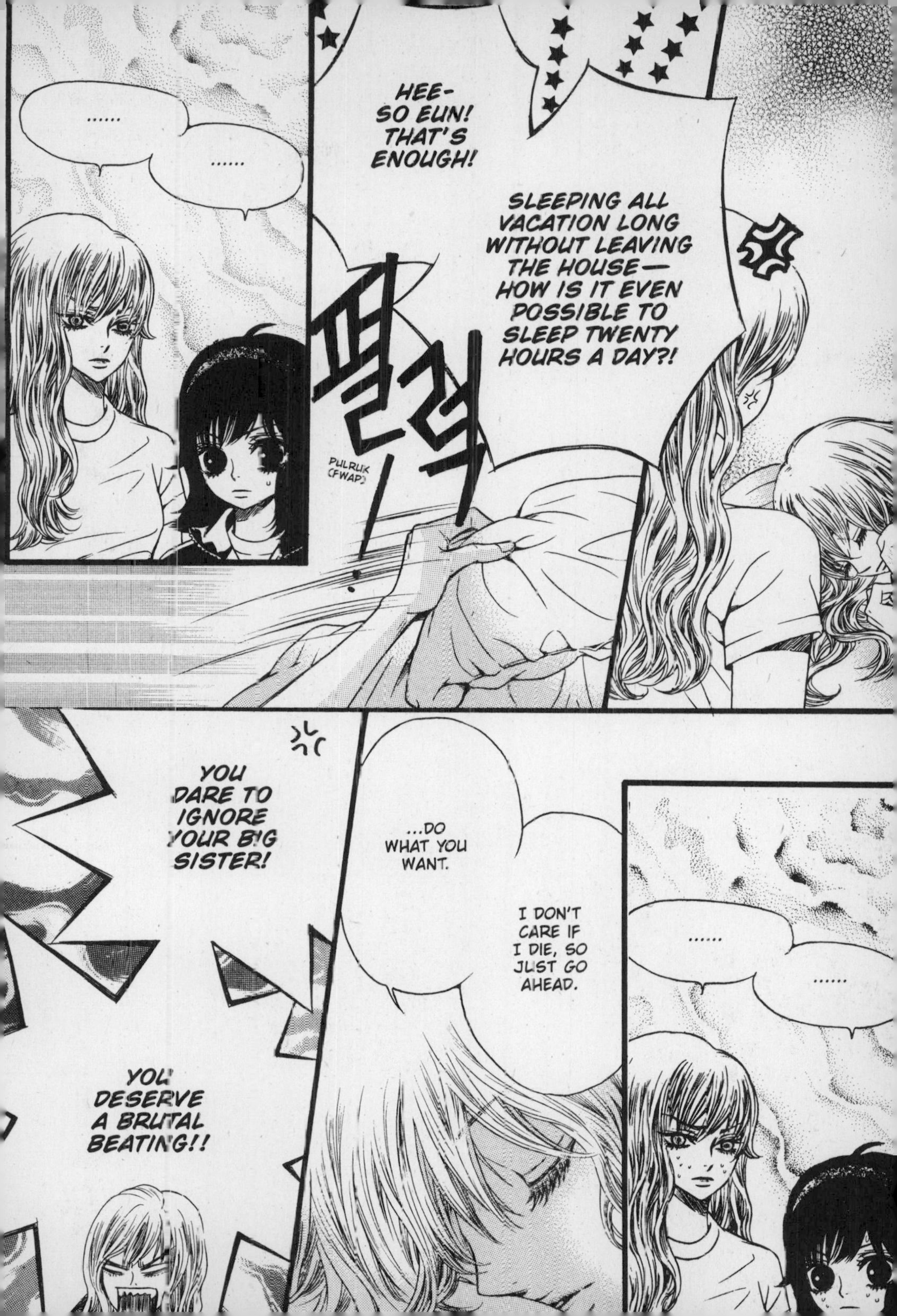
......
......
HEE-SO EUN! THAT'S ENOUGH!
SLEEPING ALL VACATION LONG WITHOUT LEAVING THE HOUSE—HOW IS IT EVEN POSSIBLE TO SLEEP TWENTY HOURS A DAY?!
펄럭
PULRUK (FWAP)
YOU DARE TO IGNORE YOUR BIG SISTER!
YOU DESERVE A BRUTAL BEATING!!
...DO WHAT YOU WANT.
I DON'T CARE IF I DIE, SO JUST GO AHEAD.
......
......

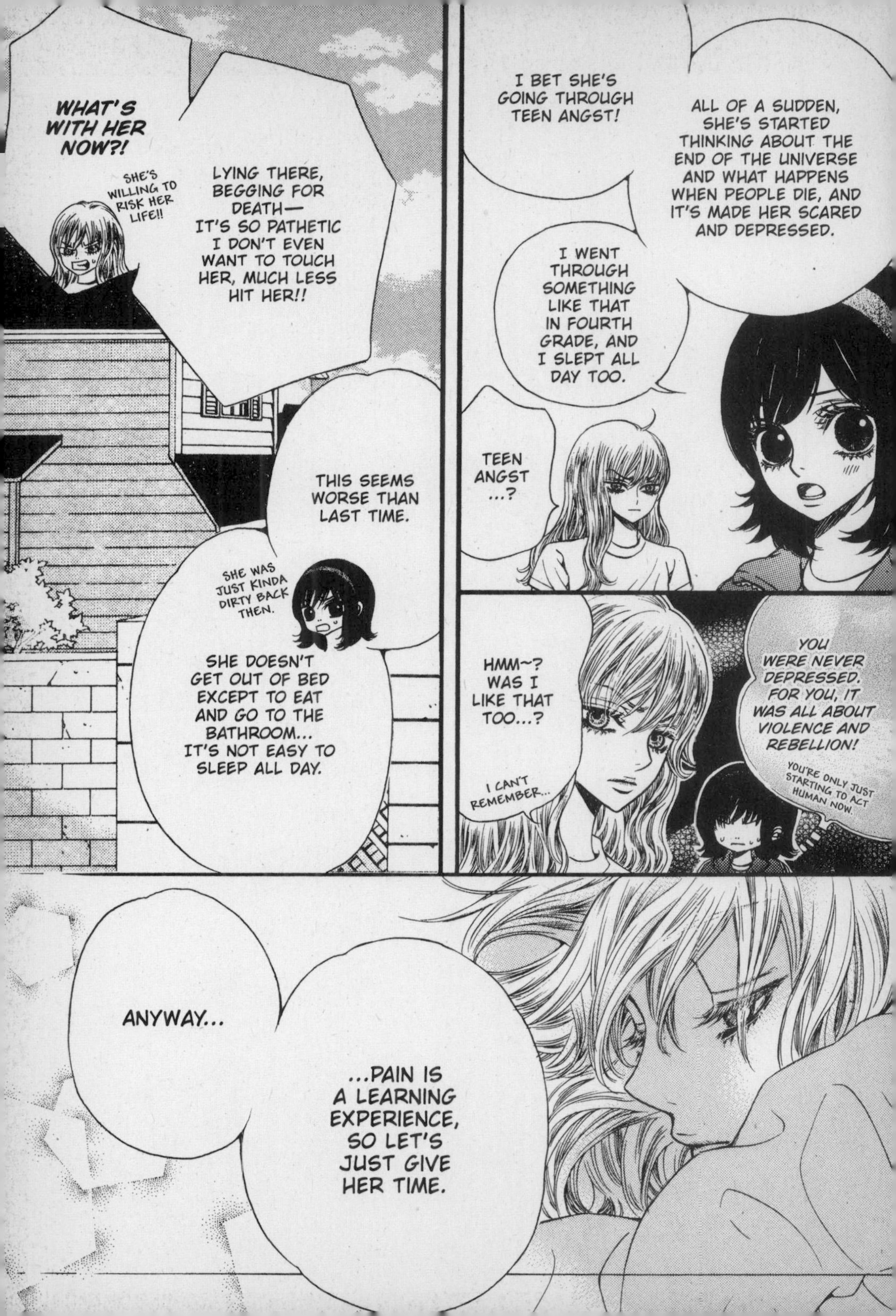
WHAT'S WITH HER NOW?!
SHE'S WILLING TO RISK HER LIFE!!
LYING THERE, BEGGING FOR DEATH— IT'S SO PATHETIC I DON'T EVEN WANT TO TOUCH HER, MUCH LESS HIT HER!!
THIS SEEMS WORSE THAN LAST TIME.
SHE WAS JUST KINDA DIRTY BACK THEN.
SHE DOESN'T GET OUT OF BED EXCEPT TO EAT AND GO TO THE BATHROOM... IT'S NOT EASY TO SLEEP ALL DAY.
I BET SHE'S GOING THROUGH TEEN ANGST!
ALL OF A SUDDEN, SHE'S STARTED THINKING ABOUT THE END OF THE UNIVERSE AND WHAT HAPPENS WHEN PEOPLE DIE, AND IT'S MADE HER SCARED AND DEPRESSED.
I WENT THROUGH SOMETHING LIKE THAT IN FOURTH GRADE, AND I SLEPT ALL DAY TOO.
TEEN ANGST ...?
HMM~? WAS I LIKE THAT TOO...?
I CAN'T REMEMBER...
YOU WERE NEVER DEPRESSED. FOR YOU, IT WAS ALL ABOUT VIOLENCE AND REBELLION!
YOU'RE ONLY JUST STARTING TO ACT HUMAN NOW.
ANYWAY...
...PAIN IS A LEARNING EXPERIENCE, SO LET'S JUST GIVE HER TIME.

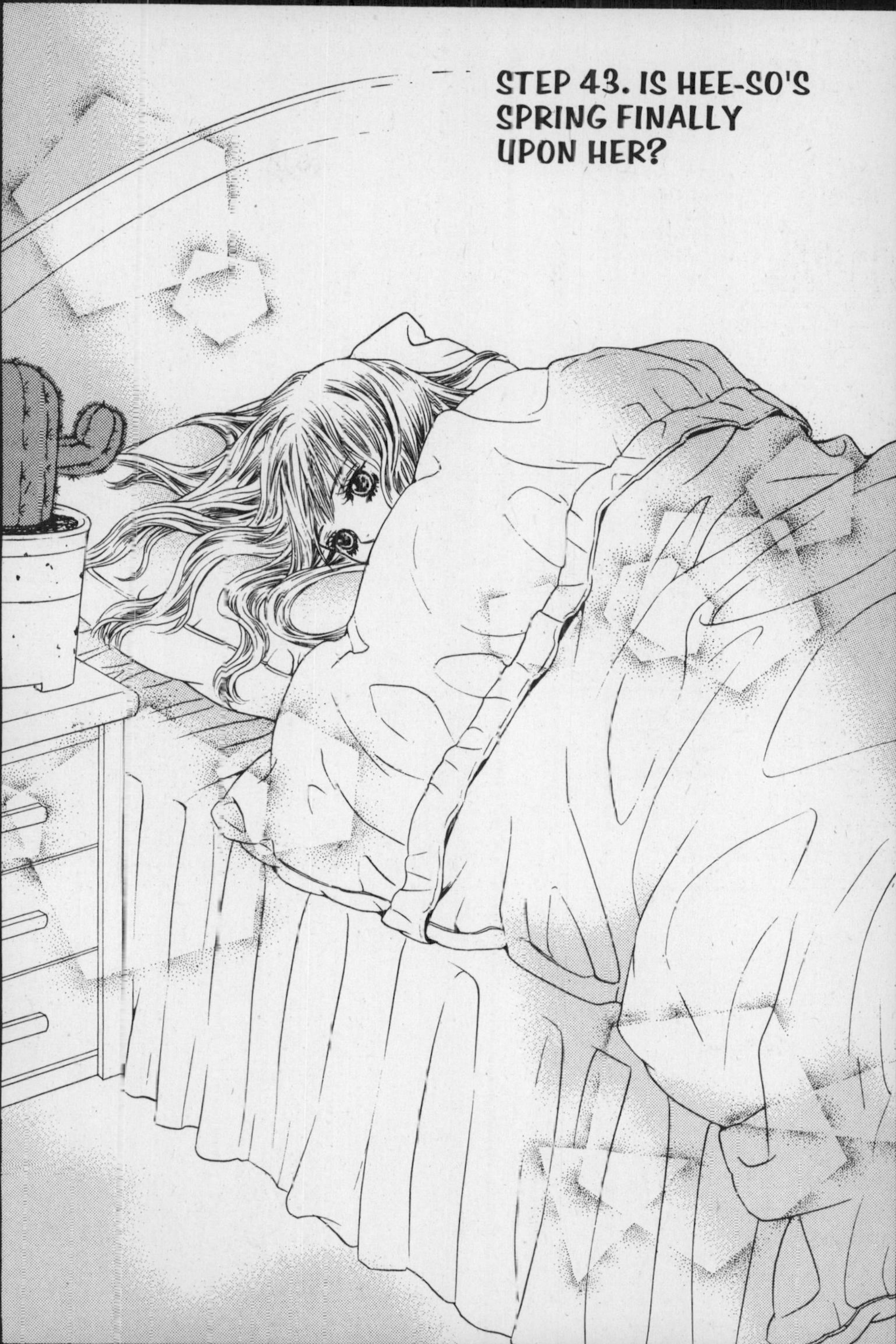
STEP 43. IS HEE-SO'S SPRING FINALLY UPON HER?

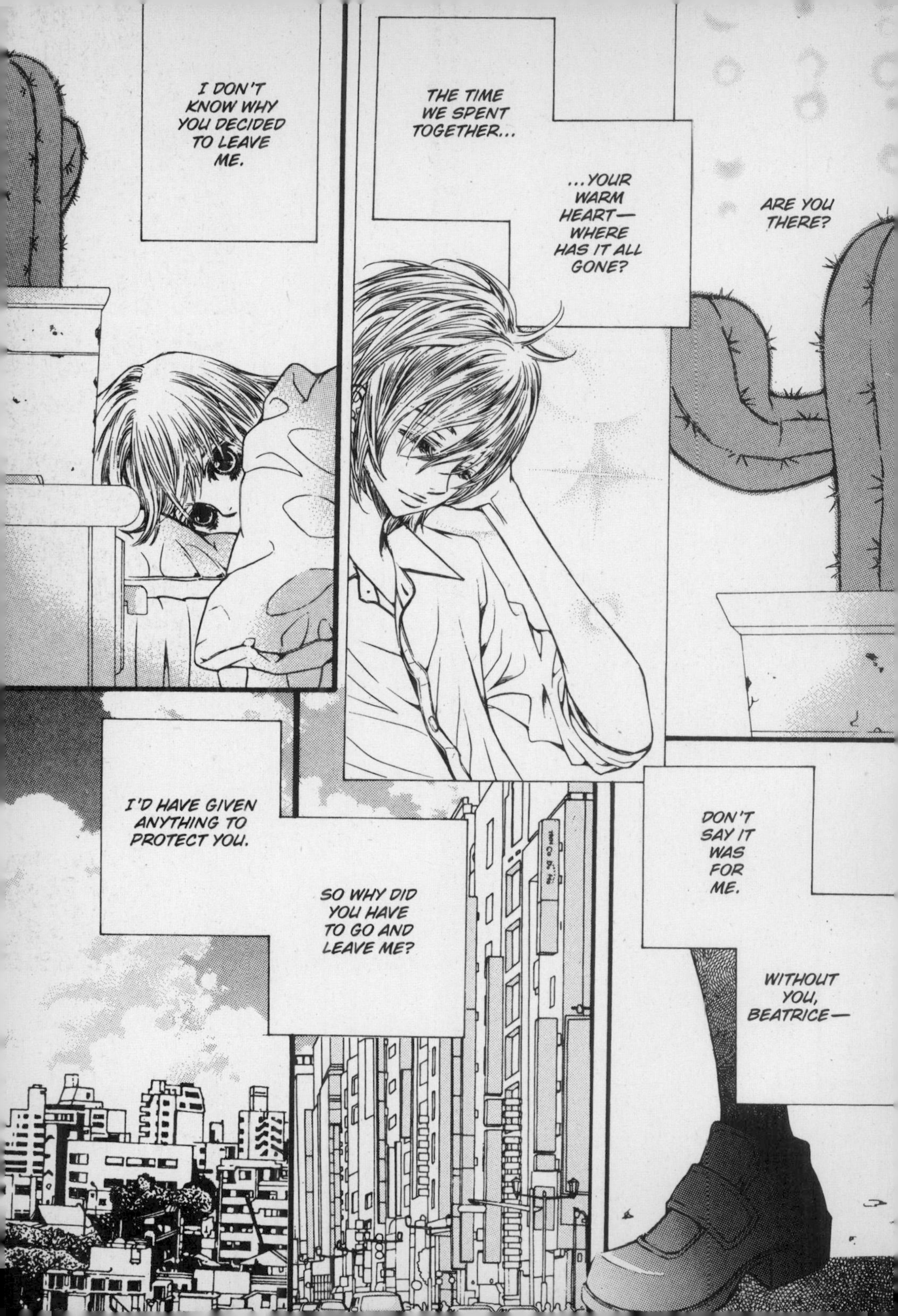
I DON'T KNOW WHY YOU DECIDED TO LEAVE ME.
THE TIME WE SPENT TOGETHER...
...YOUR WARM HEART—WHERE HAS IT ALL GONE?
ARE YOU THERE?
I'D HAVE GIVEN ANYTHING TO PROTECT YOU.
SO WHY DID YOU HAVE TO GO AND LEAVE ME?
DON'T SAY IT WAS FOR ME.
WITHOUT YOU, BEATRICE—

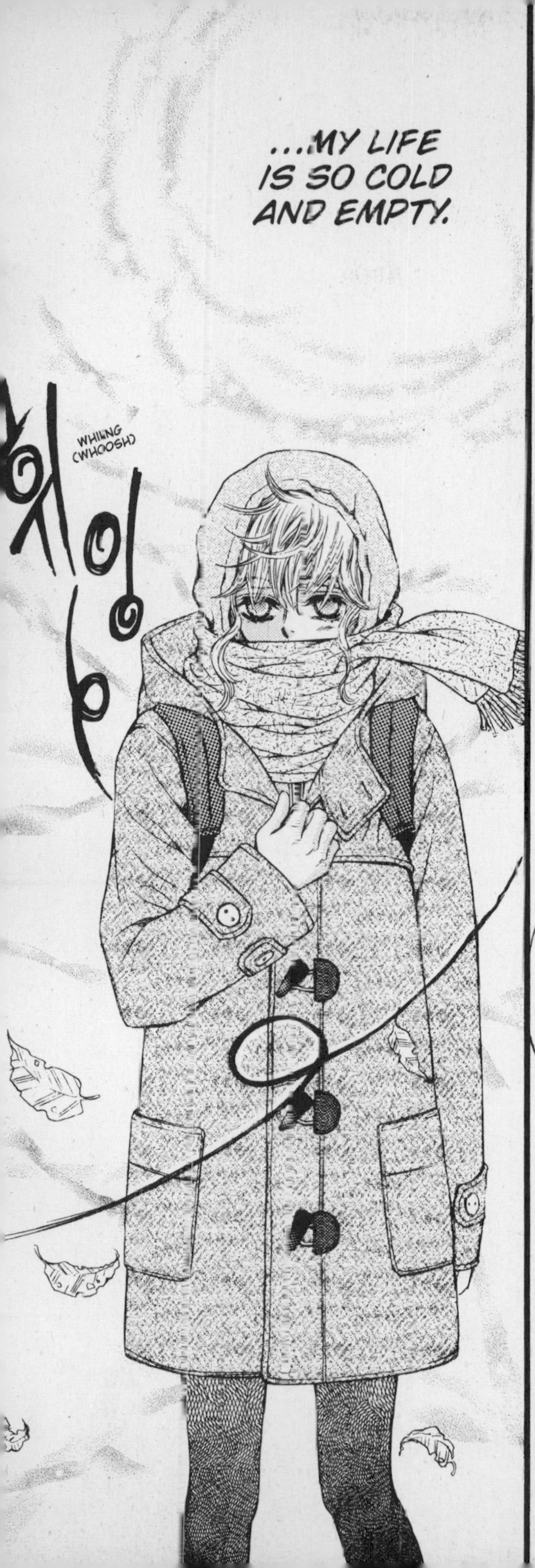
...MY LIFE IS SO COLD AND EMPTY.
WHIING (WHOOSH)

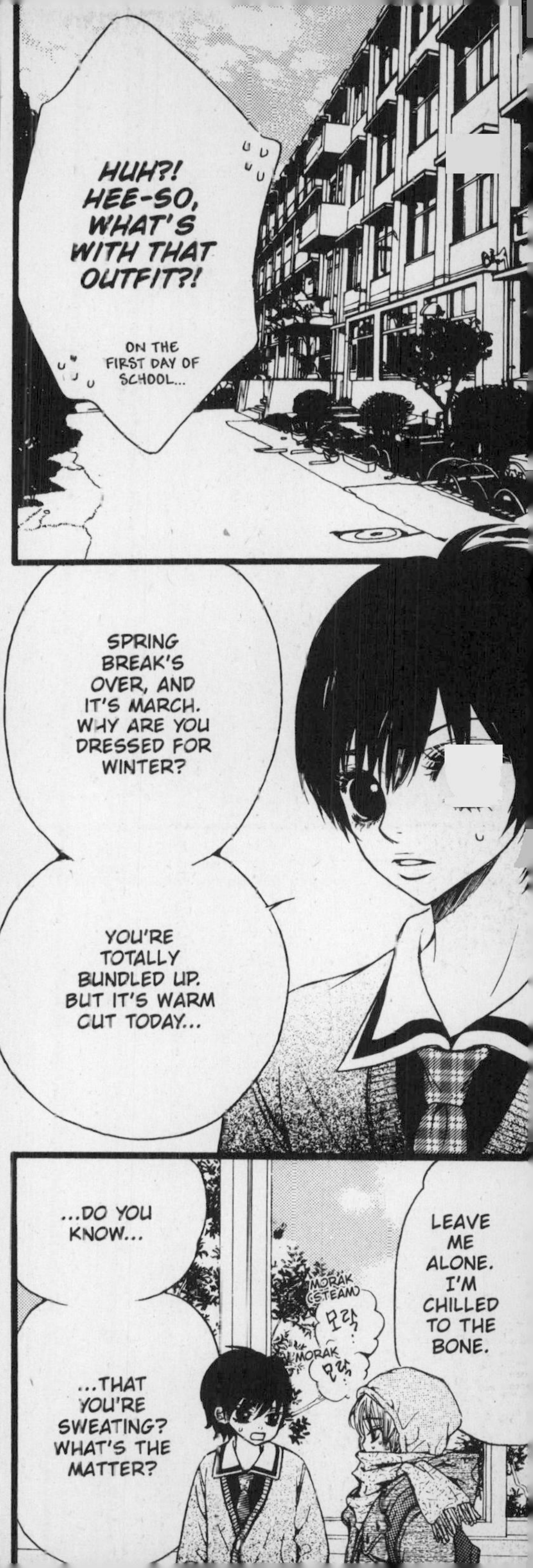
HUH?! HEE-SO, WHAT'S WITH THAT OUTFIT?!
ON THE FIRST DAY OF SCHOOL...
SPRING BREAK'S OVER, AND IT'S MARCH. WHY ARE YOU DRESSED FOR WINTER?
YOU'RE TOTALLY BUNDLED UP. BUT IT'S WARM OUT TODAY...
...DO YOU KNOW...
LEAVE ME ALONE. I'M CHILLED TO THE BONE.
MORAK (STEAM)
모락
MORAK
모락
...THAT YOU'RE SWEATING? WHAT'S THE MATTER?

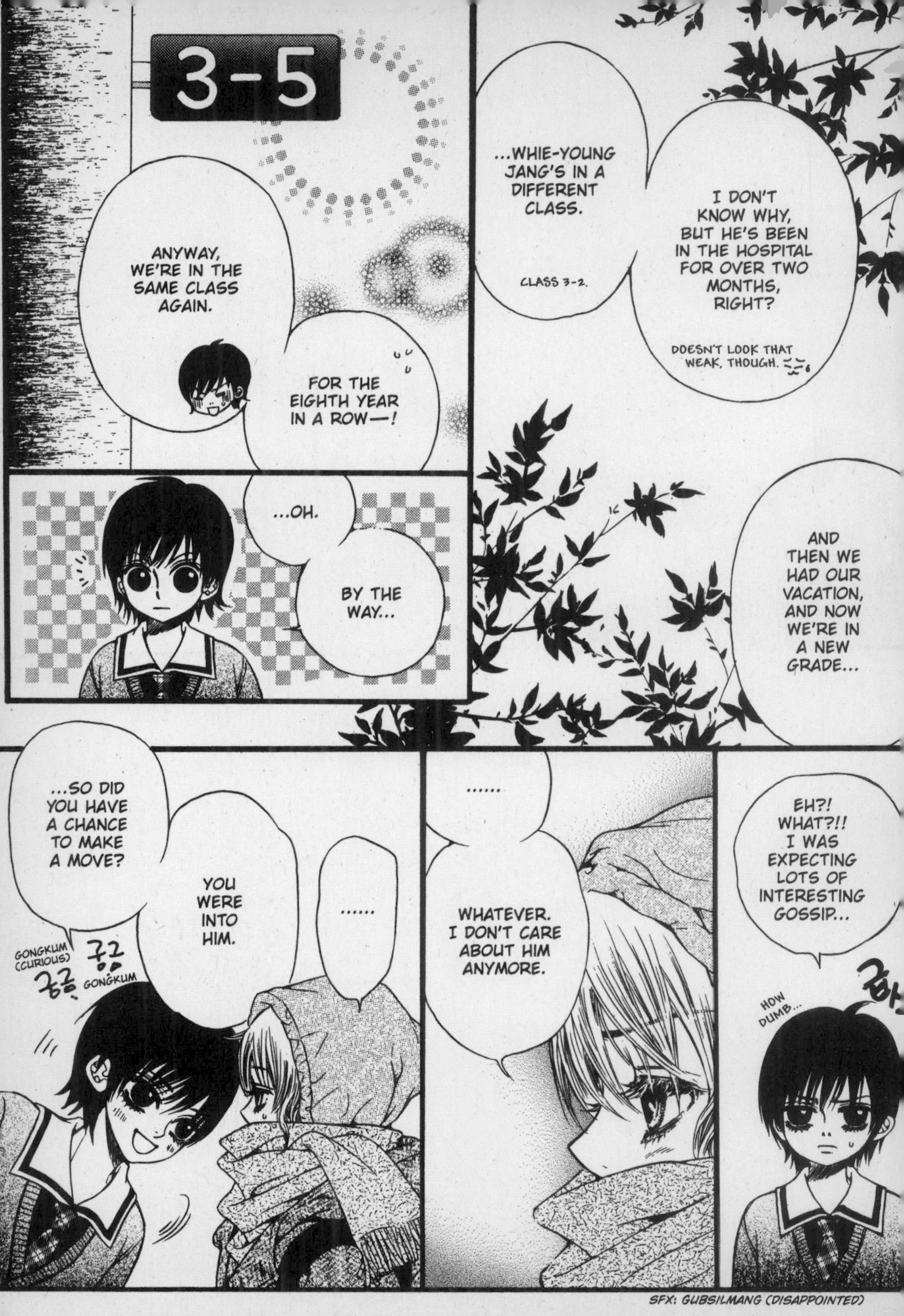
3-5
ANYWAY, WE'RE IN THE SAME CLASS AGAIN.
FOR THE EIGHTH YEAR IN A ROW—!
...OH.
BY THE WAY...
...WHIE-YOUNG JANG'S IN A DIFFERENT CLASS.
CLASS 3-2.
I DON'T KNOW WHY, BUT HE'S BEEN IN THE HOSPITAL FOR OVER TWO MONTHS, RIGHT?
DOESN'T LOOK THAT WEAK, THOUGH.
AND THEN WE HAD OUR VACATION, AND NOW WE'RE IN A NEW GRADE...
...SO DID YOU HAVE A CHANCE TO MAKE A MOVE?
YOU WERE INTO HIM.
......
GONGKUM (CURIOUS)
궁금
궁금
GONGKUM
......
WHATEVER. I DON'T CARE ABOUT HIM ANYMORE.
EH?! WHAT?!! I WAS EXPECTING LOTS OF INTERESTING GOSSIP...
HOW DUMB...
SFX: GUBSILMANG (DISAPPOINTED)

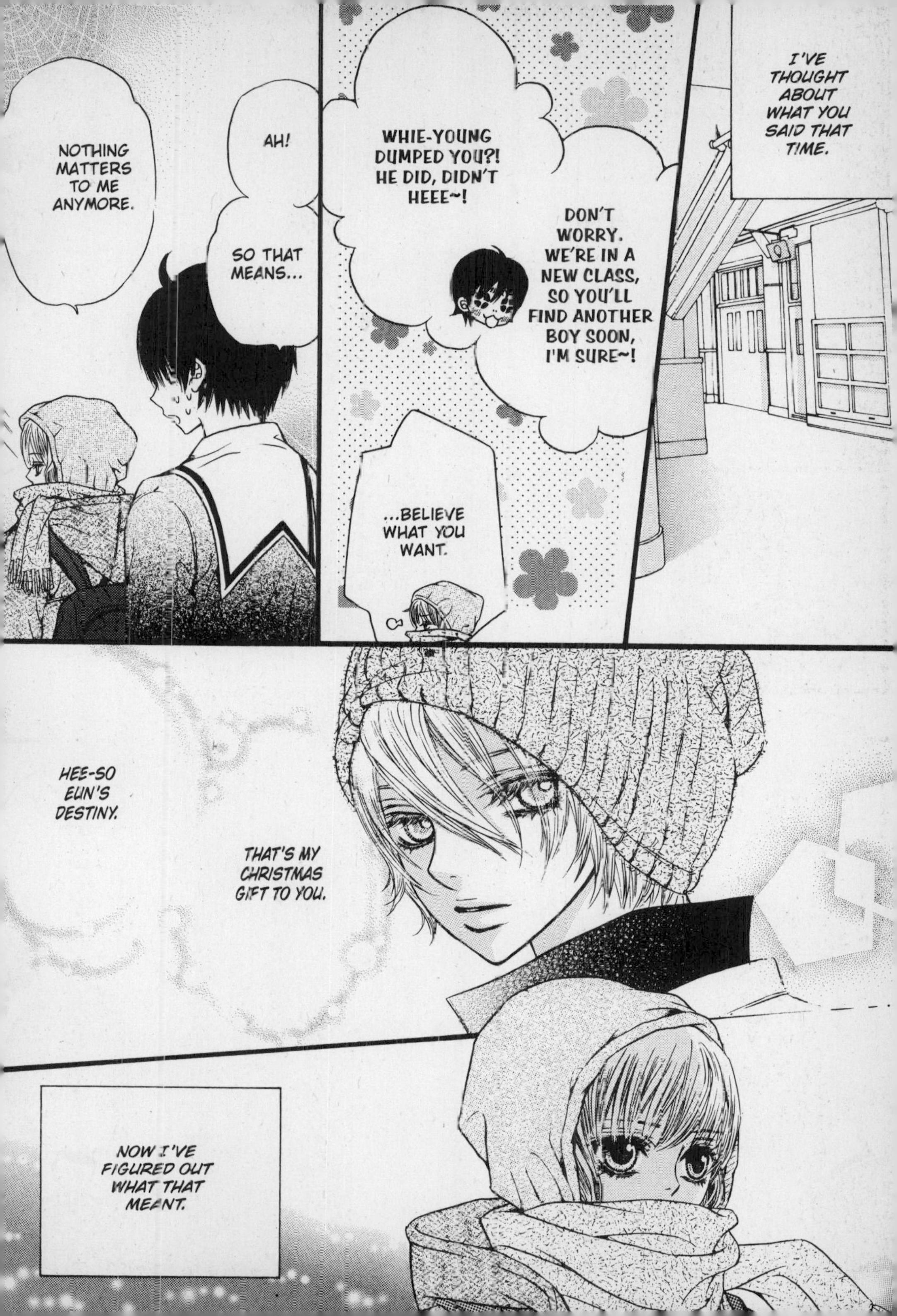
NOTHING MATTERS TO ME ANYMORE.
AH!
SO THAT MEANS...
WHIE-YOUNG DUMPED YOU?! HE DID, DIDN'T HEEE~!
DON'T WORRY. WE'RE IN A NEW CLASS, SO YOU'LL FIND ANOTHER BOY SOON, I'M SURE~!
...BELIEVE WHAT YOU WANT.
I'VE THOUGHT ABOUT WHAT YOU SAID THAT TIME.
HEE-SO EUN'S DESTINY.
THAT'S MY CHRISTMAS GIFT TO YOU.
NOW I'VE FIGURED OUT WHAT THAT MEANT.

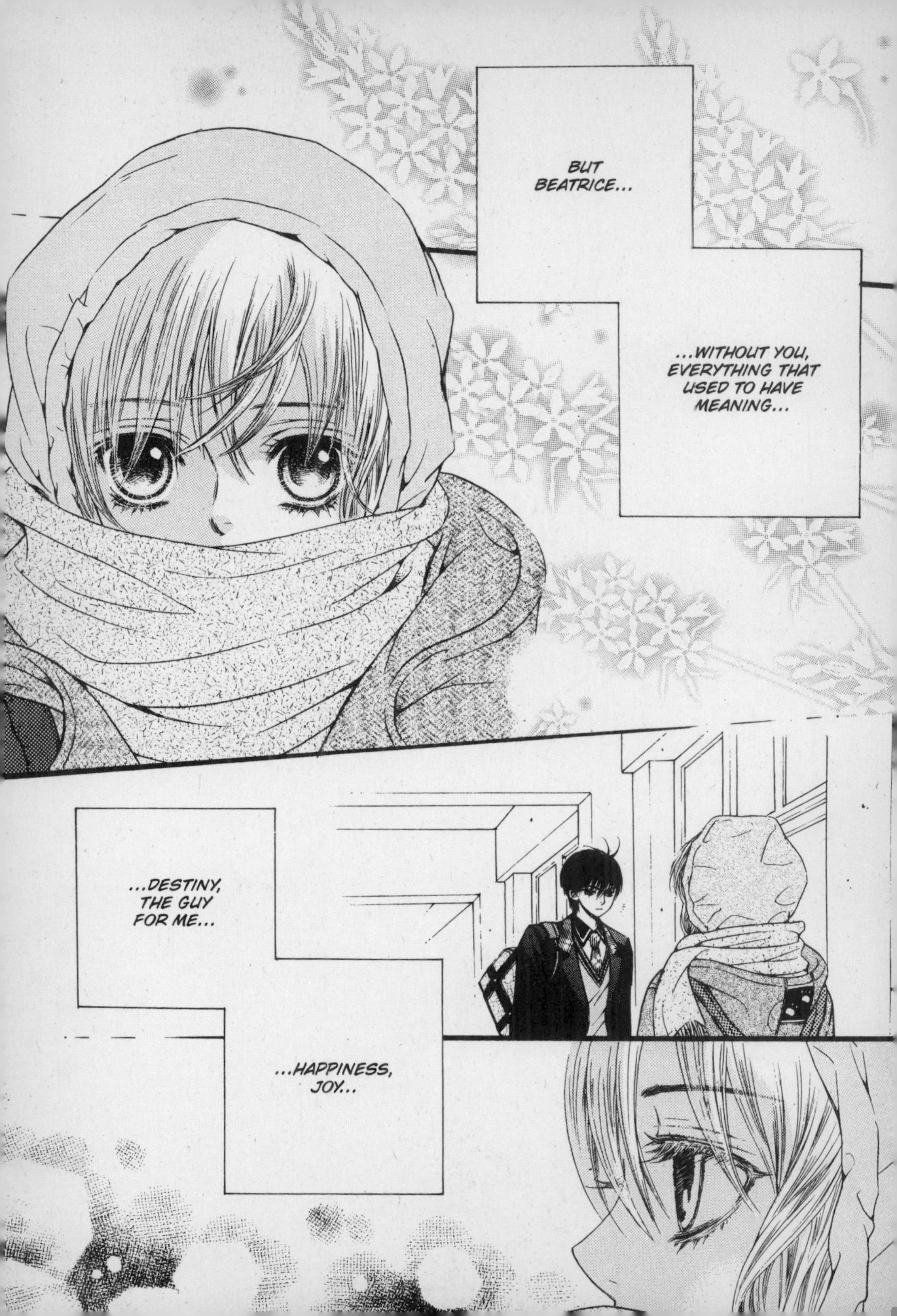
BUT BEATRICE...
...WITHOUT YOU, EVERYTHING THAT USED TO HAVE MEANING...
...DESTINY, THE GUY FOR ME...
...HAPPINESS, JOY...

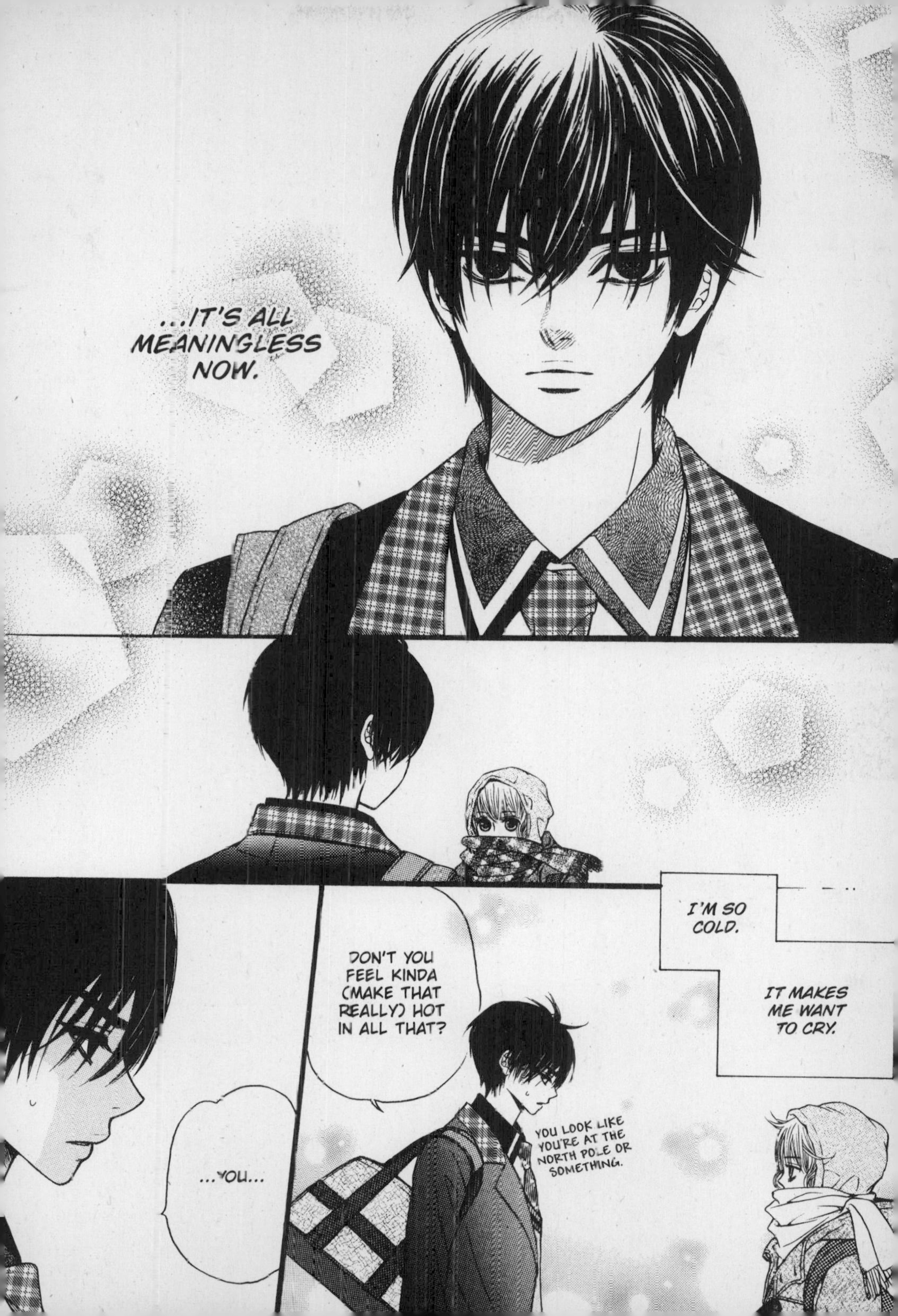
...IT'S ALL MEANINGLESS NOW.
...YOU...
DON'T YOU FEEL KINDA (MAKE THAT REALLY) HOT IN ALL THAT?
I'M SO COLD.
IT MAKES ME WANT TO CRY.
YOU LOOK LIKE YOU'RE AT THE NORTH POLE OR SOMETHING.

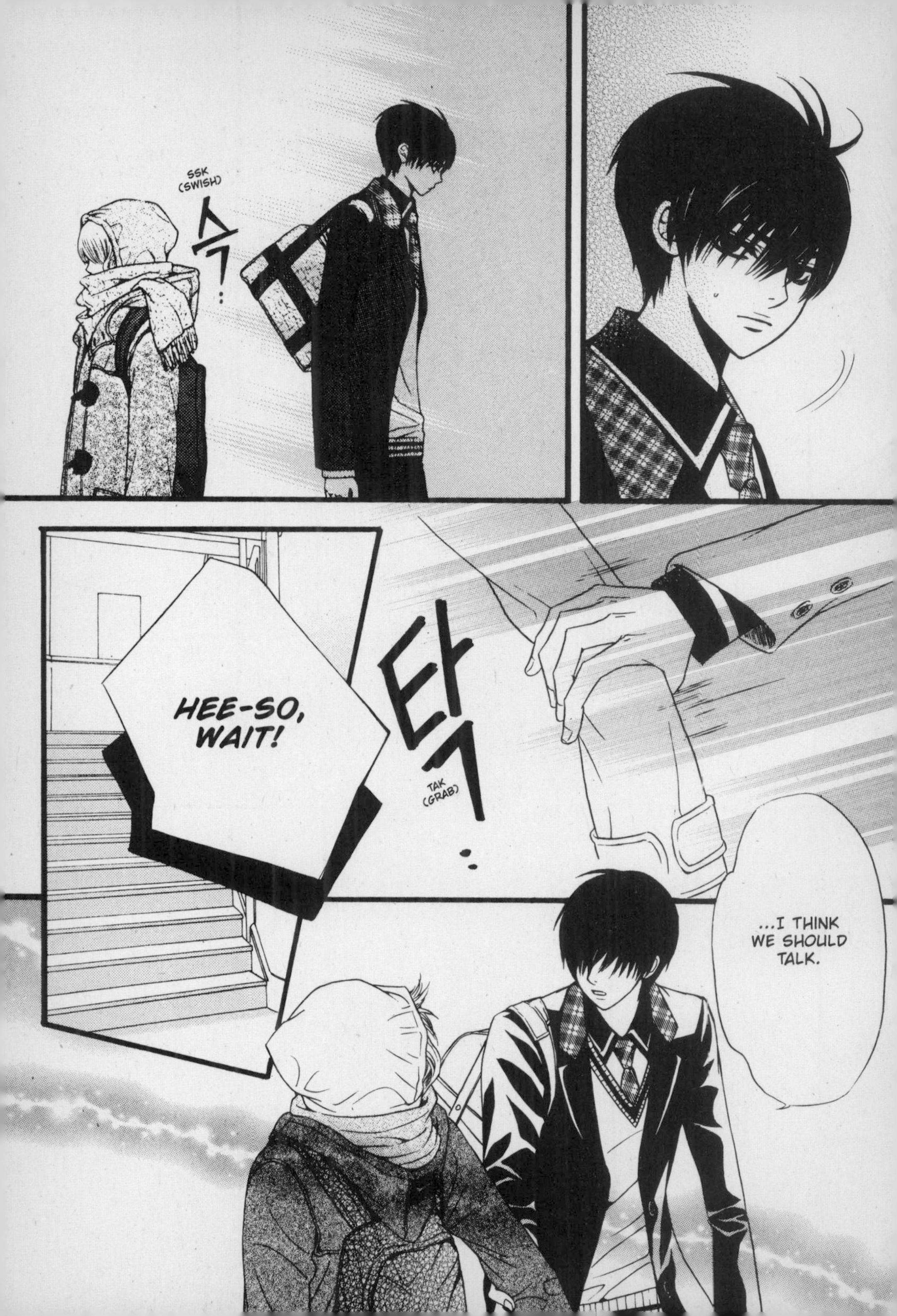

SSK (SWISH)
스-
HEE-SO, WAIT!
탁
TAK (GRAB)
...I THINK WE SHOULD TALK.

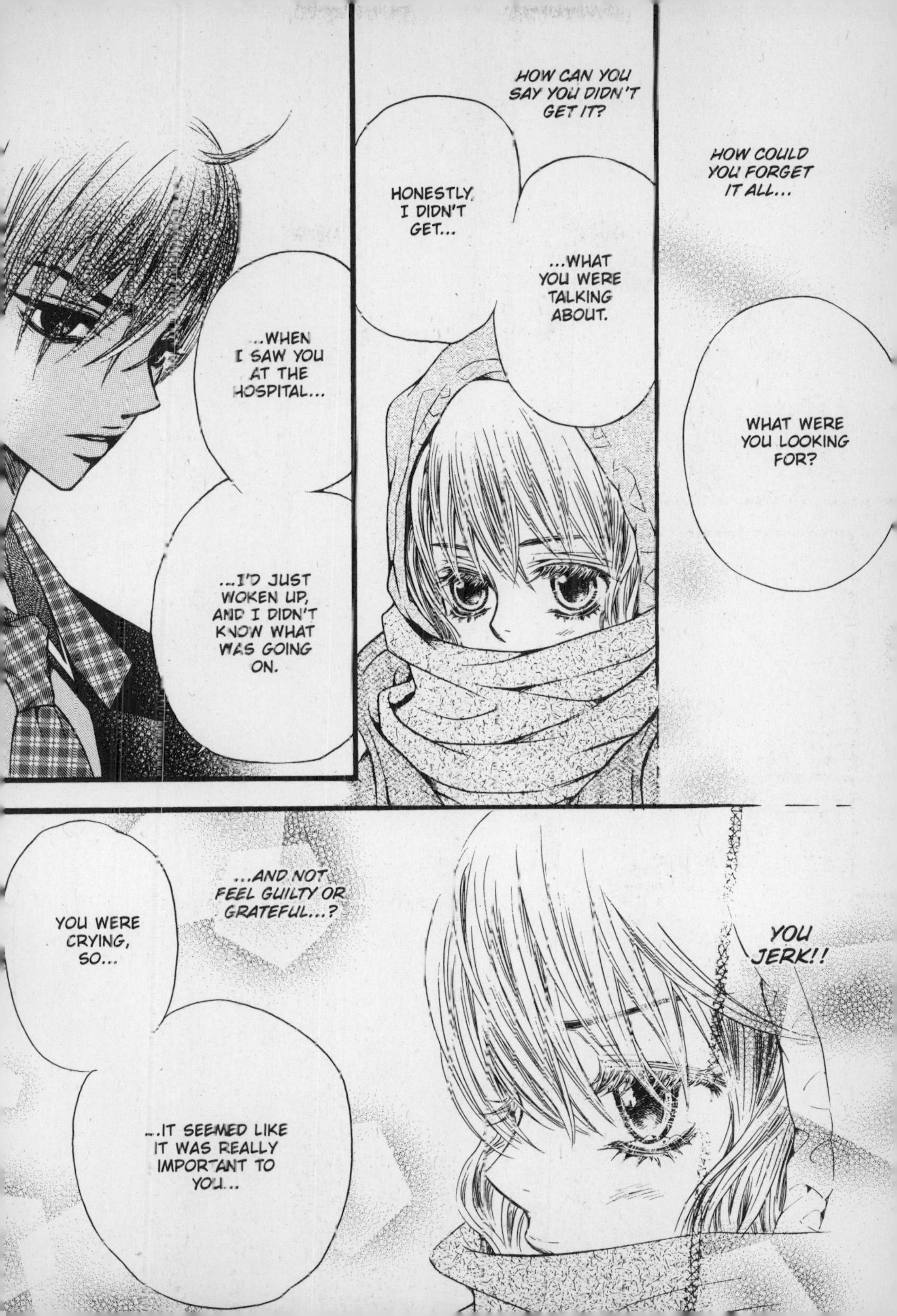
...WHEN I SAW YOU AT THE HOSPITAL...
...I'D JUST WOKEN UP, AND I DIDN'T KNOW WHAT WAS GOING ON.
HOW CAN YOU SAY YOU DIDN'T GET IT?
HONESTLY, I DIDN'T GET...
...WHAT YOU WERE TALKING ABOUT.
HOW COULD YOU FORGET IT ALL...
WHAT WERE YOU LOOKING FOR?
YOU WERE CRYING, SO...
...IT SEEMED LIKE IT WAS REALLY IMPORTANT TO YOU...
...AND NOT FEEL GUILTY OR GRATEFUL...?
YOU JERK!!

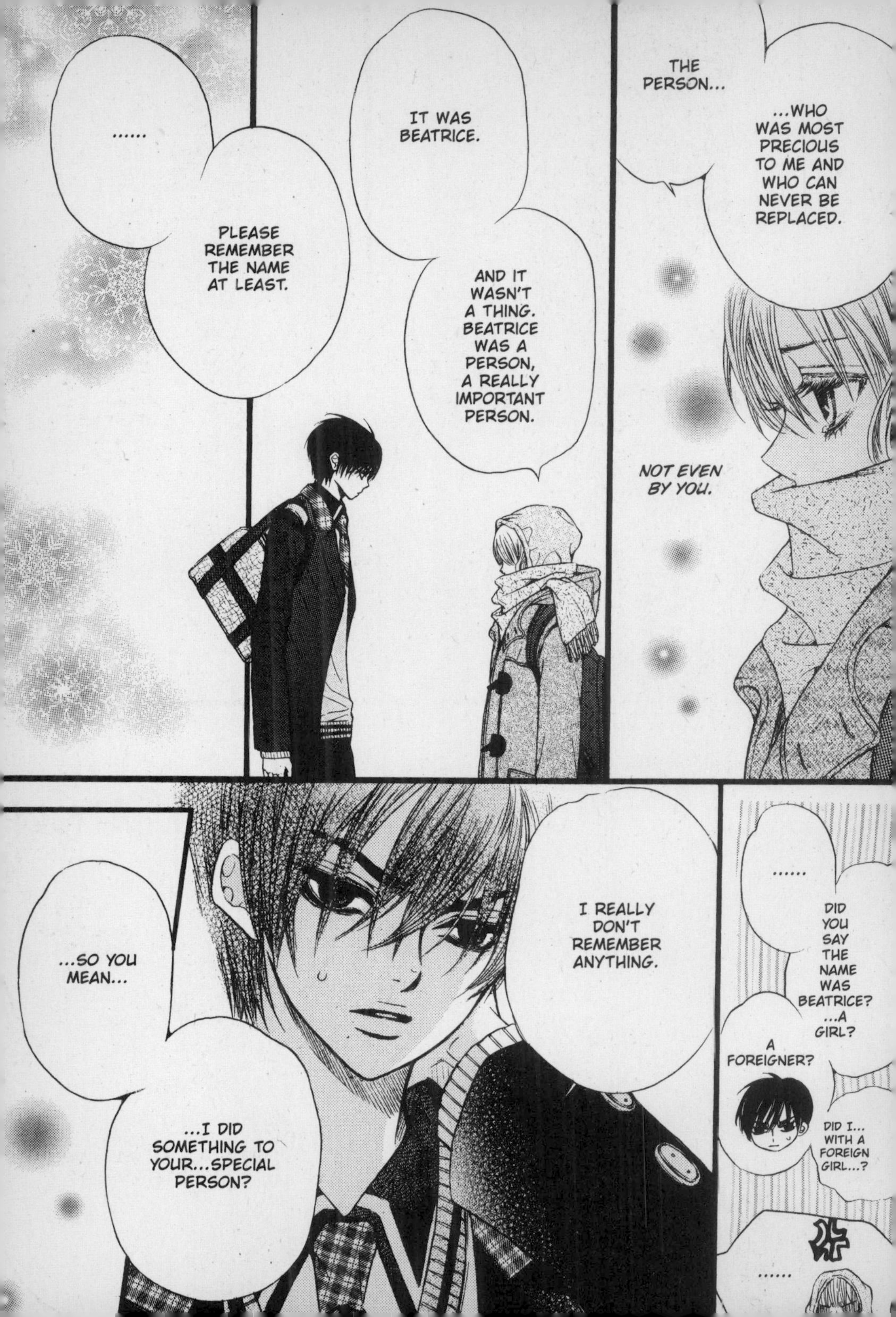
......
PLEASE REMEMBER THE NAME AT LEAST.
IT WAS BEATRICE.
AND IT WASN'T A THING. BEATRICE WAS A PERSON, A REALLY IMPORTANT PERSON.
THE PERSON...
...WHO WAS MOST PRECIOUS TO ME AND WHO CAN NEVER BE REPLACED.
NOT EVEN BY YOU.
...SO YOU MEAN...
...I DID SOMETHING TO YOUR...SPECIAL PERSON?
I REALLY DON'T REMEMBER ANYTHING.
......
DID YOU SAY THE NAME WAS BEATRICE? ...A GIRL?
A FOREIGNER?
DID I... WITH A FOREIGN GIRL...?
......

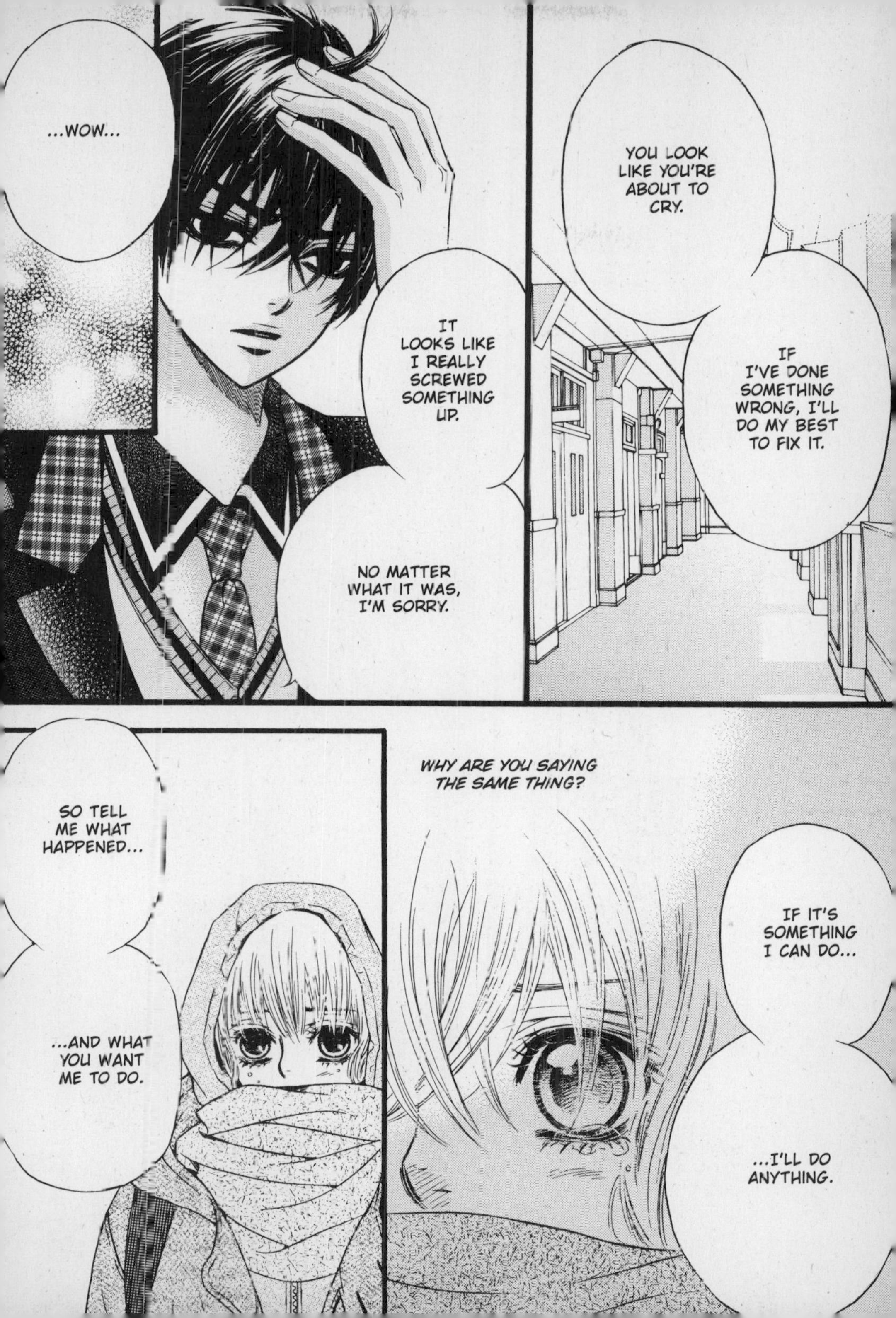
...WOW...
IT LOOKS LIKE I REALLY SCREWED SOMETHING UP.
NO MATTER WHAT IT WAS, I'M SORRY.
YOU LOOK LIKE YOU'RE ABOUT TO CRY.
IF I'VE DONE SOMETHING WRONG, I'LL DO MY BEST TO FIX IT.
SO TELL ME WHAT HAPPENED...
...AND WHAT YOU WANT ME TO DO.
WHY ARE YOU SAYING THE SAME THING?
IF IT'S SOMETHING I CAN DO...
...I'LL DO ANYTHING.

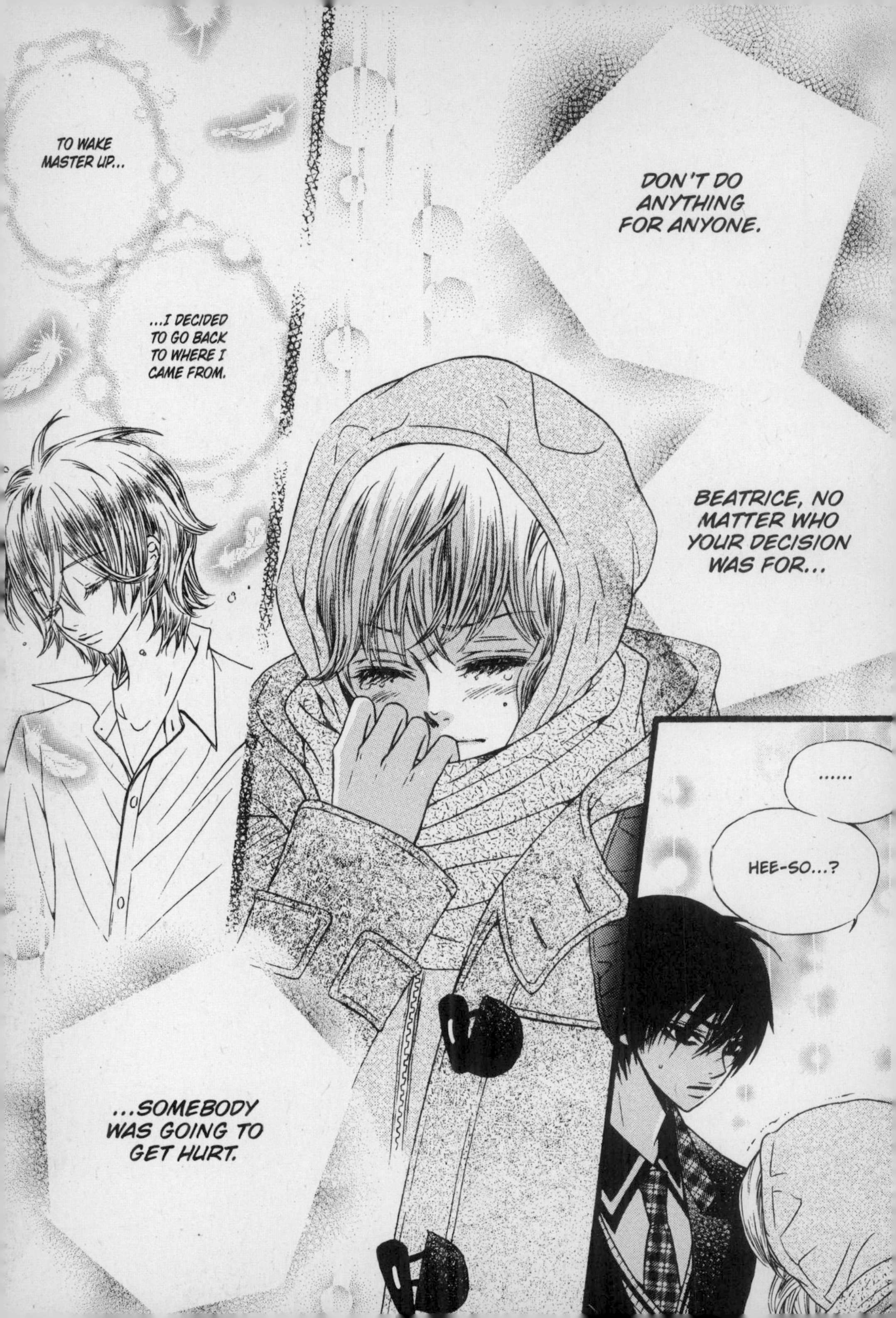
TO WAKE MASTER UP...
...I DECIDED TO GO BACK TO WHERE I CAME FROM.
DON'T DO ANYTHING FOR ANYONE.
BEATRICE, NO MATTER WHO YOUR DECISION WAS FOR...
...SOMEBODY WAS GOING TO GET HURT.
......
HEE-SO...?

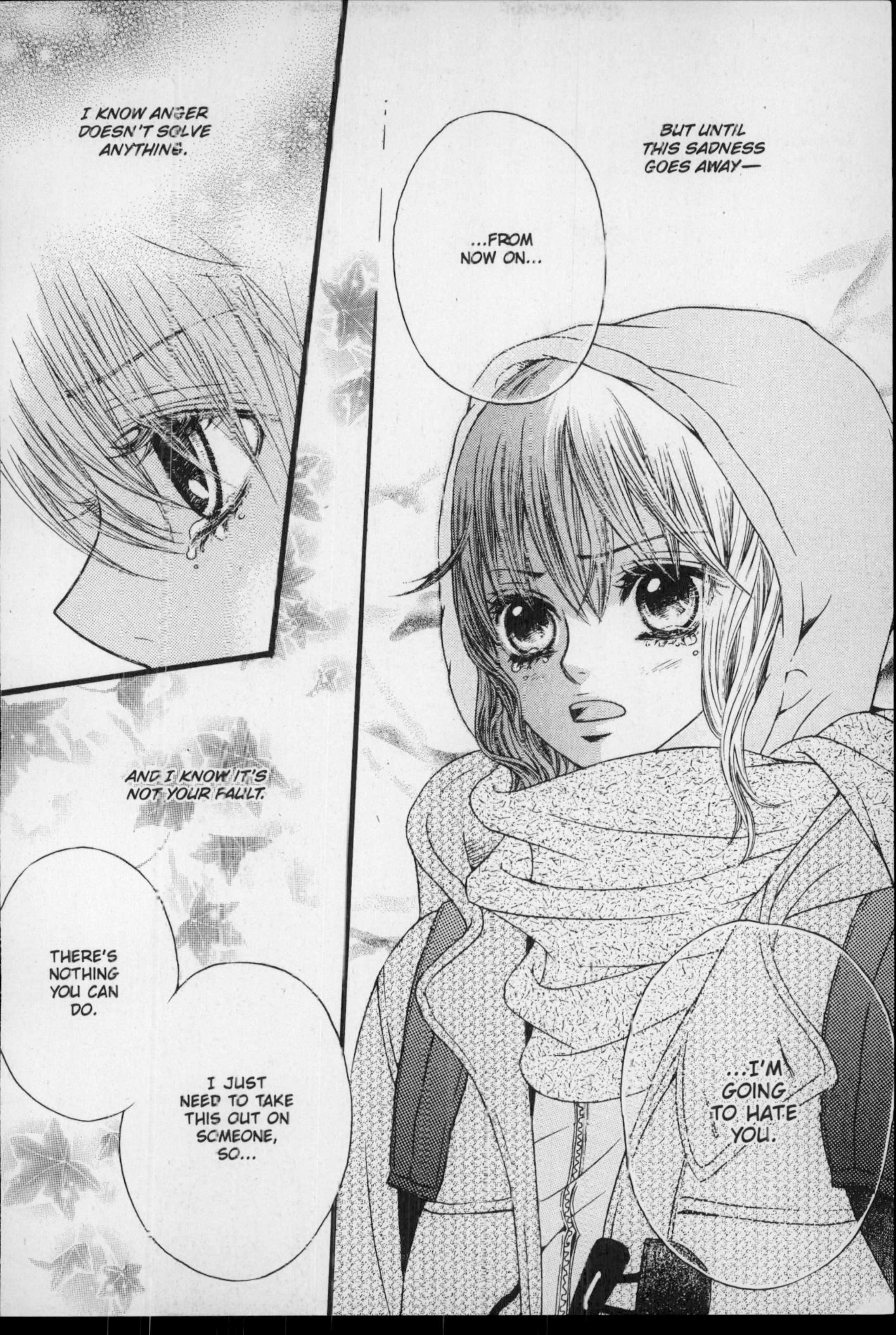
I KNOW ANGER DOESN'T SOLVE ANYTHING.
AND I KNOW IT'S NOT YOUR FAULT.
THERE'S NOTHING YOU CAN DO.
I JUST NEED TO TAKE THIS OUT ON SOMEONE, SO...
BUT UNTIL THIS SADNESS GOES AWAY—
...FROM NOW ON...
...I'M GOING TO HATE YOU.

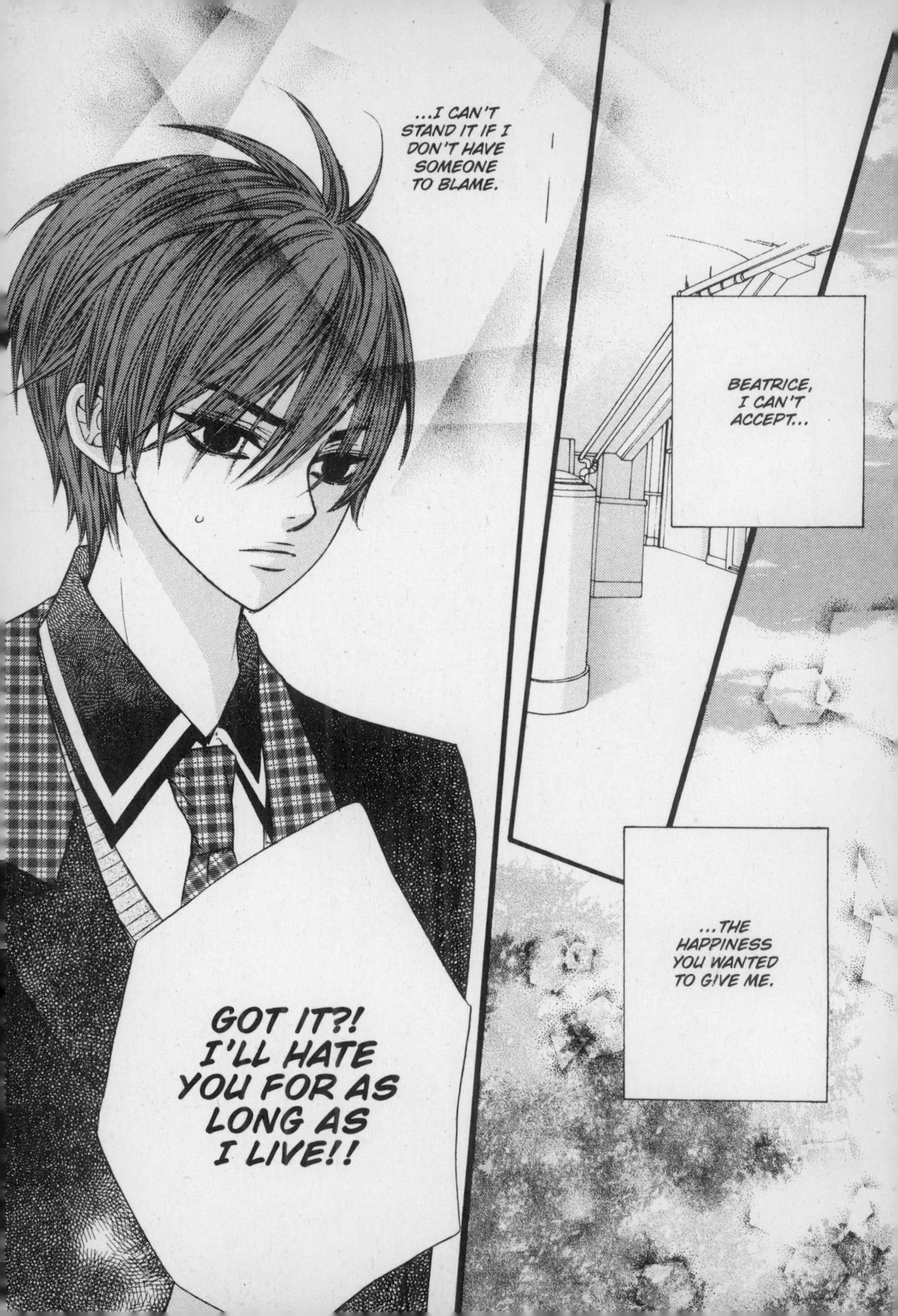
...I CAN'T STAND IT IF I DON'T HAVE SOMEONE TO BLAME.
GOT IT?! I'LL HATE YOU FOR AS LONG AS I LIVE!!
BEATRICE, I CAN'T ACCEPT...
...THE HAPPINESS YOU WANTED TO GIVE ME.

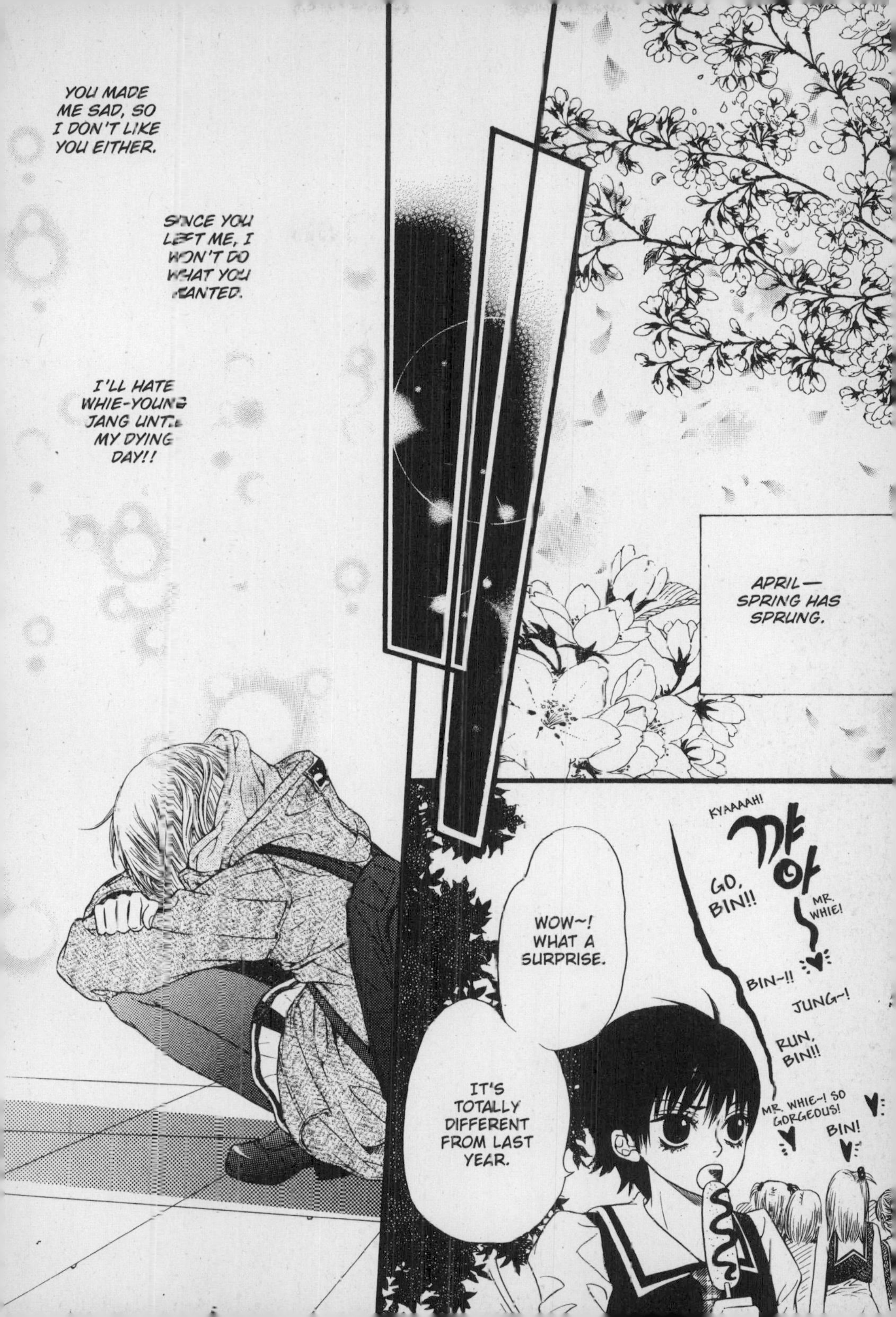
YOU MADE ME SAD, SO I DON'T LIKE YOU EITHER.
SINCE YOU LE?T ME, I WON'T DO WHAT YOU WANTED.
I'LL HATE WHIE-YOUNG JANG UNTIL MY DYING DAY!!
APRIL— SPRING HAS SPRUNG.
WOW~! WHAT A SURPRISE.
IT'S TOTALLY DIFFERENT FROM LAST YEAR.
KYAAAAH!
꺄아~
GO, BIN!!
MR. WHIE!
BIN~!!
JUNG~!
RUN, BIN!!
MR. WHIE~! SO GORGEOUS!
BIN!

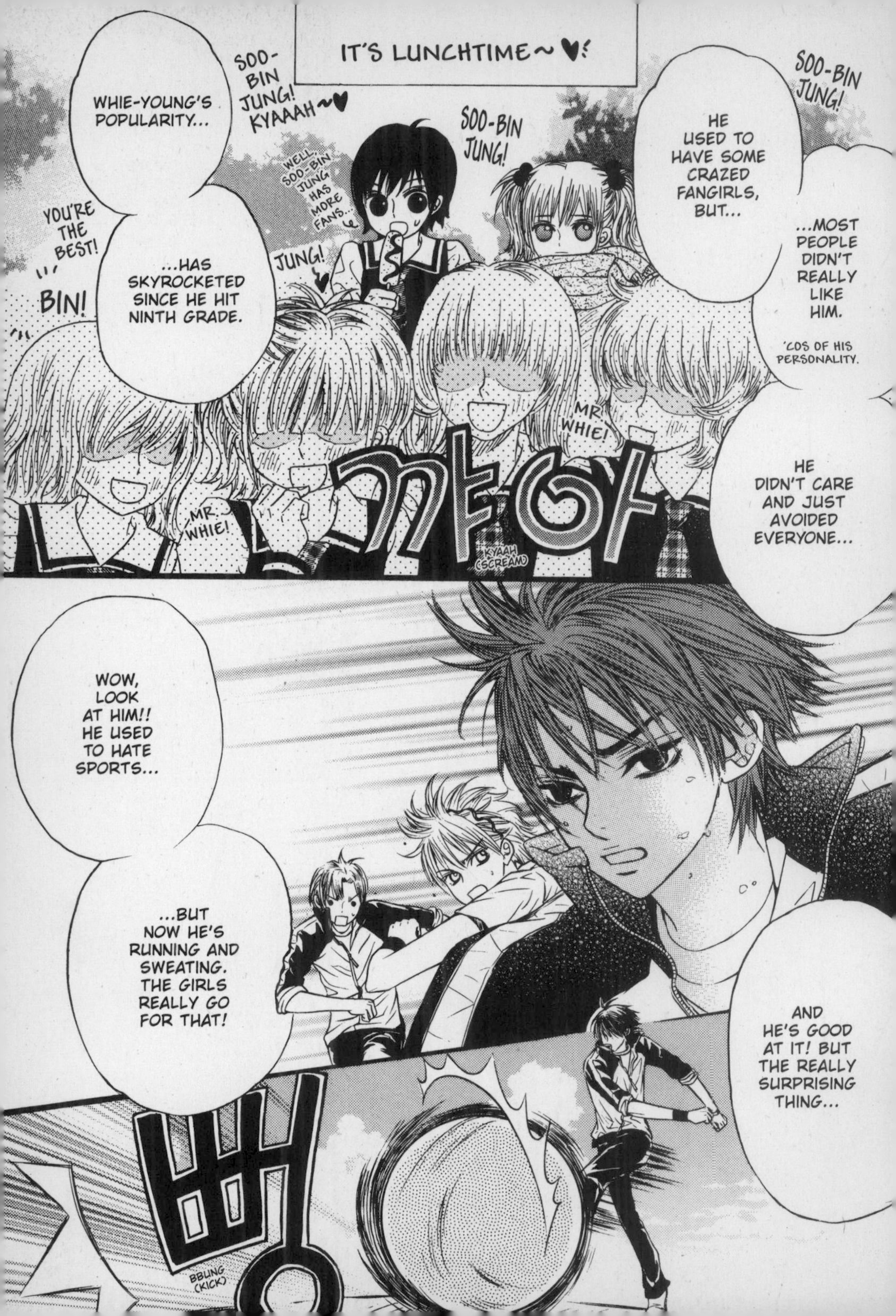
IT'S LUNCHTIME~♥!
WHIE-YOUNG'S POPULARITY...
SOO-BIN JUNG! KYAAAH~♥
YOU'RE THE BEST!
BIN!
...HAS SKYROCKETED SINCE HE HIT NINTH GRADE.
WELL, SOO-BIN JUNG HAS MORE FANS...
JUNG!
SOO-BIN JUNG!
MR. WHIE!
MR. WHIE!
KYAAH (SCREAM)
SOO-BIN JUNG!
HE USED TO HAVE SOME CRAZED FANGIRLS, BUT...
...MOST PEOPLE DIDN'T REALLY LIKE HIM.
'COS OF HIS PERSONALITY.
HE DIDN'T CARE AND JUST AVOIDED EVERYONE...
WOW, LOOK AT HIM!! HE USED TO HATE SPORTS...
...BUT NOW HE'S RUNNING AND SWEATING. THE GIRLS REALLY GO FOR THAT!
AND HE'S GOOD AT IT! BUT THE REALLY SURPRISING THING...
BBUNG (KICK)

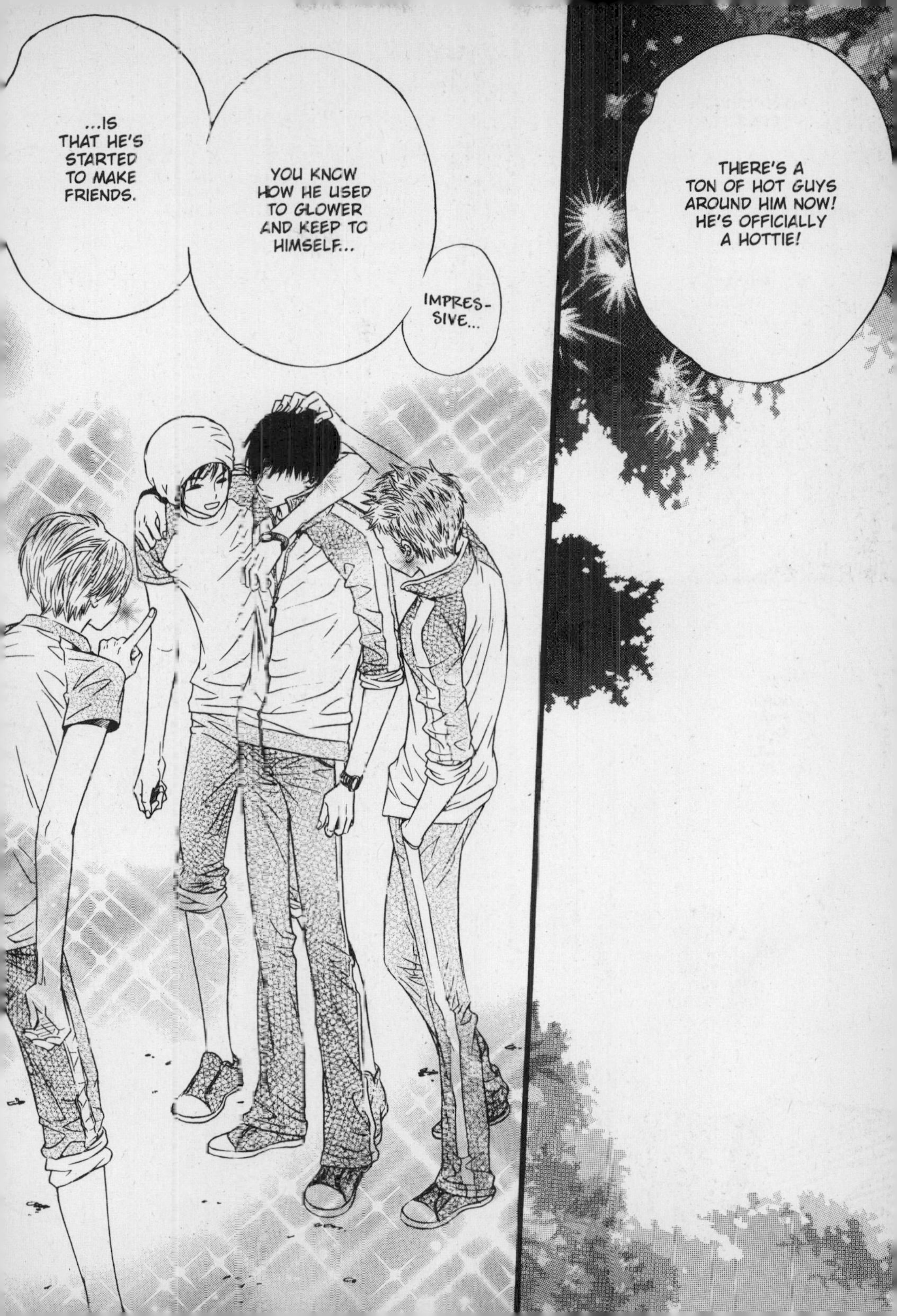
...IS THAT HE'S STARTED TO MAKE FRIENDS.
YOU KNOW HOW HE USED TO GLOWER AND KEEP TO HIMSELF...
IMPRES-SIVE...
THERE'S A TON OF HOT GUYS AROUND HIM NOW! HE'S OFFICIALLY A HOTTIE!

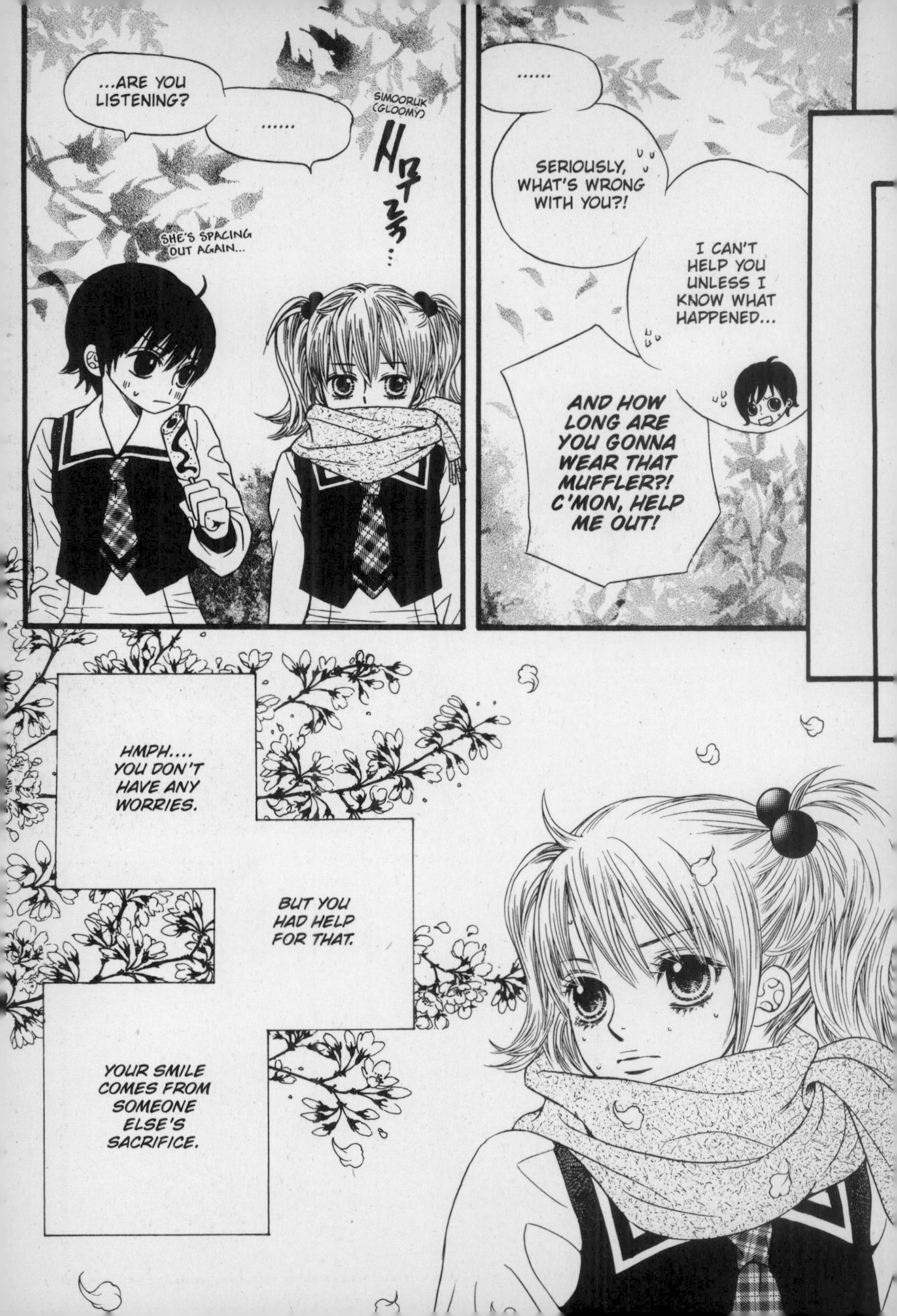
...ARE YOU LISTENING?
......
SHE'S SPACING OUT AGAIN...
SIMOORUK (GLOOMY)
시무룩...
......
SERIOUSLY, WHAT'S WRONG WITH YOU?!
I CAN'T HELP YOU UNLESS I KNOW WHAT HAPPENED...
AND HOW LONG ARE YOU GONNA WEAR THAT MUFFLER?! C'MON, HELP ME OUT!
HMPH.... YOU DON'T HAVE ANY WORRIES.
BUT YOU HAD HELP FOR THAT.
YOUR SMILE COMES FROM SOMEONE ELSE'S SACRIFICE.

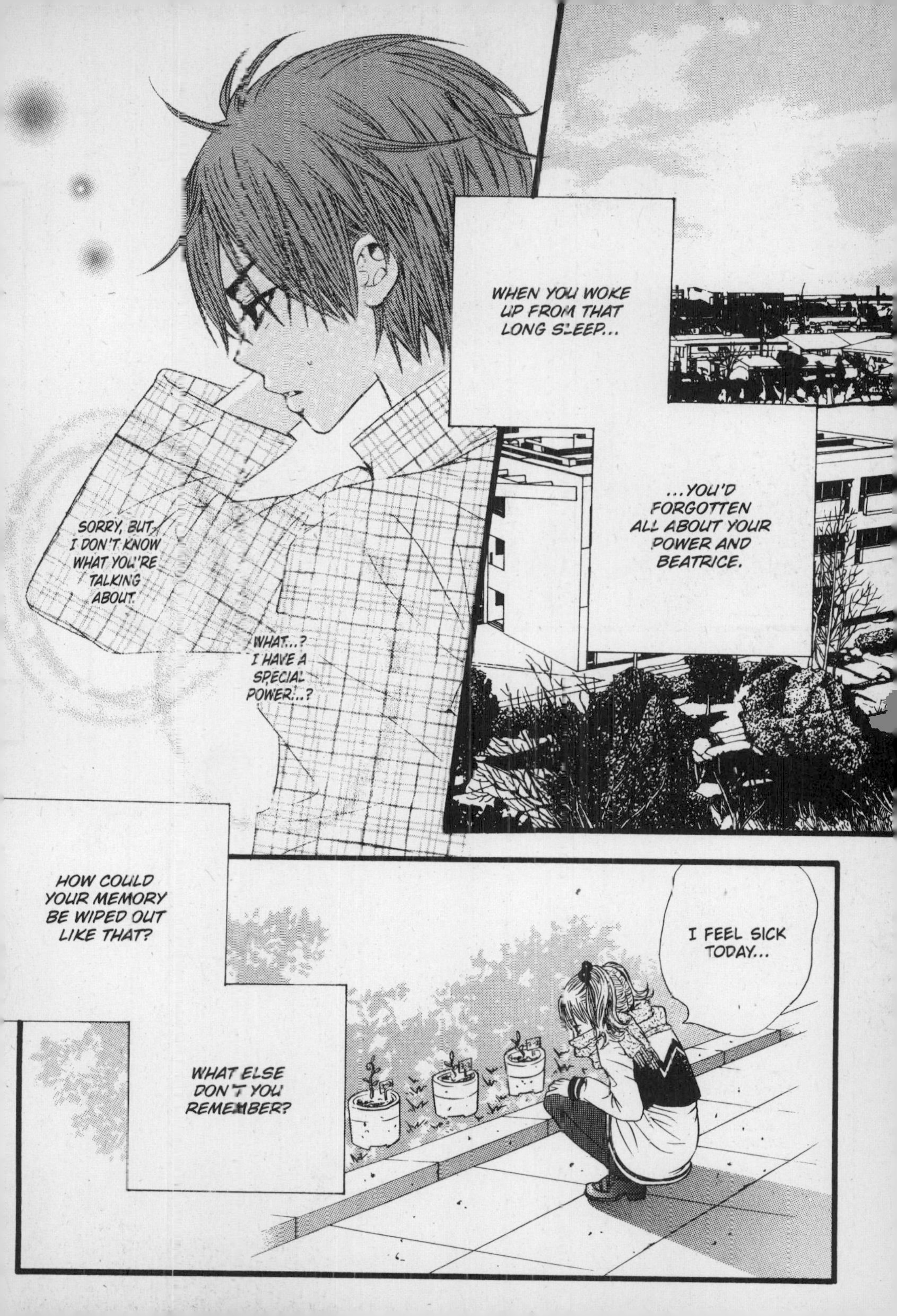
SORRY, BUT, I DON'T KNOW WHAT YOU'RE TALKING ABOUT.
WHAT...? I HAVE A SPECIAL POWER...?
WHEN YOU WOKE UP FROM THAT LONG SLEEP...
...YOU'D FORGOTTEN ALL ABOUT YOUR POWER AND BEATRICE.
HOW COULD YOUR MEMORY BE WIPED OUT LIKE THAT?
WHAT ELSE DON'T YOU REMEMBER?
I FEEL SICK TODAY...

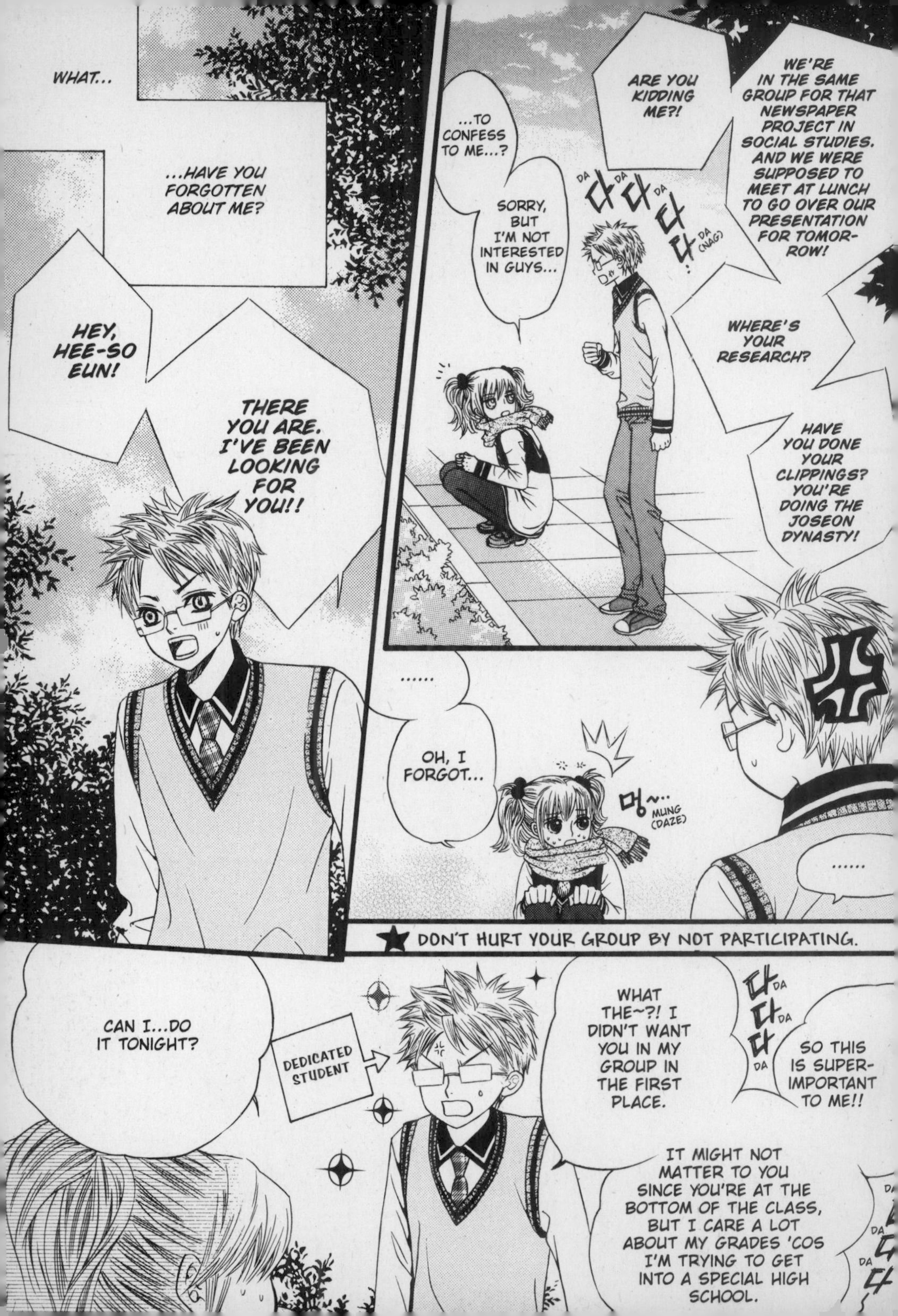
WHAT...
...HAVE YOU FORGOTTEN ABOUT ME?
HEY, HEE-SO EUN!
THERE YOU ARE. I'VE BEEN LOOKING FOR YOU!!
...TO CONFESS TO ME...?
SORRY, BUT I'M NOT INTERESTED IN GUYS...
다 DA 다 DA 다 DA 다 DA (NAG)
ARE YOU KIDDING ME?!
WE'RE IN THE SAME GROUP FOR THAT NEWSPAPER PROJECT IN SOCIAL STUDIES. AND WE WERE SUPPOSED TO MEET AT LUNCH TO GO OVER OUR PRESENTATION FOR TOMOR-ROW!
WHERE'S YOUR RESEARCH?
HAVE YOU DONE YOUR CLIPPINGS? YOU'RE DOING THE JOSEON DYNASTY!
......
OH, I FORGOT...
멍~... MUNG (DAZE)
......
DON'T HURT YOUR GROUP BY NOT PARTICIPATING.
CAN I...DO IT TONIGHT?
DEDICATED STUDENT
WHAT THE~?! I DIDN'T WANT YOU IN MY GROUP IN THE FIRST PLACE.
다 DA 다 DA 다 DA
SO THIS IS SUPER-IMPORTANT TO ME!!
IT MIGHT NOT MATTER TO YOU SINCE YOU'RE AT THE BOTTOM OF THE CLASS, BUT I CARE A LOT ABOUT MY GRADES 'COS I'M TRYING TO GET INTO A SPECIAL HIGH SCHOOL.
DA DA DA

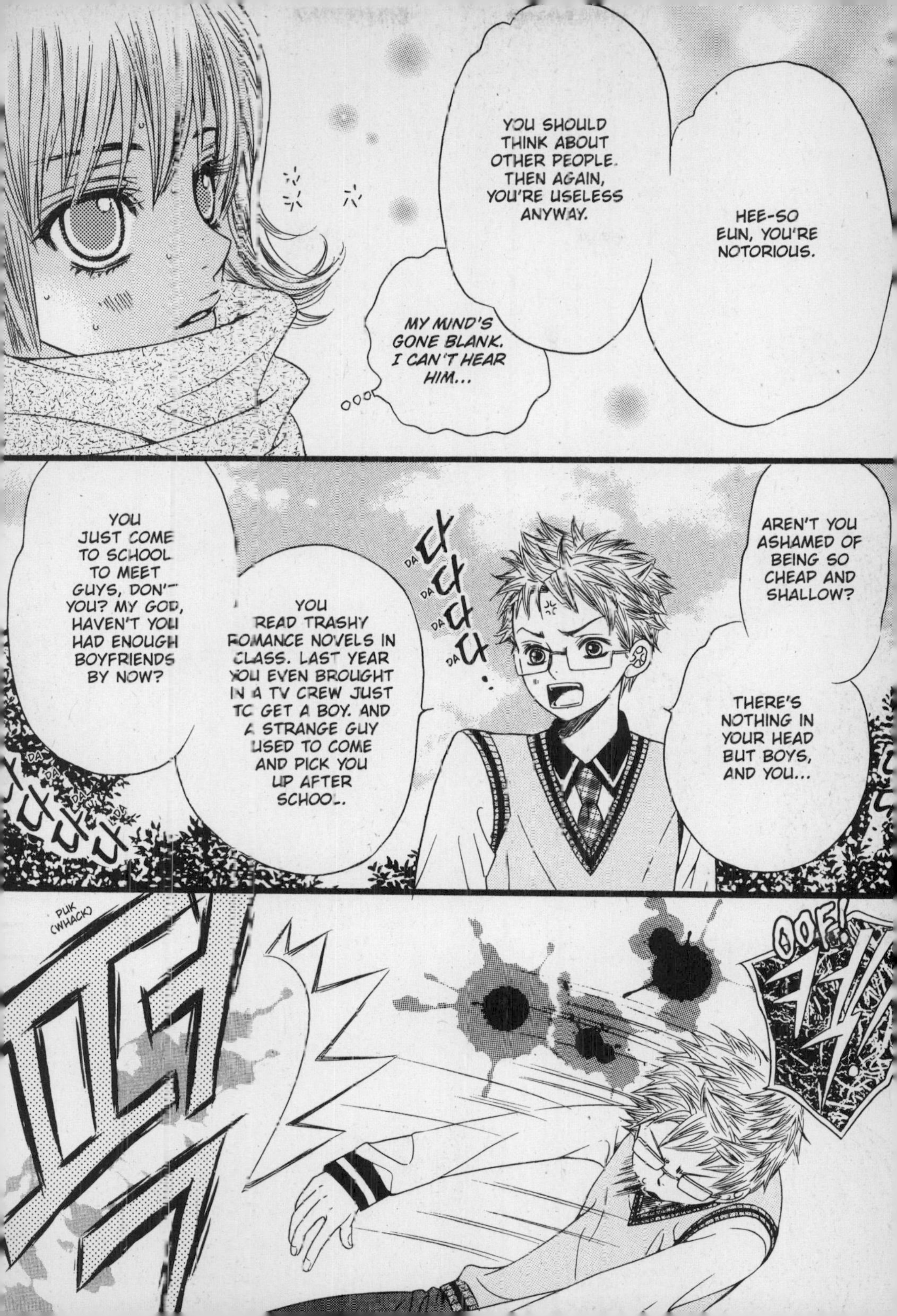

YOU SHOULD THINK ABOUT OTHER PEOPLE. THEN AGAIN, YOU'RE USELESS ANYWAY.
HEE-SO EUN, YOU'RE NOTORIOUS.
MY MIND'S GONE BLANK. I CAN'T HEAR HIM...
DA DA DA DA
YOU JUST COME TO SCHOOL TO MEET GUYS, DON'T YOU? MY GOD, HAVEN'T YOU HAD ENOUGH BOYFRIENDS BY NOW?
YOU READ TRASHY ROMANCE NOVELS IN CLASS. LAST YEAR YOU EVEN BROUGHT IN A TV CREW JUST TO GET A BOY. AND A STRANGE GUY USED TO COME AND PICK YOU UP AFTER SCHOOL.
DA DA DA DA
AREN'T YOU ASHAMED OF BEING SO CHEAP AND SHALLOW?
THERE'S NOTHING IN YOUR HEAD BUT BOYS, AND YOU...
PUK (WHACK)
OOF!

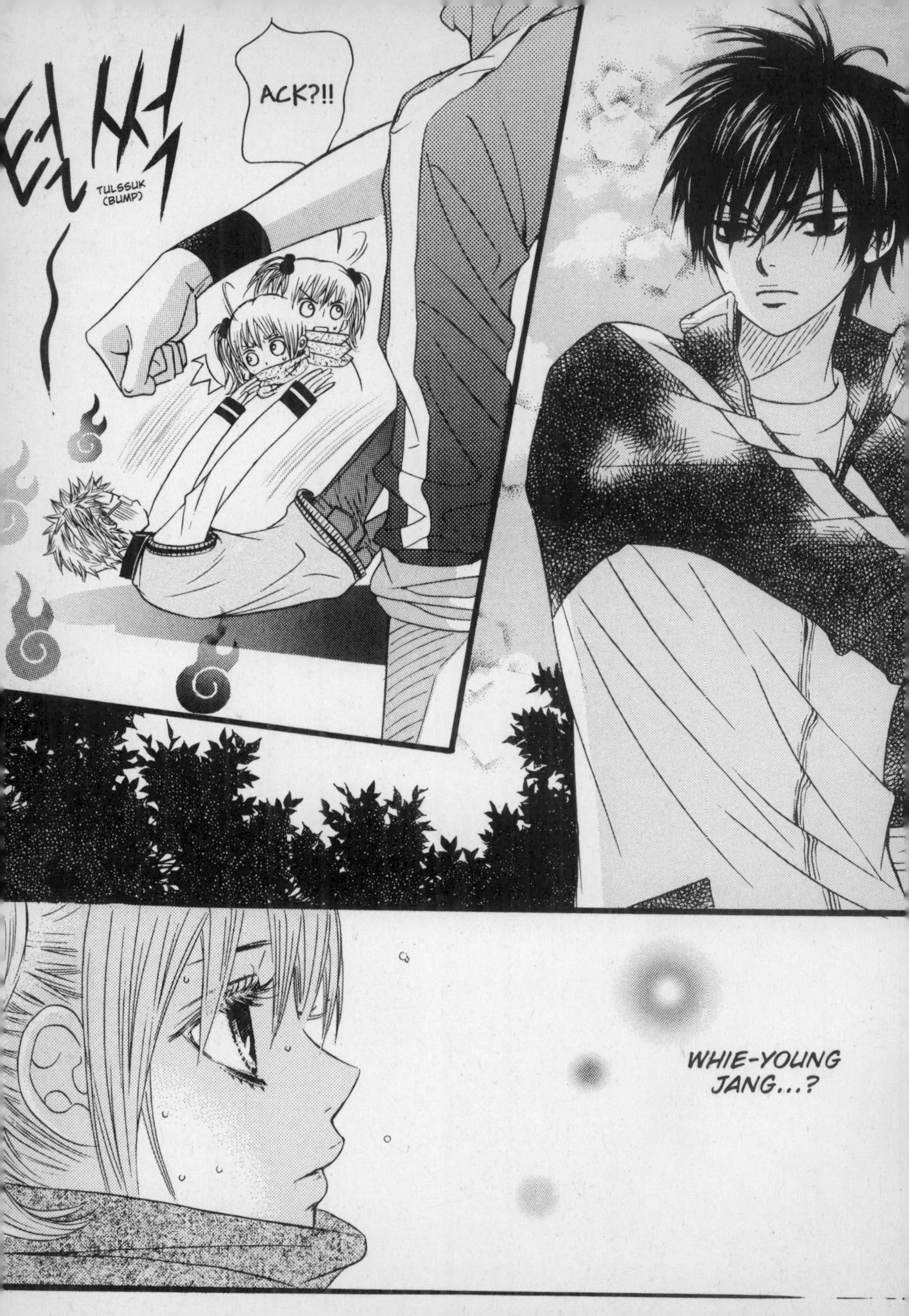
털썩
TULSSUK (BUMP)
ACK?!!
WHIE-YOUNG JANG...?

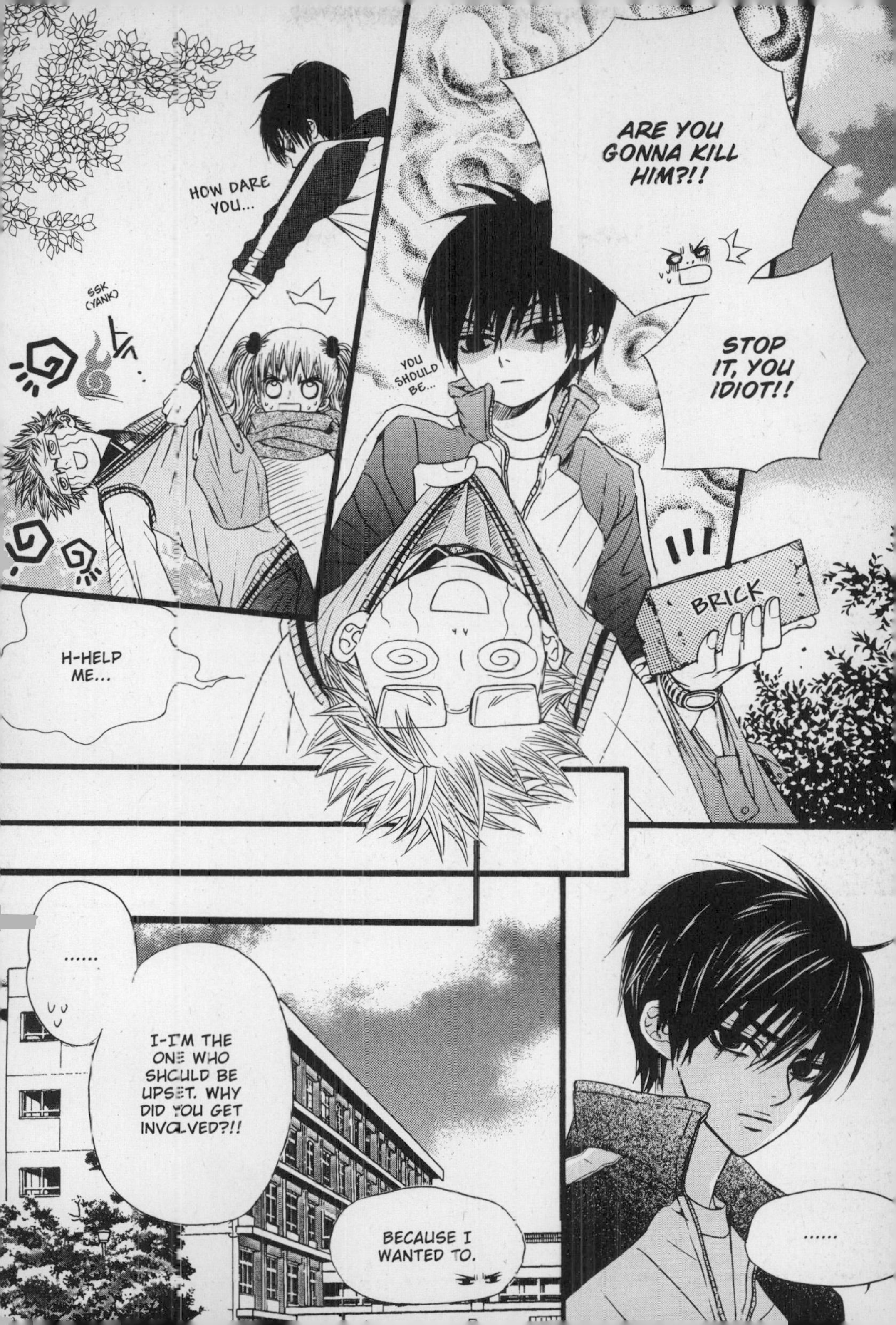
HOW DARE YOU...
SSK (YANK)
YOU SHOULD BE...
H-HELP ME...
BRICK
ARE YOU GONNA KILL HIM?!!
STOP IT, YOU IDIOT!!
......
I-I'M THE ONE WHO SHOULD BE UPSET. WHY DID YOU GET INVOLVED?!!
BECAUSE I WANTED TO.
......

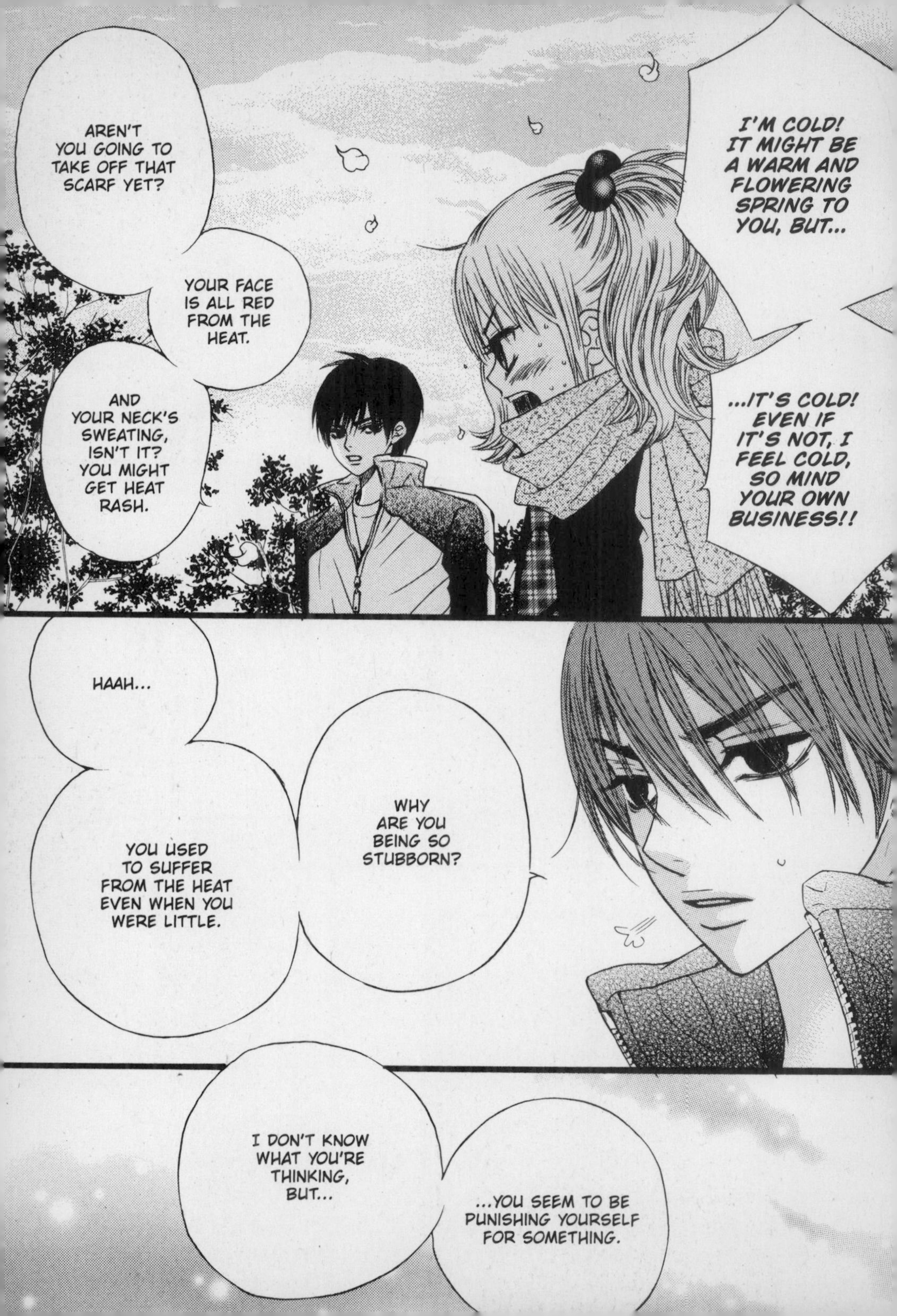
AREN'T YOU GOING TO TAKE OFF THAT SCARF YET?
YOUR FACE IS ALL RED FROM THE HEAT.
AND YOUR NECK'S SWEATING, ISN'T IT? YOU MIGHT GET HEAT RASH.
I'M COLD! IT MIGHT BE A WARM AND FLOWERING SPRING TO YOU, BUT...
...IT'S COLD! EVEN IF IT'S NOT, I FEEL COLD, SO MIND YOUR OWN BUSINESS!!
HAAH...
YOU USED TO SUFFER FROM THE HEAT EVEN WHEN YOU WERE LITTLE.
WHY ARE YOU BEING SO STUBBORN?
I DON'T KNOW WHAT YOU'RE THINKING, BUT...
...YOU SEEM TO BE PUNISHING YOURSELF FOR SOMETHING.

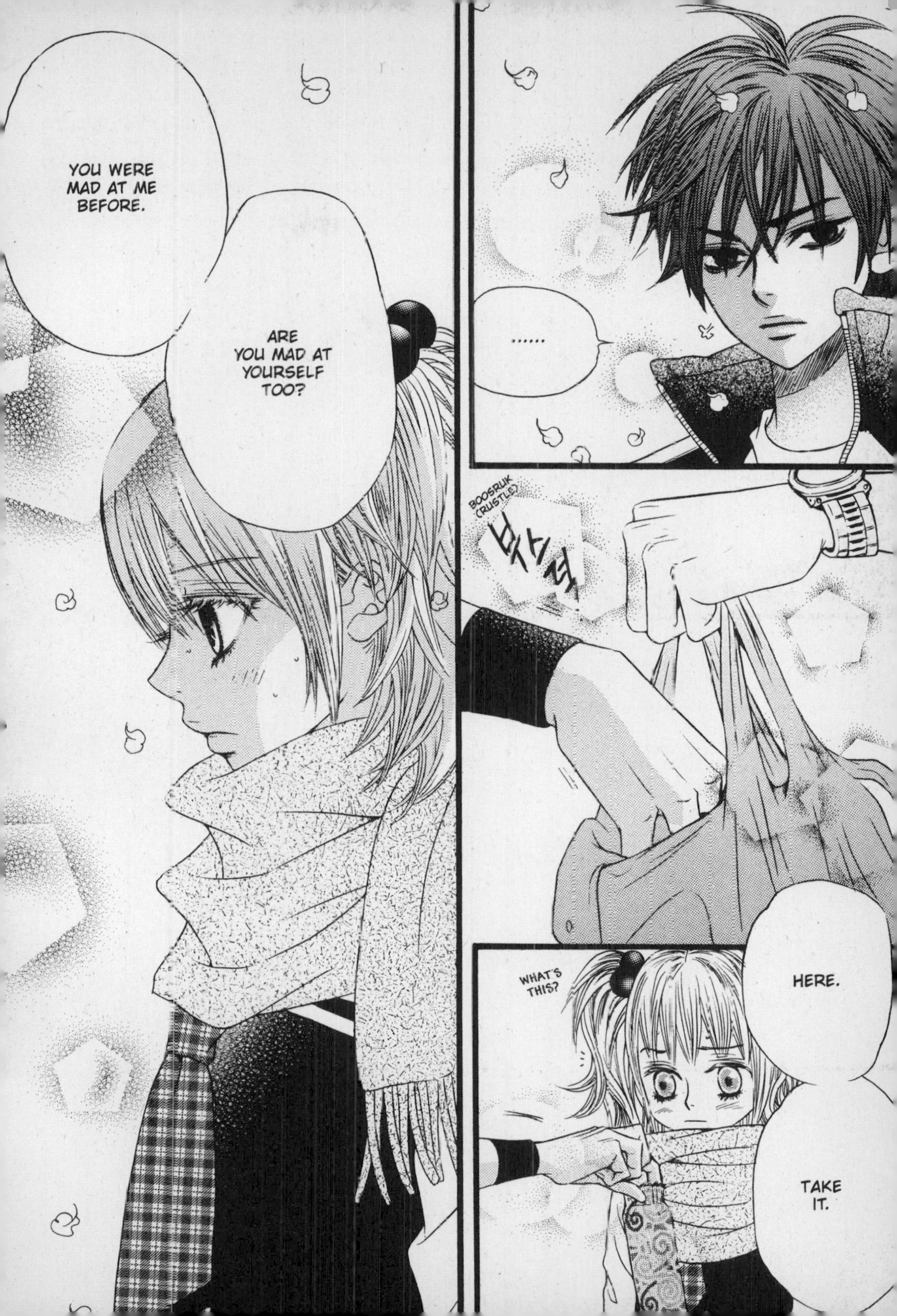
YOU WERE MAD AT ME BEFORE.
ARE YOU MAD AT YOURSELF TOO?
......
BOOSRUK (RUSTLE)
부스럭
WHAT'S THIS?
HERE.
TAKE IT.

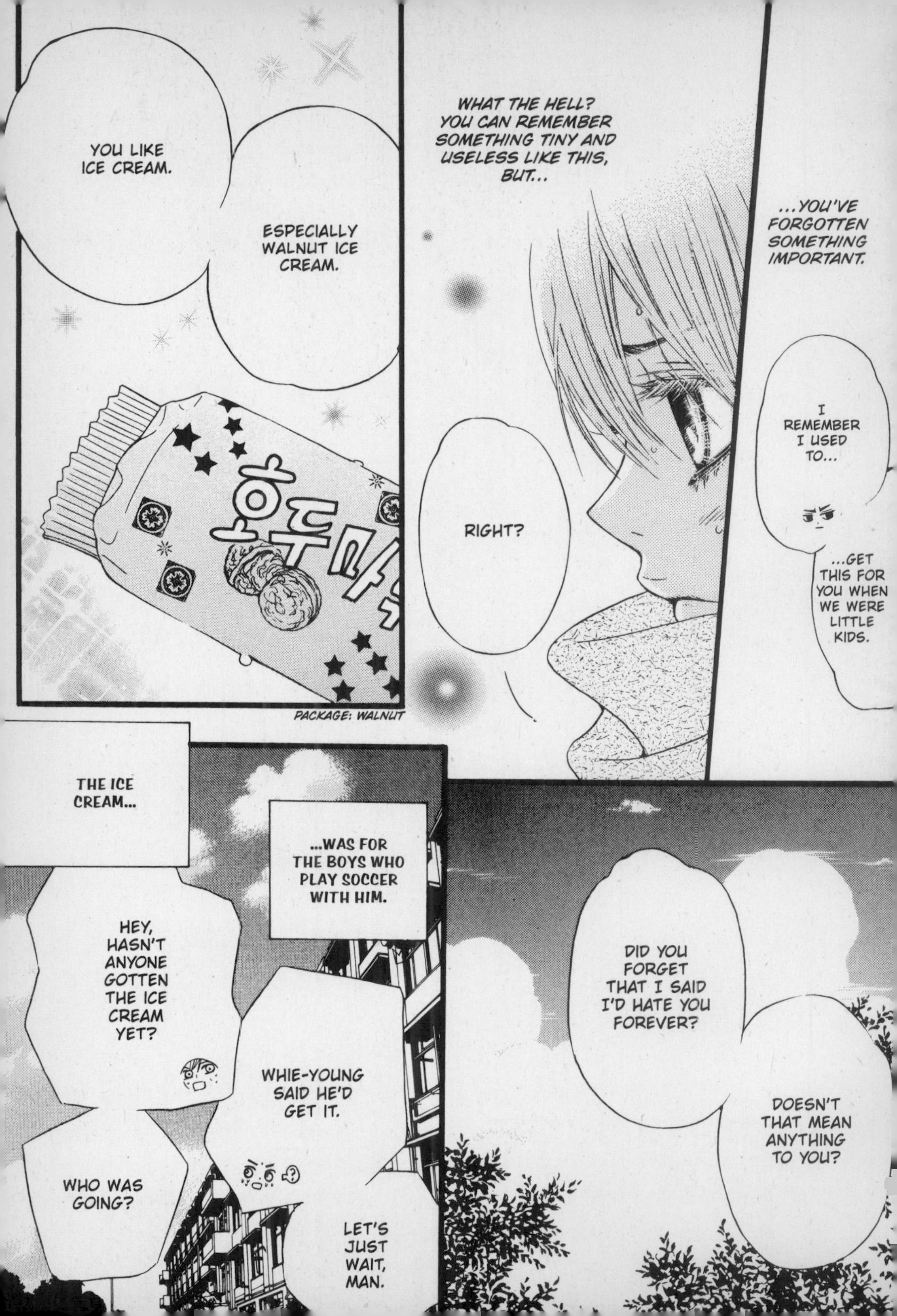
YOU LIKE ICE CREAM.
ESPECIALLY WALNUT ICE CREAM.
PACKAGE: WALNUT
WHAT THE HELL? YOU CAN REMEMBER SOMETHING TINY AND USELESS LIKE THIS, BUT...
RIGHT?
...YOU'VE FORGOTTEN SOMETHING IMPORTANT.
I REMEMBER I USED TO...
...GET THIS FOR YOU WHEN WE WERE LITTLE KIDS.
THE ICE CREAM...
...WAS FOR THE BOYS WHO PLAY SOCCER WITH HIM.
HEY, HASN'T ANYONE GOTTEN THE ICE CREAM YET?
WHIE-YOUNG SAID HE'D GET IT.
WHO WAS GOING?
LET'S JUST WAIT, MAN.
DID YOU FORGET THAT I SAID I'D HATE YOU FOREVER?
DOESN'T THAT MEAN ANYTHING TO YOU?

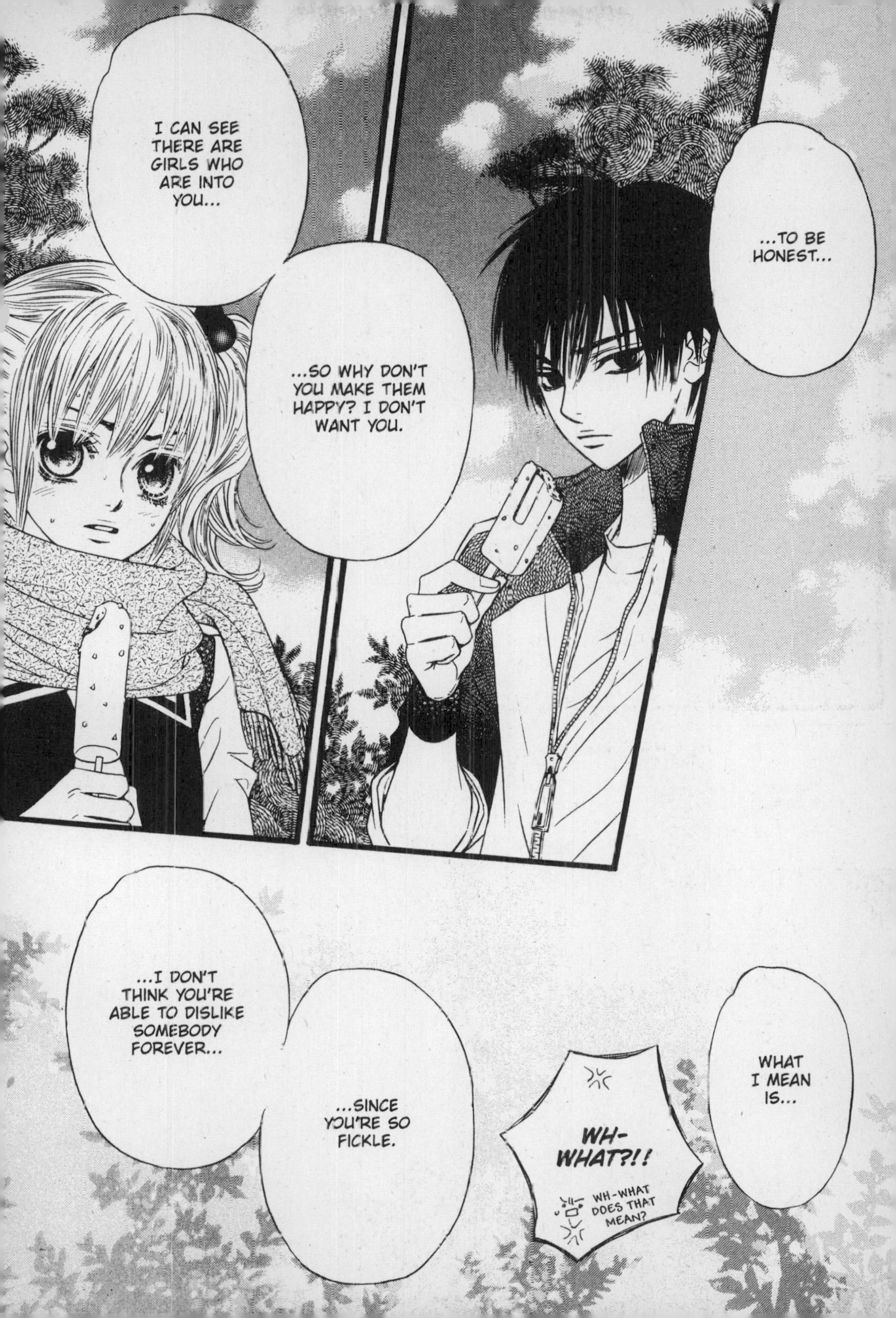

I CAN SEE THERE ARE GIRLS WHO ARE INTO YOU...
...SO WHY DON'T YOU MAKE THEM HAPPY? I DON'T WANT YOU.
...TO BE HONEST...
...I DON'T THINK YOU'RE ABLE TO DISLIKE SOMEBODY FOREVER...
...SINCE YOU'RE SO FICKLE.
WH-WHAT?!!
WH-WHAT DOES THAT MEAN?
WHAT I MEAN IS...

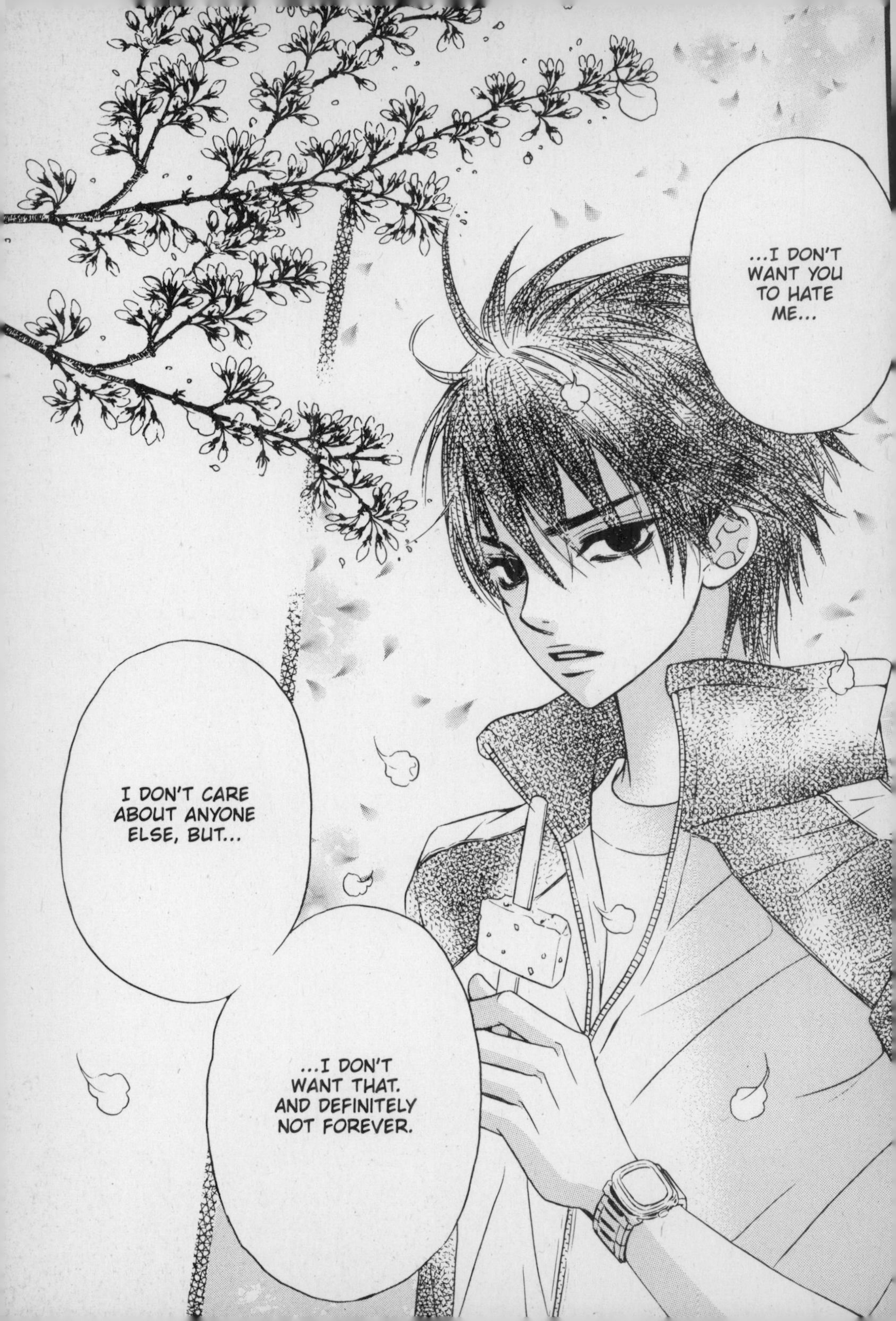
...I DON'T WANT YOU TO HATE ME...
I DON'T CARE ABOUT ANYONE ELSE, BUT...
...I DON'T WANT THAT. AND DEFINITELY NOT FOREVER.

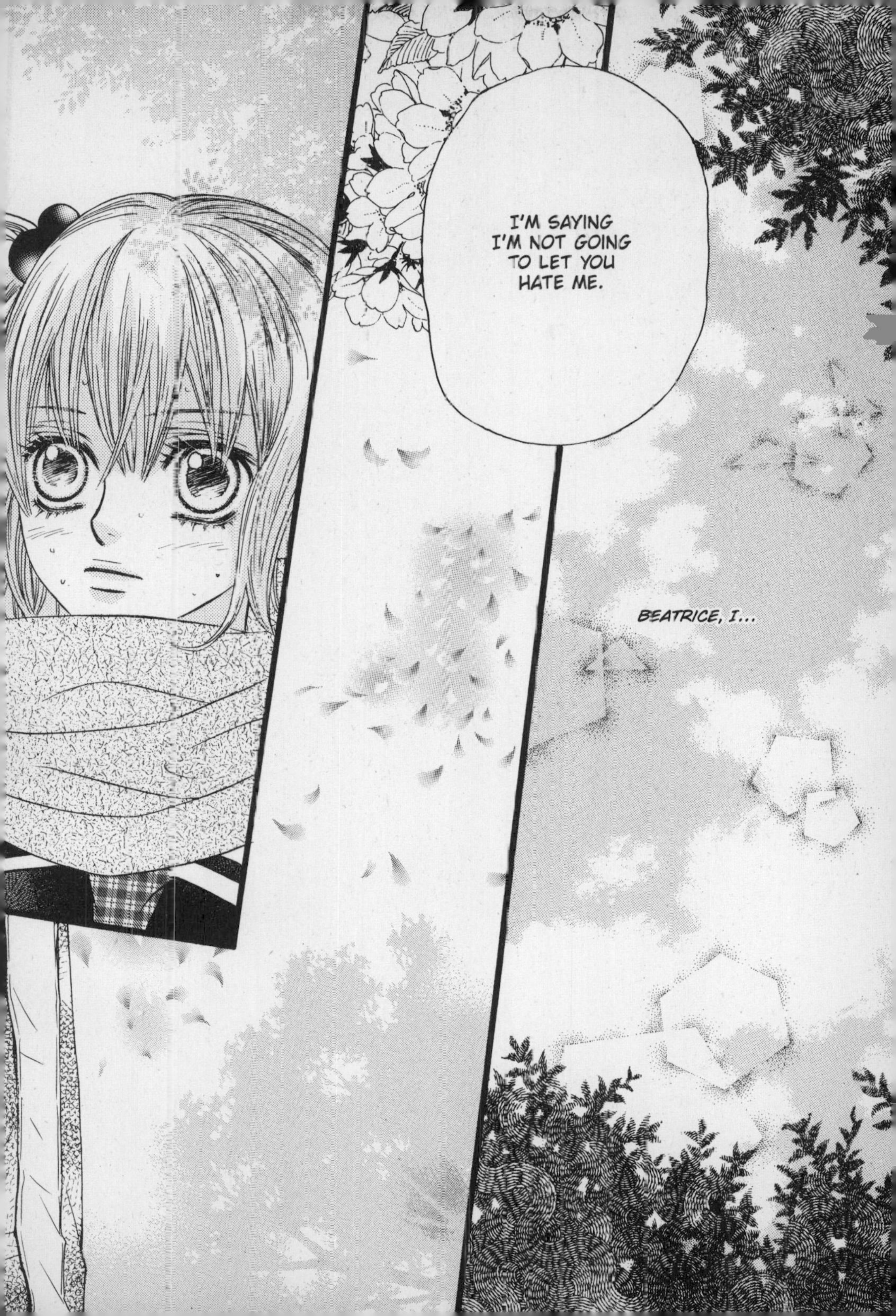
I'M SAYING I'M NOT GOING TO LET YOU HATE ME.
BEATRICE, I...

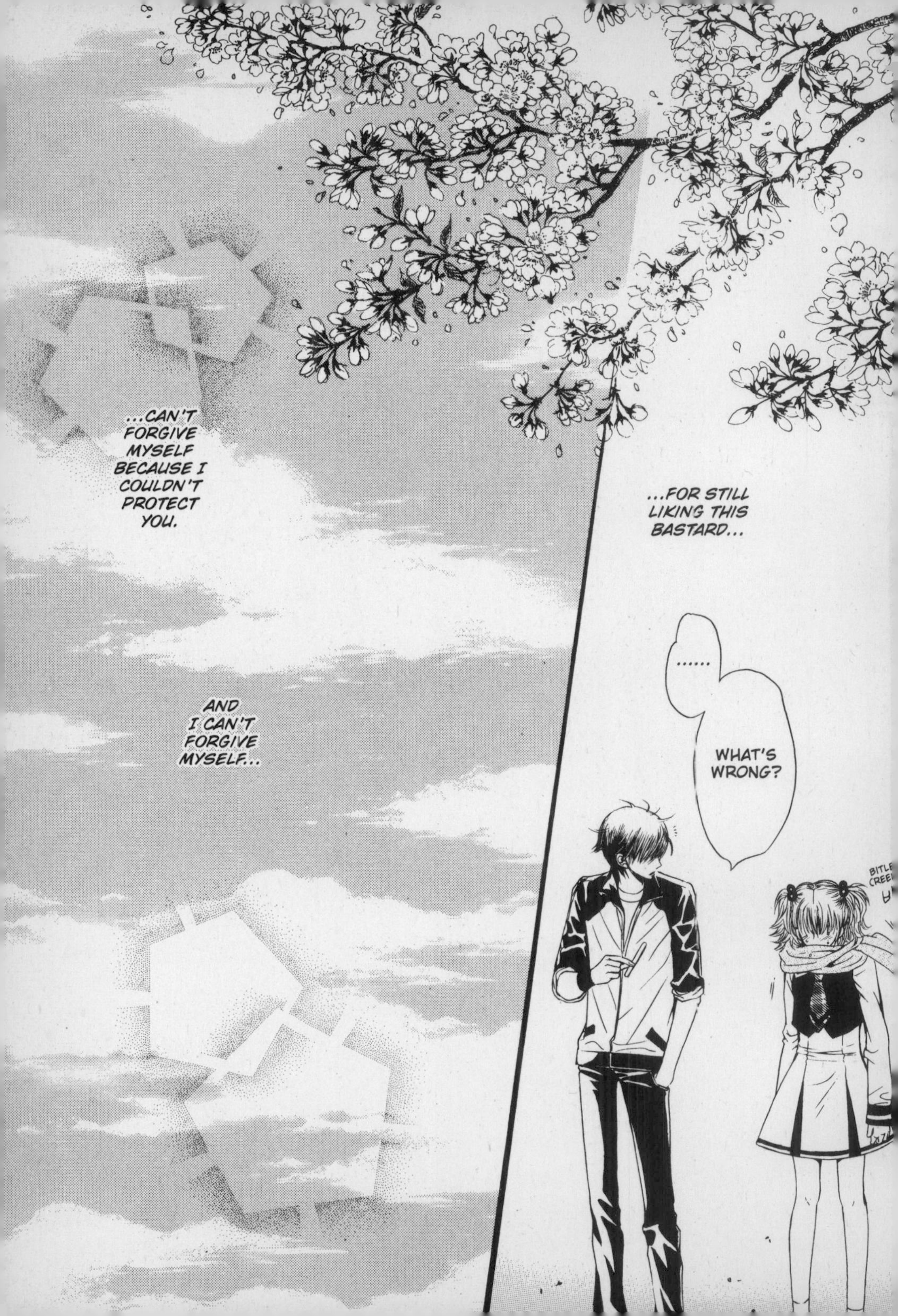
...CAN'T FORGIVE MYSELF BECAUSE I COULDN'T PROTECT YOU.
AND I CAN'T FORGIVE MYSELF...
...FOR STILL LIKING THIS BASTARD...
......
WHAT'S WRONG?

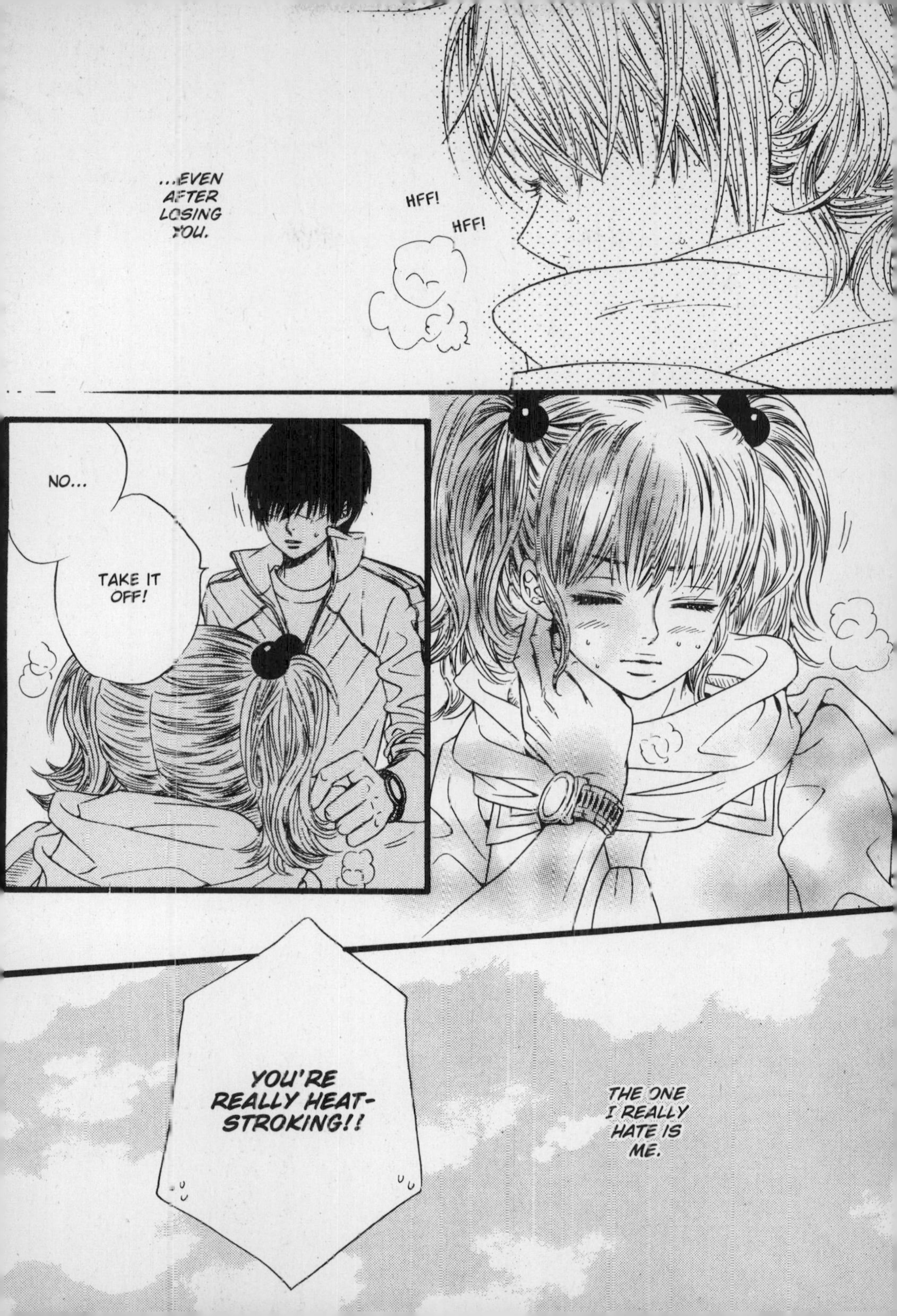
...EVEN AFTER LOSING YOU.
HFF!
HFF!
NO...
TAKE IT OFF!
YOU'RE REALLY HEAT-STROKING!!
THE ONE I REALLY HATE IS ME.

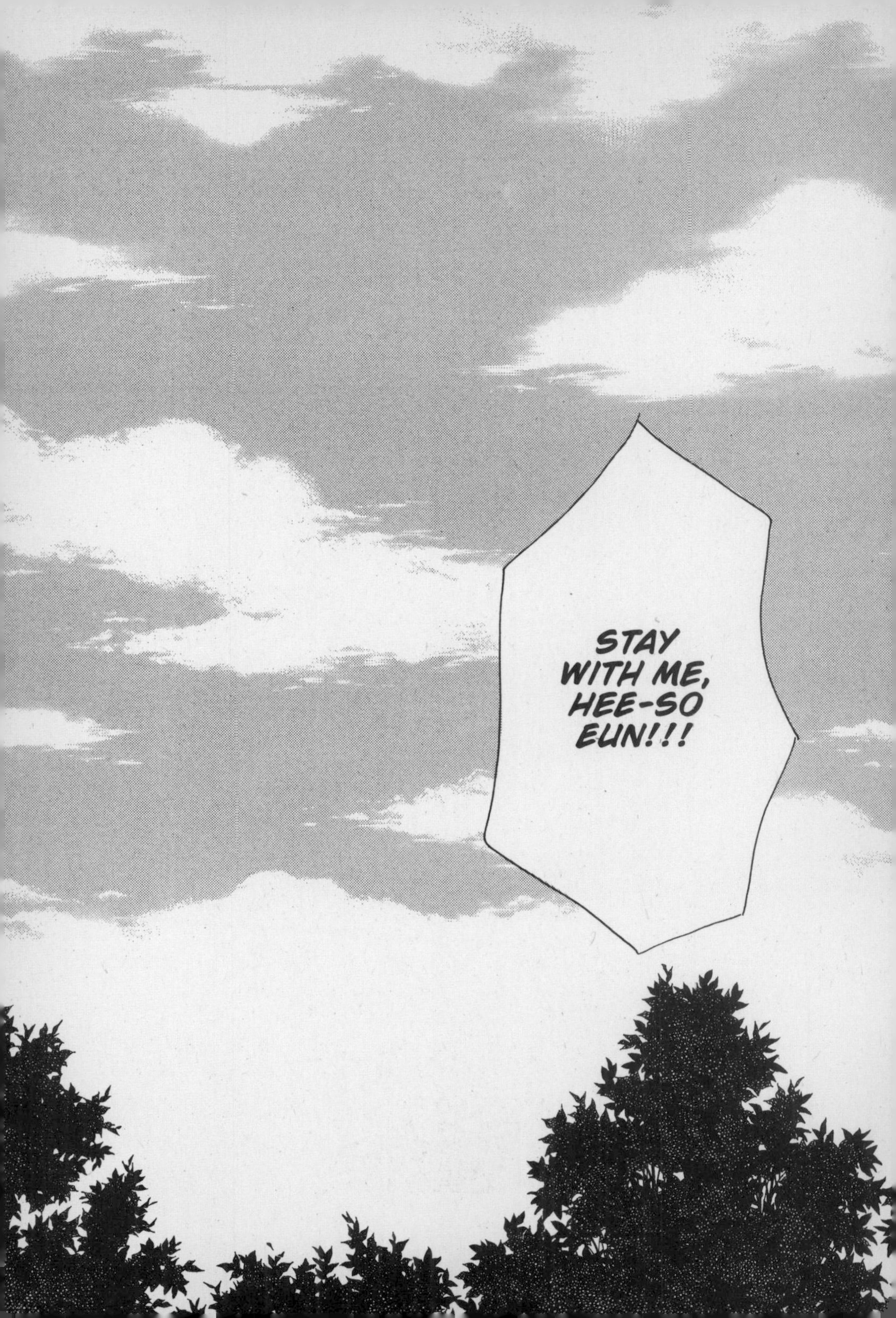
STAY WITH ME, HEE-SO EUN!!!

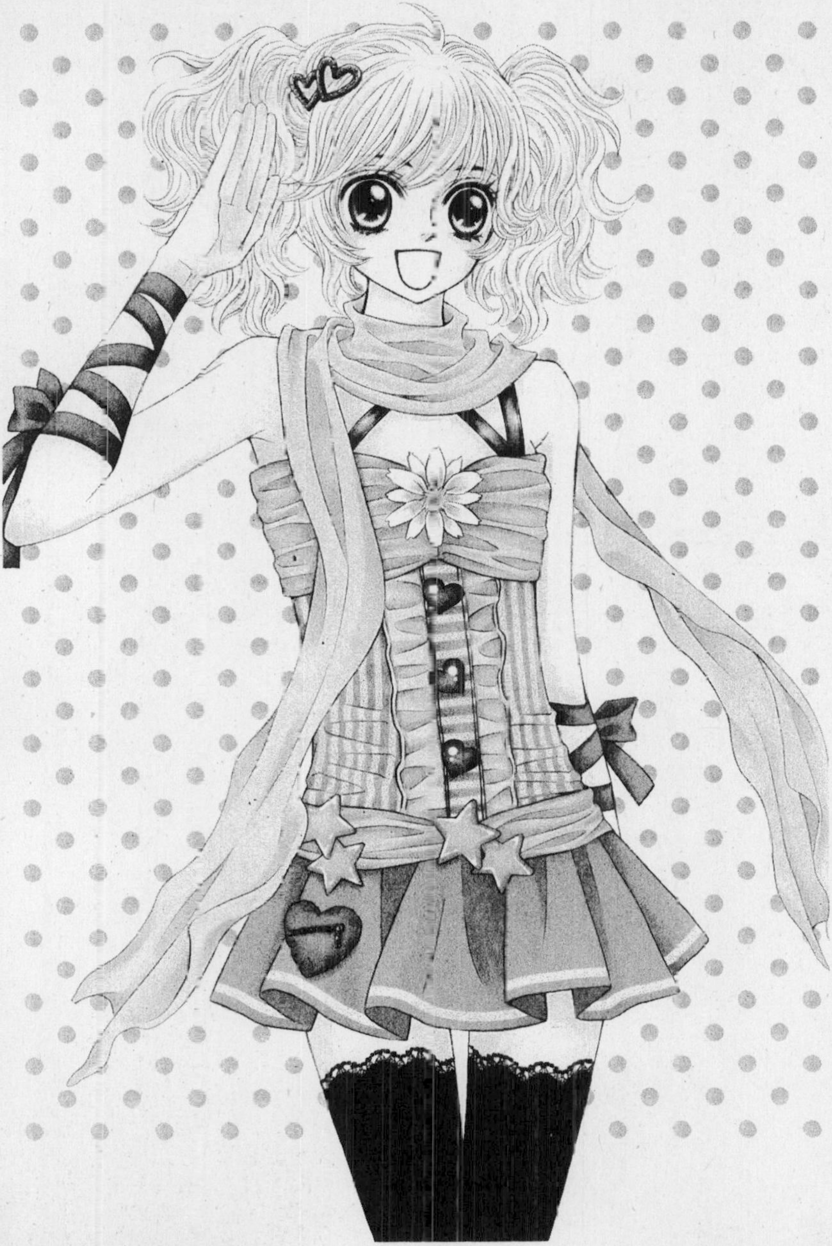

13th Boy

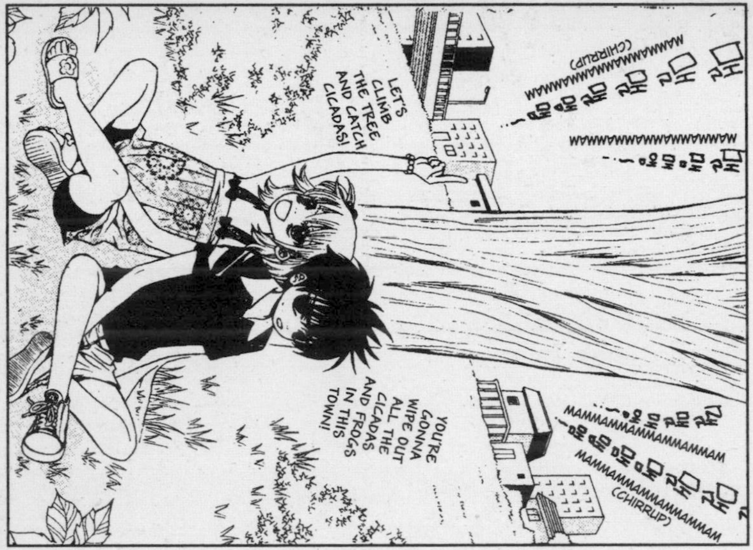
MAMMAMMAMMAMMAMMAM (CHIRRUP)
MAMMAMMAMMAMMAMMAM
MAMMAMMAMMAMMAMMAM
MAMMAMMAMMAMMAMMAM (CHIRRUP)
LET'S CLIMB THE TREE AND CATCH CICADAS!
YOU'RE GONNA WIPE OUT ALL THE CICADAS AND FROGS IN THIS TOWN!

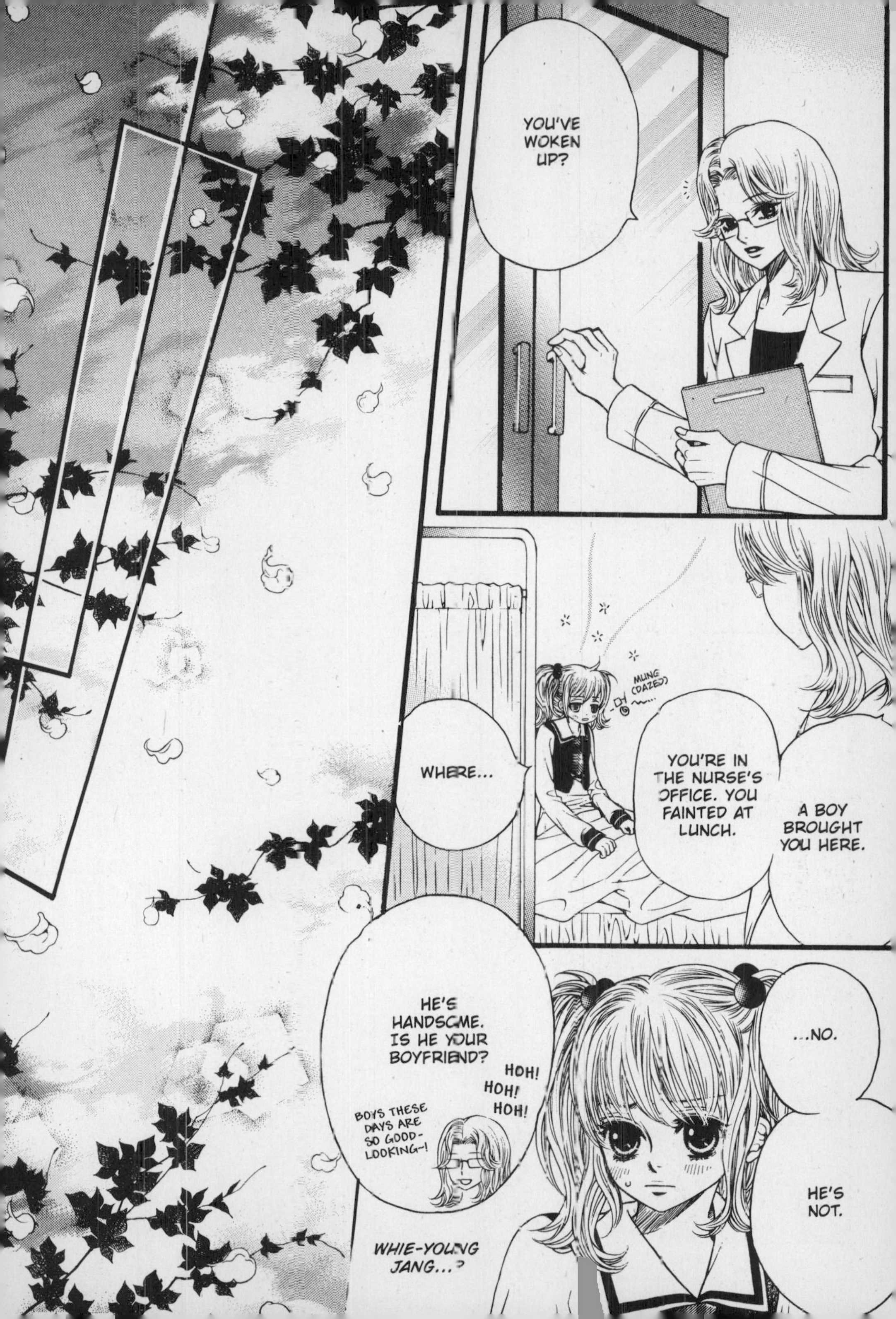
YOU'VE WOKEN UP?
WHERE...
MUNG (DAZED)
YOU'RE IN THE NURSE'S OFFICE. YOU FAINTED AT LUNCH.
A BOY BROUGHT YOU HERE.
HE'S HANDSOME. IS HE YOUR BOYFRIEND?
HOH! HOH! HOH!
BOYS THESE DAYS ARE SO GOOD-LOOKING~!
WHIE-YOUNG JANG...?
...NO.
HE'S NOT.

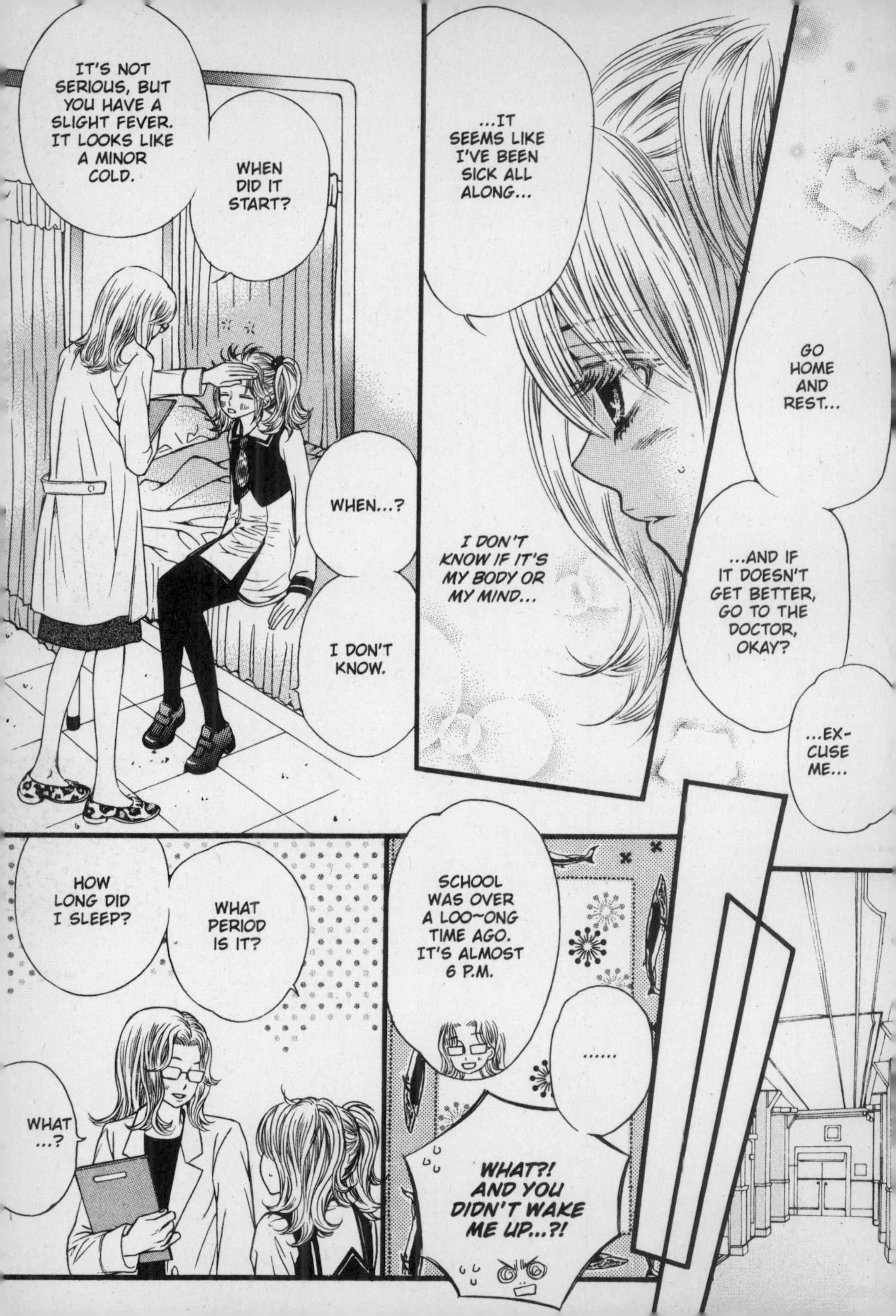
IT'S NOT SERIOUS, BUT YOU HAVE A SLIGHT FEVER. IT LOOKS LIKE A MINOR COLD.
WHEN DID IT START?
WHEN...?
I DON'T KNOW.
...IT SEEMS LIKE I'VE BEEN SICK ALL ALONG...
I DON'T KNOW IF IT'S MY BODY OR MY MIND...
GO HOME AND REST...
...AND IF IT DOESN'T GET BETTER, GO TO THE DOCTOR, OKAY?
...EX-CUSE ME...
HOW LONG DID I SLEEP?
WHAT PERIOD IS IT?
WHAT ...?
SCHOOL WAS OVER A LOO~ONG TIME AGO. IT'S ALMOST 6 P.M.
......
WHAT?! AND YOU DIDN'T WAKE ME UP...?!

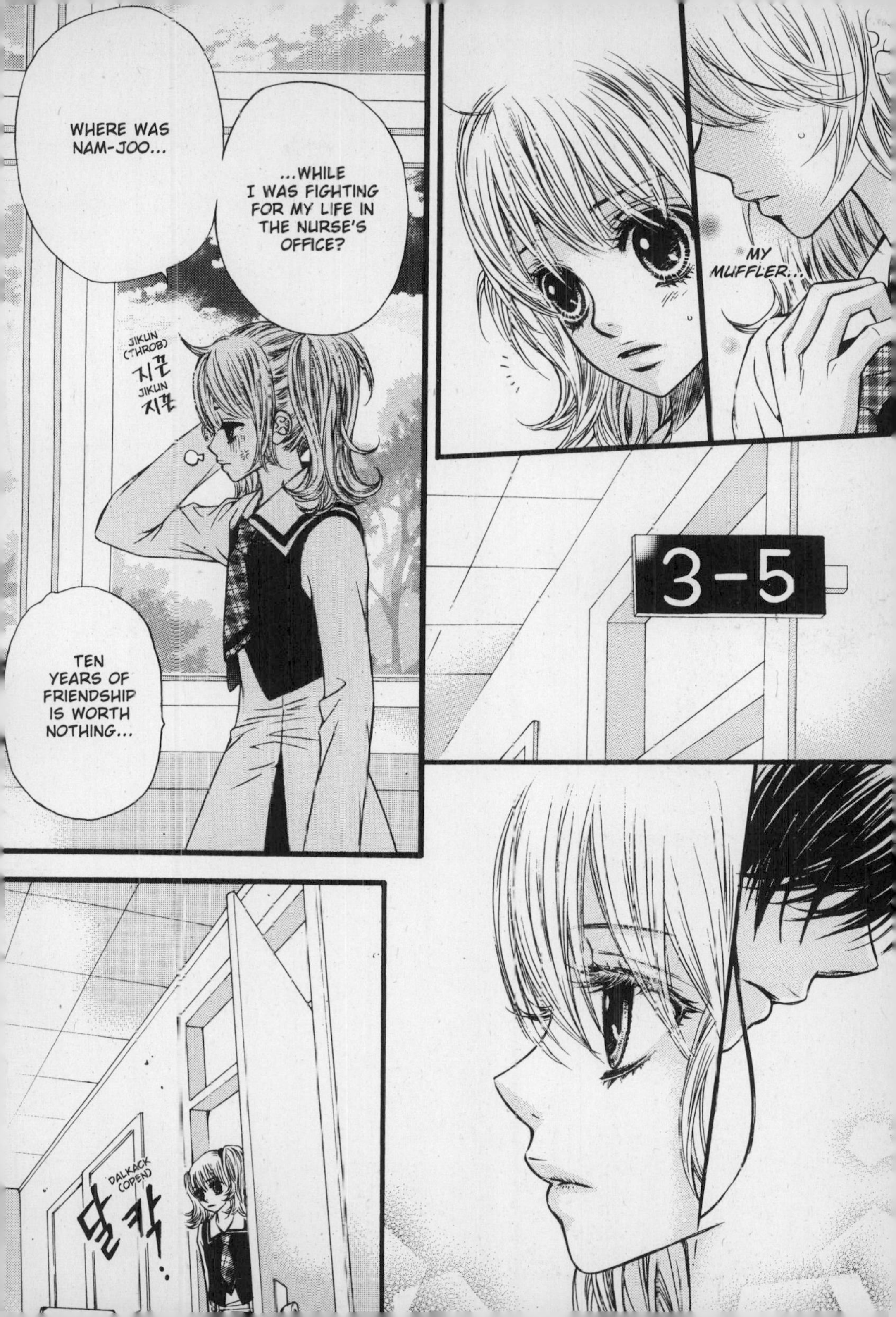
WHERE WAS NAM-JOO...
...WHILE I WAS FIGHTING FOR MY LIFE IN THE NURSE'S OFFICE?
JIKUN (THROB)
지끈
JIKUN
지끈
TEN YEARS OF FRIENDSHIP IS WORTH NOTHING...
MY MUFFLER...
3-5
DALKACK (OPEN)
달칵!

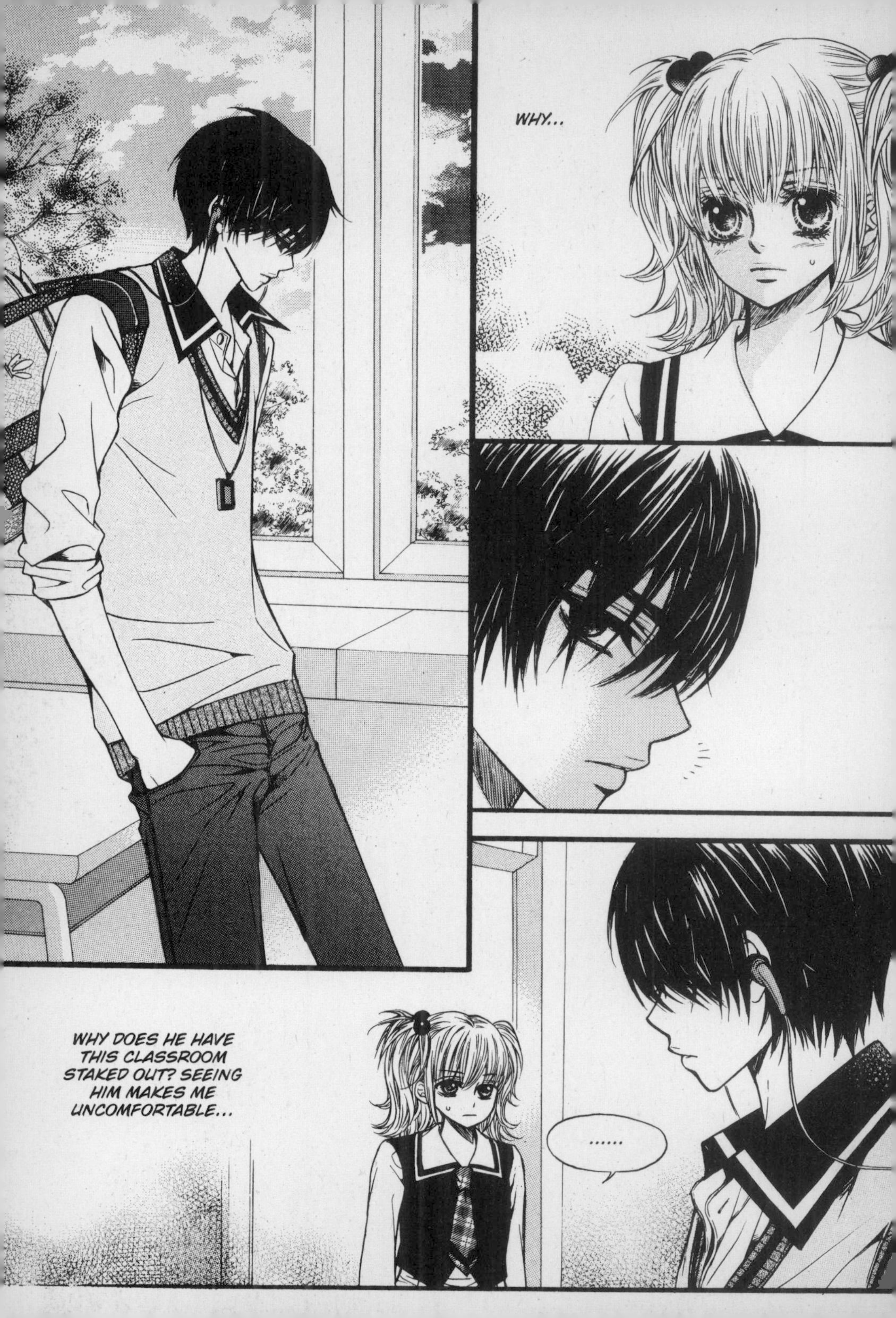
WHY...
WHY DOES HE HAVE THIS CLASSROOM STAKED OUT? SEEING HIM MAKES ME UNCOMFORTABLE...
......

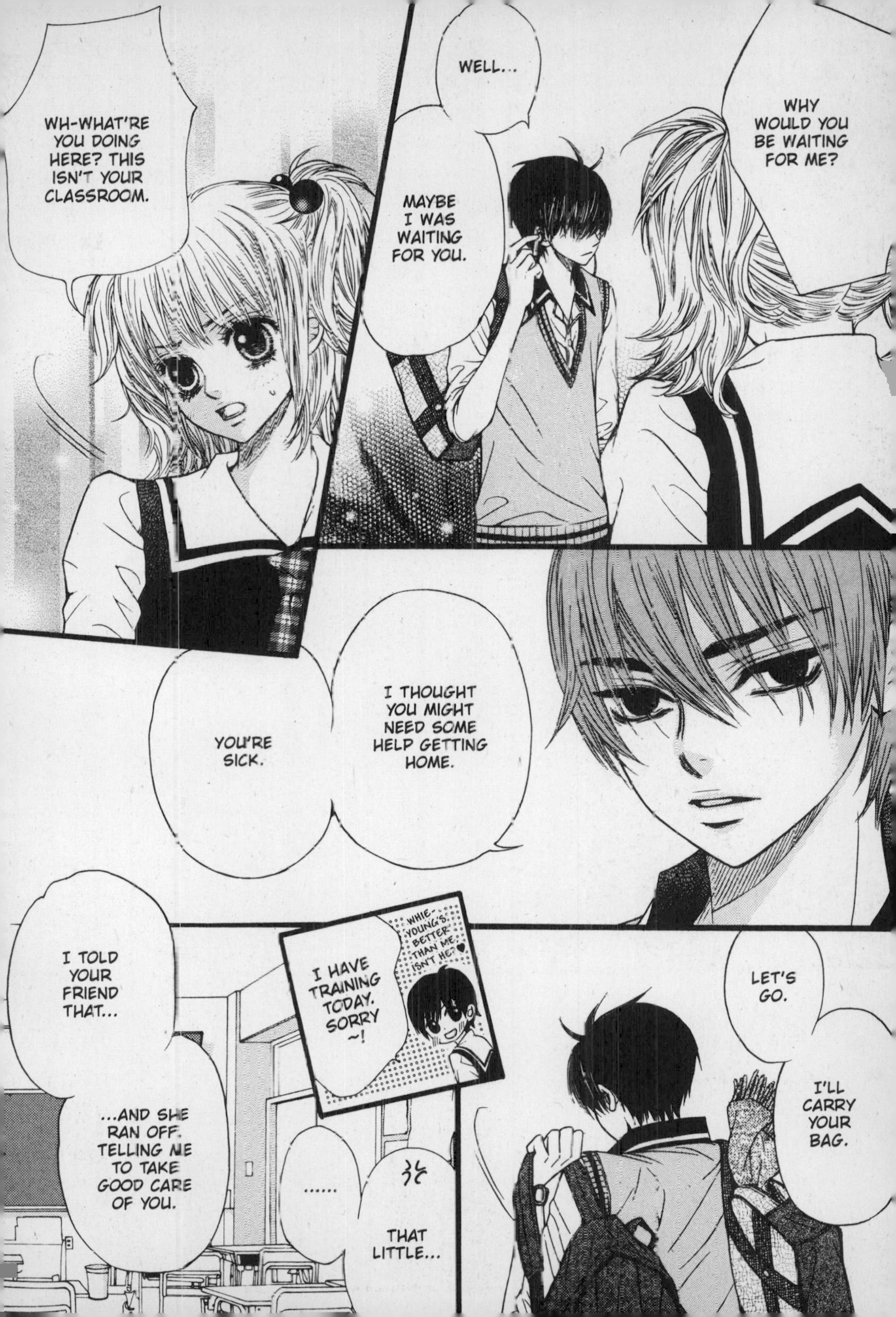
WH-WHAT'RE YOU DOING HERE? THIS ISN'T YOUR CLASSROOM.
WELL...
MAYBE I WAS WAITING FOR YOU.
WHY WOULD YOU BE WAITING FOR ME?
YOU'RE SICK.
I THOUGHT YOU MIGHT NEED SOME HELP GETTING HOME.
I TOLD YOUR FRIEND THAT...
I HAVE TRAINING TODAY. SORRY ~!
WHIE-YOUNG'S BETTER THAN ME, ISN'T HE? ♥
...AND SHE RAN OFF, TELLING ME TO TAKE GOOD CARE OF YOU.
......
THAT LITTLE...
LET'S GO.
I'LL CARRY YOUR BAG.

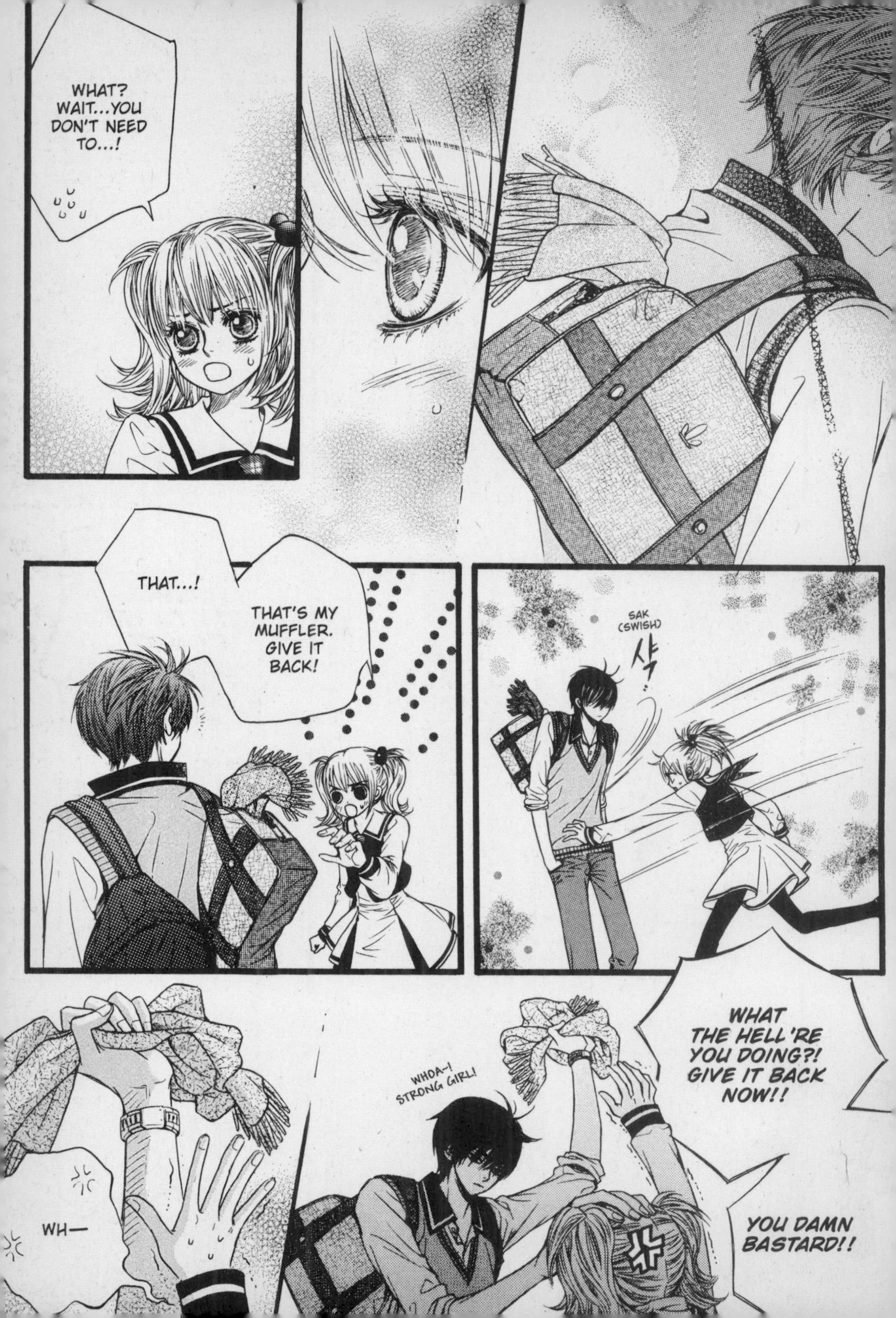
WHAT? WAIT...YOU DON'T NEED TO...!
THAT...!
THAT'S MY MUFFLER. GIVE IT BACK!
SAK (SWISH)
샥
WH—
WHOA~! STRONG GIRL!
WHAT THE HELL 'RE YOU DOING?! GIVE IT BACK NOW!!
YOU DAMN BASTARD!!

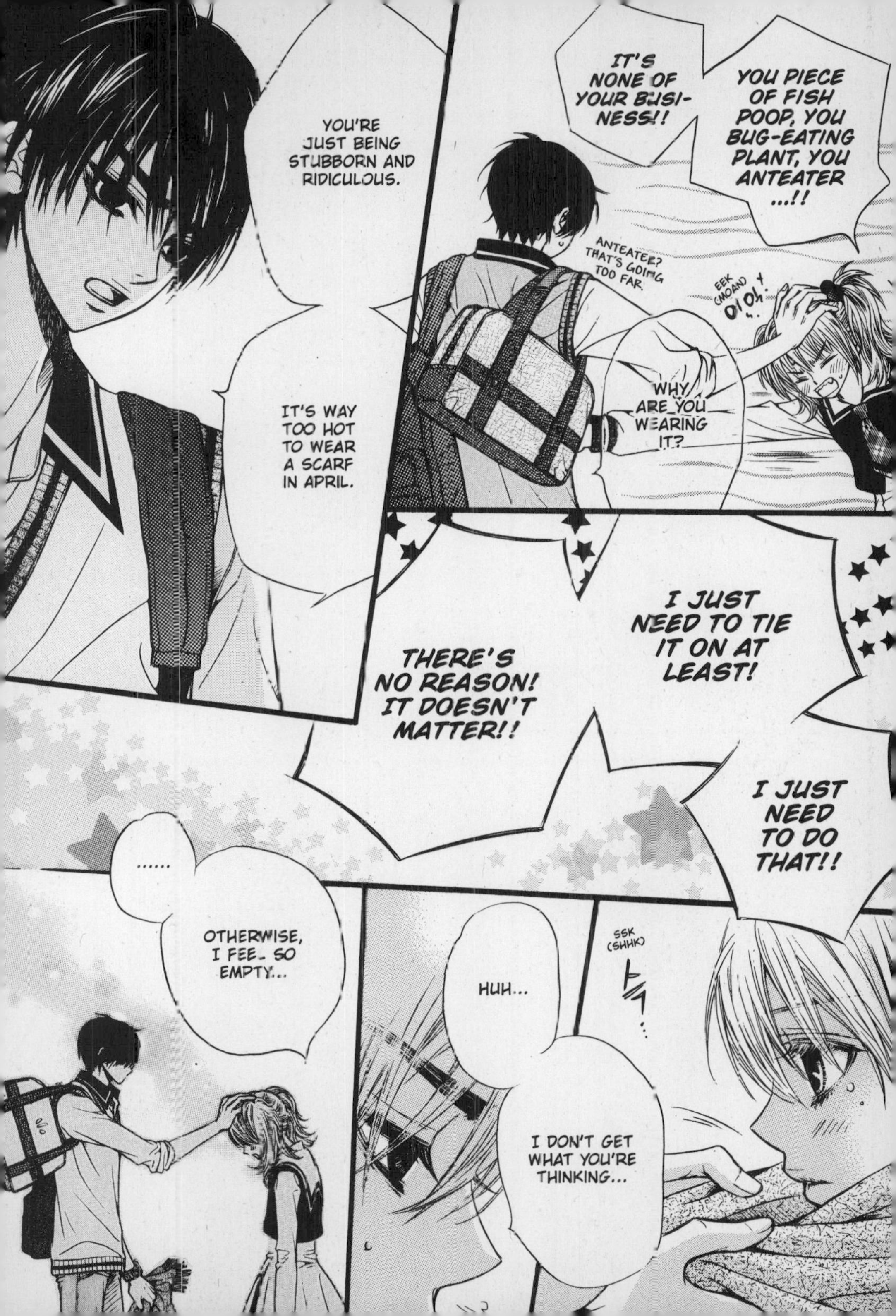
YOU'RE JUST BEING STUBBORN AND RIDICULOUS.
IT'S WAY TOO HOT TO WEAR A SCARF IN APRIL.
IT'S NONE OF YOUR BUSINESS!!
YOU PIECE OF FISH POOP, YOU BUG-EATING PLANT, YOU ANTEATER ...!!
ANTEATER? THAT'S GOING TOO FAR.
EEK (MOAN)
WHY ARE YOU WEARING IT?
THERE'S NO REASON! IT DOESN'T MATTER!!
I JUST NEED TO TIE IT ON AT LEAST!
I JUST NEED TO DO THAT!!
......
OTHERWISE, I FEEL SO EMPTY...
HUH...
SSK (SHHK)
I DON'T GET WHAT YOU'RE THINKING...

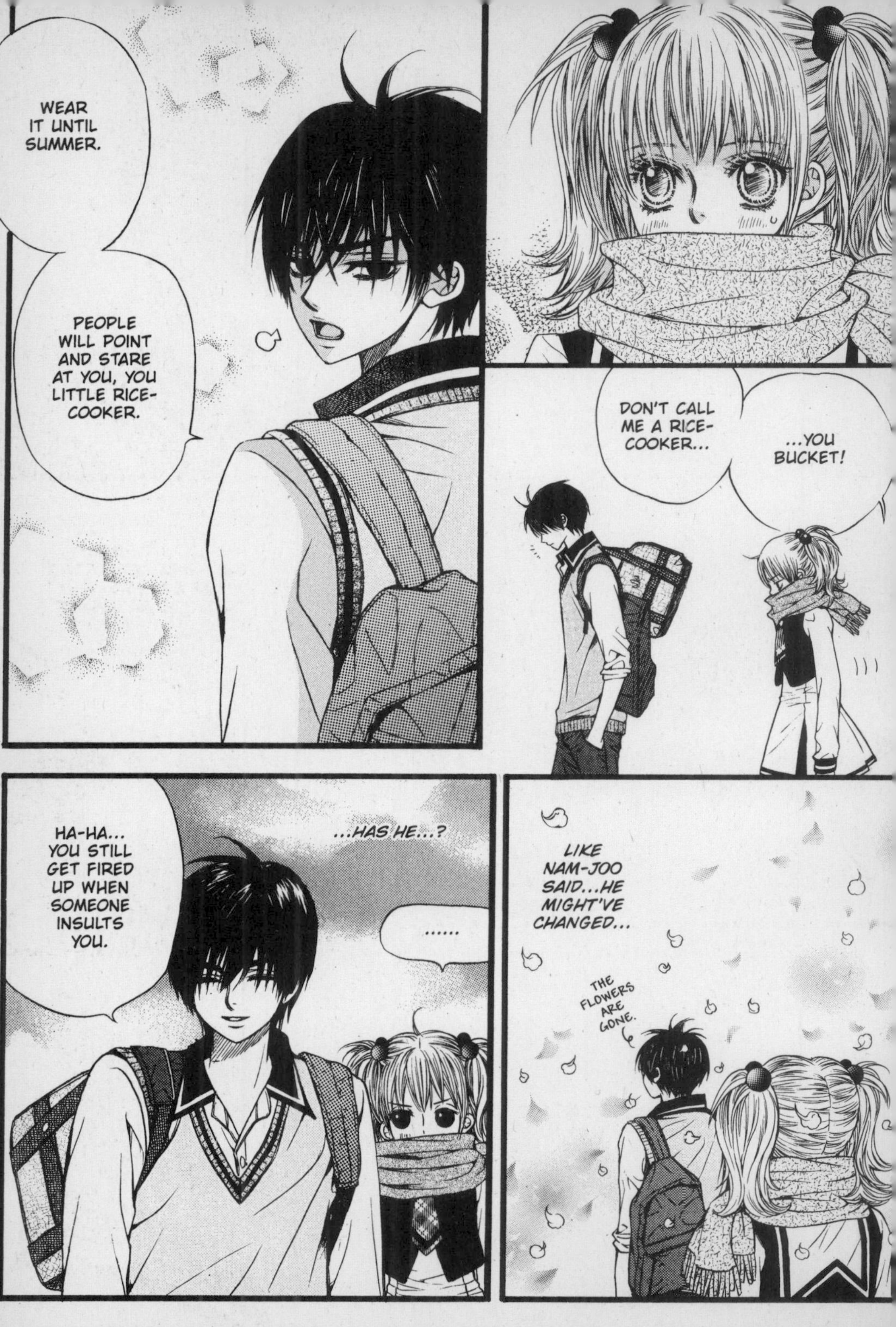
WEAR IT UNTIL SUMMER.
PEOPLE WILL POINT AND STARE AT YOU, YOU LITTLE RICE-COOKER.
DON'T CALL ME A RICE-COOKER...
...YOU BUCKET!
HA-HA... YOU STILL GET FIRED UP WHEN SOMEONE INSULTS YOU.
...HAS HE...?
......
LIKE NAM-JOO SAID...HE MIGHT'VE CHANGED...
THE FLOWERS ARE GONE.

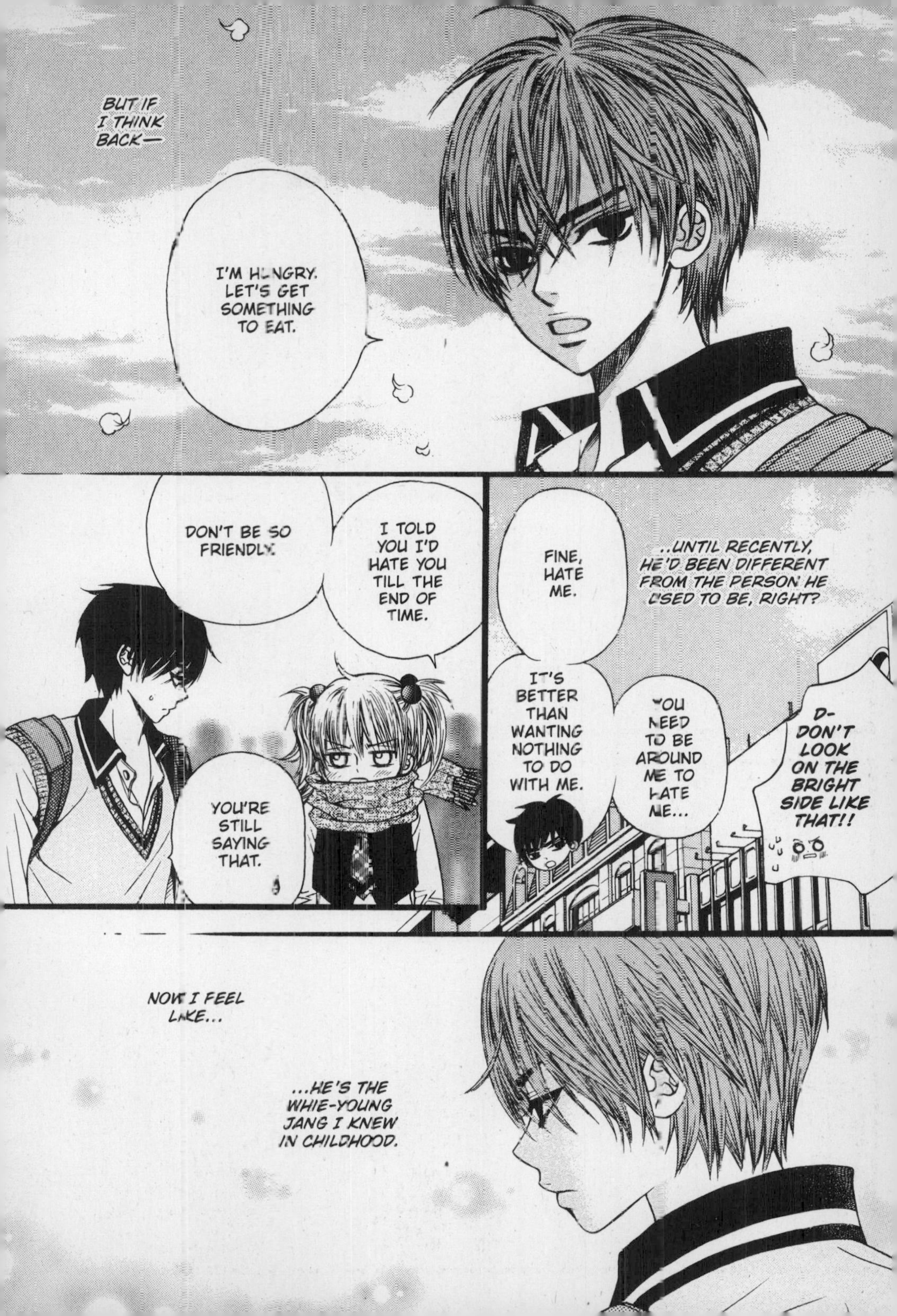
BUT IF I THINK BACK—
I'M HUNGRY. LET'S GET SOMETHING TO EAT.
DON'T BE SO FRIENDLY.
I TOLD YOU I'D HATE YOU TILL THE END OF TIME.
YOU'RE STILL SAYING THAT.
FINE, HATE ME.
...UNTIL RECENTLY, HE'D BEEN DIFFERENT FROM THE PERSON HE USED TO BE, RIGHT?
IT'S BETTER THAN WANTING NOTHING TO DO WITH ME.
YOU NEED TO BE AROUND ME TO HATE ME...
D-DON'T LOOK ON THE BRIGHT SIDE LIKE THAT!!
NOW I FEEL LIKE...
...HE'S THE WHIE-YOUNG JANG I KNEW IN CHILDHOOD.

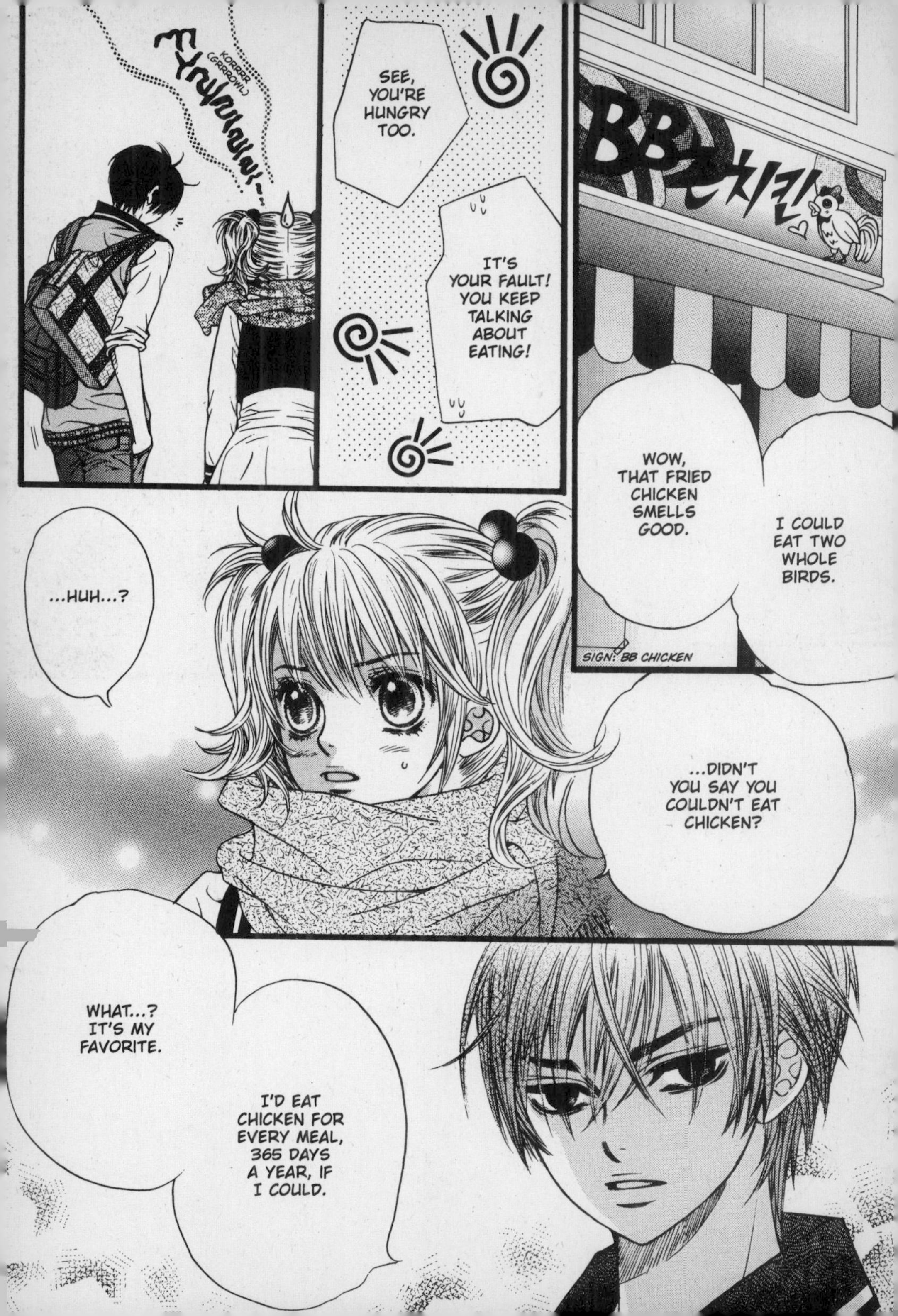
KORRRR (GRRRROWL)
SEE, YOU'RE HUNGRY TOO.
IT'S YOUR FAULT! YOU KEEP TALKING ABOUT EATING!
BB 치킨
WOW, THAT FRIED CHICKEN SMELLS GOOD.
I COULD EAT TWO WHOLE BIRDS.
SIGN: BB CHICKEN
...HUH...?
...DIDN'T YOU SAY YOU COULDN'T EAT CHICKEN?
WHAT...? IT'S MY FAVORITE.
I'D EAT CHICKEN FOR EVERY MEAL, 365 DAYS A YEAR, IF I COULD.

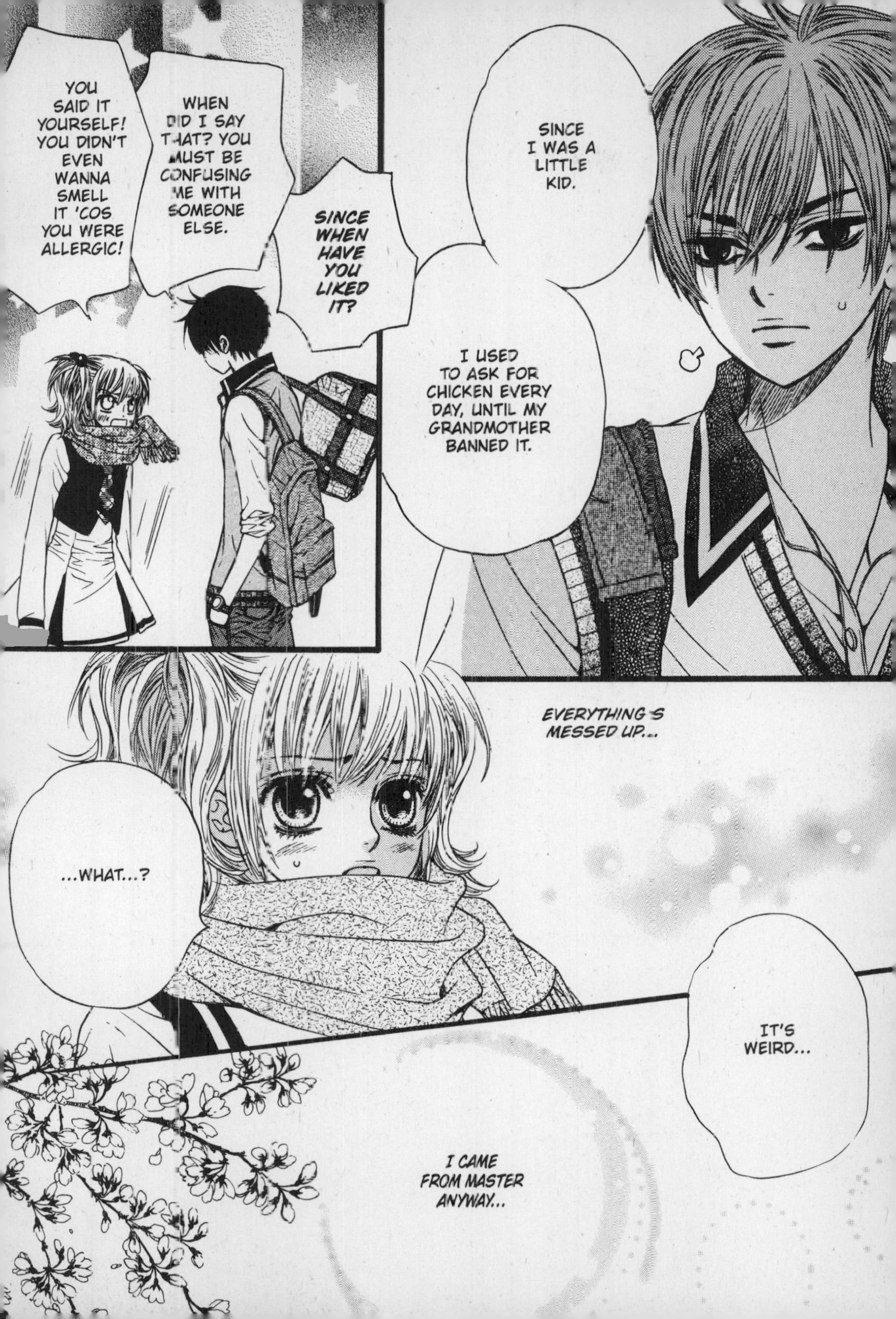
SINCE I WAS A LITTLE KID.
I USED TO ASK FOR CHICKEN EVERY DAY, UNTIL MY GRANDMOTHER BANNED IT.
SINCE WHEN HAVE YOU LIKED IT?
WHEN DID I SAY THAT? YOU MUST BE CONFUSING ME WITH SOMEONE ELSE.
YOU SAID IT YOURSELF! YOU DIDN'T EVEN WANNA SMELL IT 'COS YOU WERE ALLERGIC!
EVERYTHING'S MESSED UP...
...WHAT...?
IT'S WEIRD...
I CAME FROM MASTER ANYWAY...

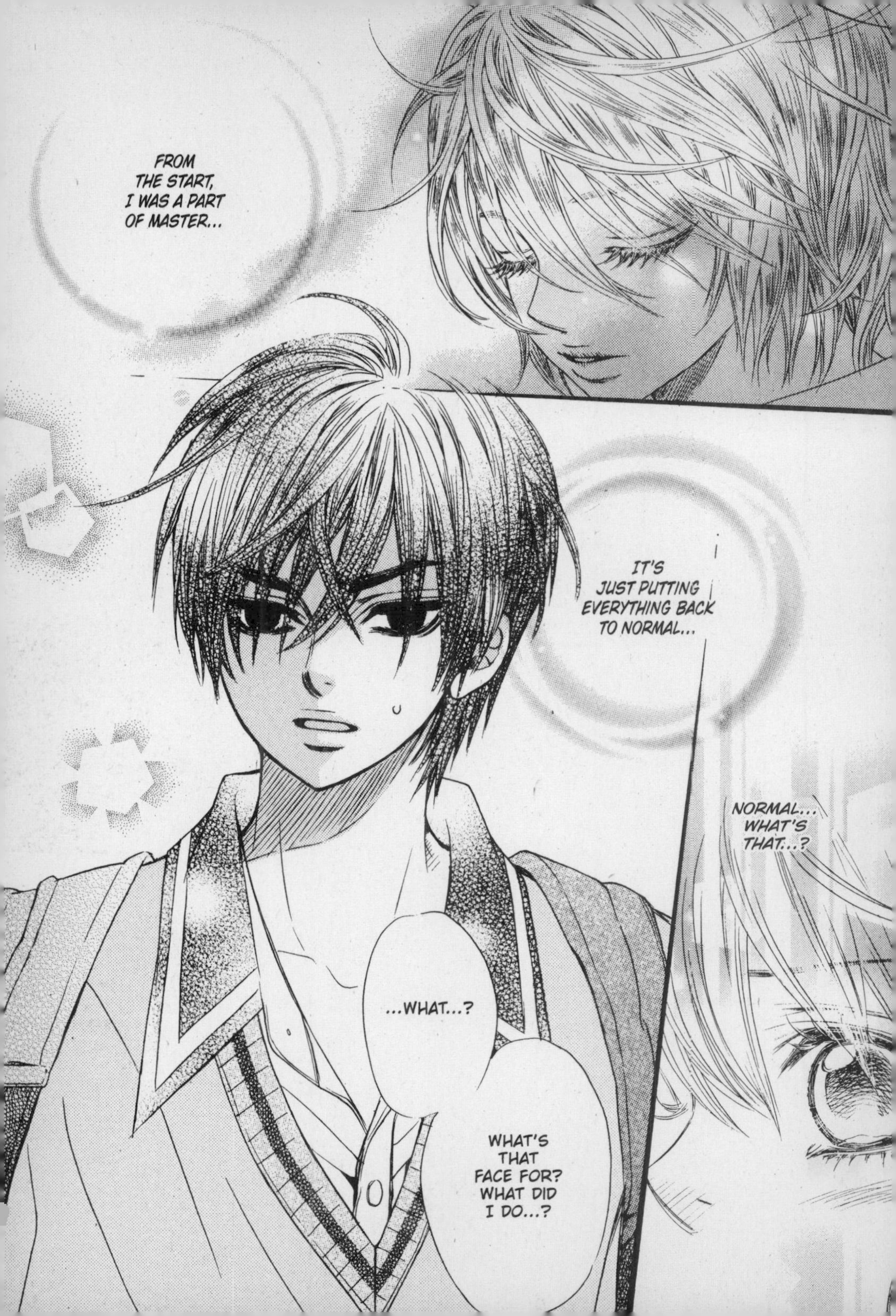
FROM THE START, I WAS A PART OF MASTER...
IT'S JUST PUTTING EVERYTHING BACK TO NORMAL...
...WHAT...?
WHAT'S THAT FACE FOR? WHAT DID I DO...?
NORMAL... WHAT'S THAT...?

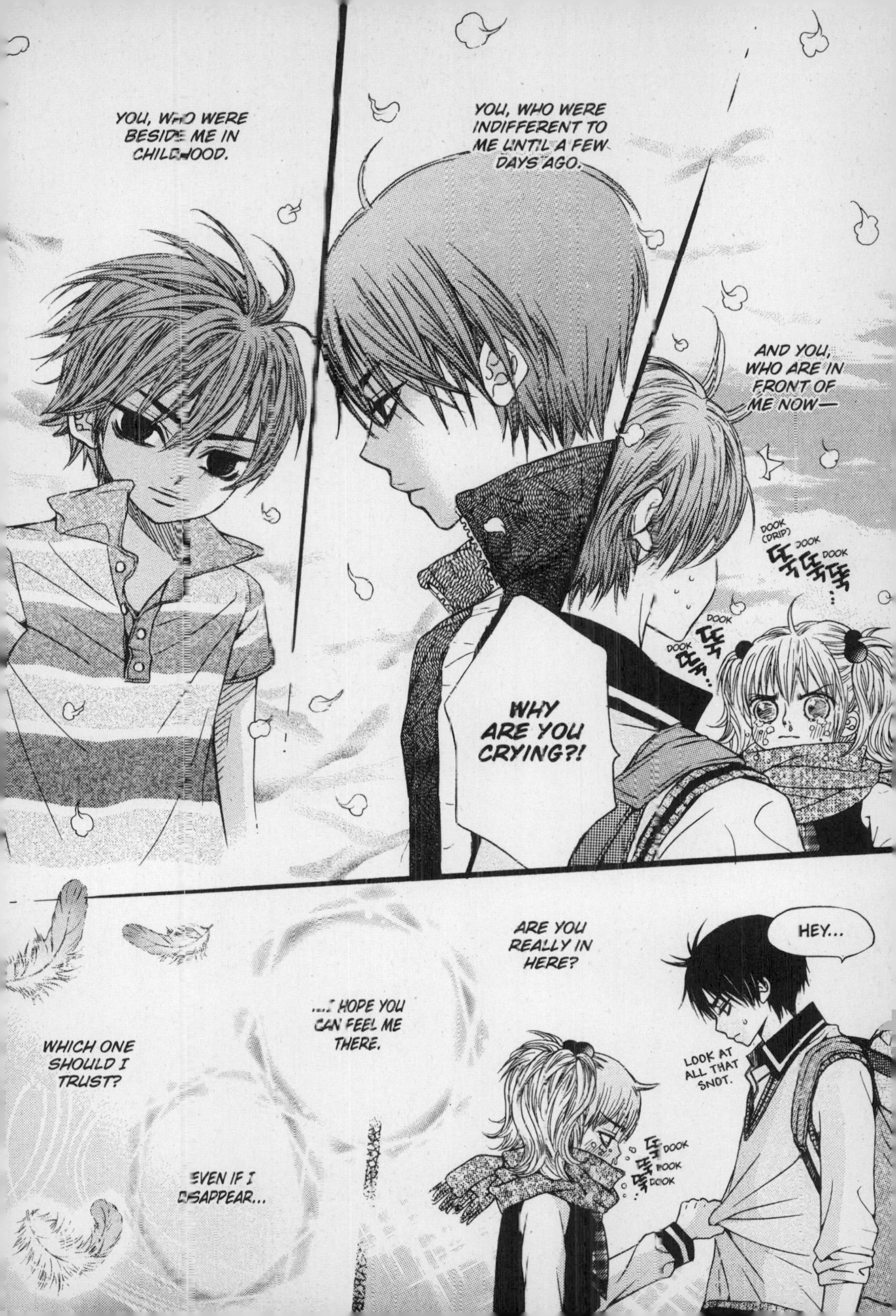

YOU, WHO WERE BESIDE ME IN CHILDHOOD.
YOU, WHO WERE INDIFFERENT TO ME UNTIL A FEW DAYS AGO.
AND YOU, WHO ARE IN FRONT OF ME NOW—
뚝뚝뚝...
DOOK (DRIP) DOOK DOOK
뚝뚝...
DOOK DOOK
WHY ARE YOU CRYING?!
ARE YOU REALLY IN HERE?
HEY...
...I HOPE YOU CAN FEEL ME THERE.
WHICH ONE SHOULD I TRUST?
LOOK AT ALL THAT SNOT.
뚝뚝뚝
DOOK DOOK DOOK
EVEN IF I DISAPPEAR...

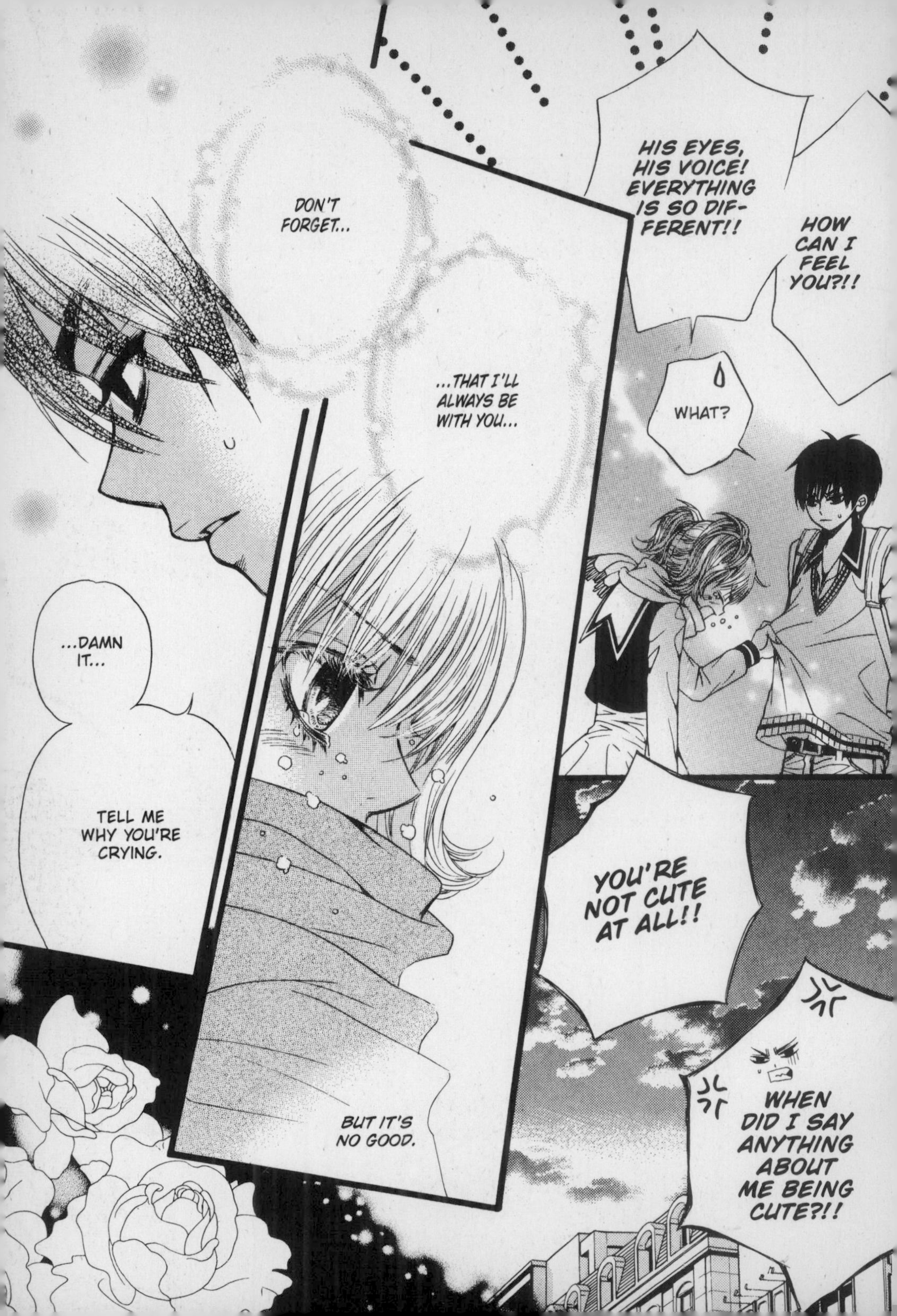
DON'T FORGET...
...DAMN IT...
TELL ME WHY YOU'RE CRYING.
...THAT I'LL ALWAYS BE WITH YOU...
BUT IT'S NO GOOD.
HIS EYES, HIS VOICE! EVERYTHING IS SO DIF-FERENT!!
HOW CAN I FEEL YOU?!!
WHAT?
YOU'RE NOT CUTE AT ALL!!
WHEN DID I SAY ANYTHING ABOUT ME BEING CUTE?!!

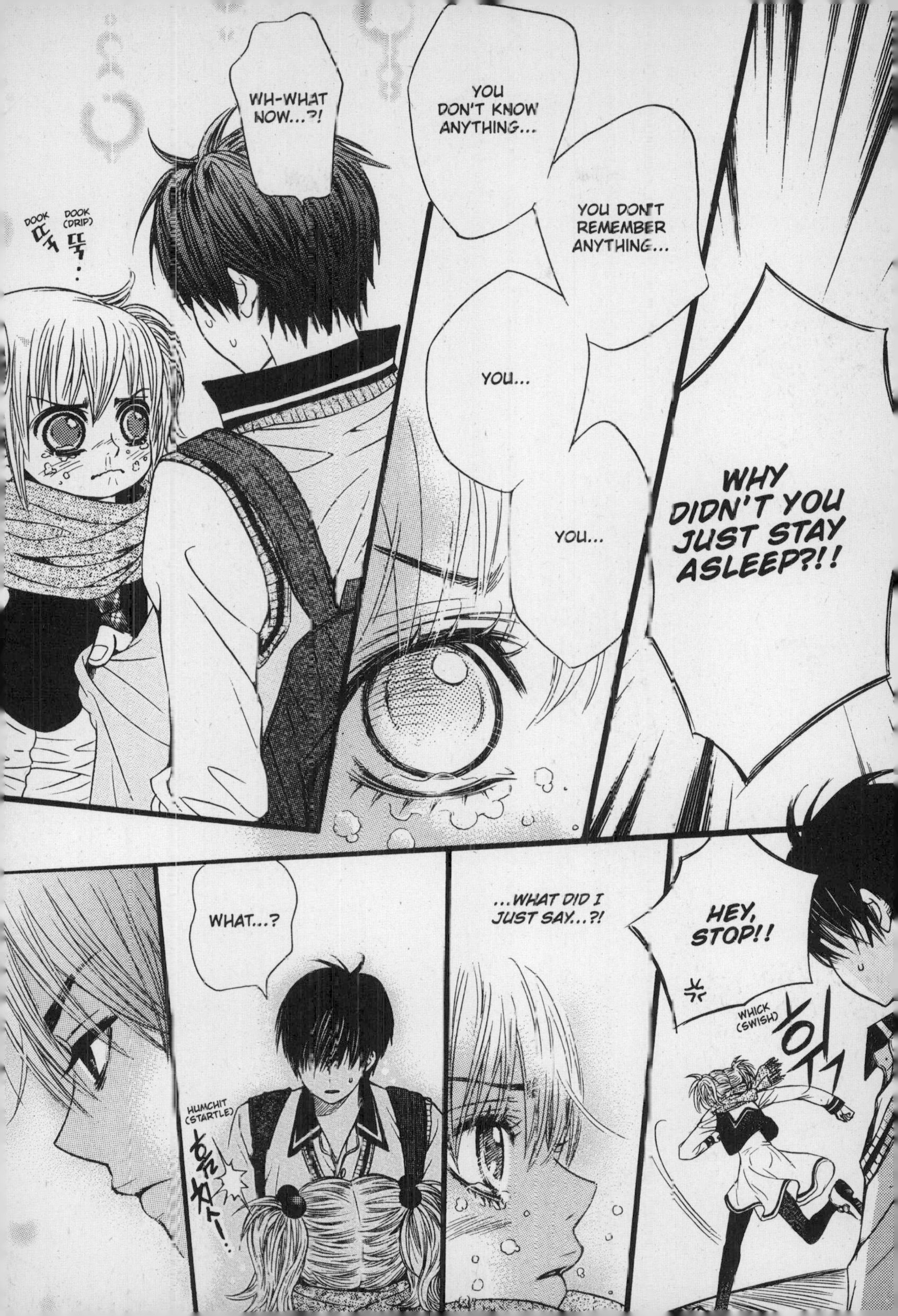

DOOK DOOK (DRIP)
WH-WHAT NOW...?!
YOU DON'T KNOW ANYTHING...
YOU DON'T REMEMBER ANYTHING...
YOU...
YOU...
WHY DIDN'T YOU JUST STAY ASLEEP?!!
WHAT...?
HUMCHIT (STARTLE)
...WHAT DID I JUST SAY...?!
HEY, STOP!!
WHICK (SWISH)

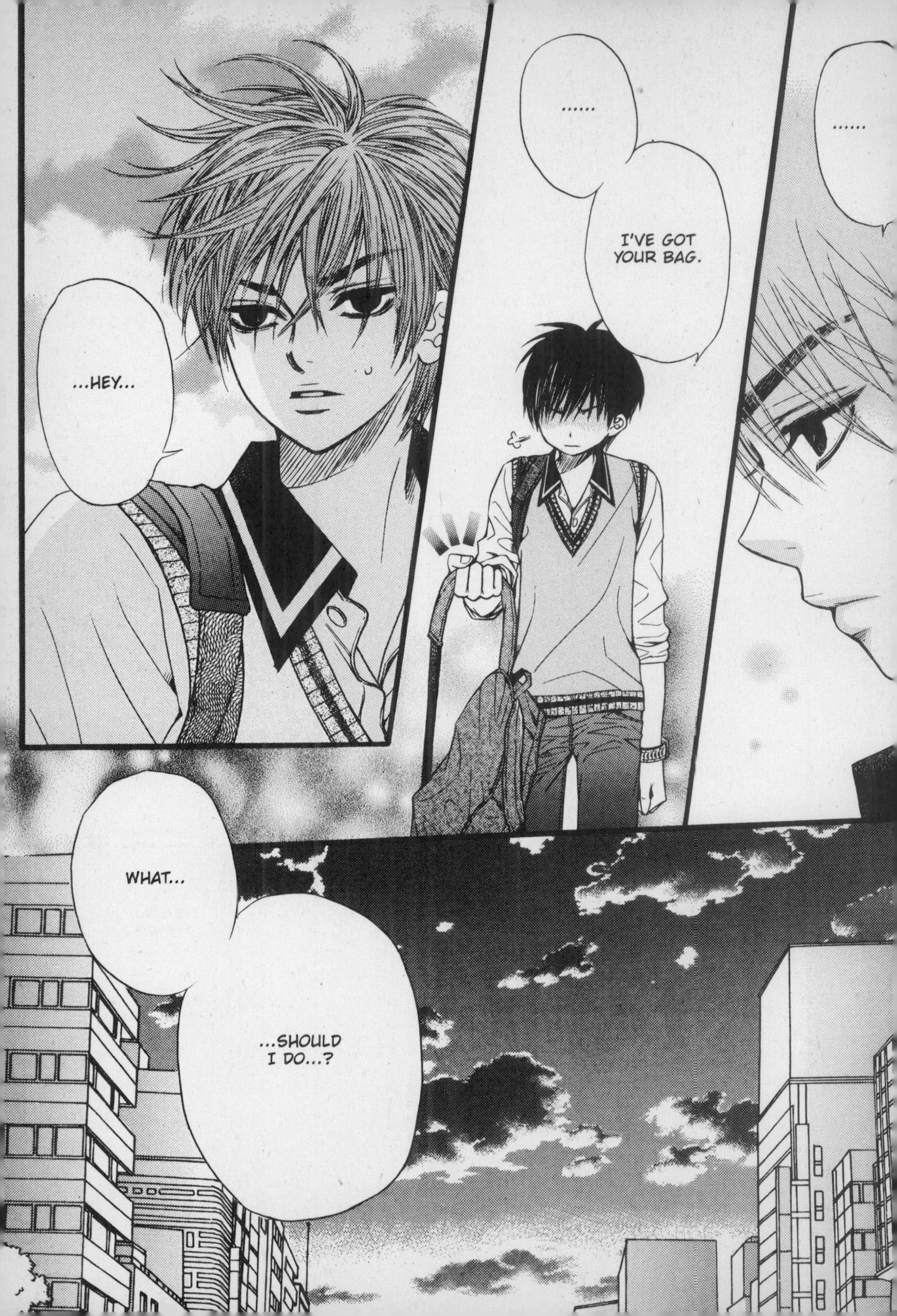
...HEY...
......
I'VE GOT YOUR BAG.
......
WHAT...
...SHOULD I DO...?

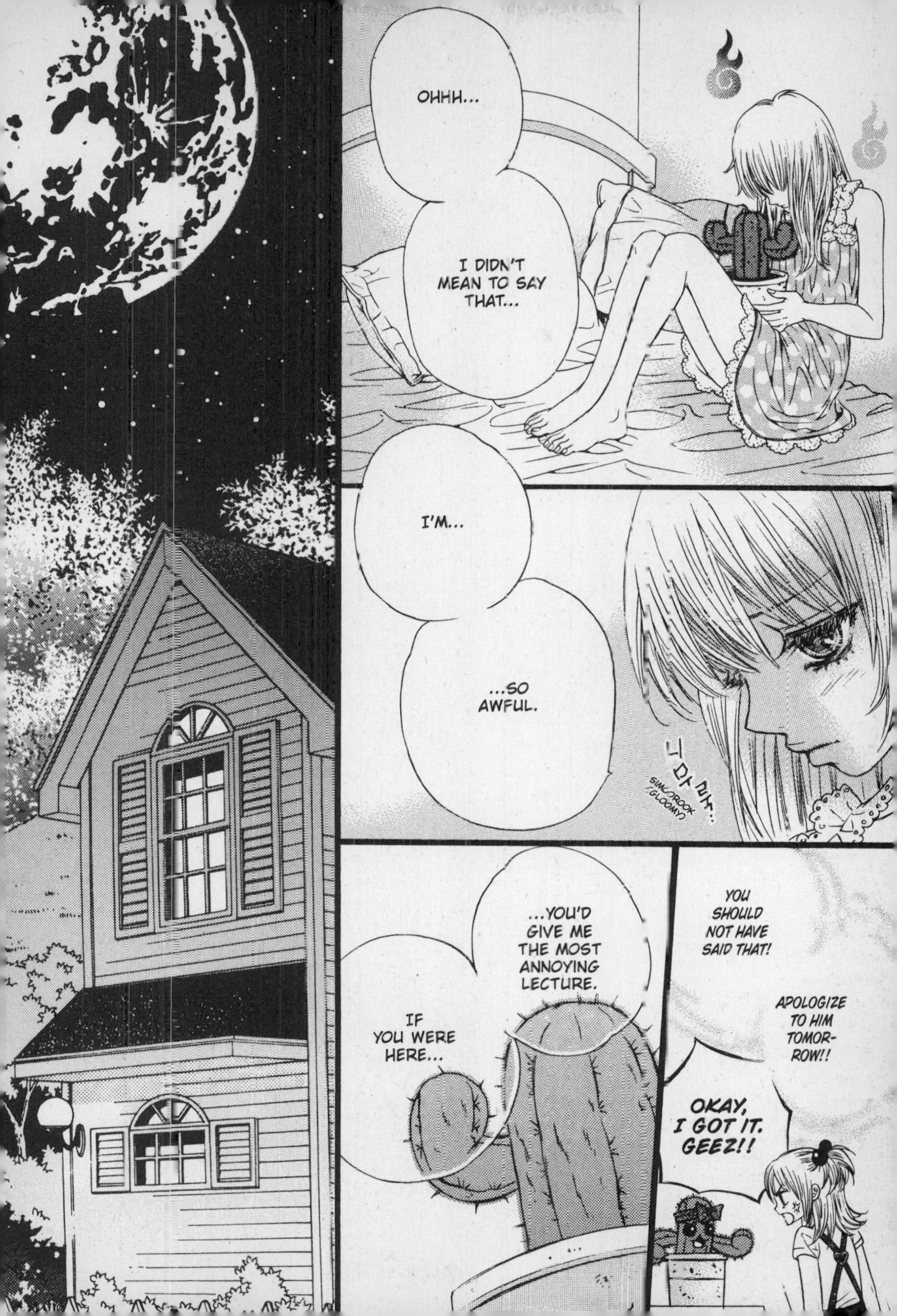
OHHH...
I DIDN'T MEAN TO SAY THAT...
I'M...
...SO AWFUL.
SIMOROOK (GLOOMY)
IF YOU WERE HERE...
...YOU'D GIVE ME THE MOST ANNOYING LECTURE.
YOU SHOULD NOT HAVE SAID THAT!
APOLOGIZE TO HIM TOMOR-ROW!!
OKAY, I GOT IT. GEEZ!!

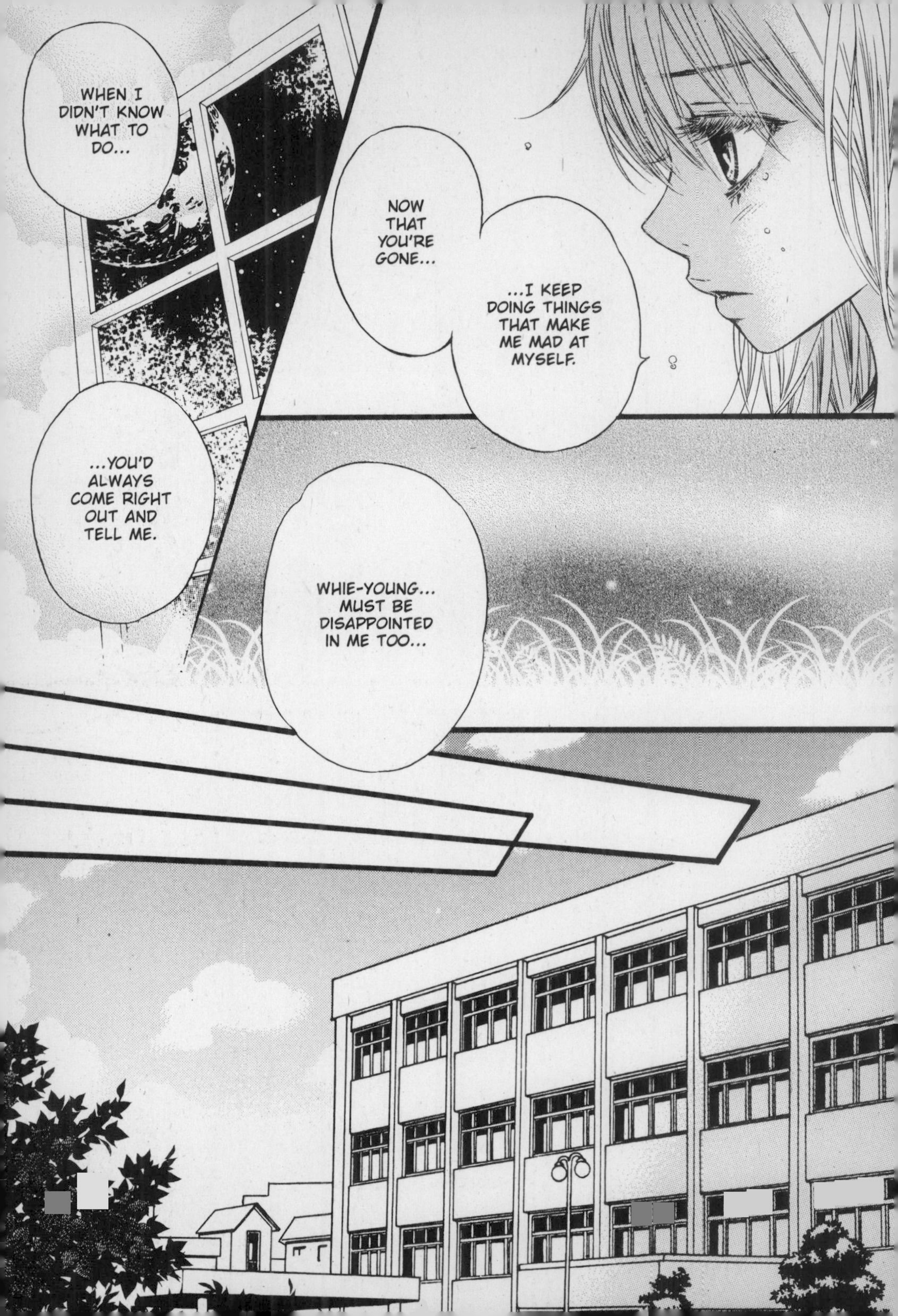
WHEN I DIDN'T KNOW WHAT TO DO...
...YOU'D ALWAYS COME RIGHT OUT AND TELL ME.
NOW THAT YOU'RE GONE...
...I KEEP DOING THINGS THAT MAKE ME MAD AT MYSELF.
WHIE-YOUNG... MUST BE DISAPPOINTED IN ME TOO...

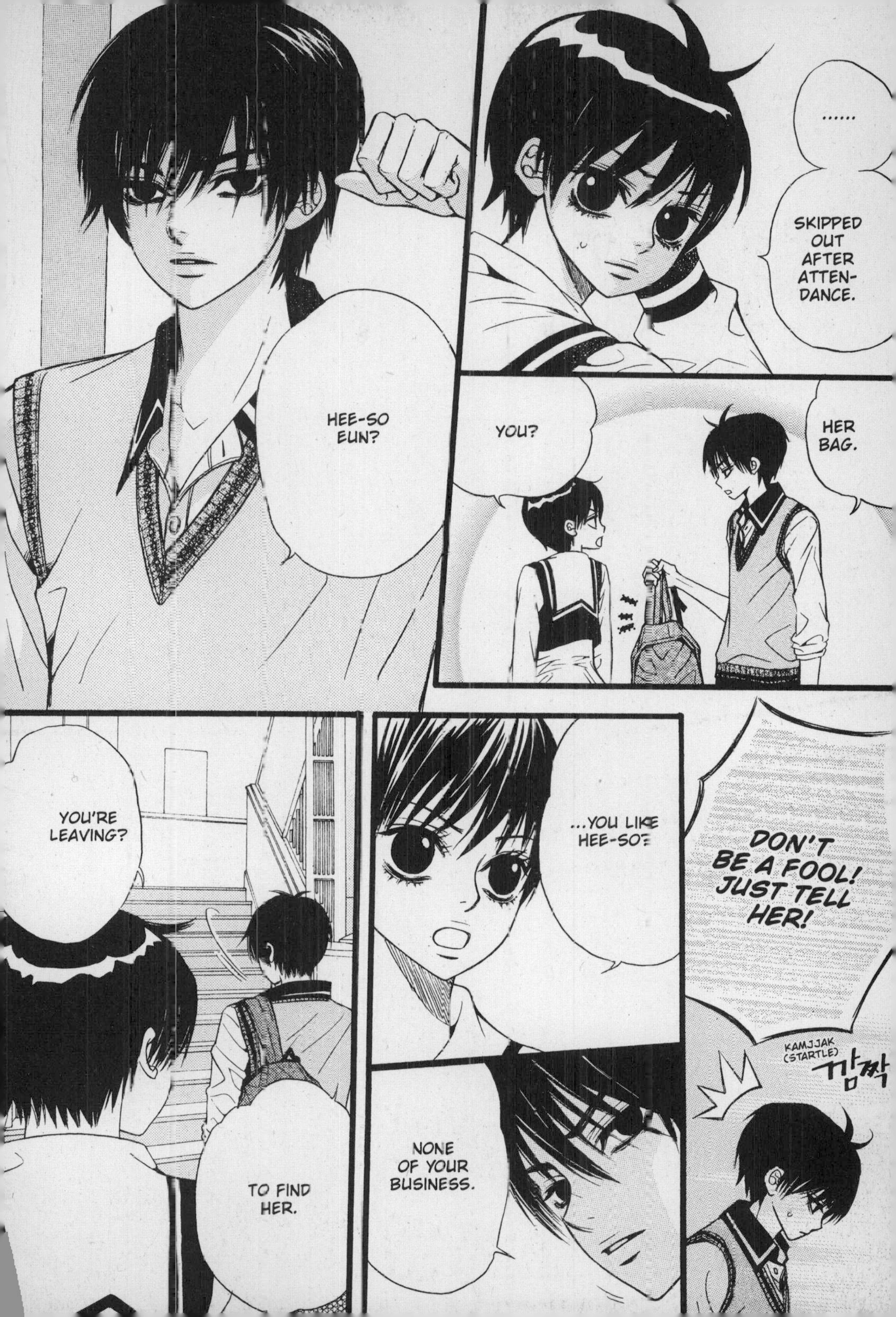
HEE-SO EUN?
......
SKIPPED OUT AFTER ATTEN-DANCE.
YOU?
HER BAG.
YOU'RE LEAVING?
TO FIND HER.
...YOU LIKE HEE-SO?
NONE OF YOUR BUSINESS.
DON'T BE A FOOL! JUST TELL HER!
KAMJJAK (STARTLE)
깜짝

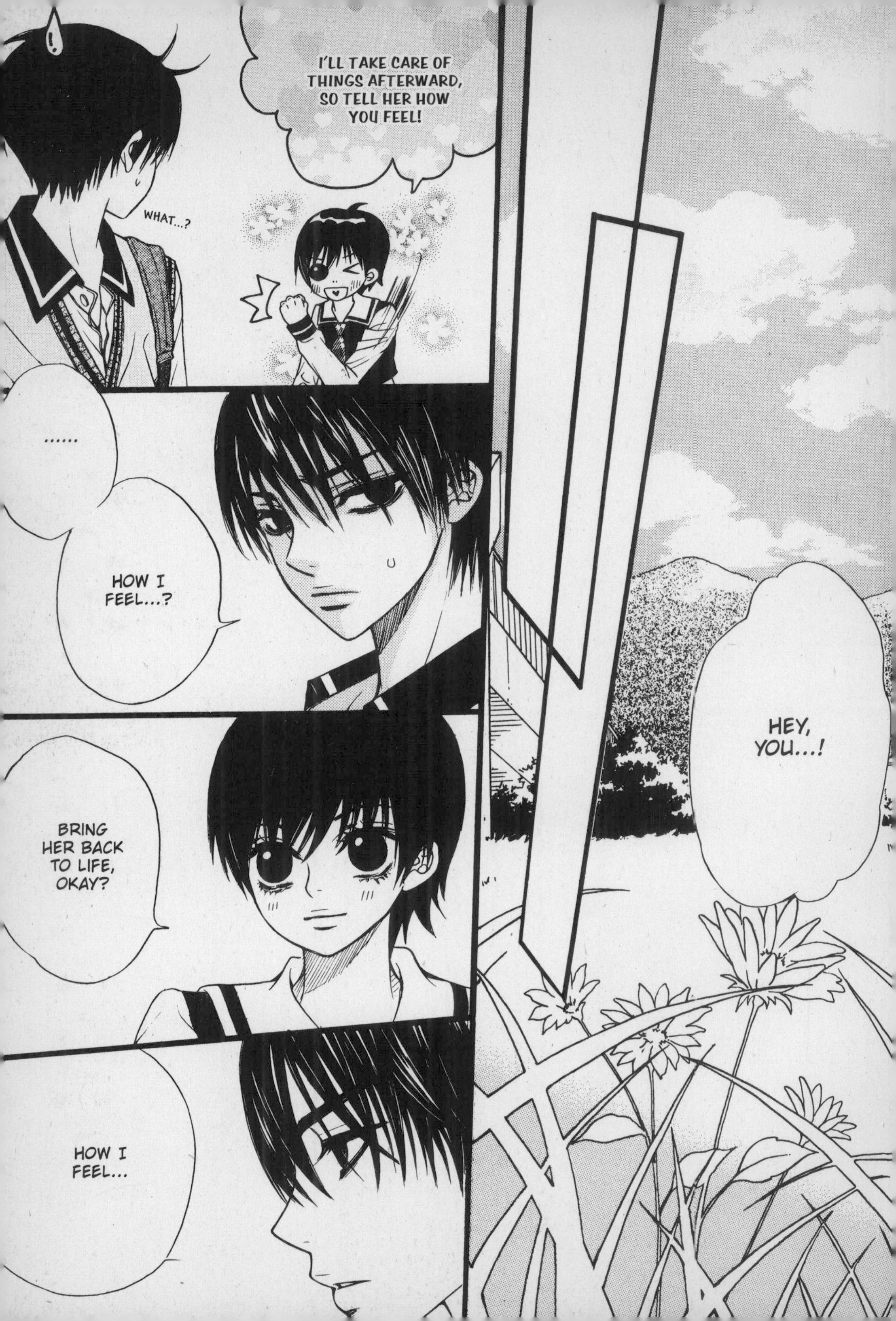
I'LL TAKE CARE OF THINGS AFTERWARD, SO TELL HER HOW YOU FEEL!
WHAT...?
......
HOW I FEEL...?
BRING HER BACK TO LIFE, OKAY?
HOW I FEEL...
HEY, YOU...!

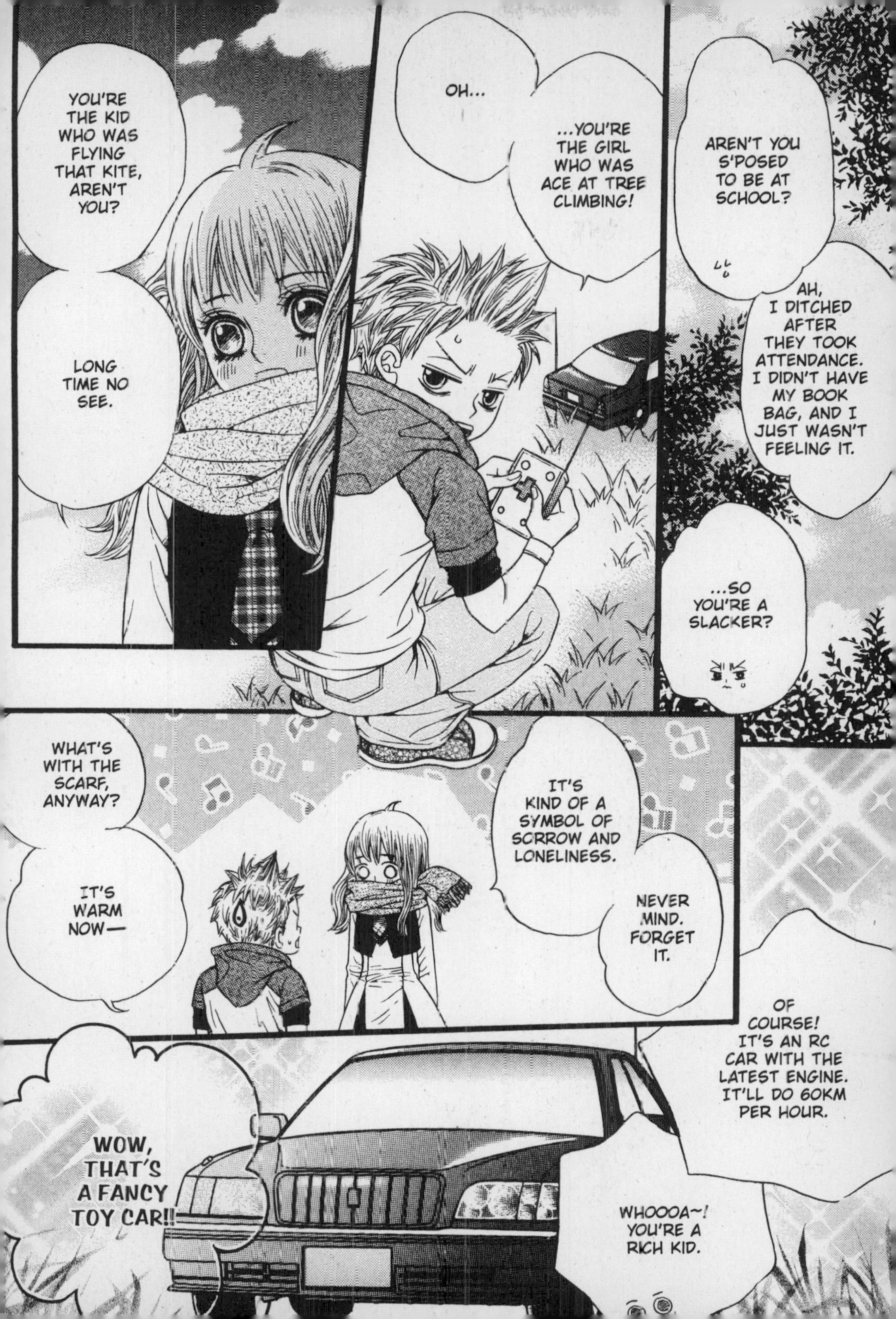
YOU'RE THE KID WHO WAS FLYING THAT KITE, AREN'T YOU?
LONG TIME NO SEE.
OH...
...YOU'RE THE GIRL WHO WAS ACE AT TREE CLIMBING!
AREN'T YOU S'POSED TO BE AT SCHOOL?
AH, I DITCHED AFTER THEY TOOK ATTENDANCE. I DIDN'T HAVE MY BOOK BAG, AND I JUST WASN'T FEELING IT.
...SO YOU'RE A SLACKER?
WHAT'S WITH THE SCARF, ANYWAY?
IT'S WARM NOW—
IT'S KIND OF A SYMBOL OF SCRROW AND LONELINESS.
NEVER MIND. FORGET IT.
WOW, THAT'S A FANCY TOY CAR!!
OF COURSE! IT'S AN RC CAR WITH THE LATEST ENGINE. IT'LL DO 60KM PER HOUR.
WHOOOA~! YOU'RE A RICH KID.

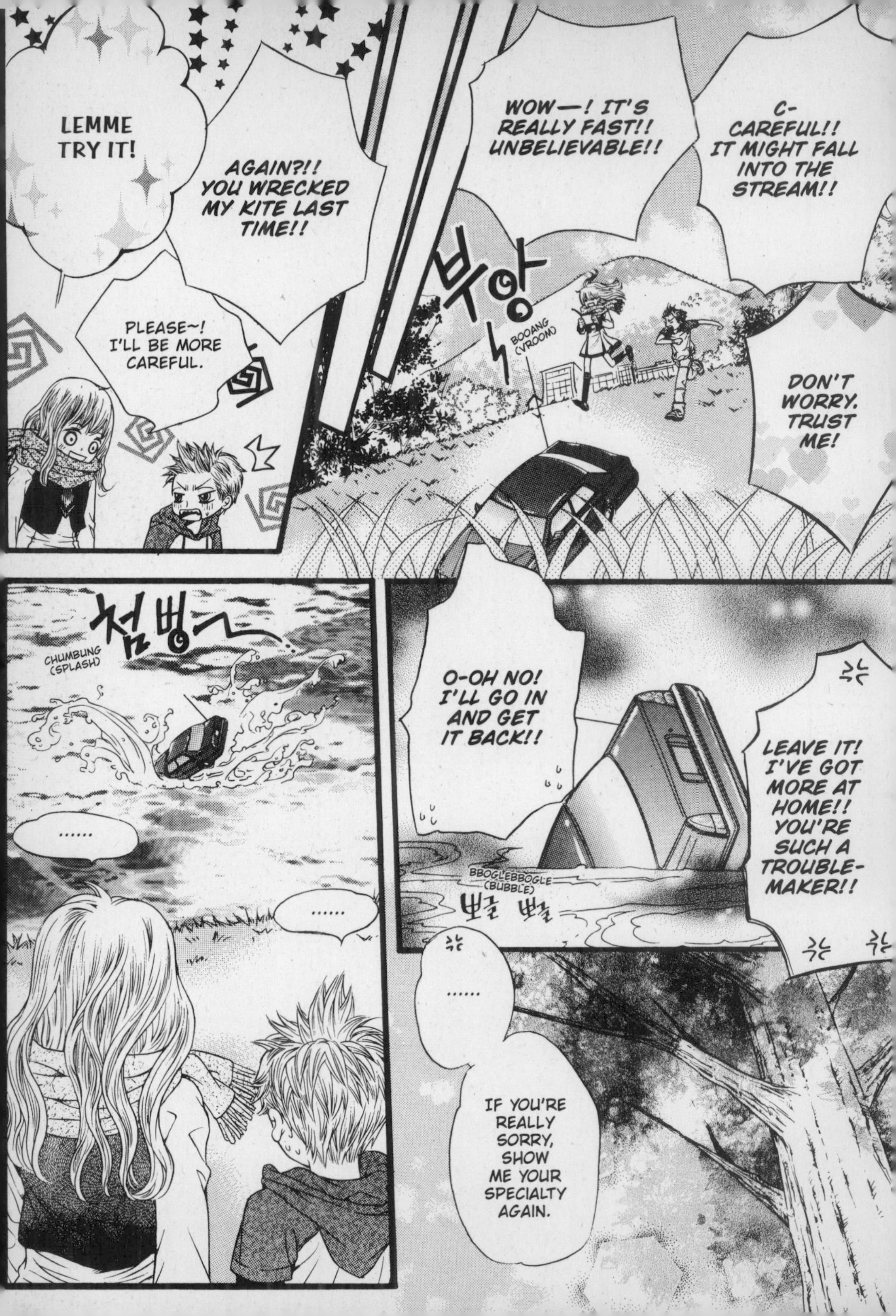
LEMME TRY IT!
AGAIN?!! YOU WRECKED MY KITE LAST TIME!!
PLEASE~! I'LL BE MORE CAREFUL.
WOW—! IT'S REALLY FAST!! UNBELIEVABLE!!
C-CAREFUL!! IT MIGHT FALL INTO THE STREAM!!
부앙
BOOANG (VROOM)
DON'T WORRY. TRUST ME!
첨벙
CHUMBUNG (SPLASH)
......
......
O-OH NO! I'LL GO IN AND GET IT BACK!!
LEAVE IT! I'VE GOT MORE AT HOME!! YOU'RE SUCH A TROUBLE-MAKER!!
BBOGLEBBOGLE (BUBBLE)
뽀글 뽀글
......
IF YOU'RE REALLY SORRY, SHOW ME YOUR SPECIALTY AGAIN.

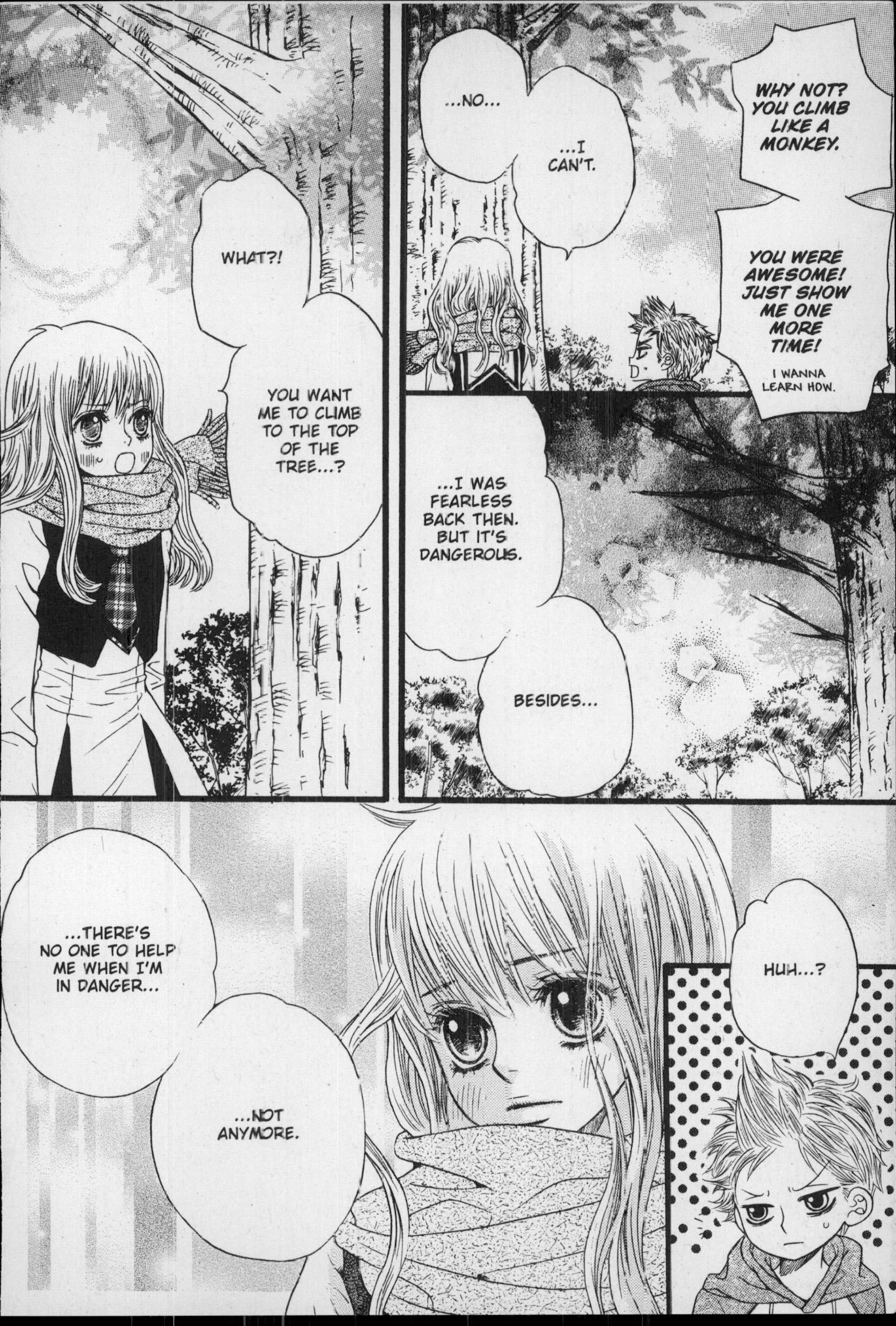
WHAT?!
YOU WANT ME TO CLIMB TO THE TOP OF THE TREE...?
...NO...
...I CAN'T.
WHY NOT? YOU CLIMB LIKE A MONKEY.
YOU WERE AWESOME! JUST SHOW ME ONE MORE TIME!
I WANNA LEARN HOW.
...I WAS FEARLESS BACK THEN. BUT IT'S DANGEROUS.
BESIDES...
...THERE'S NO ONE TO HELP ME WHEN I'M IN DANGER...
...NOT ANYMORE.
HUH...?

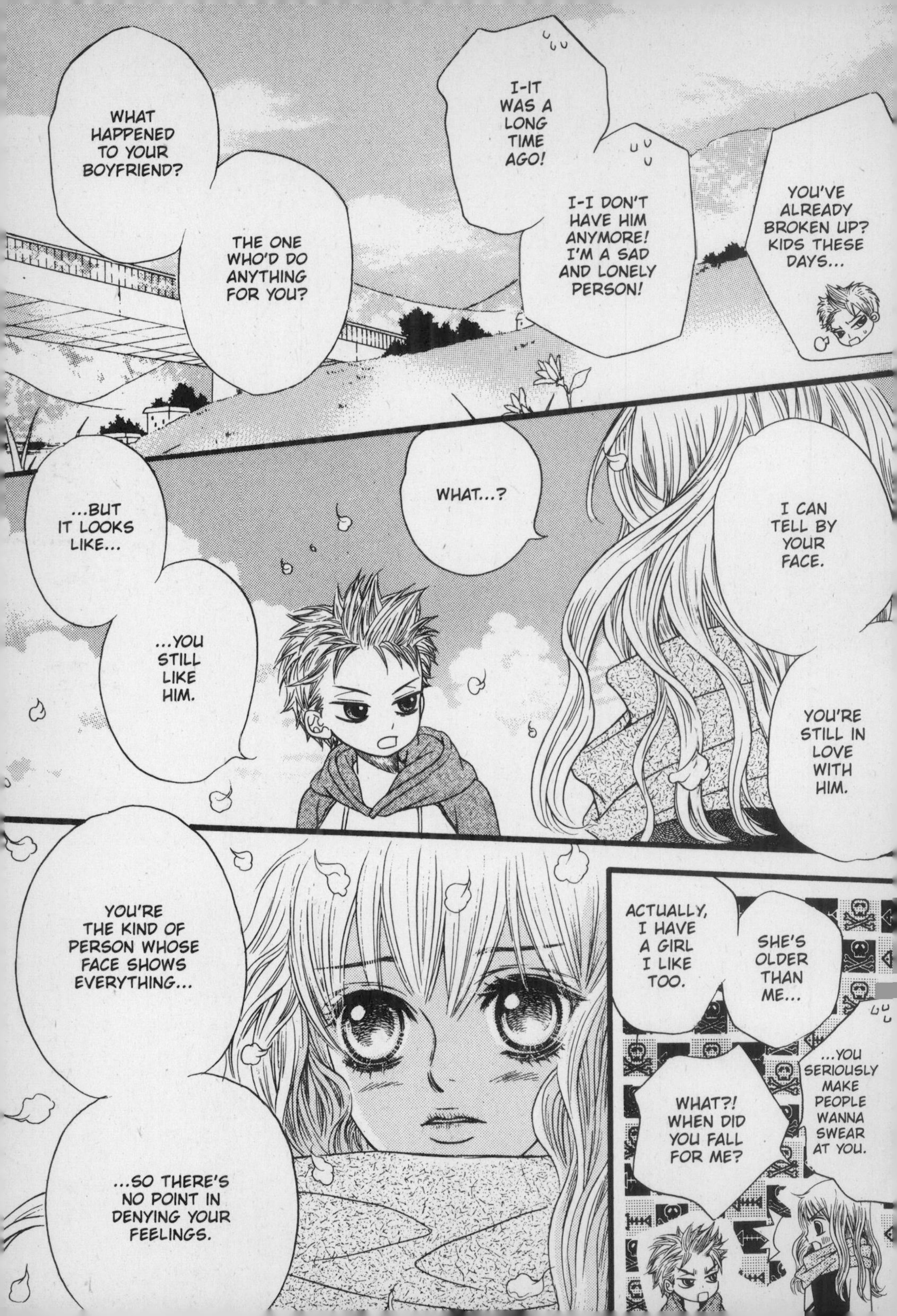
WHAT HAPPENED TO YOUR BOYFRIEND?
THE ONE WHO'D DO ANYTHING FOR YOU?
I-IT WAS A LONG TIME AGO!
I-I DON'T HAVE HIM ANYMORE! I'M A SAD AND LONELY PERSON!
YOU'VE ALREADY BROKEN UP? KIDS THESE DAYS...
...BUT IT LOOKS LIKE...
...YOU STILL LIKE HIM.
WHAT...?
I CAN TELL BY YOUR FACE.
YOU'RE STILL IN LOVE WITH HIM.
YOU'RE THE KIND OF PERSON WHOSE FACE SHOWS EVERYTHING...
...SO THERE'S NO POINT IN DENYING YOUR FEELINGS.
ACTUALLY, I HAVE A GIRL I LIKE TOO.
SHE'S OLDER THAN ME...
WHAT?! WHEN DID YOU FALL FOR ME?
...YOU SERIOUSLY MAKE PEOPLE WANNA SWEAR AT YOU.

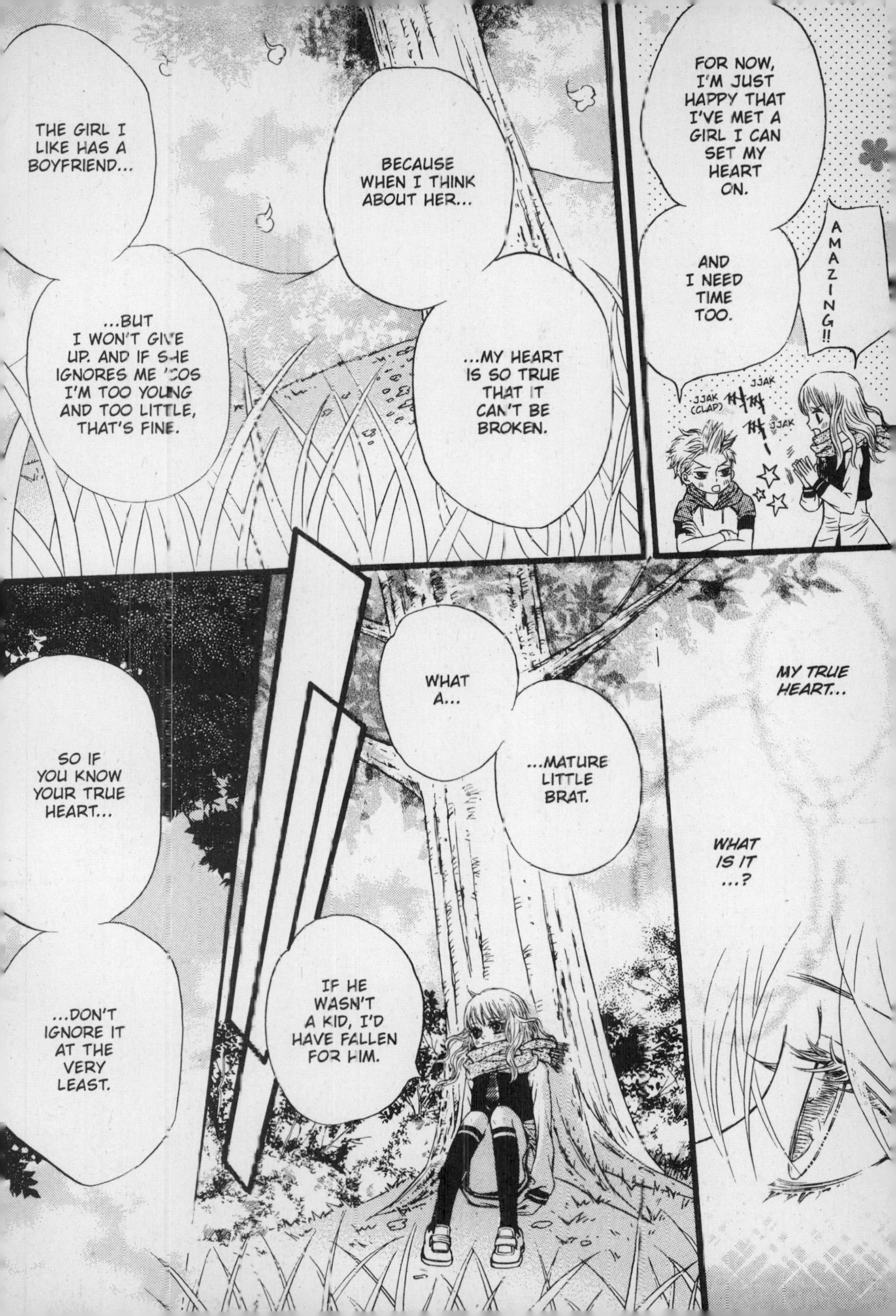
THE GIRL I LIKE HAS A BOYFRIEND...
...BUT I WON'T GIVE UP. AND IF SHE IGNORES ME 'COS I'M TOO YOUNG AND TOO LITTLE, THAT'S FINE.
BECAUSE WHEN I THINK ABOUT HER...
...MY HEART IS SO TRUE THAT IT CAN'T BE BROKEN.
FOR NOW, I'M JUST HAPPY THAT I'VE MET A GIRL I CAN SET MY HEART ON.
AND I NEED TIME TOO.
AMAZING!!
JJAK (CLAP)
JJAK
JJAK
SO IF YOU KNOW YOUR TRUE HEART...
...DON'T IGNORE IT AT THE VERY LEAST.
WHAT A...
...MATURE LITTLE BRAT.
IF HE WASN'T A KID, I'D HAVE FALLEN FOR HIM.
MY TRUE HEART...
WHAT IS IT ...?

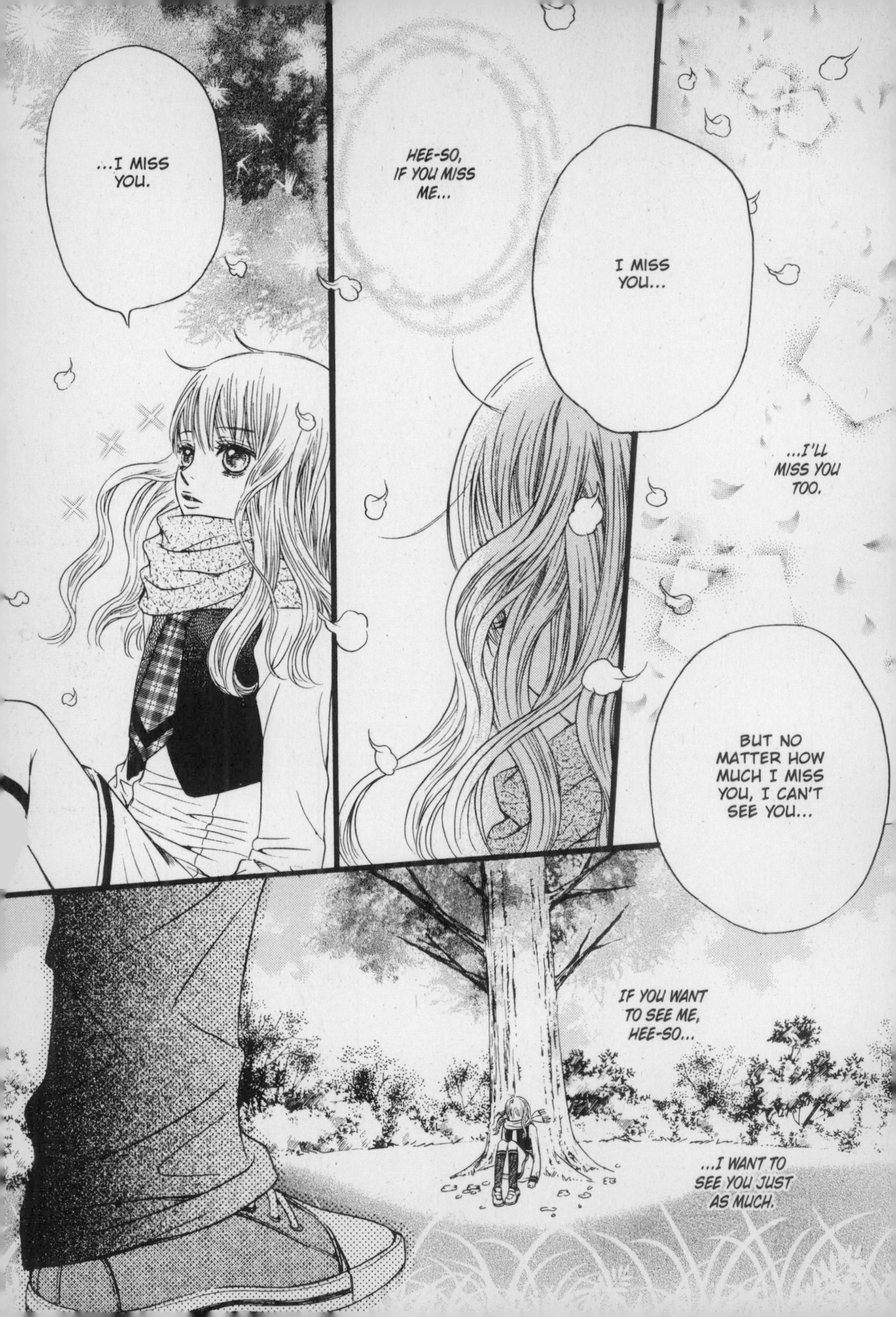

...I MISS YOU.
HEE-SO, IF YOU MISS ME...
I MISS YOU...
...I'LL MISS YOU TOO.
BUT NO MATTER HOW MUCH I MISS YOU, I CAN'T SEE YOU...
IF YOU WANT TO SEE ME, HEE-SO...
...I WANT TO SEE YOU JUST AS MUCH.

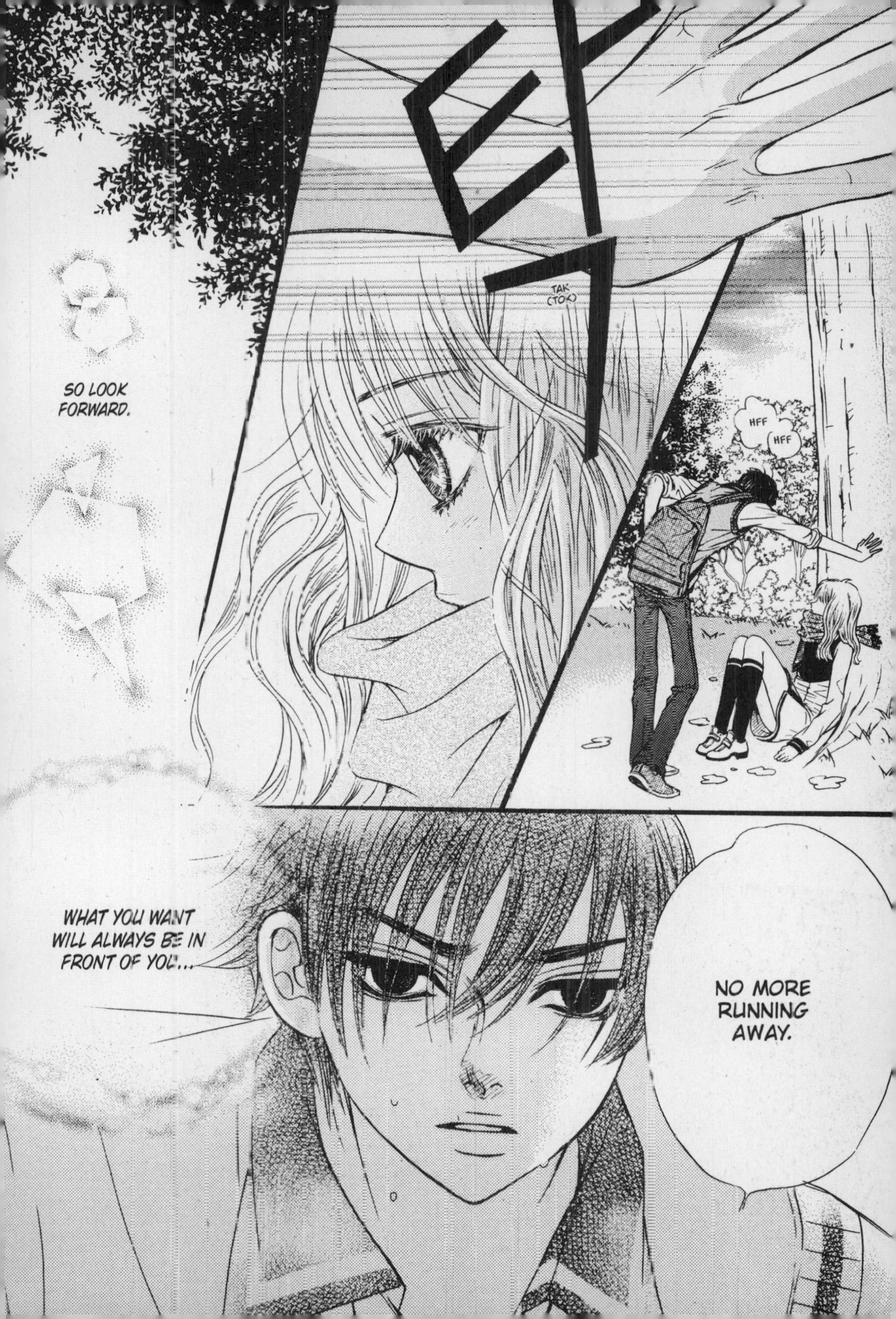

SO LOOK FORWARD.
TAK (TOK)
HFF
HFF
WHAT YOU WANT WILL ALWAYS BE IN FRONT OF YOU...
NO MORE RUNNING AWAY.

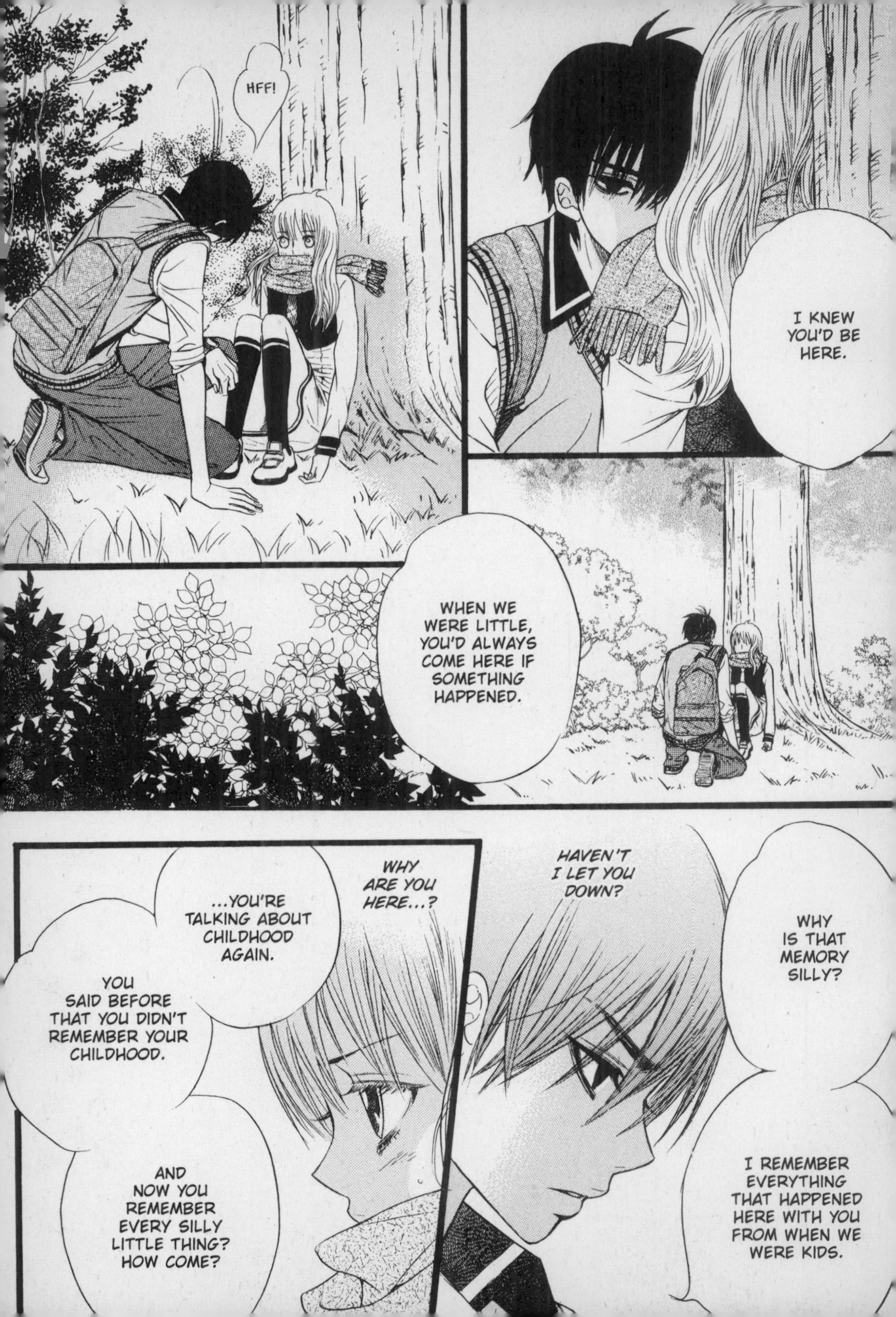
HFF!
I KNEW YOU'D BE HERE.
WHEN WE WERE LITTLE, YOU'D ALWAYS COME HERE IF SOMETHING HAPPENED.
...YOU'RE TALKING ABOUT CHILDHOOD AGAIN.
WHY ARE YOU HERE...?
HAVEN'T I LET YOU DOWN?
YOU SAID BEFORE THAT YOU DIDN'T REMEMBER YOUR CHILDHOOD.
WHY IS THAT MEMORY SILLY?
AND NOW YOU REMEMBER EVERY SILLY LITTLE THING? HOW COME?
I REMEMBER EVERYTHING THAT HAPPENED HERE WITH YOU FROM WHEN WE WERE KIDS.

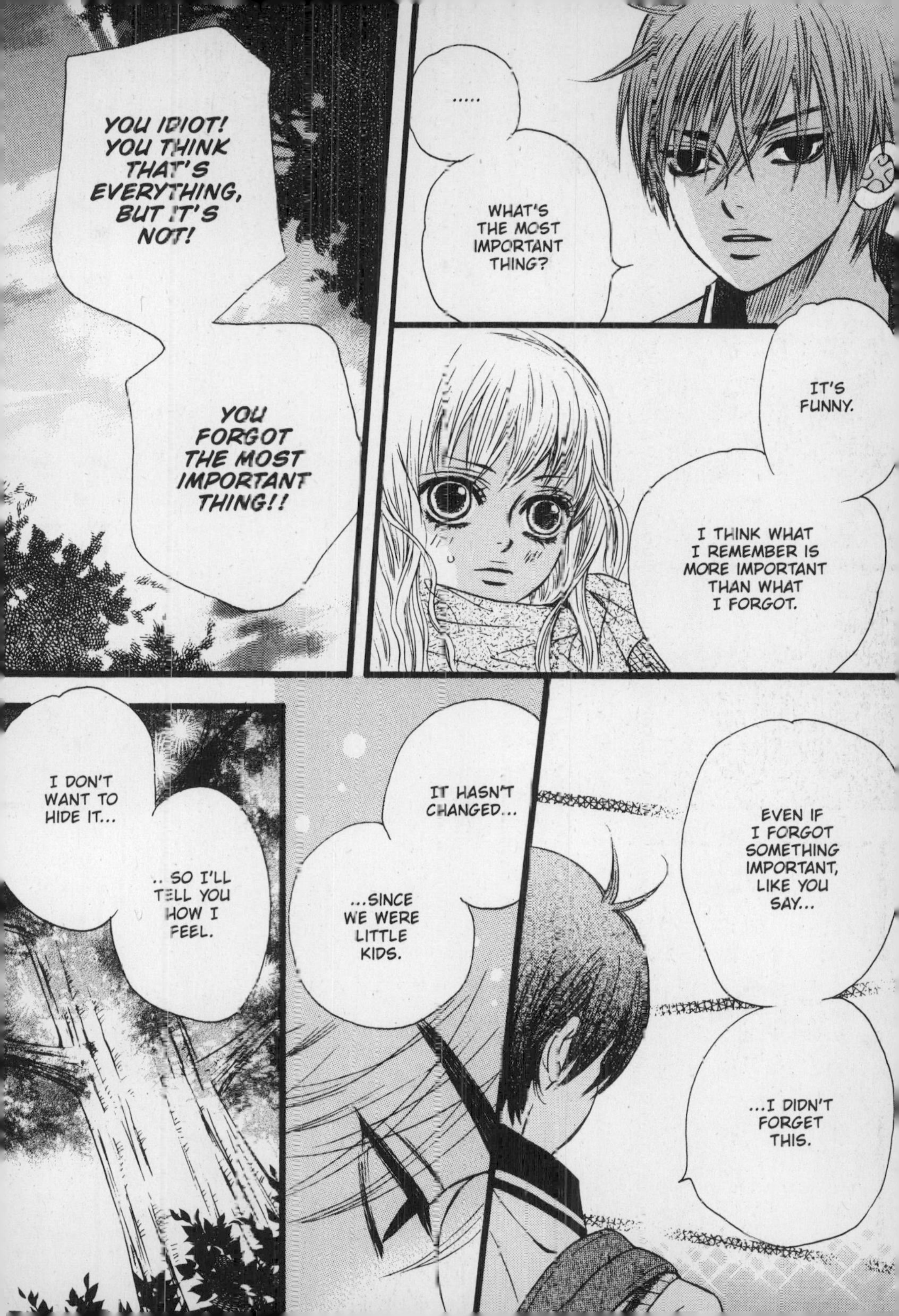
YOU IDIOT! YOU THINK THAT'S EVERYTHING, BUT IT'S NOT!
YOU FORGOT THE MOST IMPORTANT THING!!
.....
WHAT'S THE MOST IMPORTANT THING?
IT'S FUNNY.
I THINK WHAT I REMEMBER IS MORE IMPORTANT THAN WHAT I FORGOT.
I DON'T WANT TO HIDE IT...
...SO I'LL TELL YOU HOW I FEEL.
IT HASN'T CHANGED...
...SINCE WE WERE LITTLE KIDS.
EVEN IF I FORGOT SOMETHING IMPORTANT, LIKE YOU SAY...
...I DIDN'T FORGET THIS.

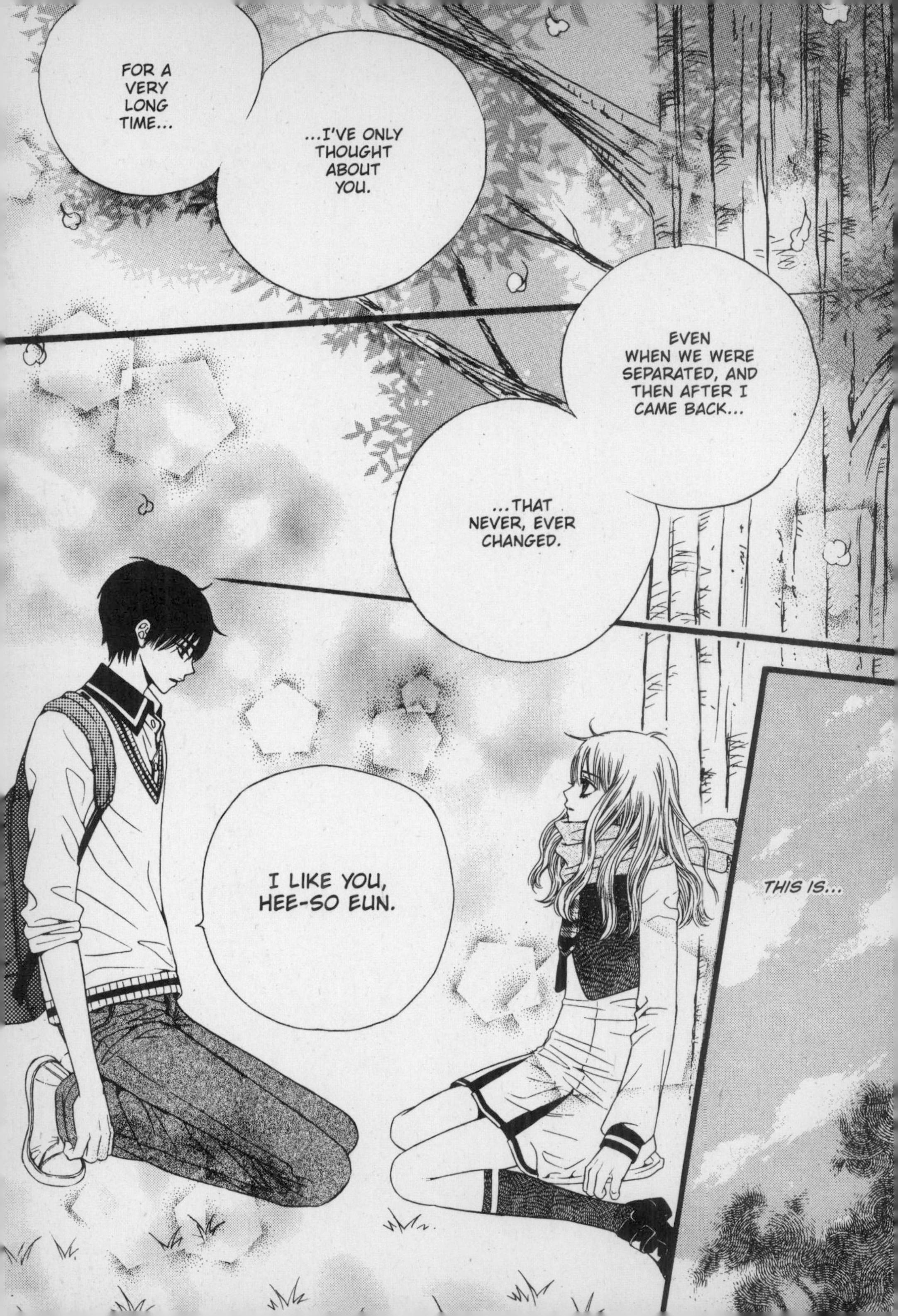
FOR A VERY LONG TIME...
...I'VE ONLY THOUGHT ABOUT YOU.
EVEN WHEN WE WERE SEPARATED, AND THEN AFTER I CAME BACK...
...THAT NEVER, EVER CHANGED.
I LIKE YOU, HEE-SO EUN.
THIS IS...

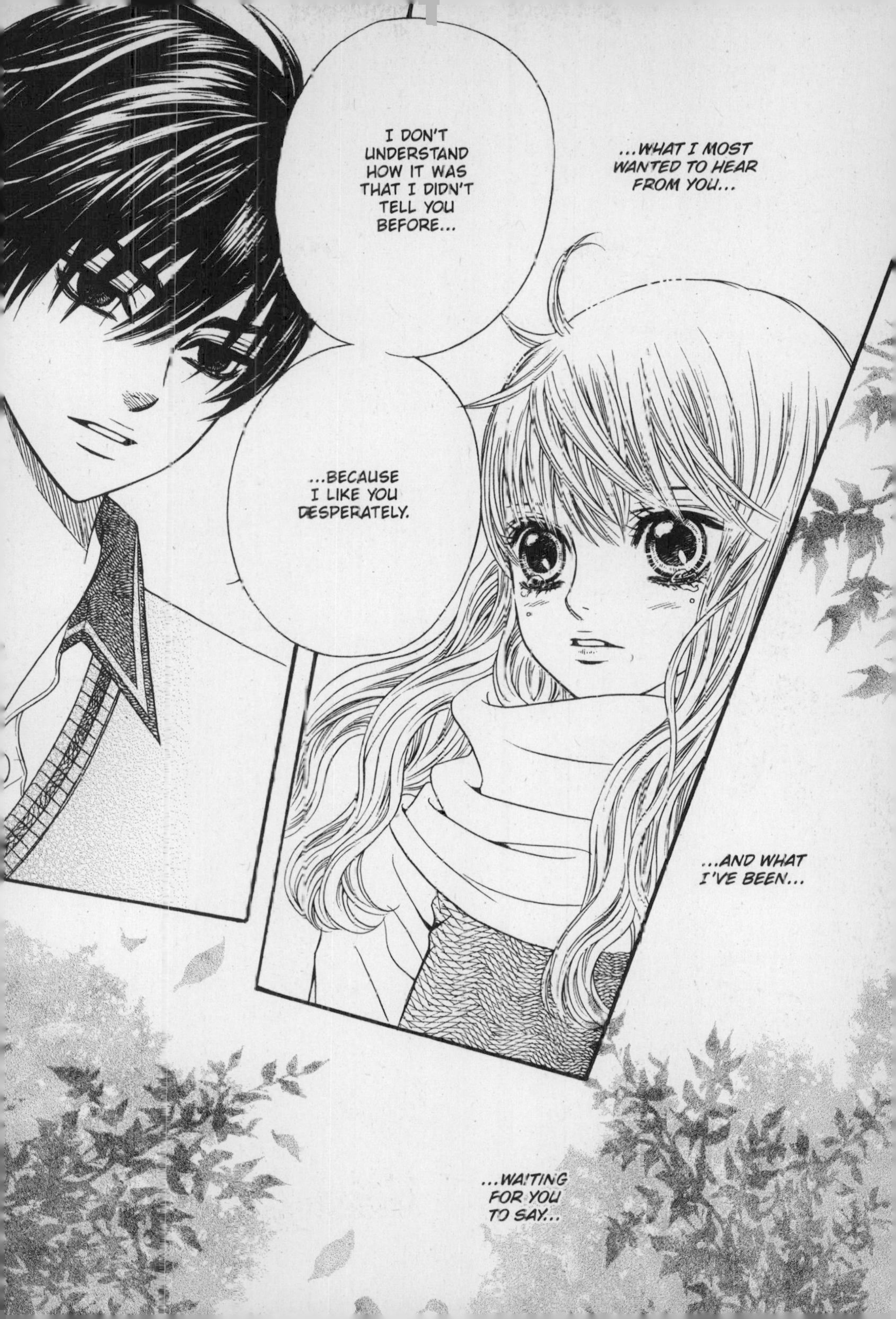
I DON'T UNDERSTAND HOW IT WAS THAT I DIDN'T TELL YOU BEFORE...
...BECAUSE I LIKE YOU DESPERATELY.
...WHAT I MOST WANTED TO HEAR FROM YOU...
...AND WHAT I'VE BEEN...
...WAITING FOR YOU TO SAY...

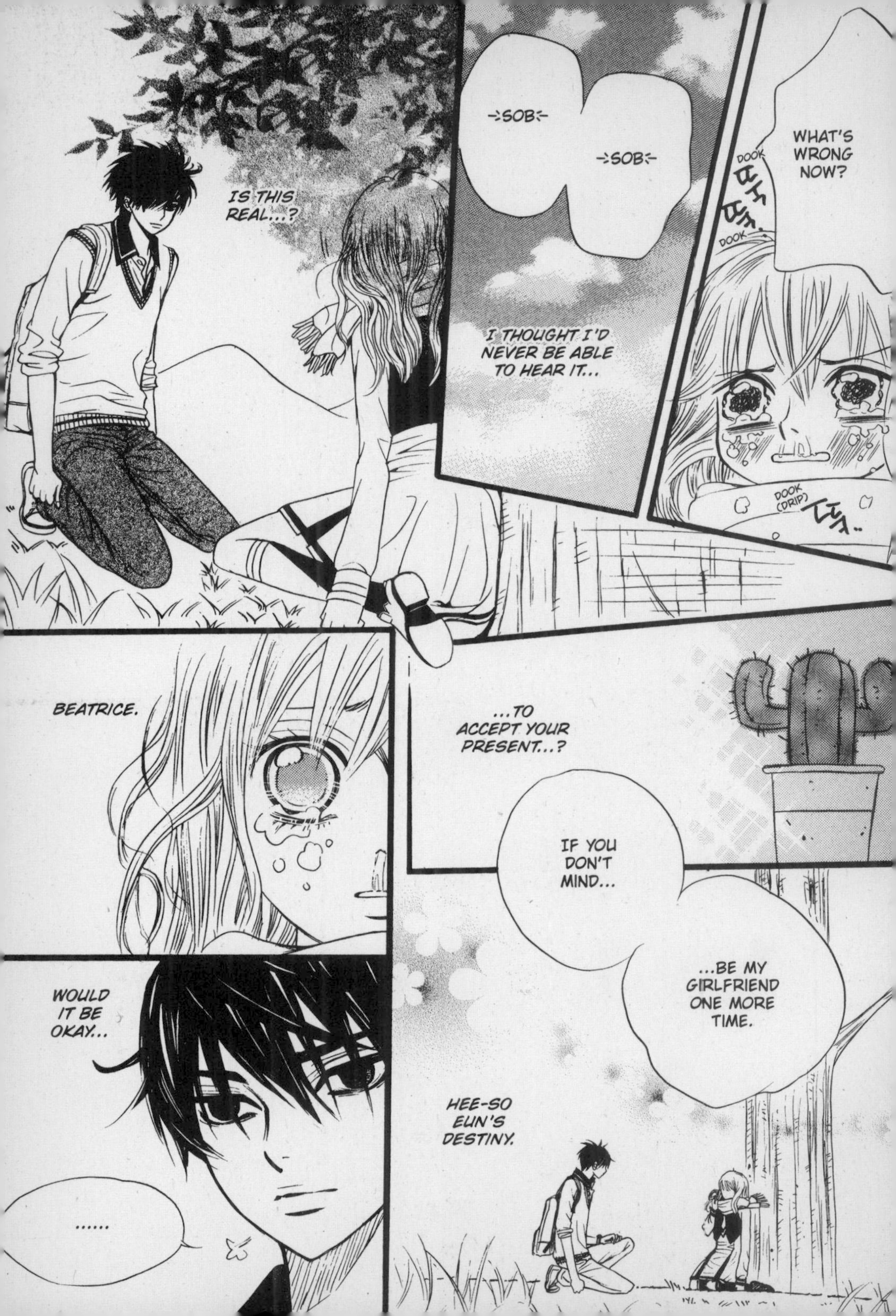
IS THIS REAL...?
-SOB-
-SOB-
I THOUGHT I'D NEVER BE ABLE TO HEAR IT...
WHAT'S WRONG NOW?
DOOK
DOOK
DOOK (DRIP)
BEATRICE.
WOULD IT BE OKAY...
......
...TO ACCEPT YOUR PRESENT...?
IF YOU DON'T MIND...
...BE MY GIRLFRIEND ONE MORE TIME.
HEE-SO EUN'S DESTINY.

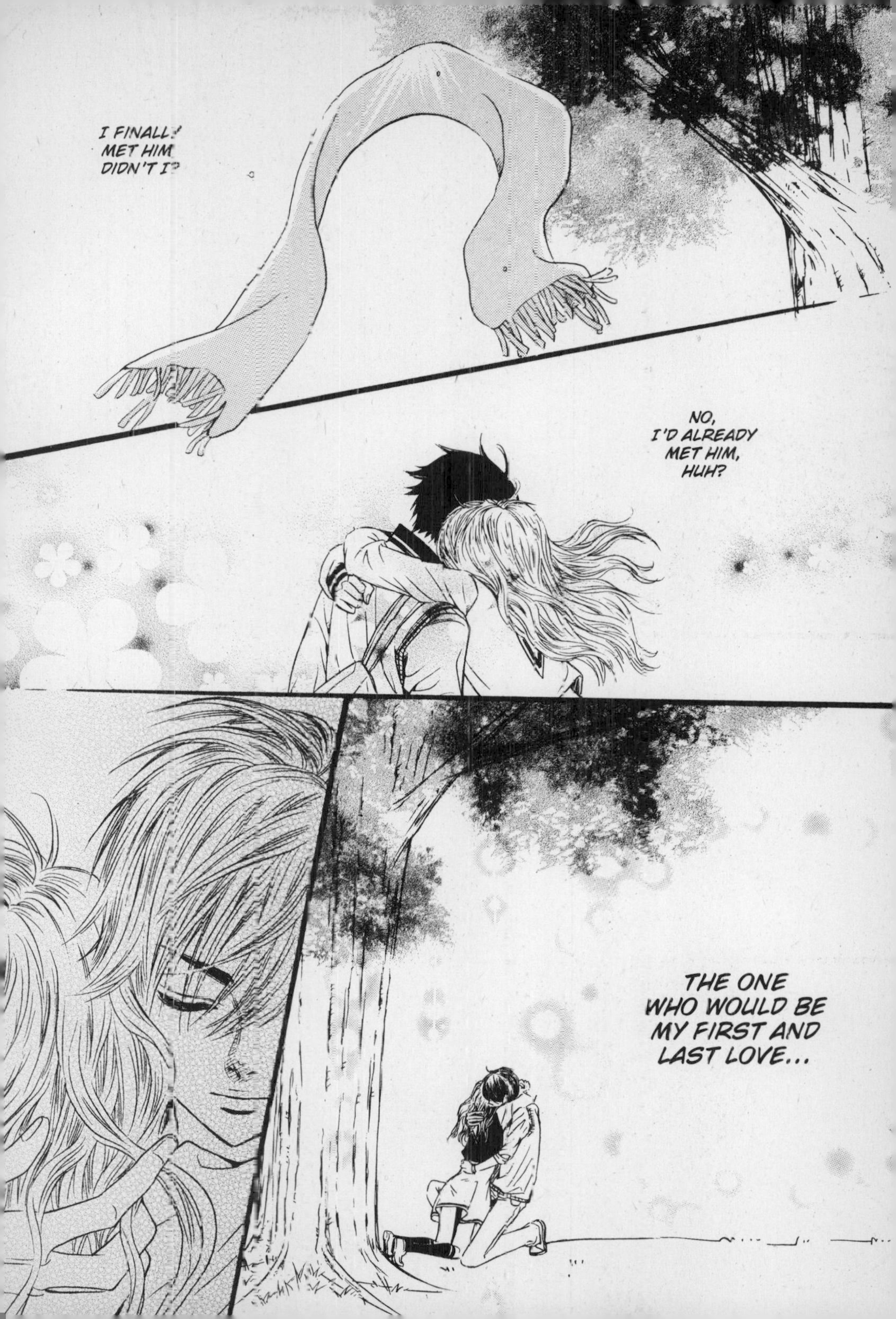
I FINALLY MET HIM DIDN'T I?
NO, I'D ALREADY MET HIM, HUH?
THE ONE WHO WOULD BE MY FIRST AND LAST LOVE...

13th Boy

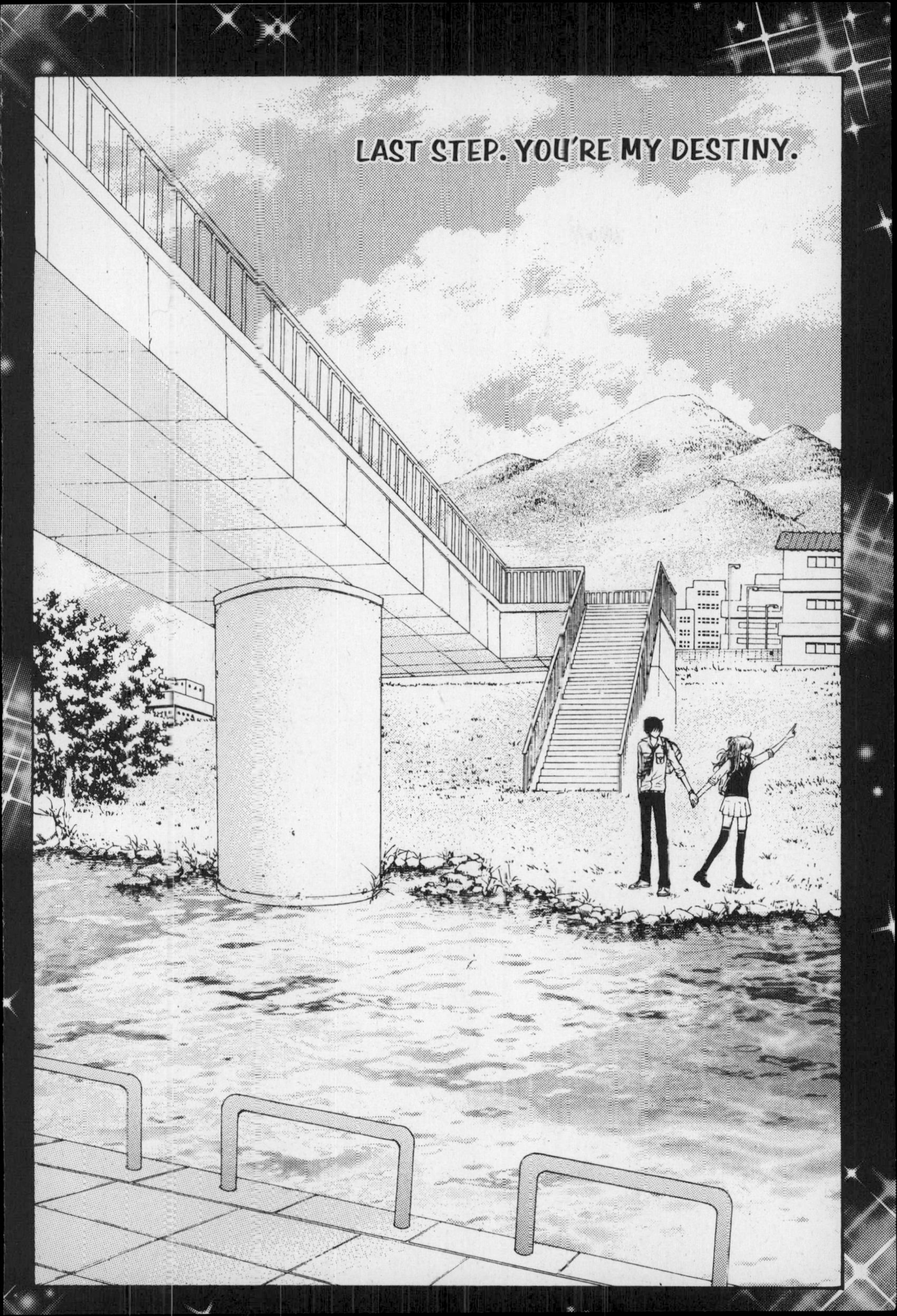
LAST STEP. YOU'RE MY DESTINY.

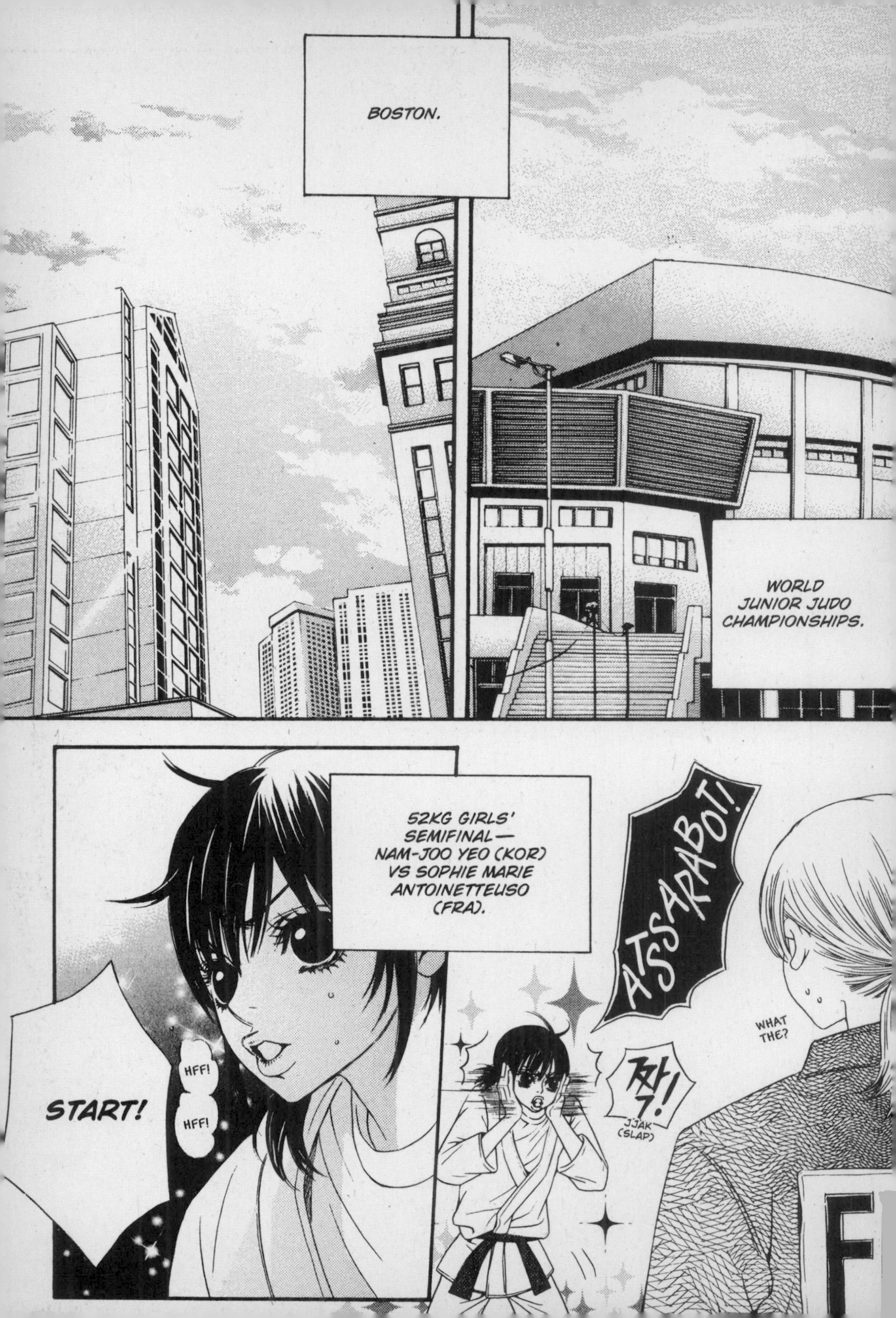
BOSTON.
WORLD JUNIOR JUDO CHAMPIONSHIPS.
52KG GIRLS' SEMIFINAL—NAM-JOO YEO (KOR) VS SOPHIE MARIE ANTOINETTEUSO (FRA).
HFF!
HFF!
START!
ATSSARABOT!
짝!
JJAK (SLAP)
WHAT THE?

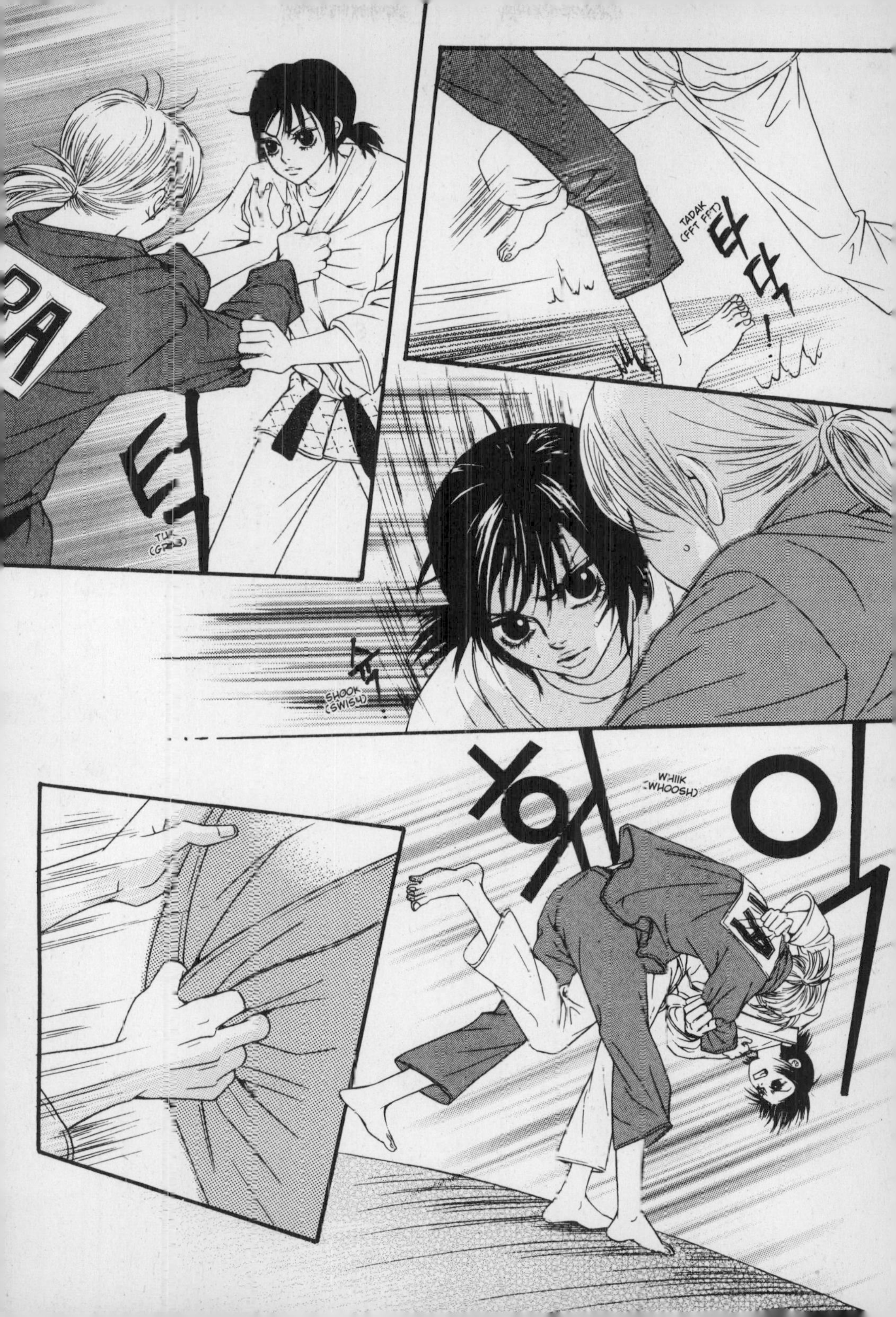
TU
TADAK (FFT FFT)
타닥!
SHOOK (SWISH)
WHIIK (WHOOSH)

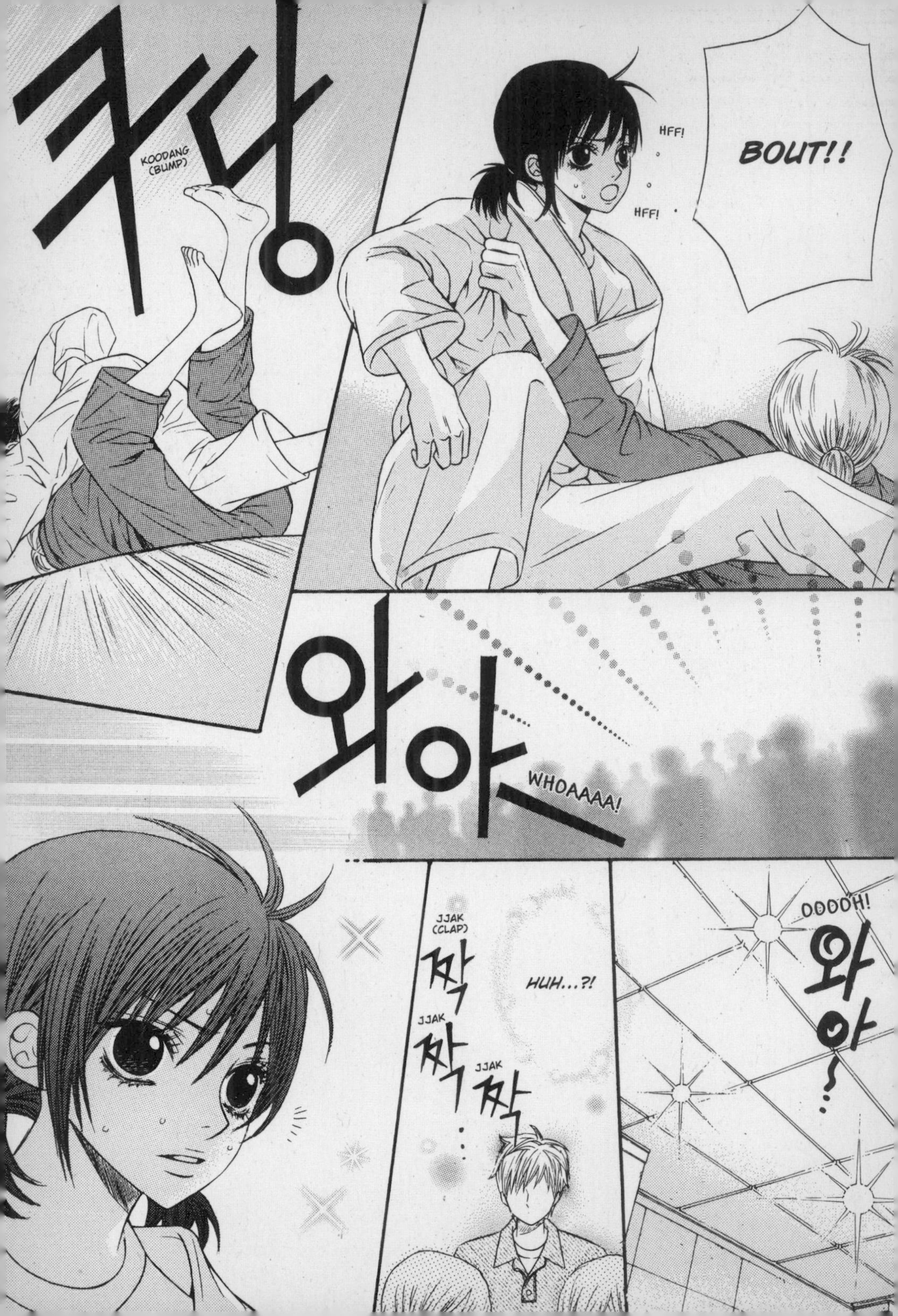
쿠당
KOODANG (BUMP)
HFF!
HFF!
BOUT!!
와아
WHOAAAA!
짝
JJAK (CLAP)
짝
JJAK
짝
JJAK
HUH...?!
와아~...
OOOOH!

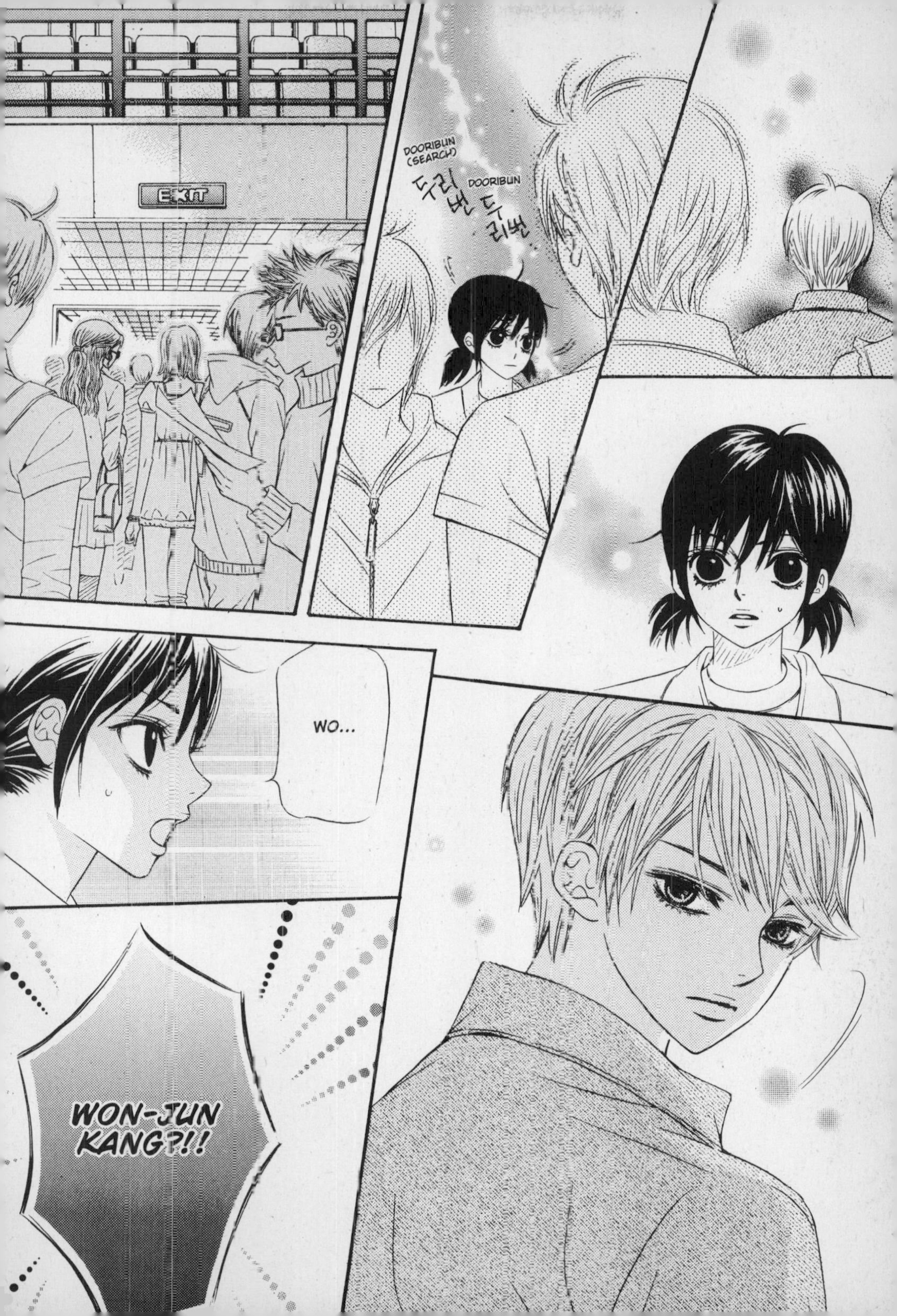
EXIT
DOORIBUN (SEARCH)
두리번
DOORIBUN
두리번
WO...
WON-JUN KANG?!!

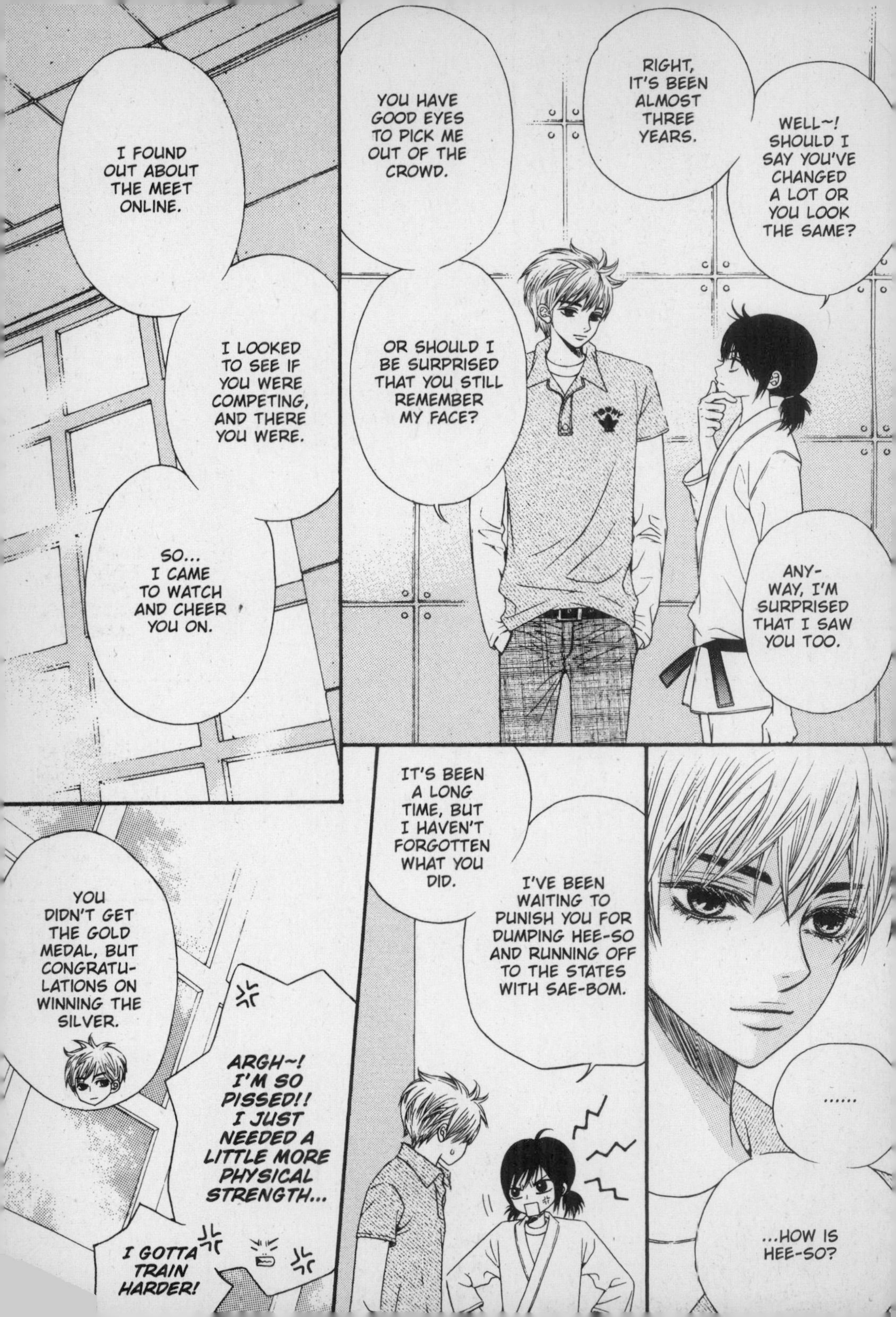
I FOUND OUT ABOUT THE MEET ONLINE.
I LOOKED TO SEE IF YOU WERE COMPETING, AND THERE YOU WERE.
SO... I CAME TO WATCH AND CHEER YOU ON.
YOU HAVE GOOD EYES TO PICK ME OUT OF THE CROWD.
RIGHT, IT'S BEEN ALMOST THREE YEARS.
WELL~! SHOULD I SAY YOU'VE CHANGED A LOT OR YOU LOOK THE SAME?
OR SHOULD I BE SURPRISED THAT YOU STILL REMEMBER MY FACE?
ANY-WAY, I'M SURPRISED THAT I SAW YOU TOO.
YOU DIDN'T GET THE GOLD MEDAL, BUT CONGRATU-LATIONS ON WINNING THE SILVER.
ARGH~! I'M SO PISSED!! I JUST NEEDED A LITTLE MORE PHYSICAL STRENGTH...
I GOTTA TRAIN HARDER!
IT'S BEEN A LONG TIME, BUT I HAVEN'T FORGOTTEN WHAT YOU DID.
I'VE BEEN WAITING TO PUNISH YOU FOR DUMPING HEE-SO AND RUNNING OFF TO THE STATES WITH SAE-BOM.
......
...HOW IS HEE-SO?

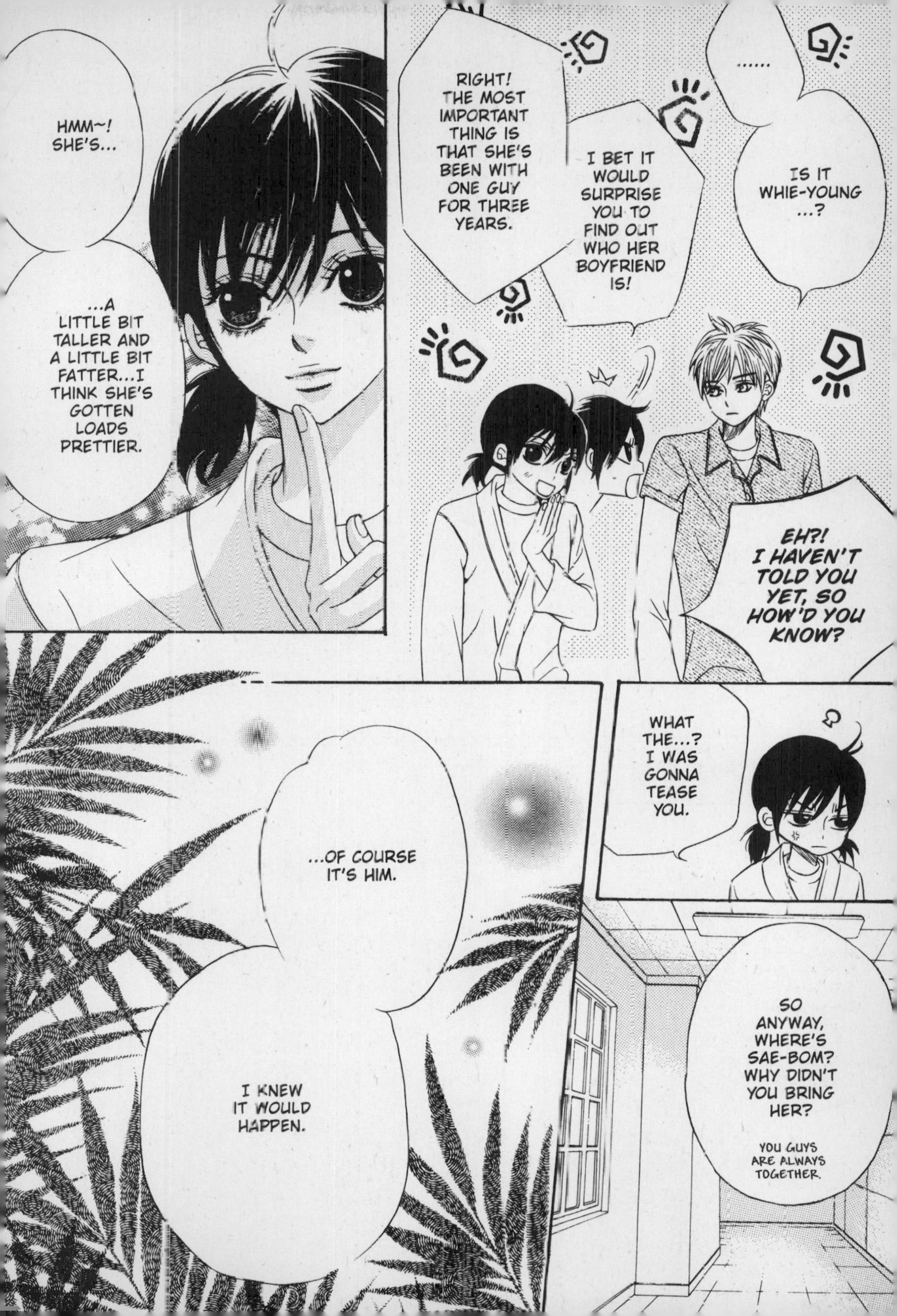
HMM~! SHE'S...
...A LITTLE BIT TALLER AND A LITTLE BIT FATTER...I THINK SHE'S GOTTEN LOADS PRETTIER.
RIGHT! THE MOST IMPORTANT THING IS THAT SHE'S BEEN WITH ONE GUY FOR THREE YEARS.
I BET IT WOULD SURPRISE YOU TO FIND OUT WHO HER BOYFRIEND IS!
......
IS IT WHIE-YOUNG ...?
EH?! I HAVEN'T TOLD YOU YET, SO HOW'D YOU KNOW?
...OF COURSE IT'S HIM.
I KNEW IT WOULD HAPPEN.
WHAT THE...? I WAS GONNA TEASE YOU.
SO ANYWAY, WHERE'S SAE-BOM? WHY DIDN'T YOU BRING HER?
YOU GUYS ARE ALWAYS TOGETHER.

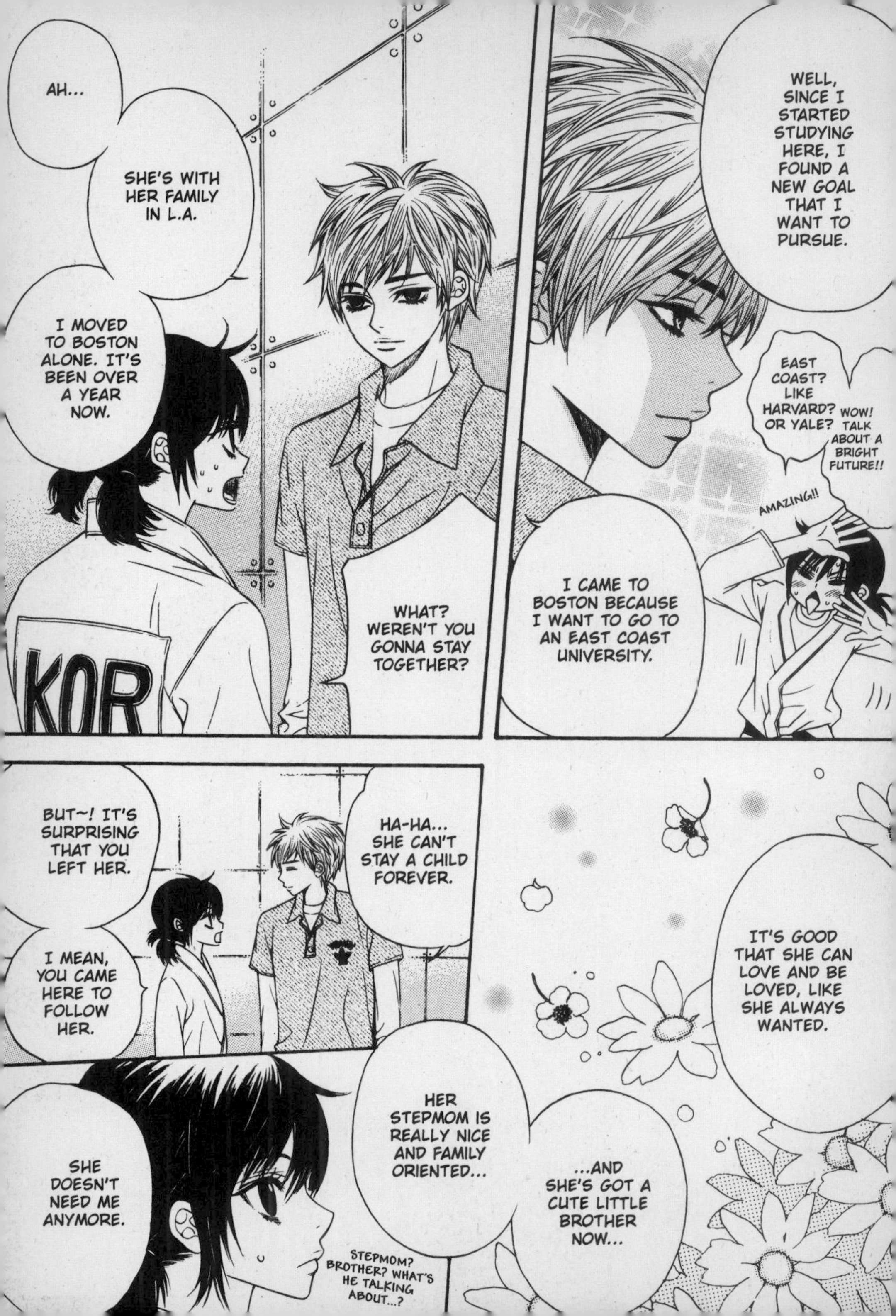
AH...
SHE'S WITH HER FAMILY IN L.A.
I MOVED TO BOSTON ALONE. IT'S BEEN OVER A YEAR NOW.
KOR
WHAT? WEREN'T YOU GONNA STAY TOGETHER?
WELL, SINCE I STARTED STUDYING HERE, I FOUND A NEW GOAL THAT I WANT TO PURSUE.
I CAME TO BOSTON BECAUSE I WANT TO GO TO AN EAST COAST UNIVERSITY.
EAST COAST? LIKE HARVARD? OR YALE?
WOW! TALK ABOUT A BRIGHT FUTURE!!
AMAZING!!
BUT~! IT'S SURPRISING THAT YOU LEFT HER.
HA-HA... SHE CAN'T STAY A CHILD FOREVER.
I MEAN, YOU CAME HERE TO FOLLOW HER.
SHE DOESN'T NEED ME ANYMORE.
HER STEPMOM IS REALLY NICE AND FAMILY ORIENTED...
...AND SHE'S GOT A CUTE LITTLE BROTHER NOW...
STEPMOM? BROTHER? WHAT'S HE TALKING ABOUT...?
IT'S GOOD THAT SHE CAN LOVE AND BE LOVED, LIKE SHE ALWAYS WANTED.

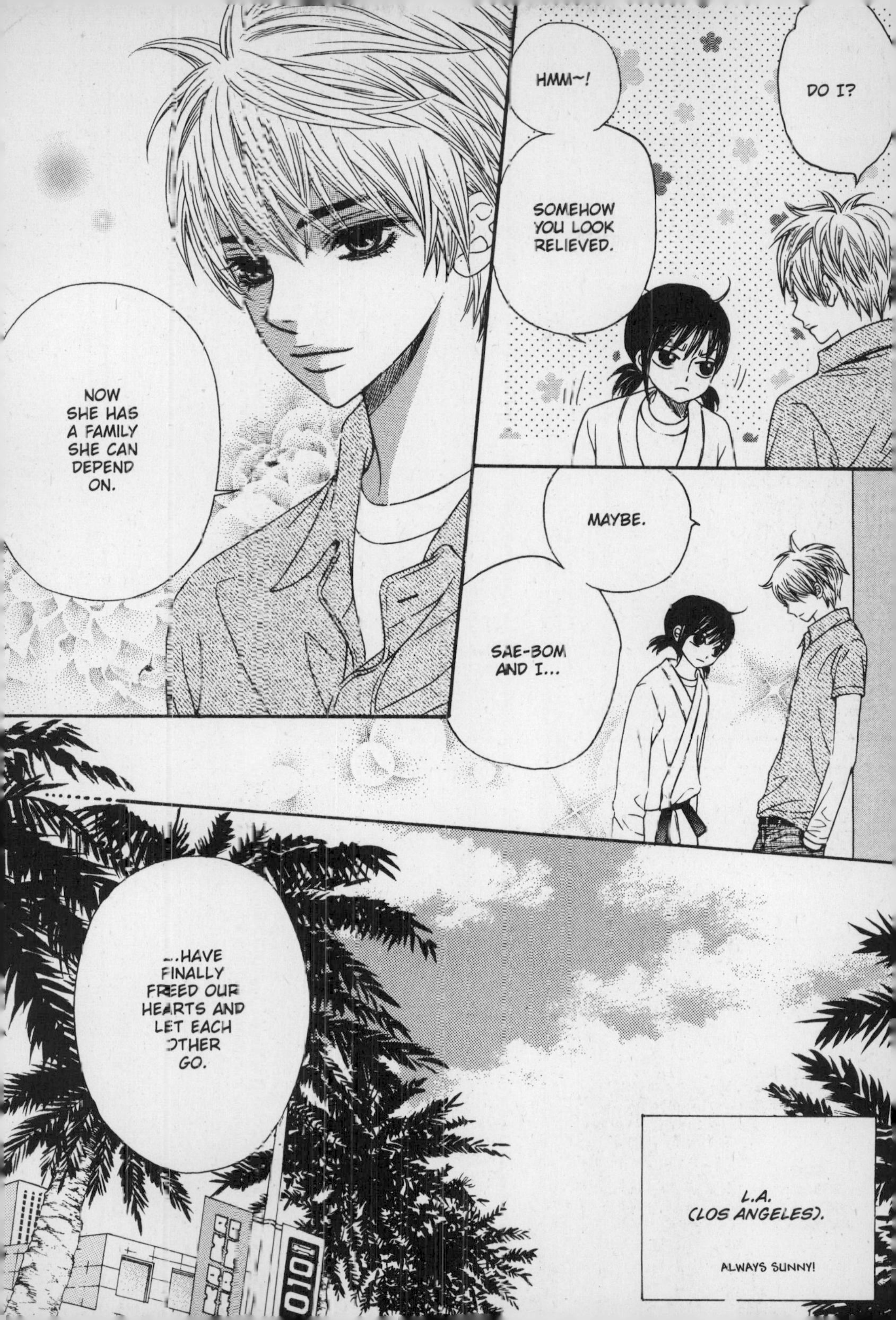
NOW SHE HAS A FAMILY SHE CAN DEPEND ON.
HMM~!
SOMEHOW YOU LOOK RELIEVED.
DO I?
MAYBE.
SAE-BOM AND I...
...HAVE FINALLY FREED OUR HEARTS AND LET EACH OTHER GO.
L.A. (LOS ANGELES).
ALWAYS SUNNY!

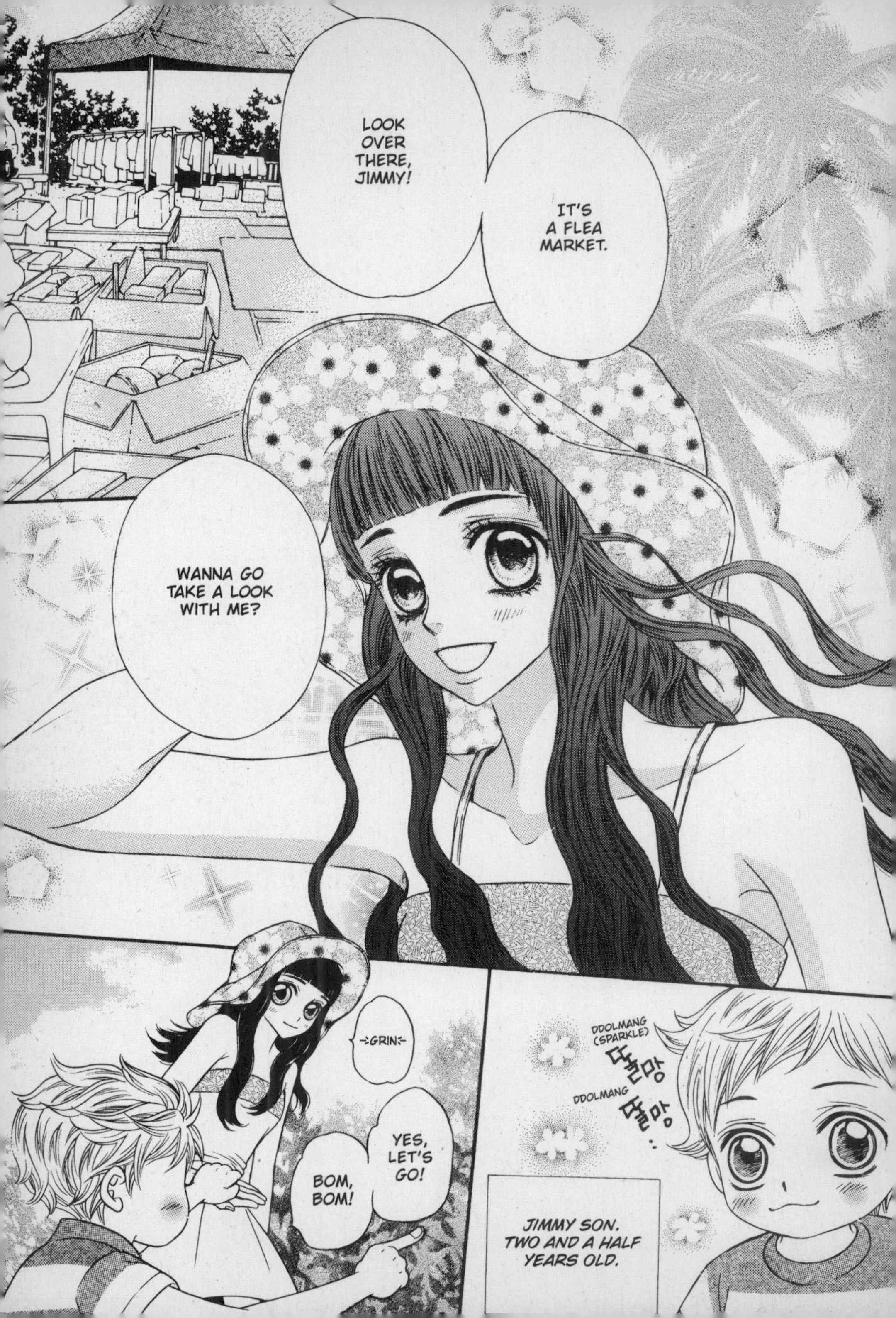
LOOK OVER THERE, JIMMY!
IT'S A FLEA MARKET.
WANNA GO TAKE A LOOK WITH ME?
~GRIN~
BOM, BOM!
YES, LET'S GO!
DDOLMANG (SPARKLE)
또올망
DDOLMANG
또올망..
JIMMY SON. TWO AND A HALF YEARS OLD.

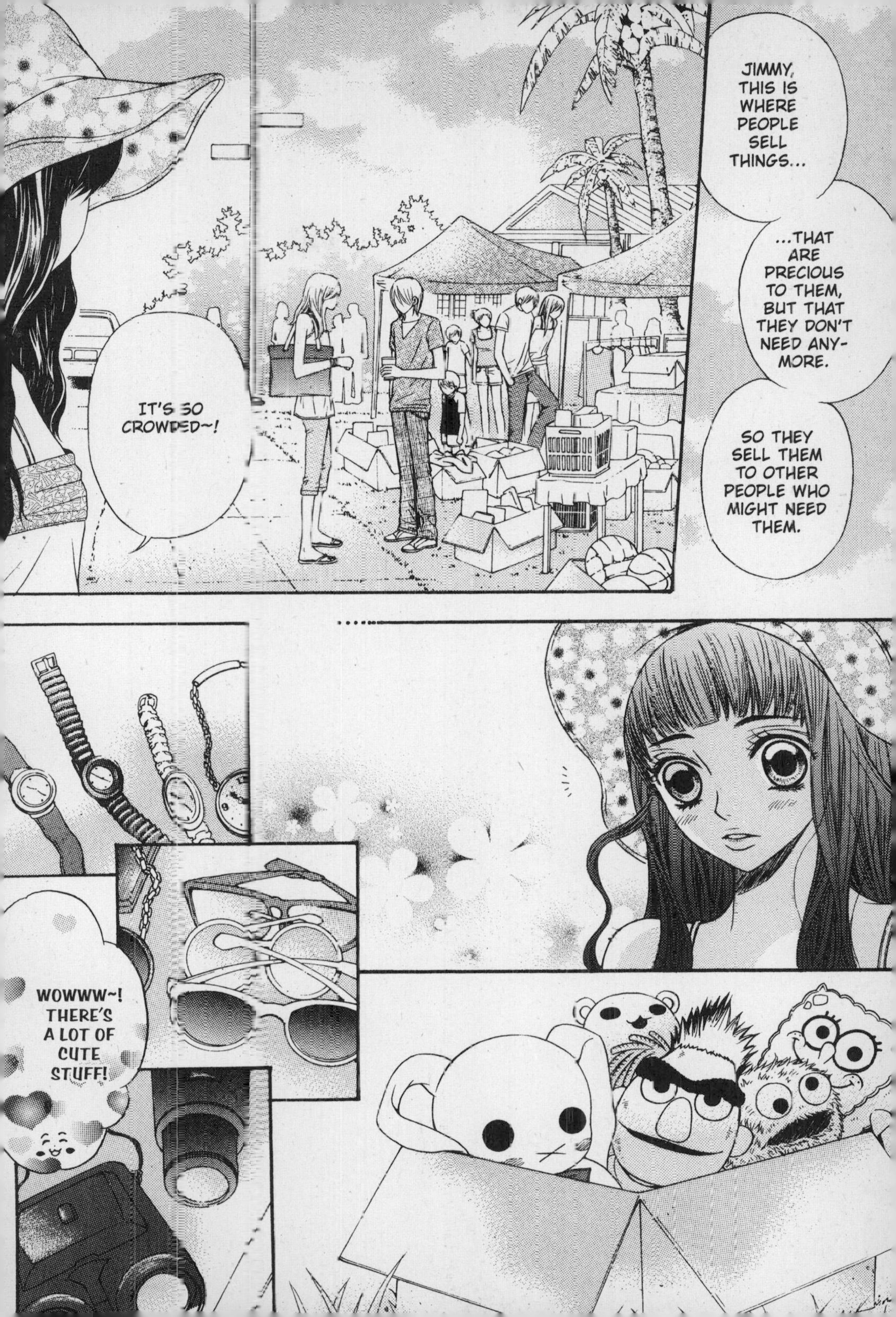
IT'S SO CROWDED~!
JIMMY, THIS IS WHERE PEOPLE SELL THINGS...
...THAT ARE PRECIOUS TO THEM, BUT THAT THEY DON'T NEED ANY-MORE.
SO THEY SELL THEM TO OTHER PEOPLE WHO MIGHT NEED THEM.
......
WOWWW~! THERE'S A LOT OF CUTE STUFF!

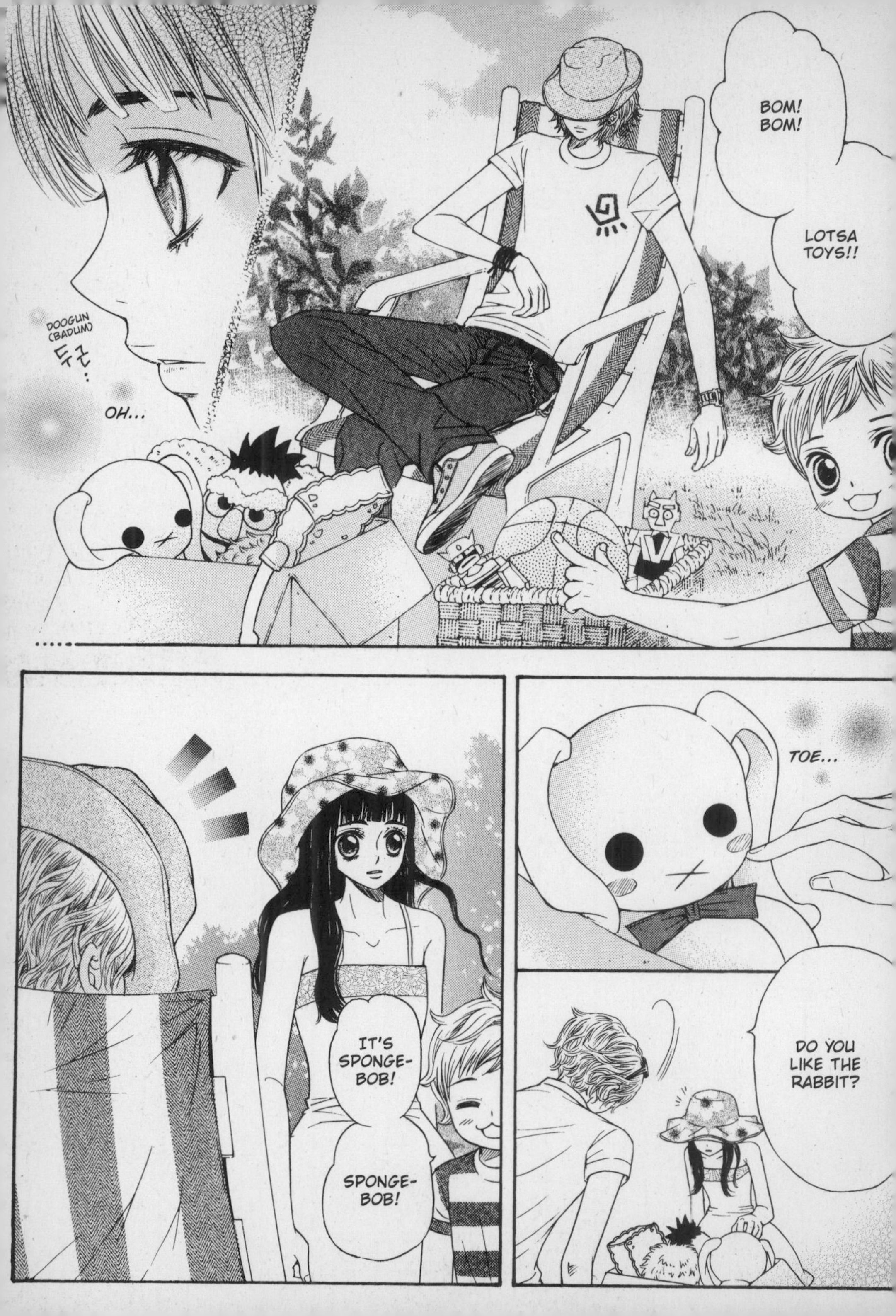
BOM! BOM!
LOTSA TOYS!!
DOOGUN (BADUM)
두근..
OH...
IT'S SPONGE-BOB!
SPONGE-BOB!
TOE...
DO YOU LIKE THE RABBIT?

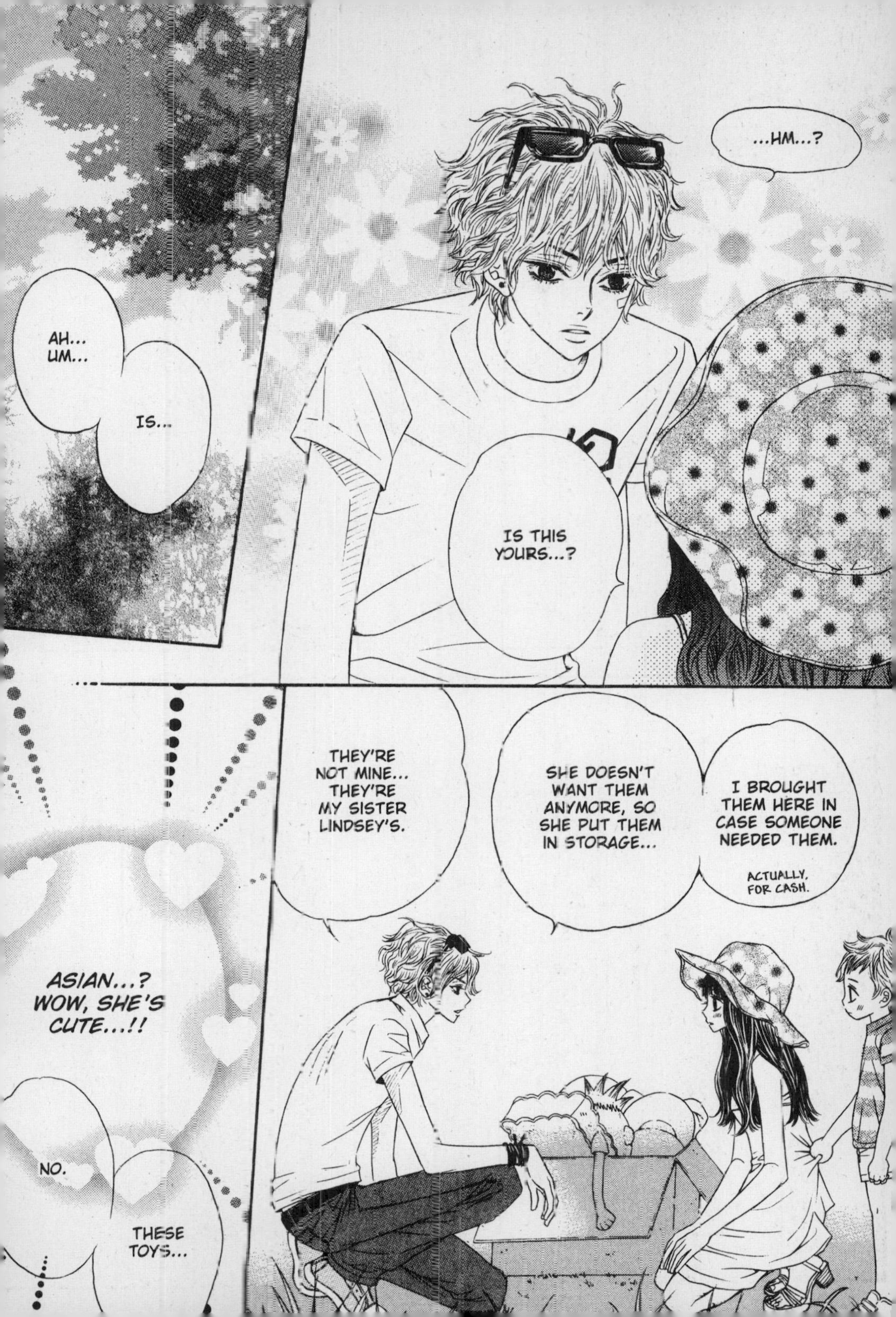
AH... UM...
IS...
...HM...?
IS THIS YOURS...?
ASIAN...? WOW, SHE'S CUTE...!!
NO.
THESE TOYS...
THEY'RE NOT MINE... THEY'RE MY SISTER LINDSEY'S.
SHE DOESN'T WANT THEM ANYMORE, SO SHE PUT THEM IN STORAGE...
I BROUGHT THEM HERE IN CASE SOMEONE NEEDED THEM.
ACTUALLY, FOR CASH.

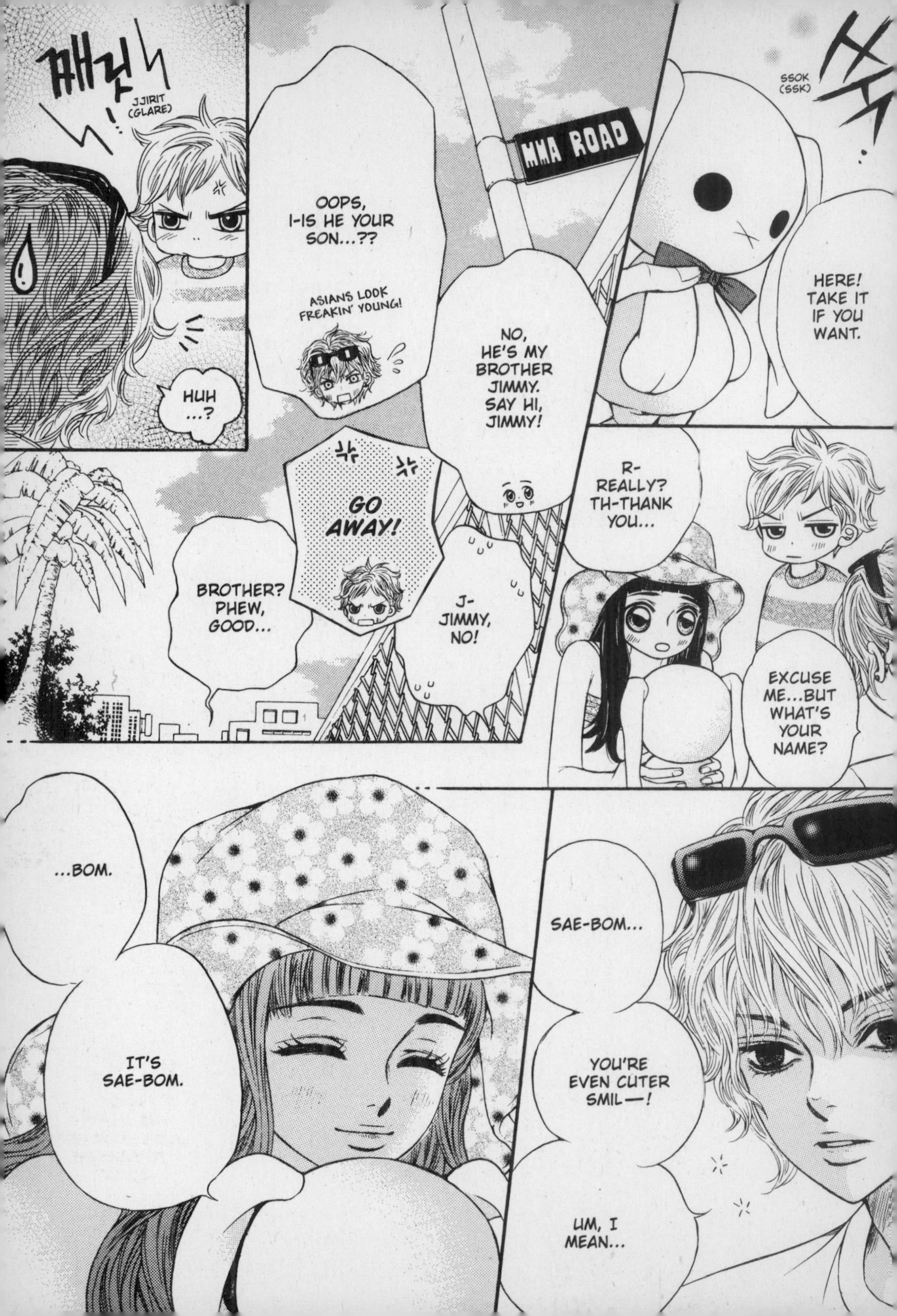
째릿
JJIRIT (GLARE)
HUH ...?
OOPS, I-IS HE YOUR SON...??
ASIANS LOOK FREAKIN' YOUNG!
NO, HE'S MY BROTHER JIMMY. SAY HI, JIMMY!
MMA ROAD
GO AWAY!
BROTHER? PHEW, GOOD...
J-JIMMY, NO!
쏙
SSOK (SSK)
HERE! TAKE IT IF YOU WANT.
R-REALLY? TH-THANK YOU...
EXCUSE ME...BUT WHAT'S YOUR NAME?
...BOM.
IT'S SAE-BOM.
SAE-BOM...
YOU'RE EVEN CUTER SMIL—!
UM, I MEAN...

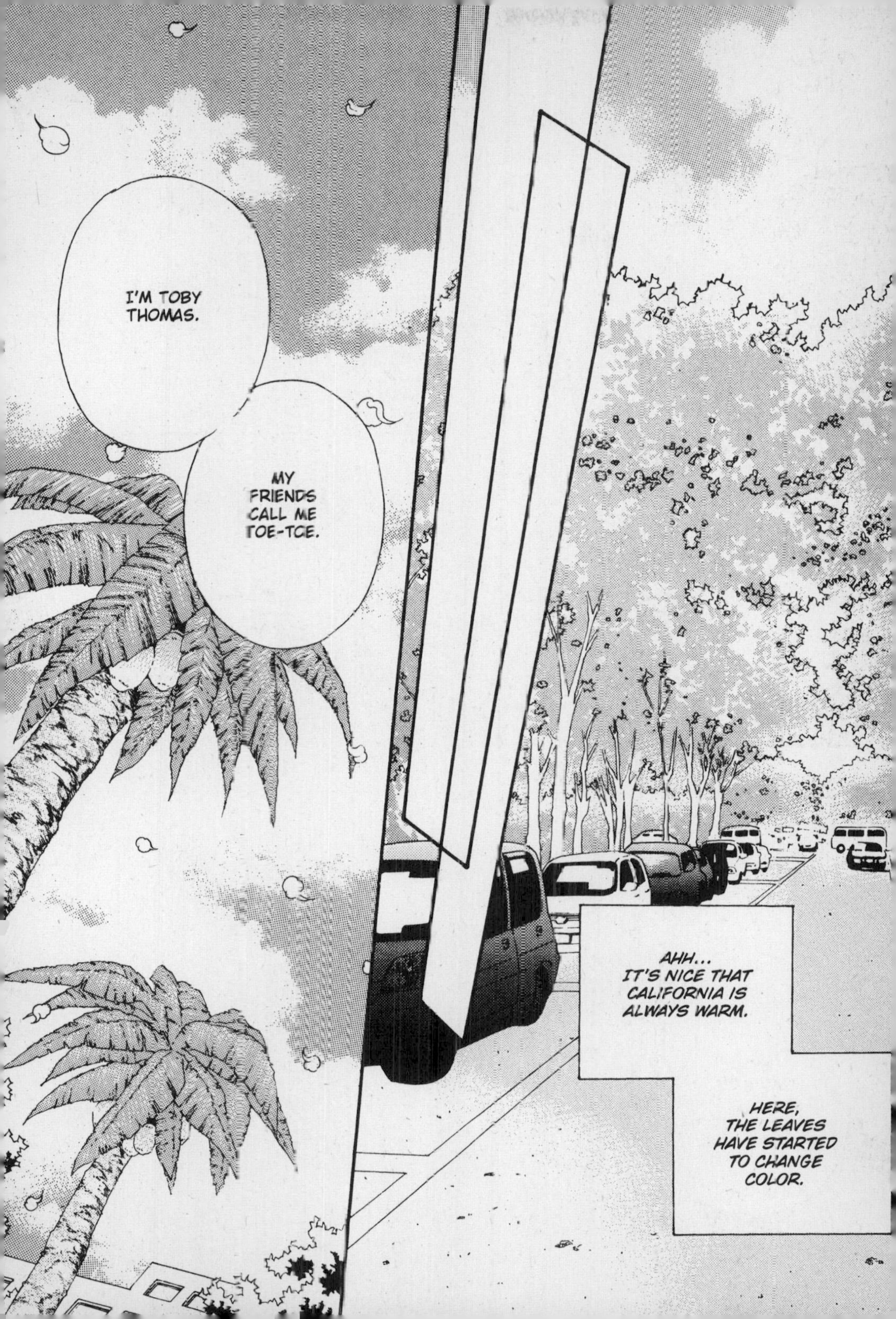
I'M TOBY THOMAS.
MY FRIENDS CALL ME TOE-TOE.
AHH... IT'S NICE THAT CALIFORNIA IS ALWAYS WARM.
HERE, THE LEAVES HAVE STARTED TO CHANGE COLOR.

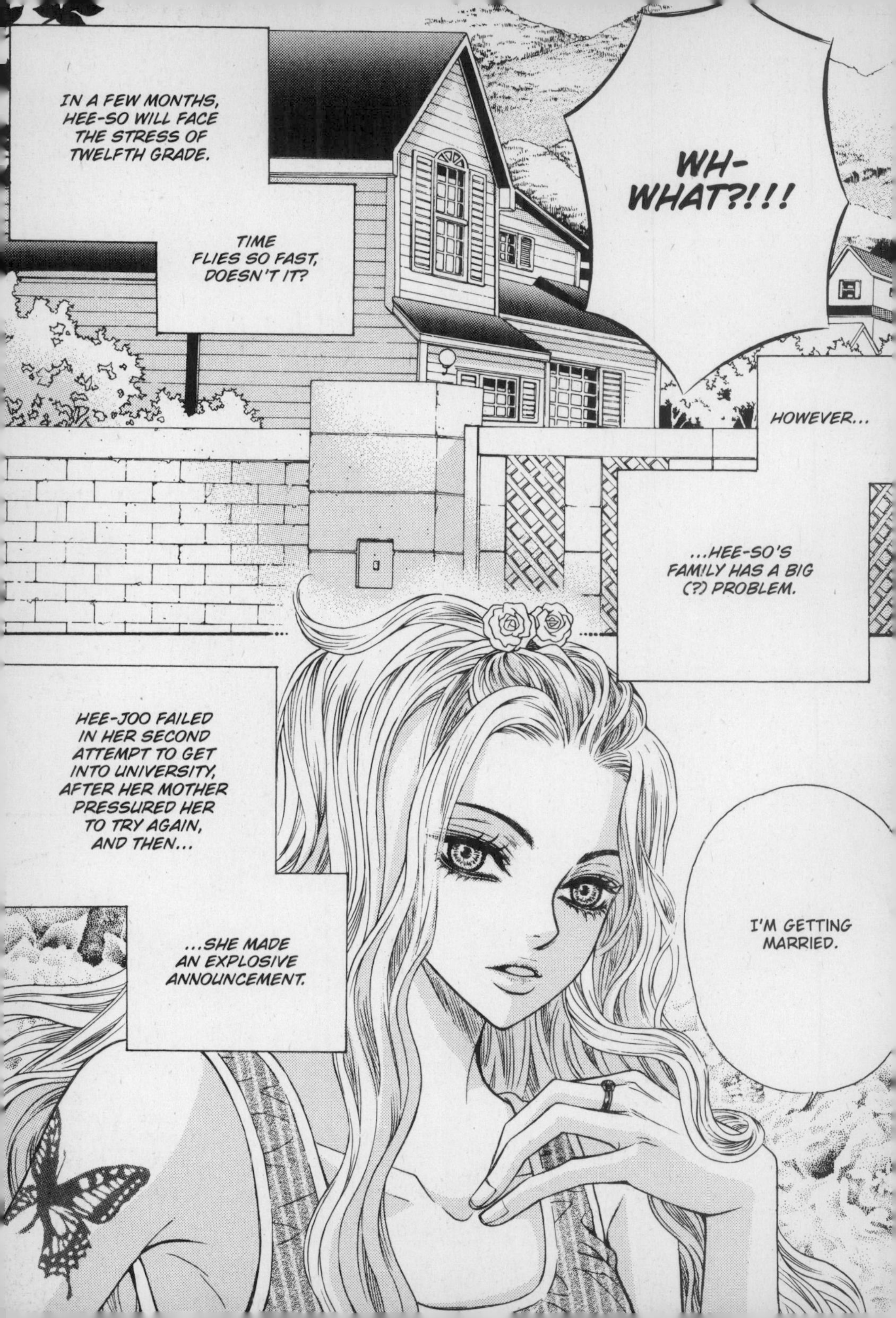
IN A FEW MONTHS, HEE-SO WILL FACE THE STRESS OF TWELFTH GRADE.
TIME FLIES SO FAST, DOESN'T IT?
HOWEVER...
...HEE-SO'S FAMILY HAS A BIG (?) PROBLEM.
HEE-JOO FAILED IN HER SECOND ATTEMPT TO GET INTO UNIVERSITY, AFTER HER MOTHER PRESSURED HER TO TRY AGAIN, AND THEN...
...SHE MADE AN EXPLOSIVE ANNOUNCEMENT.
I'M GETTING MARRIED.
WH-WHAT?!!!

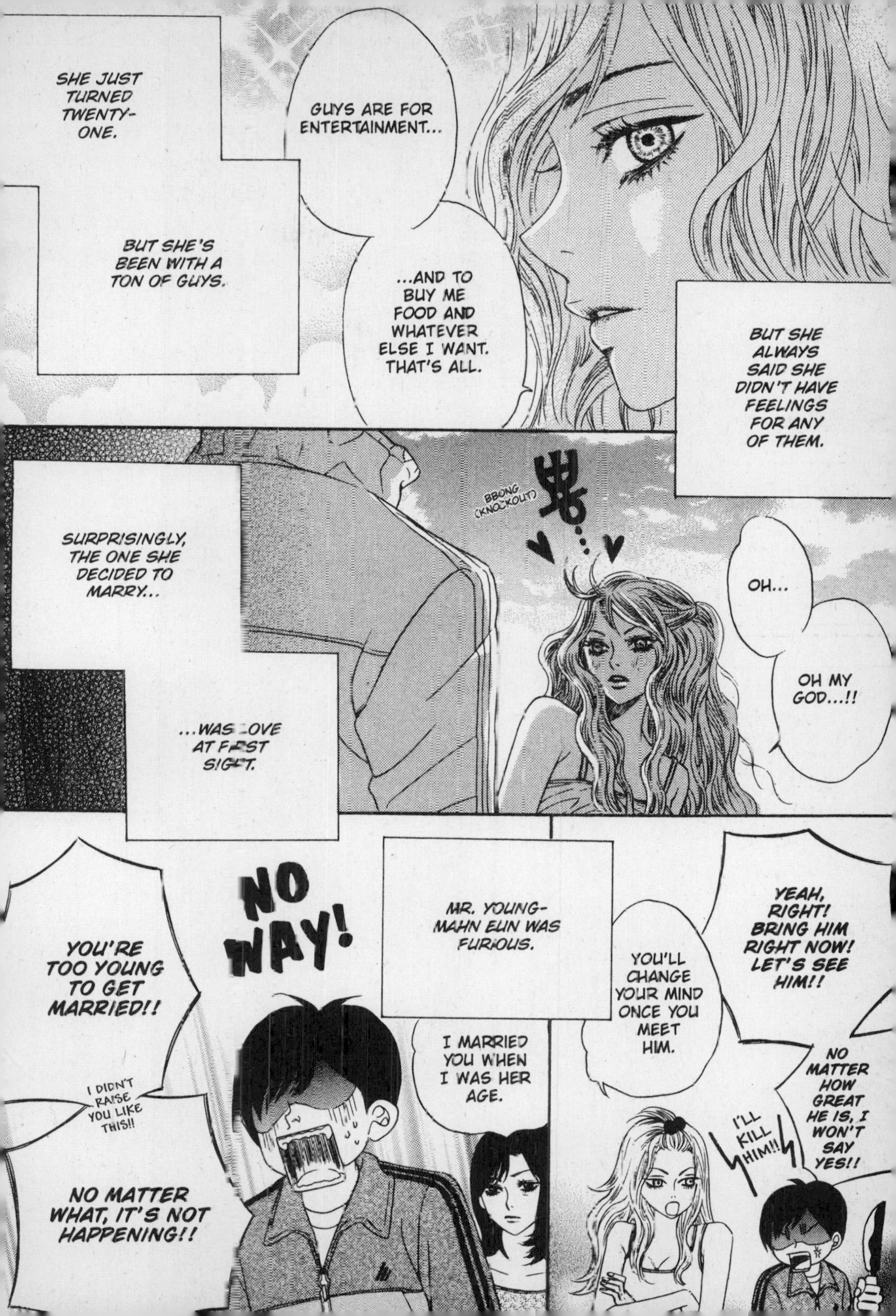
SHE JUST TURNED TWENTY-ONE.
BUT SHE'S BEEN WITH A TON OF GUYS.
GUYS ARE FOR ENTERTAINMENT...
...AND TO BUY ME FOOD AND WHATEVER ELSE I WANT. THAT'S ALL.
BUT SHE ALWAYS SAID SHE DIDN'T HAVE FEELINGS FOR ANY OF THEM.
SURPRISINGLY, THE ONE SHE DECIDED TO MARRY...
...WAS LOVE AT FIRST SIGHT.
BBONG (KNOCKOUT)
OH...
OH MY GOD...!!
NO WAY!
YOU'RE TOO YOUNG TO GET MARRIED!!
I DIDN'T RAISE YOU LIKE THIS!!
NO MATTER WHAT, IT'S NOT HAPPENING!!
MR. YOUNG-MAHN EUN WAS FURIOUS.
I MARRIED YOU WHEN I WAS HER AGE.
YOU'LL CHANGE YOUR MIND ONCE YOU MEET HIM.
YEAH, RIGHT! BRING HIM RIGHT NOW! LET'S SEE HIM!!
I'LL KILL HIM!!
NO MATTER HOW GREAT HE IS, I WON'T SAY YES!!

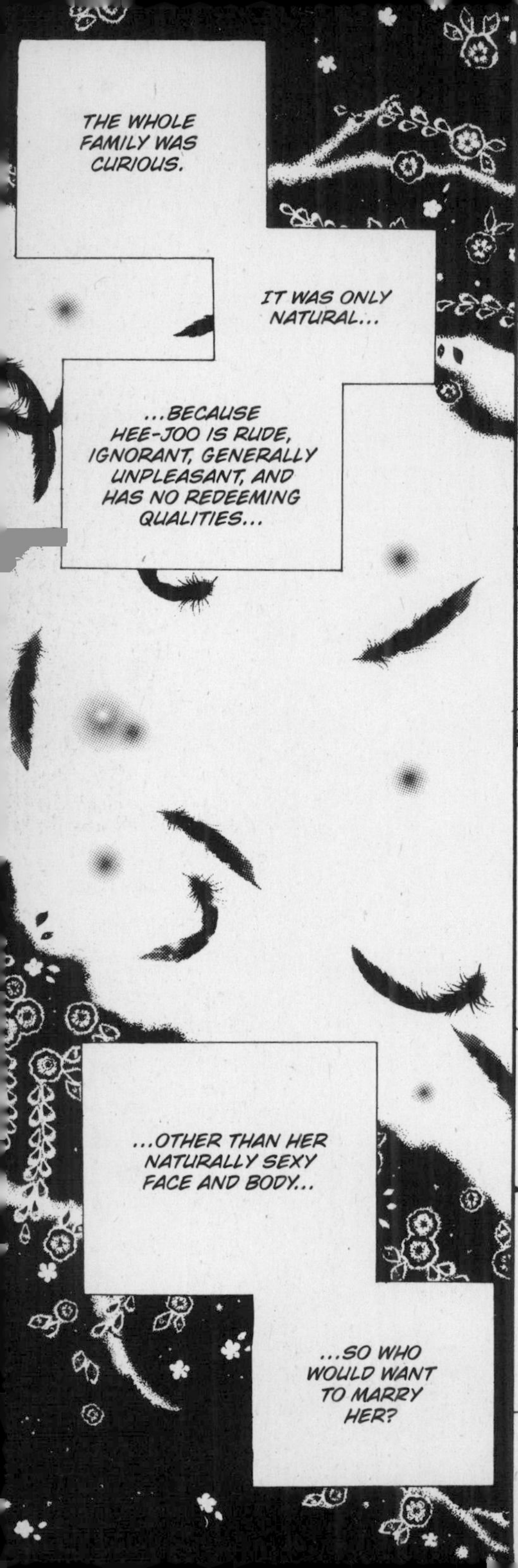
THE WHOLE FAMILY WAS CURIOUS.
IT WAS ONLY NATURAL...
...BECAUSE HEE-JOO IS RUDE, IGNORANT, GENERALLY UNPLEASANT, AND HAS NO REDEEMING QUALITIES...
...OTHER THAN HER NATURALLY SEXY FACE AND BODY...
...SO WHO WOULD WANT TO MARRY HER?
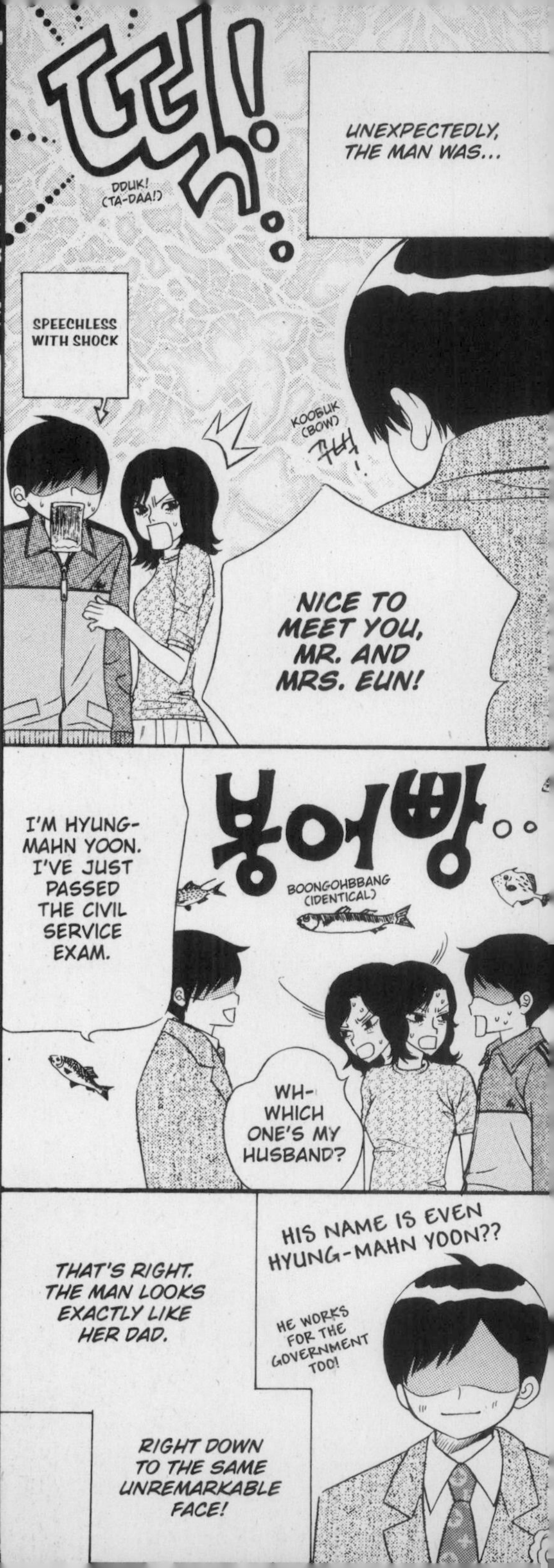
떡!
DDUK! (TA-DAA!)
UNEXPECTEDLY, THE MAN WAS...
SPEECHLESS WITH SHOCK
KOOBUK (BOW)
꾸벅
NICE TO MEET YOU, MR. AND MRS. EUN!
I'M HYUNG-MAHN YOON. I'VE JUST PASSED THE CIVIL SERVICE EXAM.
붕어빵
BOONGOHBBANG (IDENTICAL)
WH-WHICH ONE'S MY HUSBAND?
THAT'S RIGHT. THE MAN LOOKS EXACTLY LIKE HER DAD.
HIS NAME IS EVEN HYUNG-MAHN YOON??
HE WORKS FOR THE GOVERNMENT TOO!
RIGHT DOWN TO THE SAME UNREMARKABLE FACE!

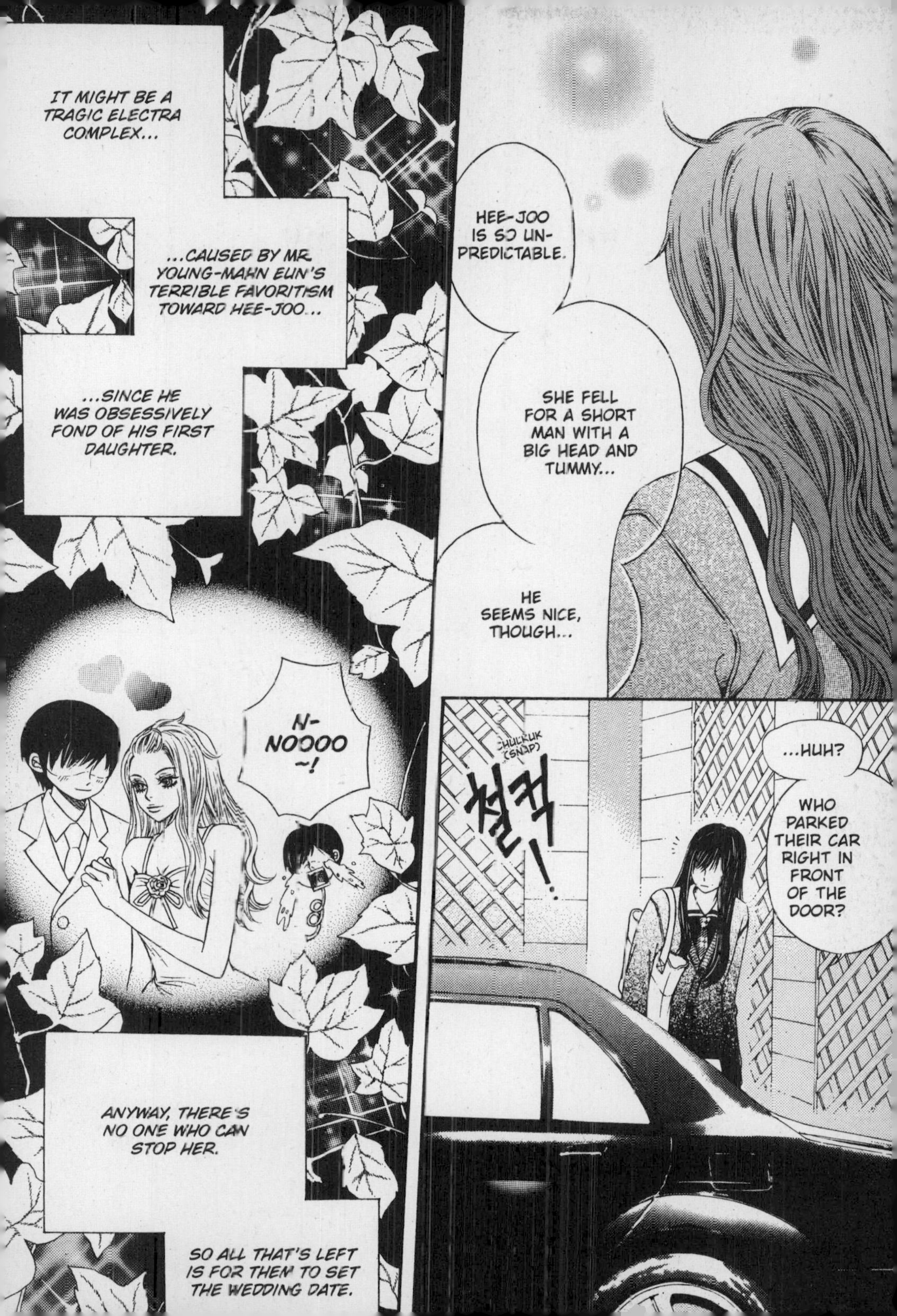
IT MIGHT BE A TRAGIC ELECTRA COMPLEX...
...CAUSED BY MR. YOUNG-MAHN EUN'S TERRIBLE FAVORITISM TOWARD HEE-JOO...
...SINCE HE WAS OBSESSIVELY FOND OF HIS FIRST DAUGHTER.
N-NOOOO~!
ANYWAY, THERE'S NO ONE WHO CAN STOP HER.
SO ALL THAT'S LEFT IS FOR THEM TO SET THE WEDDING DATE.
HEE-JOO IS SO UN-PREDICTABLE.
SHE FELL FOR A SHORT MAN WITH A BIG HEAD AND TUMMY...
HE SEEMS NICE, THOUGH...
CHULKUK (SNAP)
철컥!
...HUH?
WHO PARKED THEIR CAR RIGHT IN FRONT OF THE DOOR?

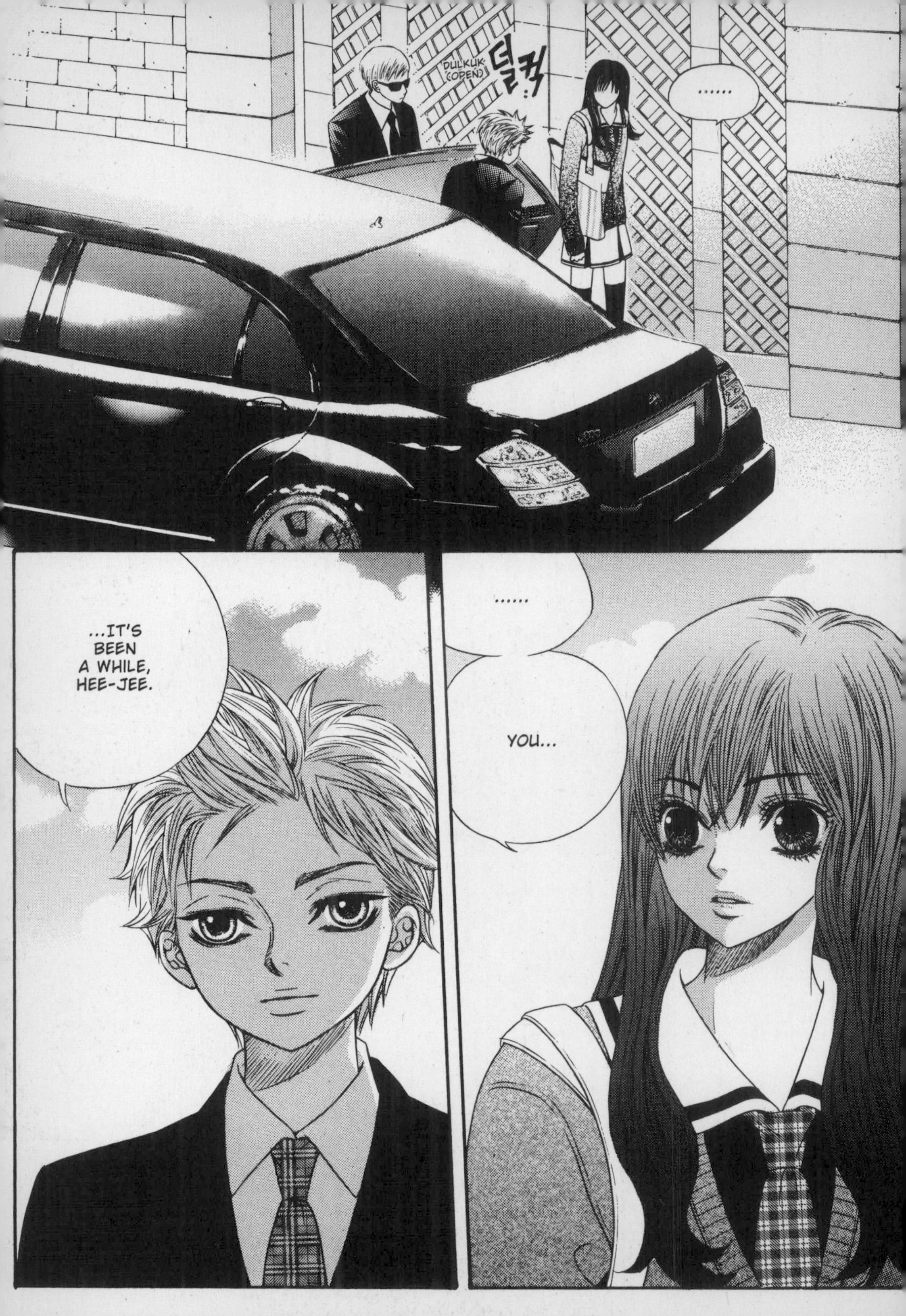
DULKUK (OPEN)
덜컥
......
...IT'S BEEN A WHILE, HEE-JEE.
......
YOU...

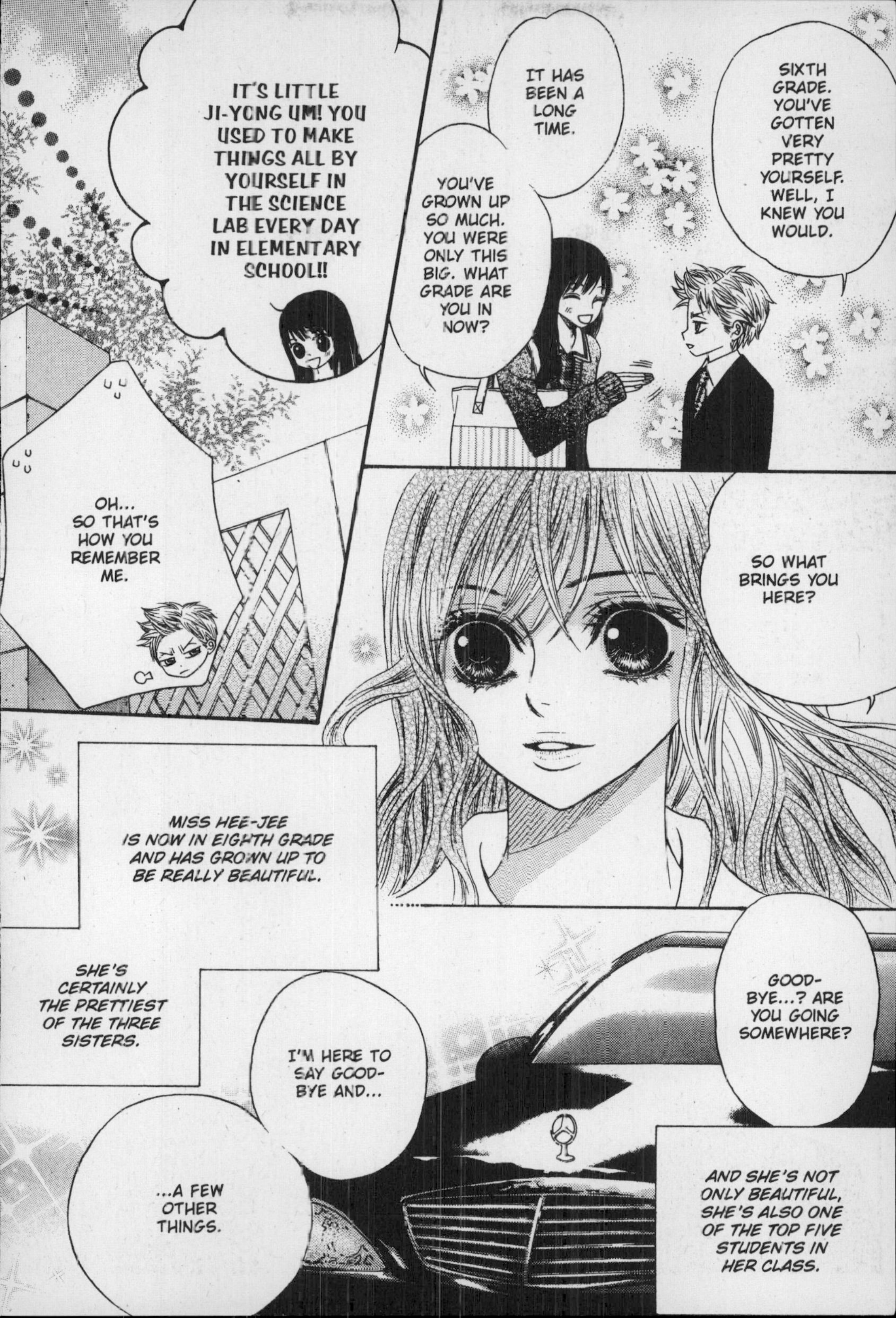
IT'S LITTLE JI-YONG UM! YOU USED TO MAKE THINGS ALL BY YOURSELF IN THE SCIENCE LAB EVERY DAY IN ELEMENTARY SCHOOL!!
IT HAS BEEN A LONG TIME.
YOU'VE GROWN UP SO MUCH. YOU WERE ONLY THIS BIG. WHAT GRADE ARE YOU IN NOW?
SIXTH GRADE. YOU'VE GOTTEN VERY PRETTY YOURSELF. WELL, I KNEW YOU WOULD.
OH... SO THAT'S HOW YOU REMEMBER ME.
SO WHAT BRINGS YOU HERE?
MISS HEE-JEE IS NOW IN EIGHTH GRADE AND HAS GROWN UP TO BE REALLY BEAUTIFUL.
SHE'S CERTAINLY THE PRETTIEST OF THE THREE SISTERS.
I'M HERE TO SAY GOOD-BYE AND...
...A FEW OTHER THINGS.
GOOD-BYE...? ARE YOU GOING SOMEWHERE?
AND SHE'S NOT ONLY BEAUTIFUL, SHE'S ALSO ONE OF THE TOP FIVE STUDENTS IN HER CLASS.

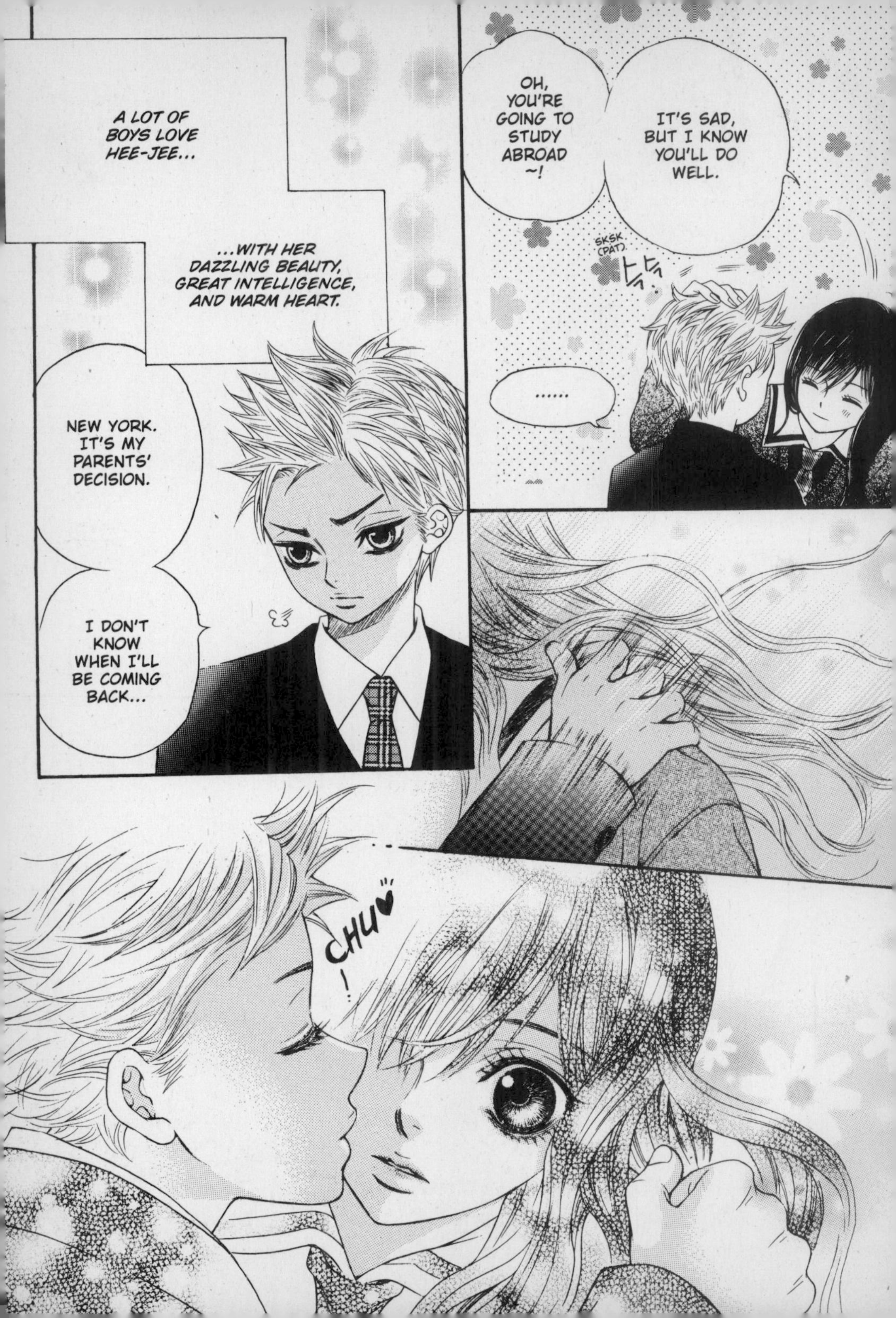
A LOT OF BOYS LOVE HEE-JEE...
...WITH HER DAZZLING BEAUTY, GREAT INTELLIGENCE, AND WARM HEART.
NEW YORK. IT'S MY PARENTS' DECISION.
I DON'T KNOW WHEN I'LL BE COMING BACK...
OH, YOU'RE GOING TO STUDY ABROAD ~!
IT'S SAD, BUT I KNOW YOU'LL DO WELL.
SKSK (PAT)
......
CHU
!

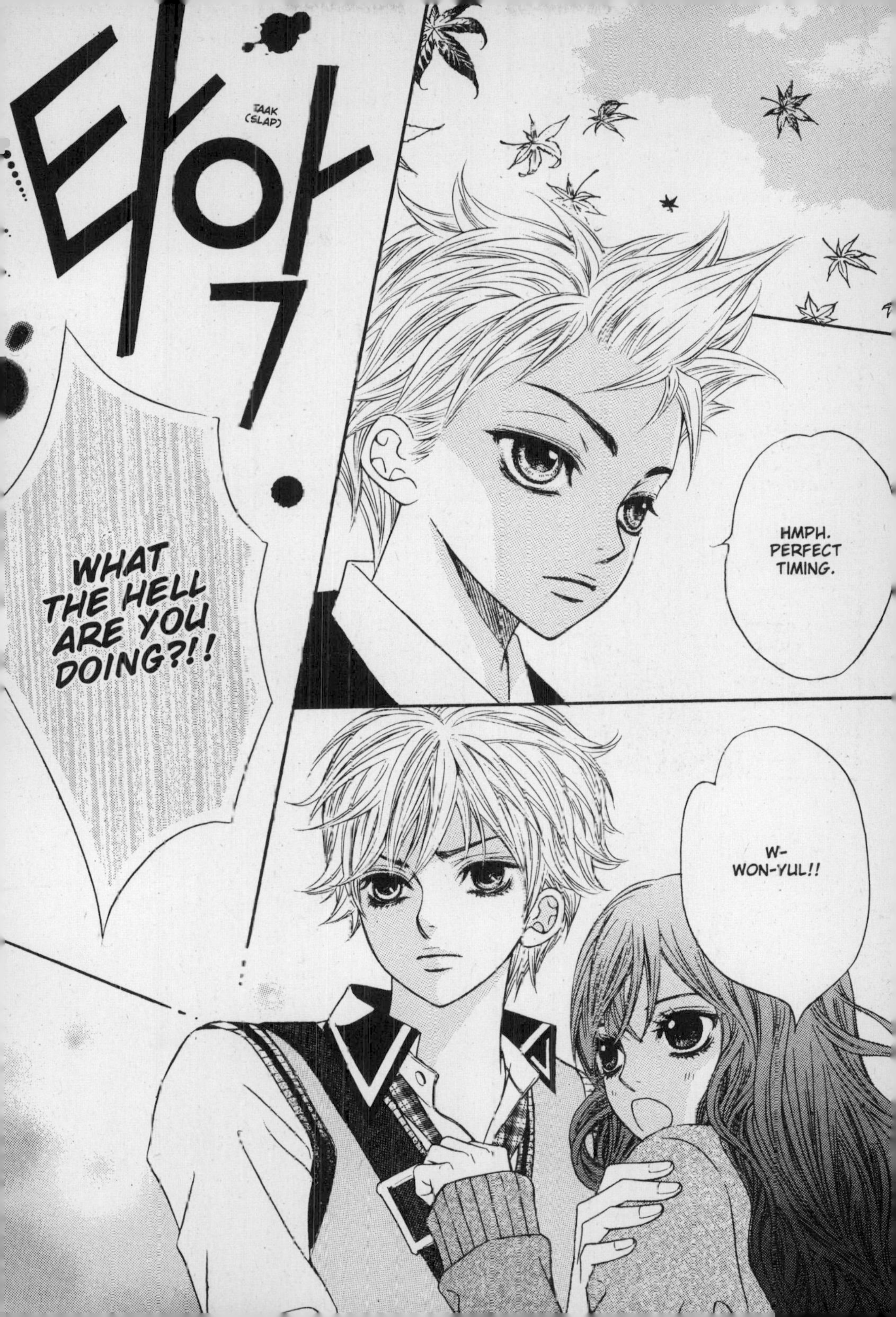
탁
TAAK (SLAP)
WHAT THE HELL ARE YOU DOING?!!
HMPH. PERFECT TIMING.
W- WON-YUL!!

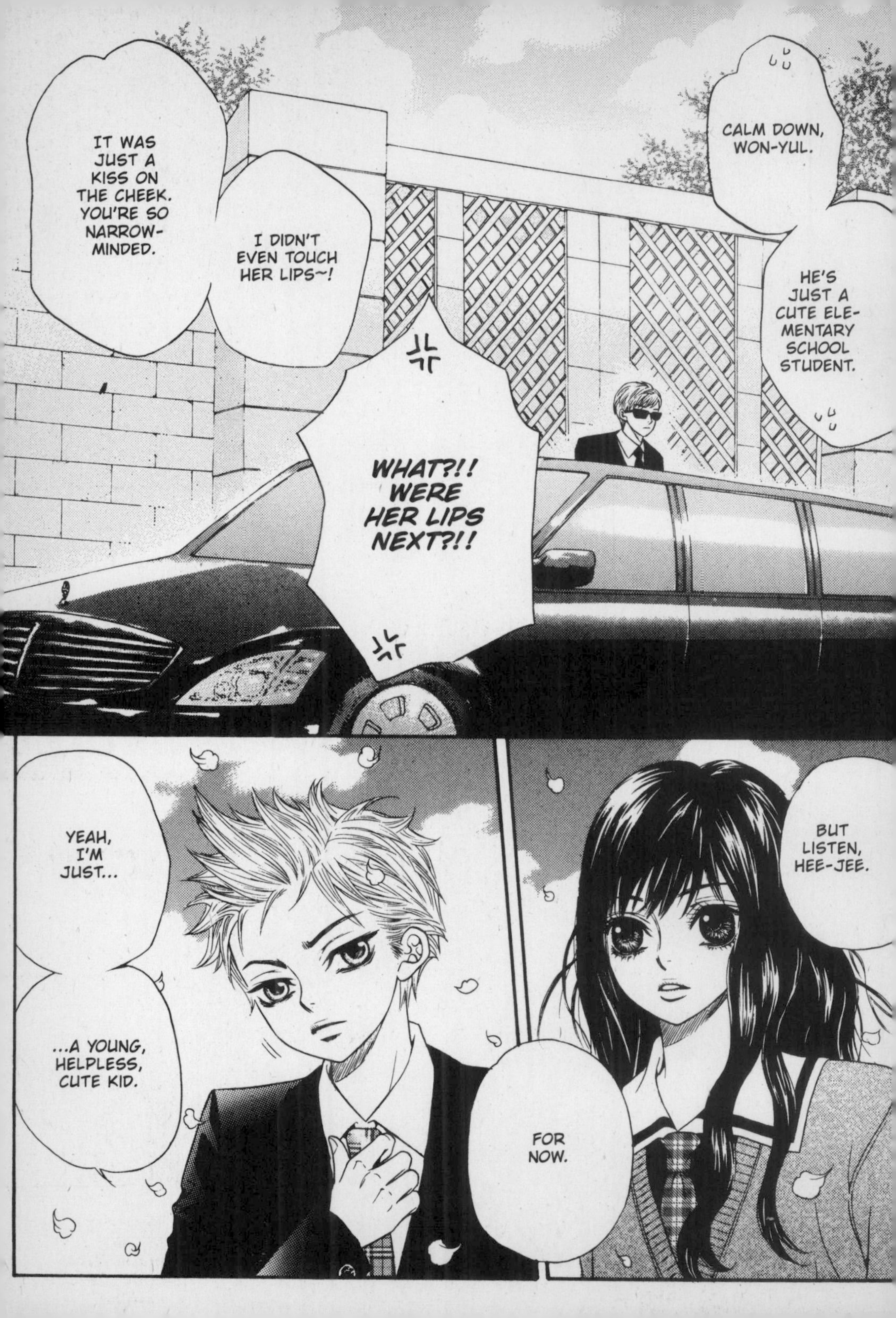
IT WAS JUST A KISS ON THE CHEEK. YOU'RE SO NARROW-MINDED.
I DIDN'T EVEN TOUCH HER LIPS~!
WHAT?!! WERE HER LIPS NEXT?!!
CALM DOWN, WON-YUL.
HE'S JUST A CUTE ELE-MENTARY SCHOOL STUDENT.
YEAH, I'M JUST...
...A YOUNG, HELPLESS, CUTE KID.
FOR NOW.
BUT LISTEN, HEE-JEE.

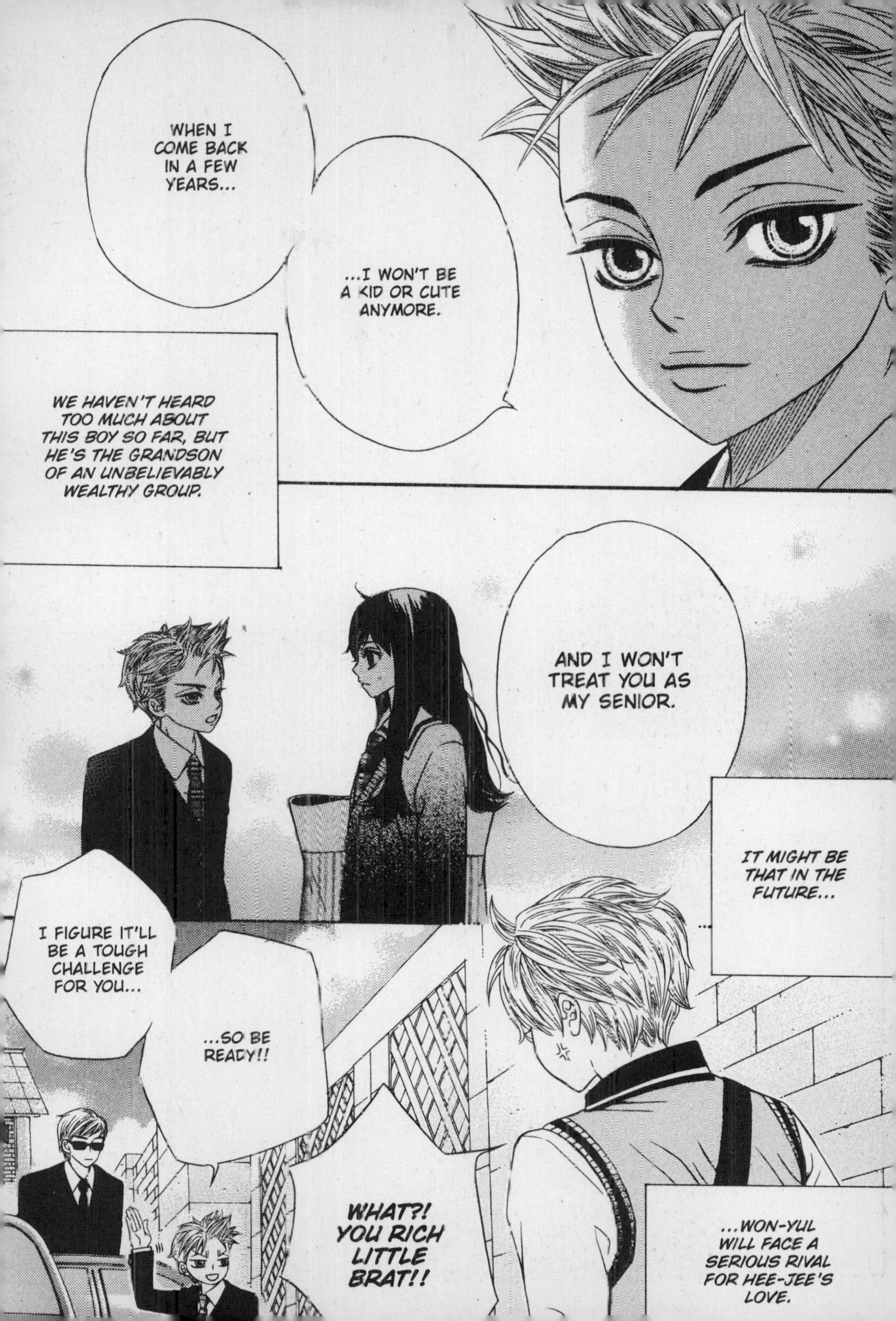

WHEN I COME BACK IN A FEW YEARS...
...I WON'T BE A KID OR CUTE ANYMORE.
WE HAVEN'T HEARD TOO MUCH ABOUT THIS BOY SO FAR, BUT HE'S THE GRANDSON OF AN UNBELIEVABLY WEALTHY GROUP.
AND I WON'T TREAT YOU AS MY SENIOR.
I FIGURE IT'LL BE A TOUGH CHALLENGE FOR YOU...
...SO BE READY!!
IT MIGHT BE THAT IN THE FUTURE...
WHAT?! YOU RICH LITTLE BRAT!!
...WON-YUL WILL FACE A SERIOUS RIVAL FOR HEE-JEE'S LOVE.

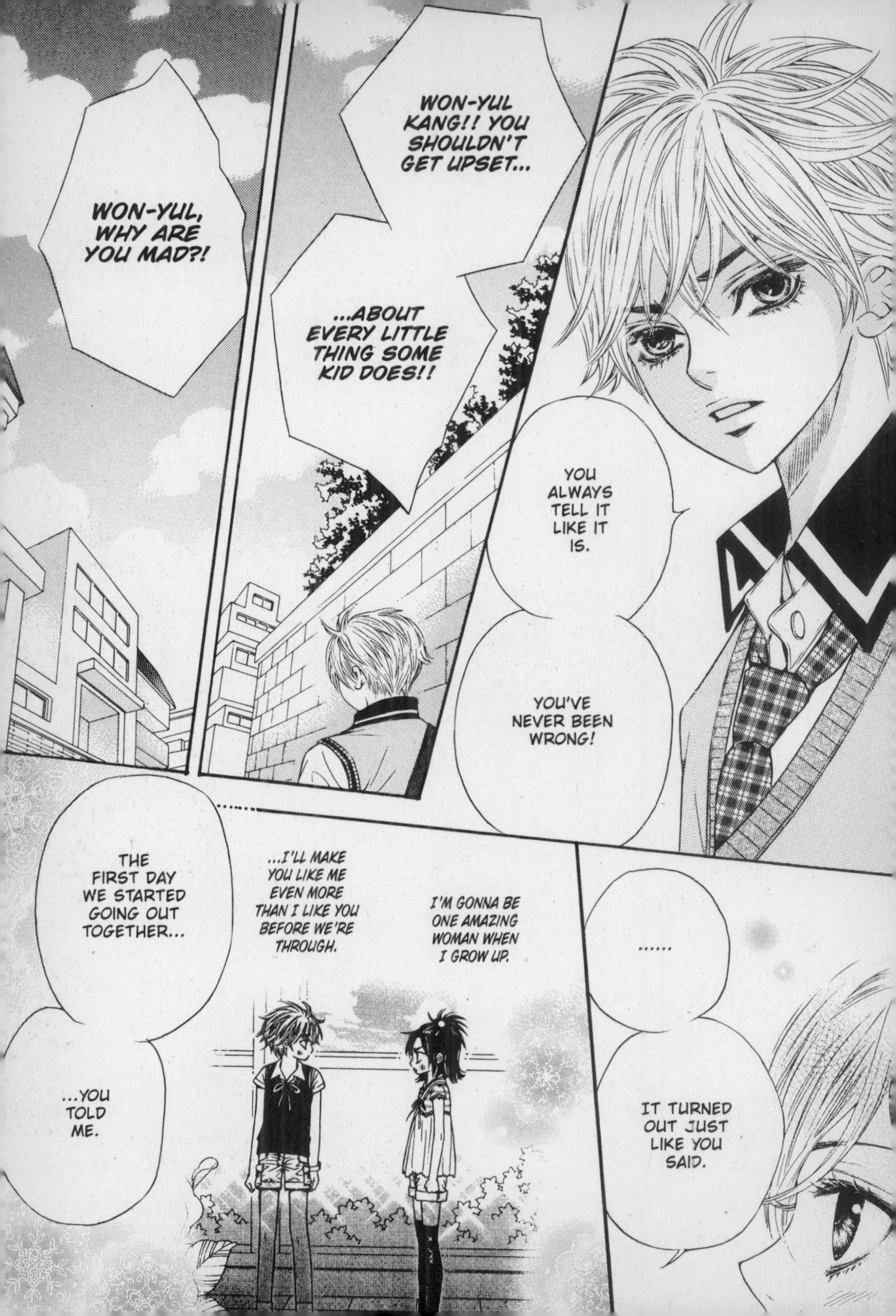
WON-YUL, WHY ARE YOU MAD?!
WON-YUL KANG!! YOU SHOULDN'T GET UPSET...
...ABOUT EVERY LITTLE THING SOME KID DOES!!
YOU ALWAYS TELL IT LIKE IT IS.
YOU'VE NEVER BEEN WRONG!
THE FIRST DAY WE STARTED GOING OUT TOGETHER...
...I'LL MAKE YOU LIKE ME EVEN MORE THAN I LIKE YOU BEFORE WE'RE THROUGH.
I'M GONNA BE ONE AMAZING WOMAN WHEN I GROW UP.
...YOU TOLD ME.
......
IT TURNED OUT JUST LIKE YOU SAID.

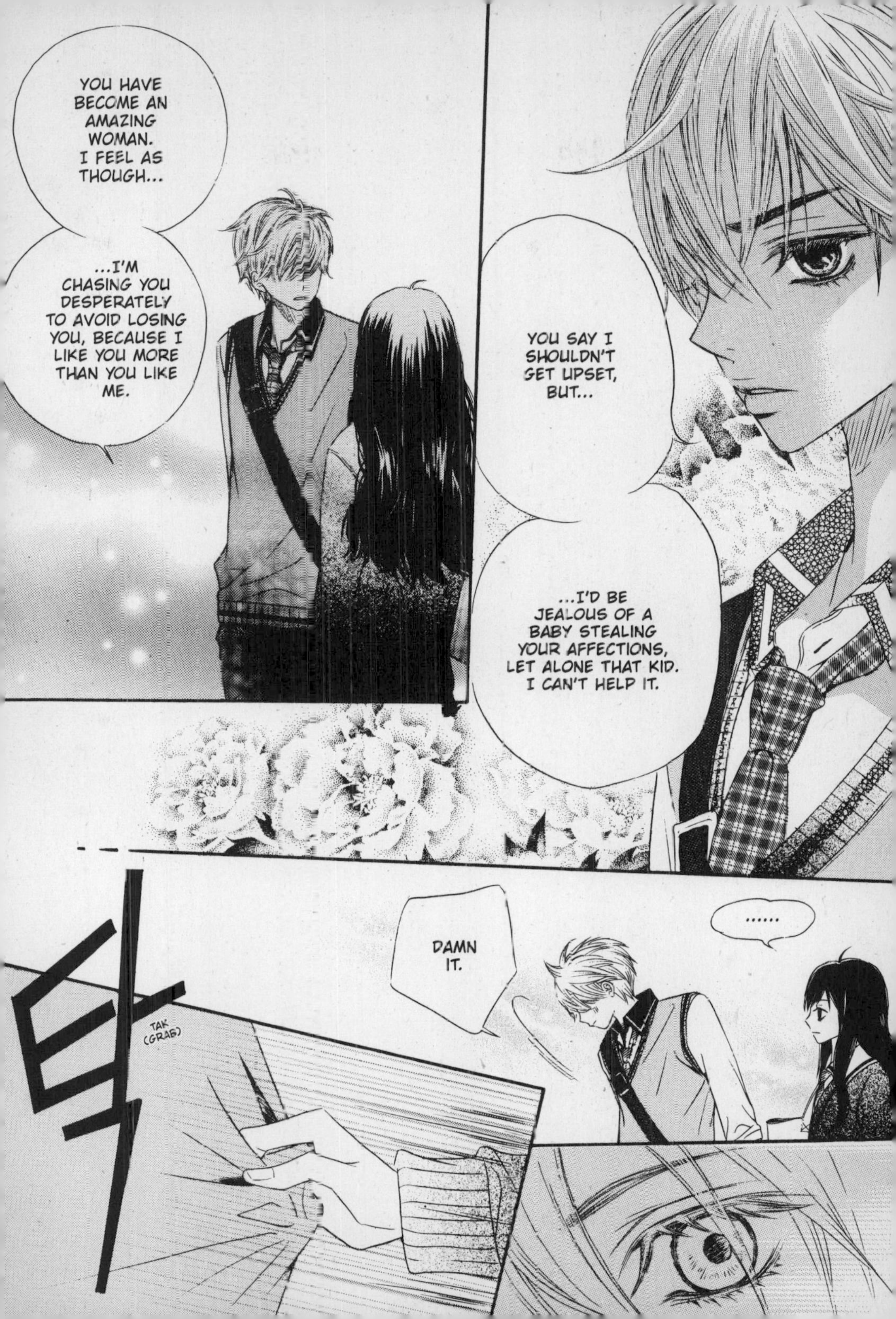
YOU SAY I SHOULDN'T GET UPSET, BUT...
...I'D BE JEALOUS OF A BABY STEALING YOUR AFFECTIONS, LET ALONE THAT KID. I CAN'T HELP IT.
YOU HAVE BECOME AN AMAZING WOMAN. I FEEL AS THOUGH...
...I'M CHASING YOU DESPERATELY TO AVOID LOSING YOU, BECAUSE I LIKE YOU MORE THAN YOU LIKE ME.
......
DAMN IT.
TAK (GRAB)

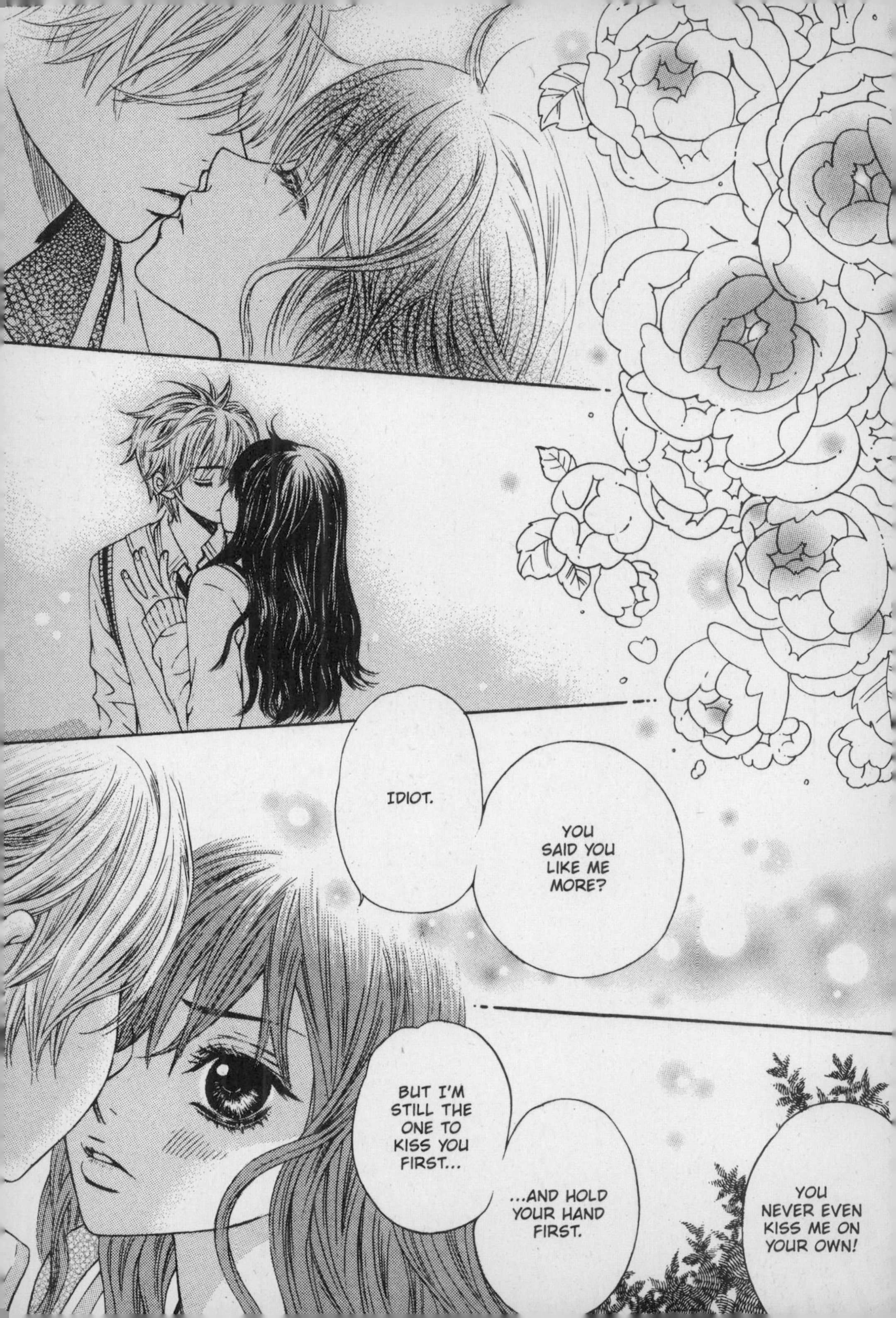
IDIOT.
YOU SAID YOU LIKE ME MORE?
BUT I'M STILL THE ONE TO KISS YOU FIRST...
...AND HOLD YOUR HAND FIRST.
YOU NEVER EVEN KISS ME ON YOUR OWN!

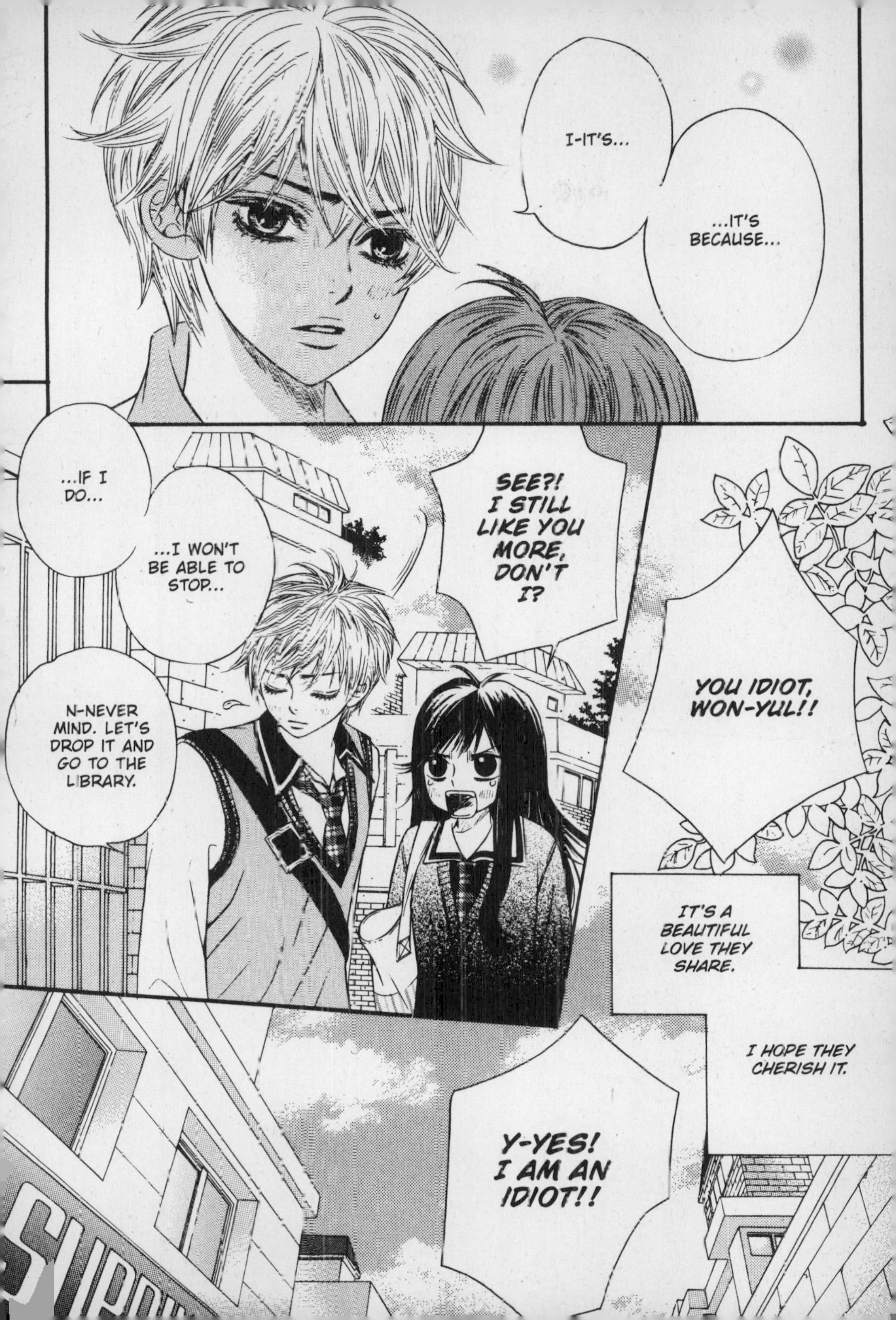
I-IT'S...
...IT'S BECAUSE...
...IF I DO...
...I WON'T BE ABLE TO STOP...
N-NEVER MIND. LET'S DROP IT AND GO TO THE LIBRARY.
SEE?! I STILL LIKE YOU MORE, DON'T I?
YOU IDIOT, WON-YUL!!
IT'S A BEAUTIFUL LOVE THEY SHARE.
Y-YES! I AM AN IDIOT!!
I HOPE THEY CHERISH IT.

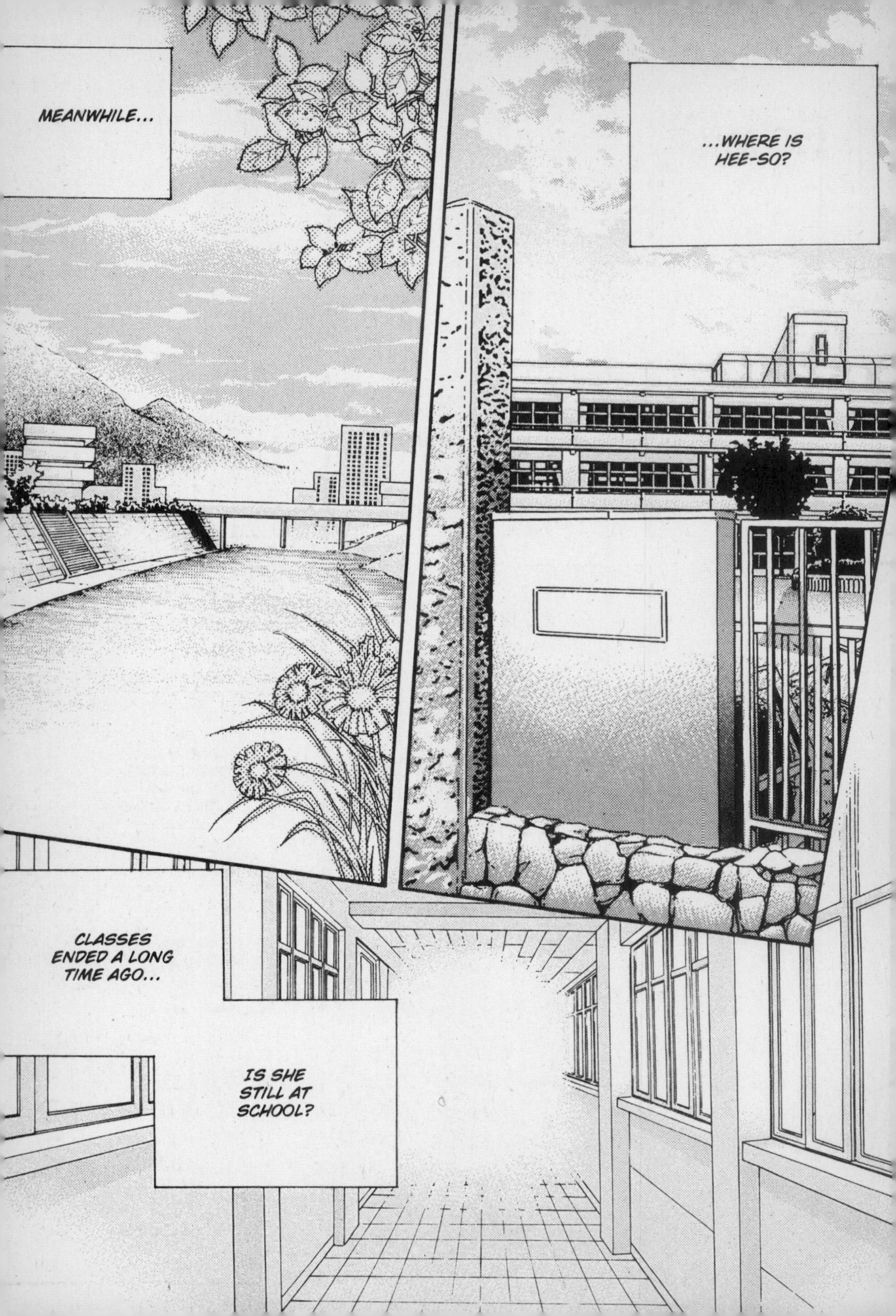
MEANWHILE...
...WHERE IS HEE-SO?
CLASSES ENDED A LONG TIME AGO...
IS SHE STILL AT SCHOOL?

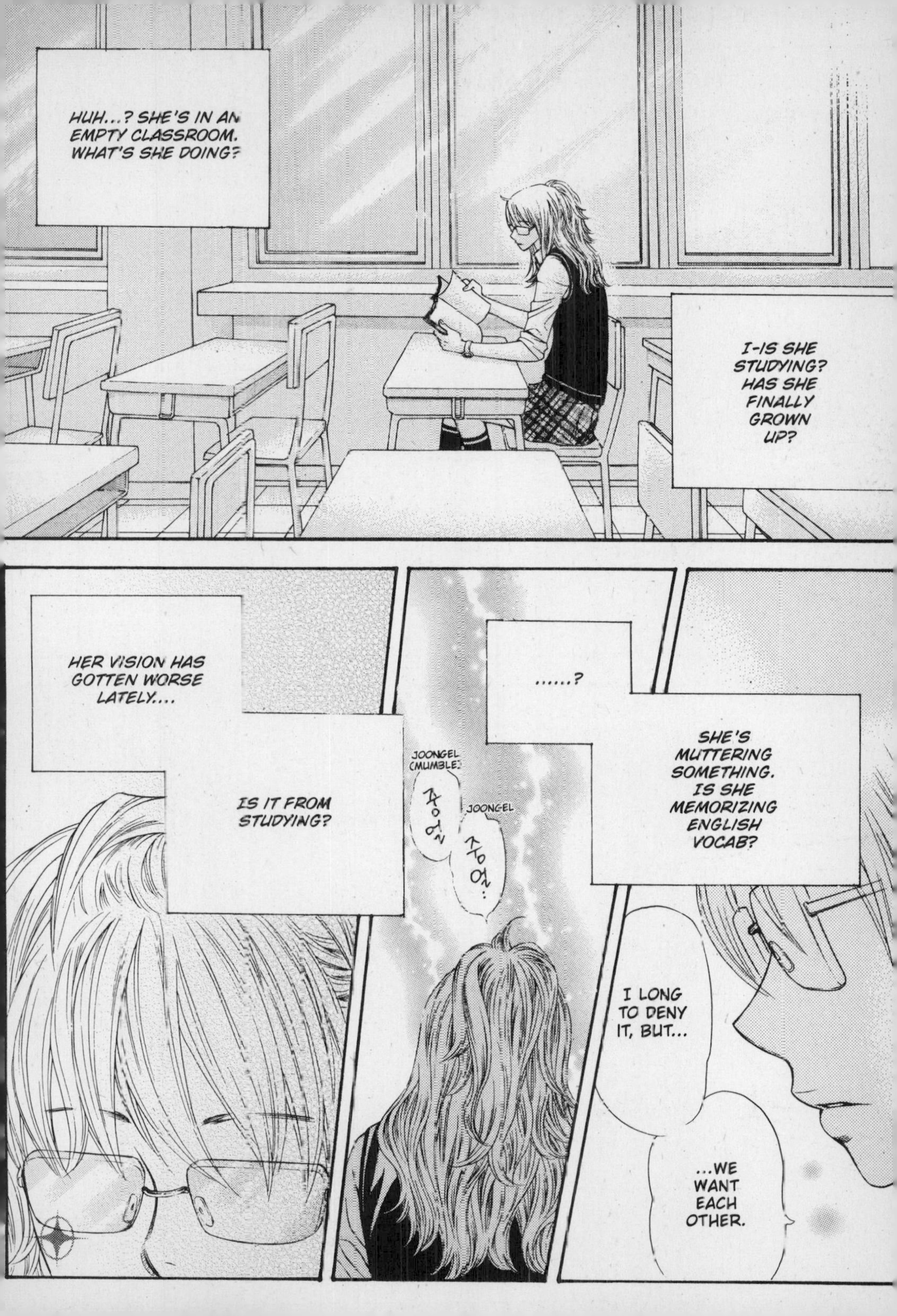
HUH...? SHE'S IN AN EMPTY CLASSROOM. WHAT'S SHE DOING?
I-IS SHE STUDYING? HAS SHE FINALLY GROWN UP?
HER VISION HAS GOTTEN WORSE LATELY....
IS IT FROM STUDYING?
JOONGEL (MUMBLE)
중얼
JOONGEL
중얼..
......?
SHE'S MUTTERING SOMETHING. IS SHE MEMORIZING ENGLISH VOCAB?
I LONG TO DENY IT, BUT...
...WE WANT EACH OTHER.

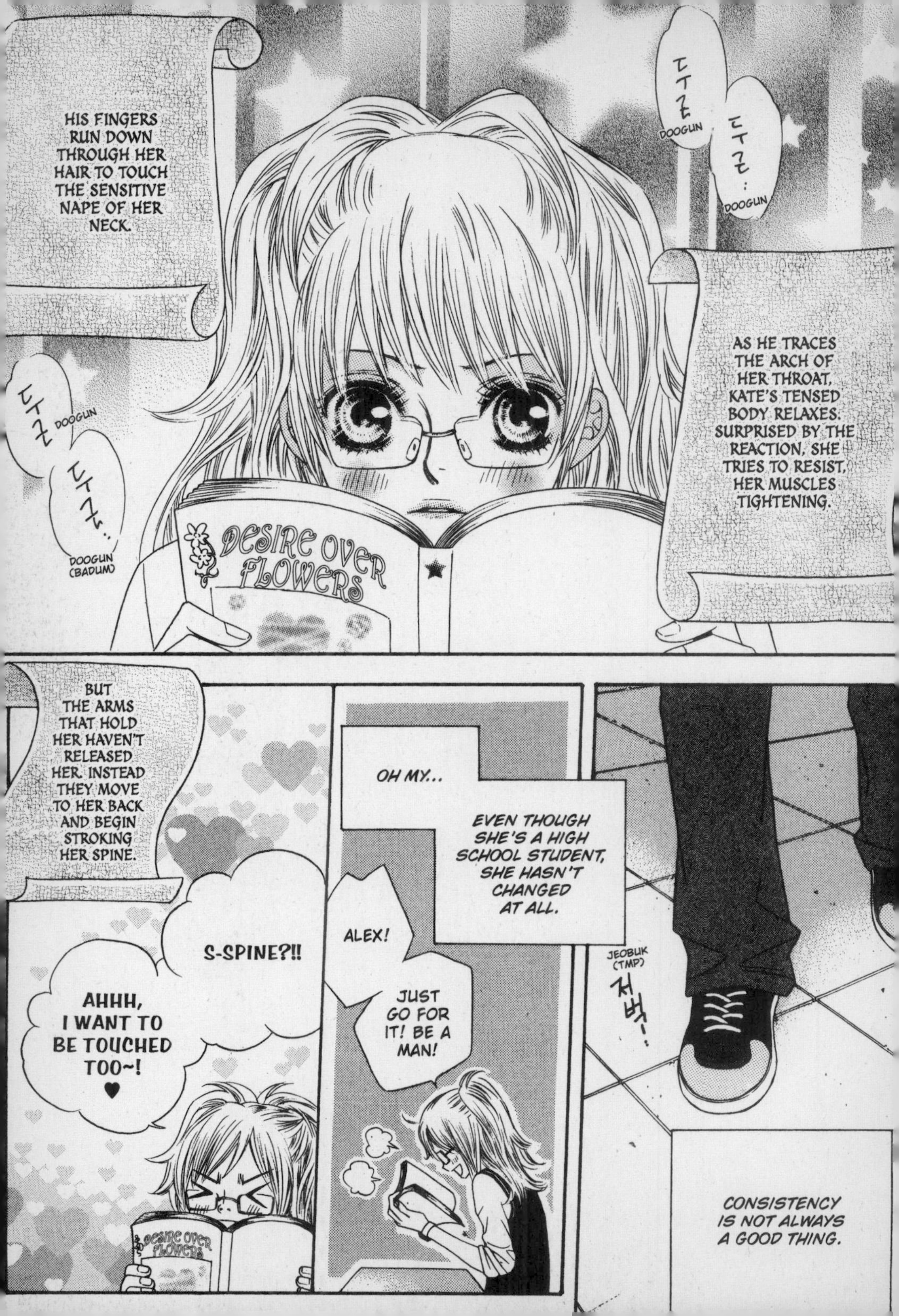
HIS FINGERS RUN DOWN THROUGH HER HAIR TO TOUCH THE SENSITIVE NAPE OF HER NECK.
두근
DOOGUN
두근..
DOOGUN
두근
DOOGUN
두근..
DOOGUN (BADUM)
DESIRE OVER FLOWERS
AS HE TRACES THE ARCH OF HER THROAT, KATE'S TENSED BODY RELAXES. SURPRISED BY THE REACTION, SHE TRIES TO RESIST, HER MUSCLES TIGHTENING.
BUT THE ARMS THAT HOLD HER HAVEN'T RELEASED HER. INSTEAD THEY MOVE TO HER BACK AND BEGIN STROKING HER SPINE.
S-SPINE?!!
AHHH, I WANT TO BE TOUCHED TOO~! ♥
DESIRE OVER FLOWERS
OH MY...
EVEN THOUGH SHE'S A HIGH SCHOOL STUDENT, SHE HASN'T CHANGED AT ALL.
ALEX!
JUST GO FOR IT! BE A MAN!
JEOBUK (TMP)
저벅
CONSISTENCY IS NOT ALWAYS A GOOD THING.

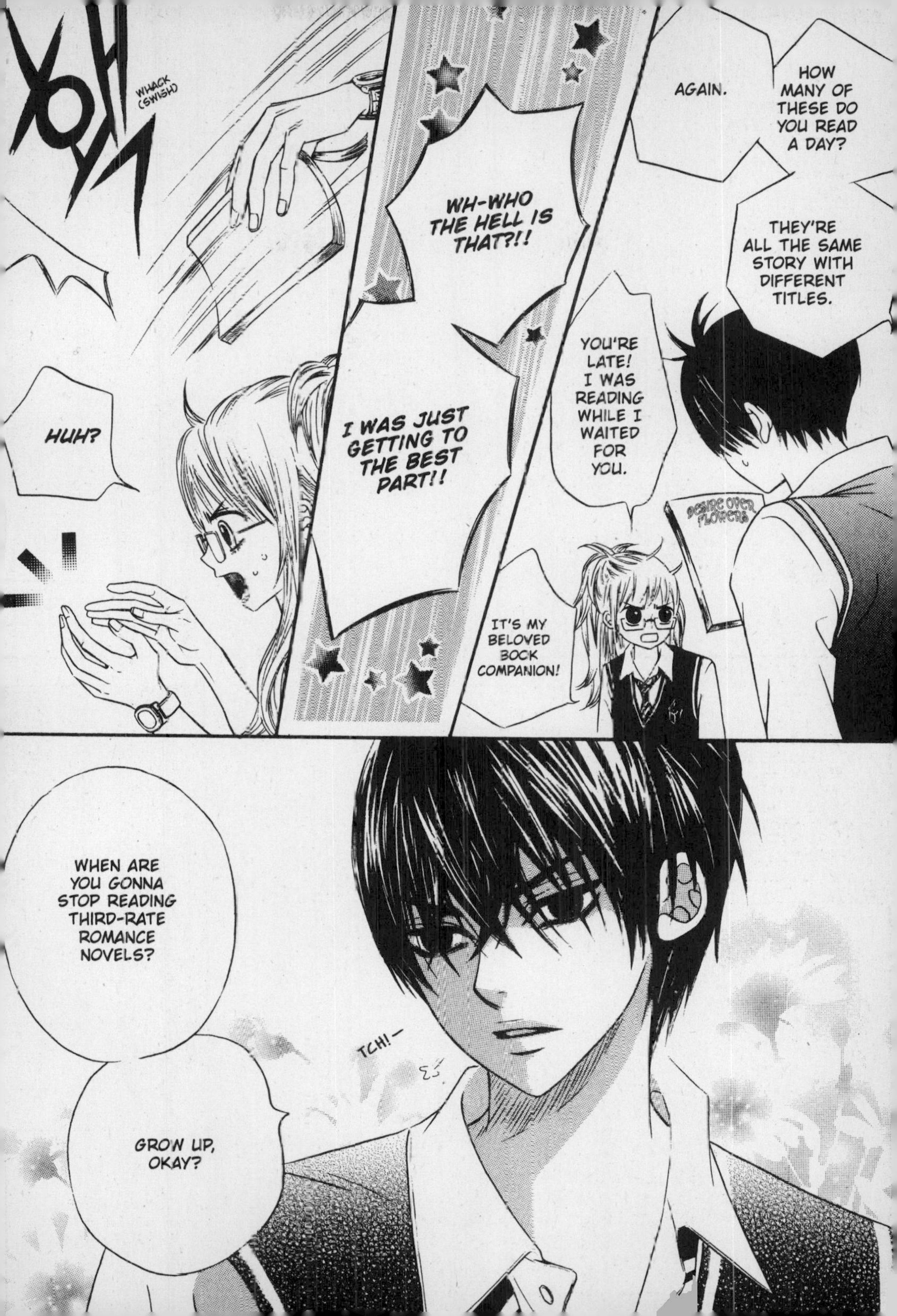

WHACK (SWISH)
HUH?
WH-WHO THE HELL IS THAT?!!
I WAS JUST GETTING TO THE BEST PART!!
AGAIN.
HOW MANY OF THESE DO YOU READ A DAY?
THEY'RE ALL THE SAME STORY WITH DIFFERENT TITLES.
YOU'RE LATE! I WAS READING WHILE I WAITED FOR YOU.
DESIRE OVER FLOWERS
IT'S MY BELOVED BOOK COMPANION!
WHEN ARE YOU GONNA STOP READING THIRD-RATE ROMANCE NOVELS?
TCH!
GROW UP, OKAY?

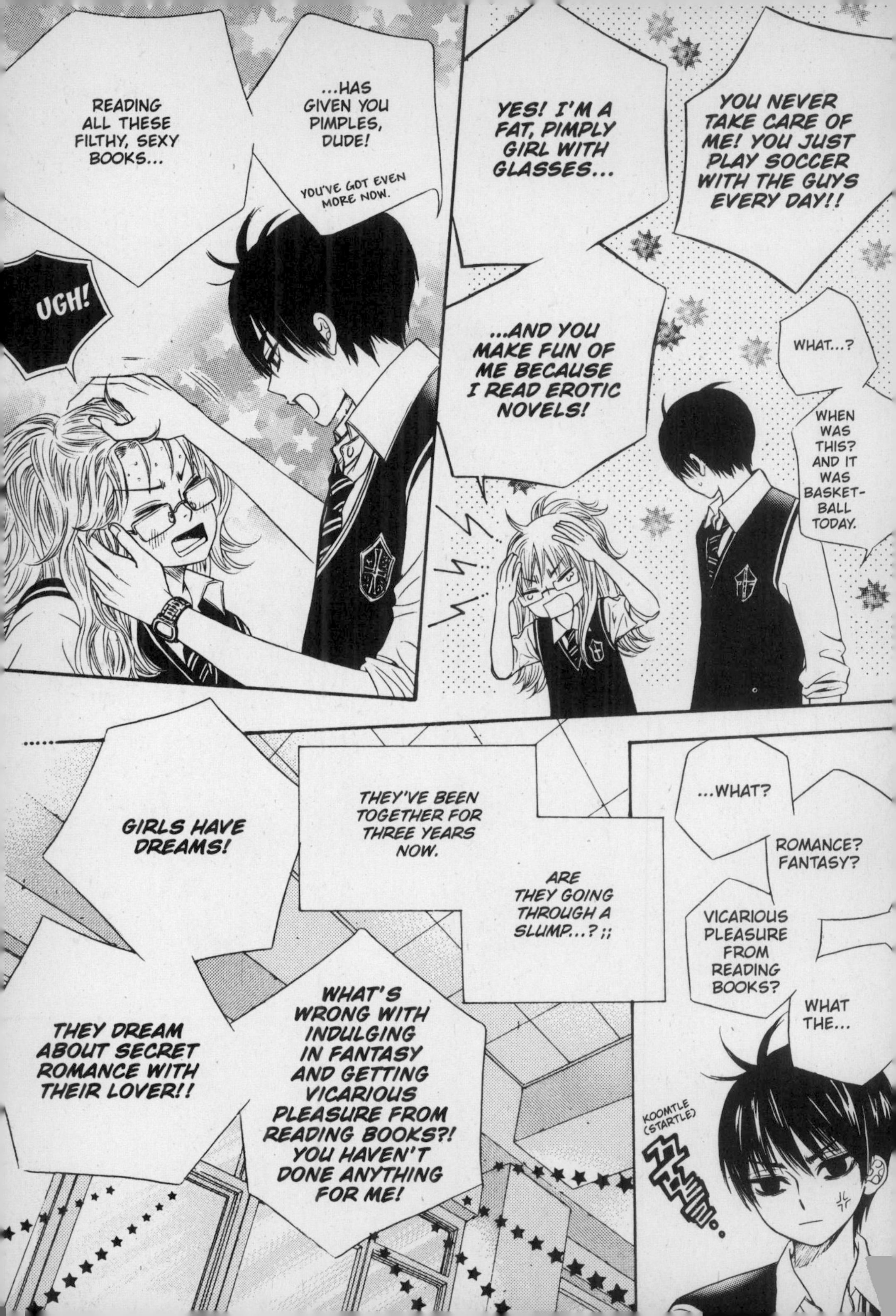

READING ALL THESE FILTHY, SEXY BOOKS...
...HAS GIVEN YOU PIMPLES, DUDE!
YOU'VE GOT EVEN MORE NOW.
UGH!
YES! I'M A FAT, PIMPLY GIRL WITH GLASSES...
YOU NEVER TAKE CARE OF ME! YOU JUST PLAY SOCCER WITH THE GUYS EVERY DAY!!
...AND YOU MAKE FUN OF ME BECAUSE I READ EROTIC NOVELS!
WHAT...?
WHEN WAS THIS? AND IT WAS BASKET-BALL TODAY.
......
GIRLS HAVE DREAMS!
THEY DREAM ABOUT SECRET ROMANCE WITH THEIR LOVER!!
WHAT'S WRONG WITH INDULGING IN FANTASY AND GETTING VICARIOUS PLEASURE FROM READING BOOKS?! YOU HAVEN'T DONE ANYTHING FOR ME!
THEY'VE BEEN TOGETHER FOR THREE YEARS NOW.
ARE THEY GOING THROUGH A SLUMP...? ;;
...WHAT?
ROMANCE? FANTASY?
VICARIOUS PLEASURE FROM READING BOOKS?
WHAT THE...
KOOMTLE (STARTLE)

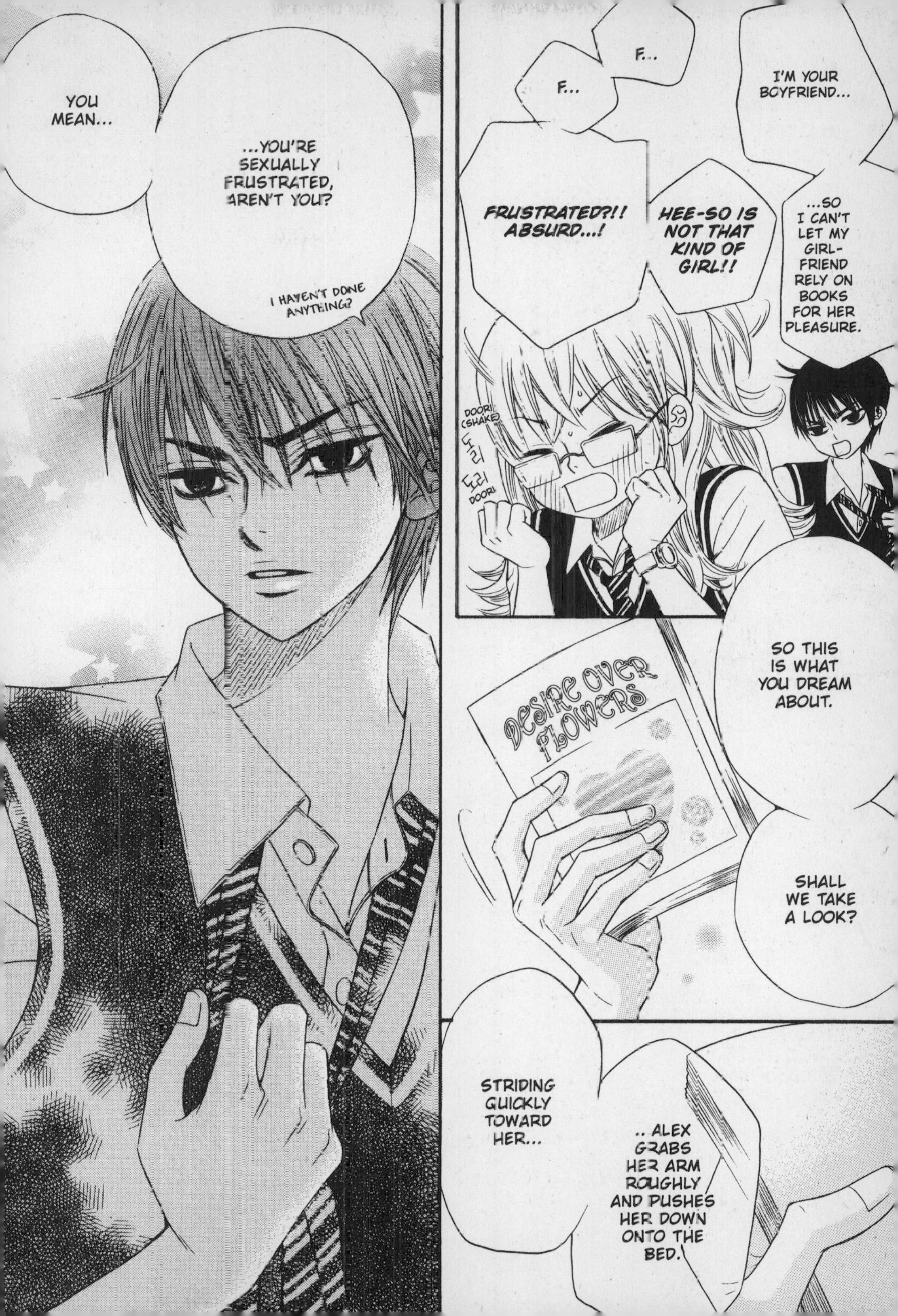
YOU MEAN...
...YOU'RE SEXUALLY FRUSTRATED, AREN'T YOU?
I HAVEN'T DONE ANYTHING?
F...
F...
I'M YOUR BOYFRIEND...
FRUSTRATED?!! ABSURD...!
HEE-SO IS NOT THAT KIND OF GIRL!!
...SO I CAN'T LET MY GIRL-FRIEND RELY ON BOOKS FOR HER PLEASURE.
DOORI (SHAKE)
DOORI
DESIRE OVER FLOWERS
SO THIS IS WHAT YOU DREAM ABOUT.
SHALL WE TAKE A LOOK?
STRIDING QUICKLY TOWARD HER...
.. ALEX GRABS HER ARM ROUGHLY AND PUSHES HER DOWN ONTO THE BED.

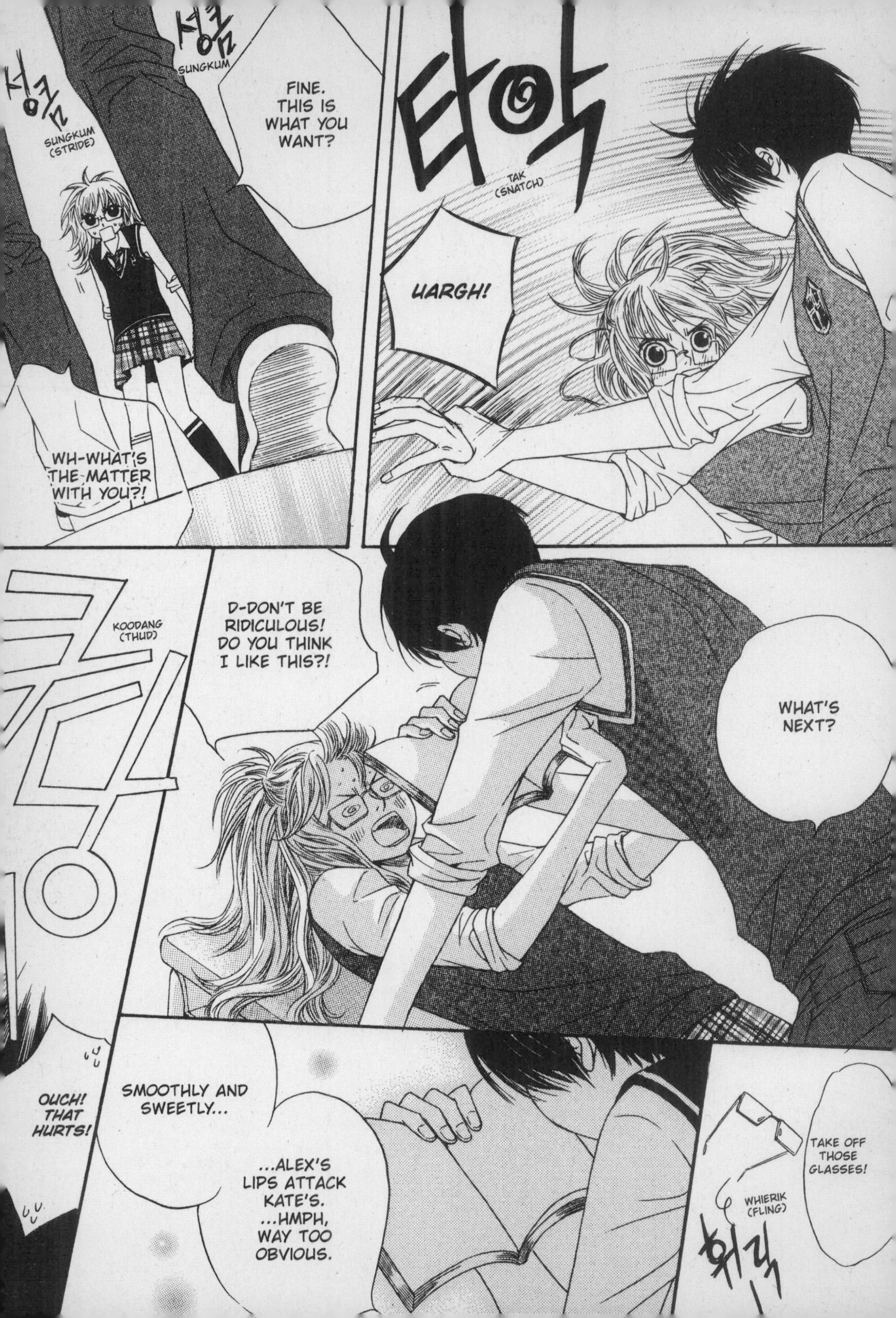
SUNGKUM
SUNGKUM (STRIDE)
FINE. THIS IS WHAT YOU WANT?
WH-WHAT'S THE MATTER WITH YOU?!
TAK (SNATCH)
UARGH!
KOODANG (THUD)
D-DON'T BE RIDICULOUS! DO YOU THINK I LIKE THIS?!
WHAT'S NEXT?
OUCH! THAT HURTS!
SMOOTHLY AND SWEETLY...
...ALEX'S LIPS ATTACK KATE'S. ...HMPH, WAY TOO OBVIOUS.
TAKE OFF THOSE GLASSES!
WHIERIK (FLING)

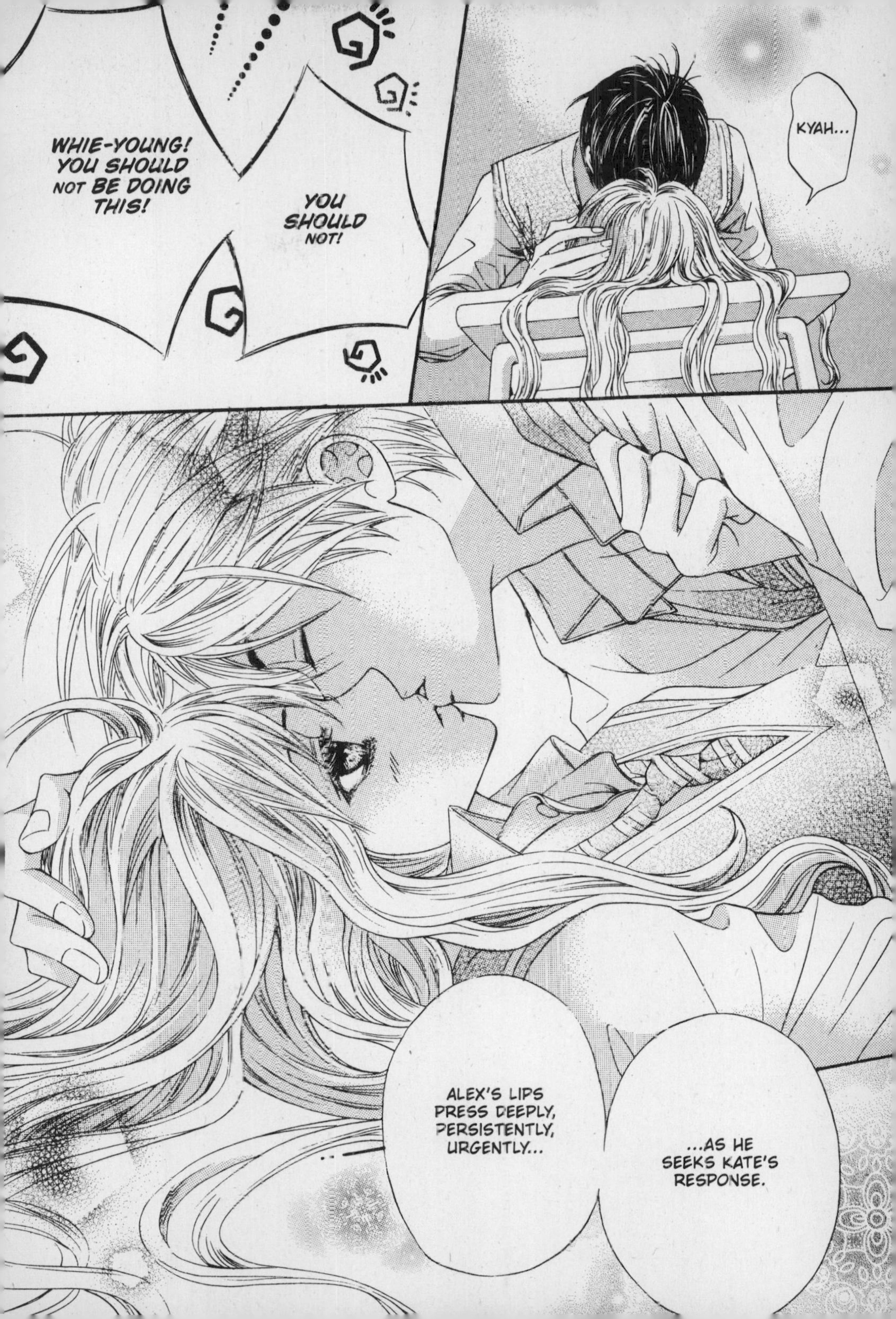
WHIE-YOUNG! YOU SHOULD NOT BE DOING THIS!
YOU SHOULD NOT!
KYAH...
ALEX'S LIPS PRESS DEEPLY, PERSISTENTLY, URGENTLY...
...AS HE SEEKS KATE'S RESPONSE.

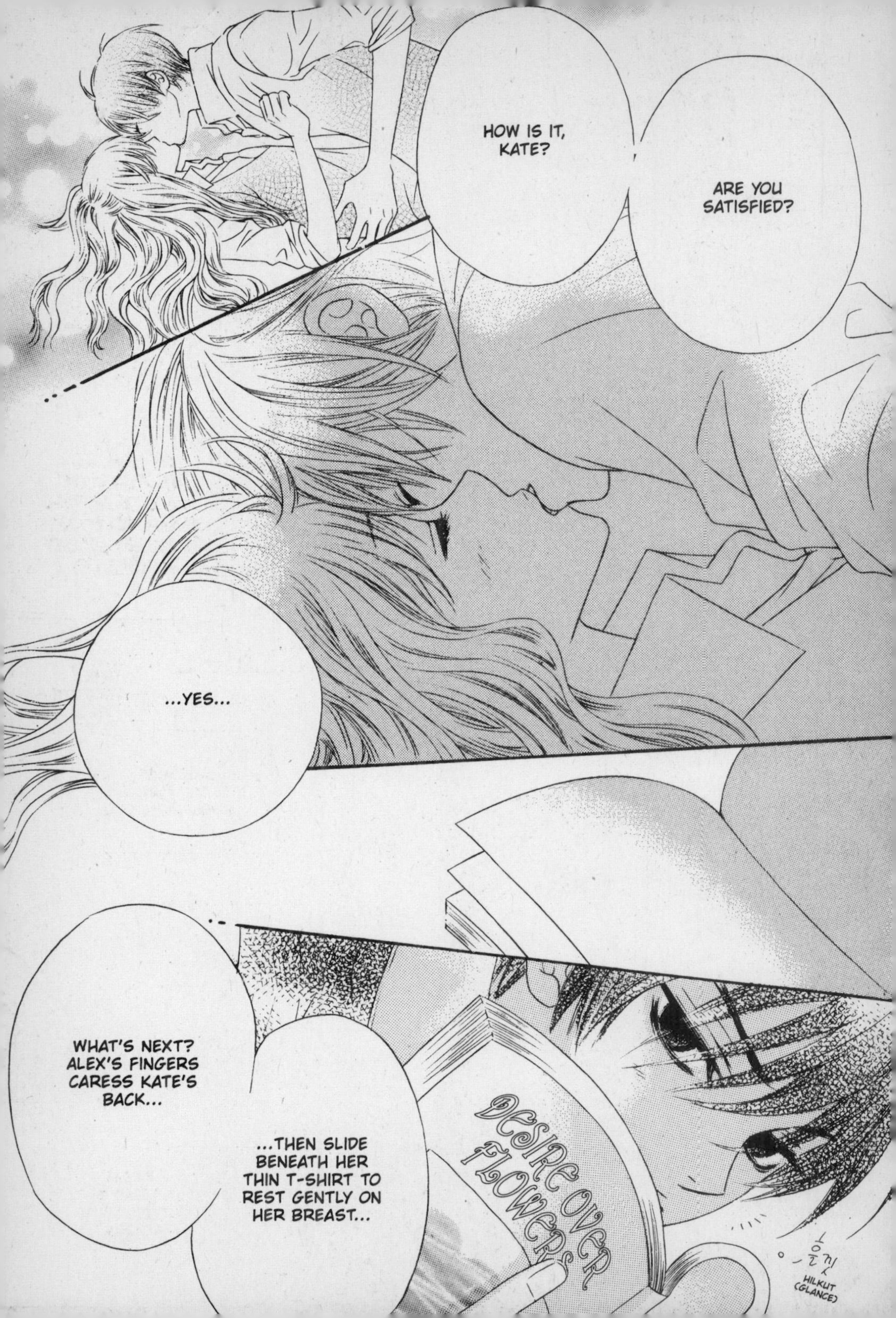
HOW IS IT, KATE?
ARE YOU SATISFIED?
...YES...
WHAT'S NEXT? ALEX'S FINGERS CARESS KATE'S BACK...
...THEN SLIDE BENEATH HER THIN T-SHIRT TO REST GENTLY ON HER BREAST...
DESIRE OVER FLOWERS
힐끗
HILKUT (GLANCE)

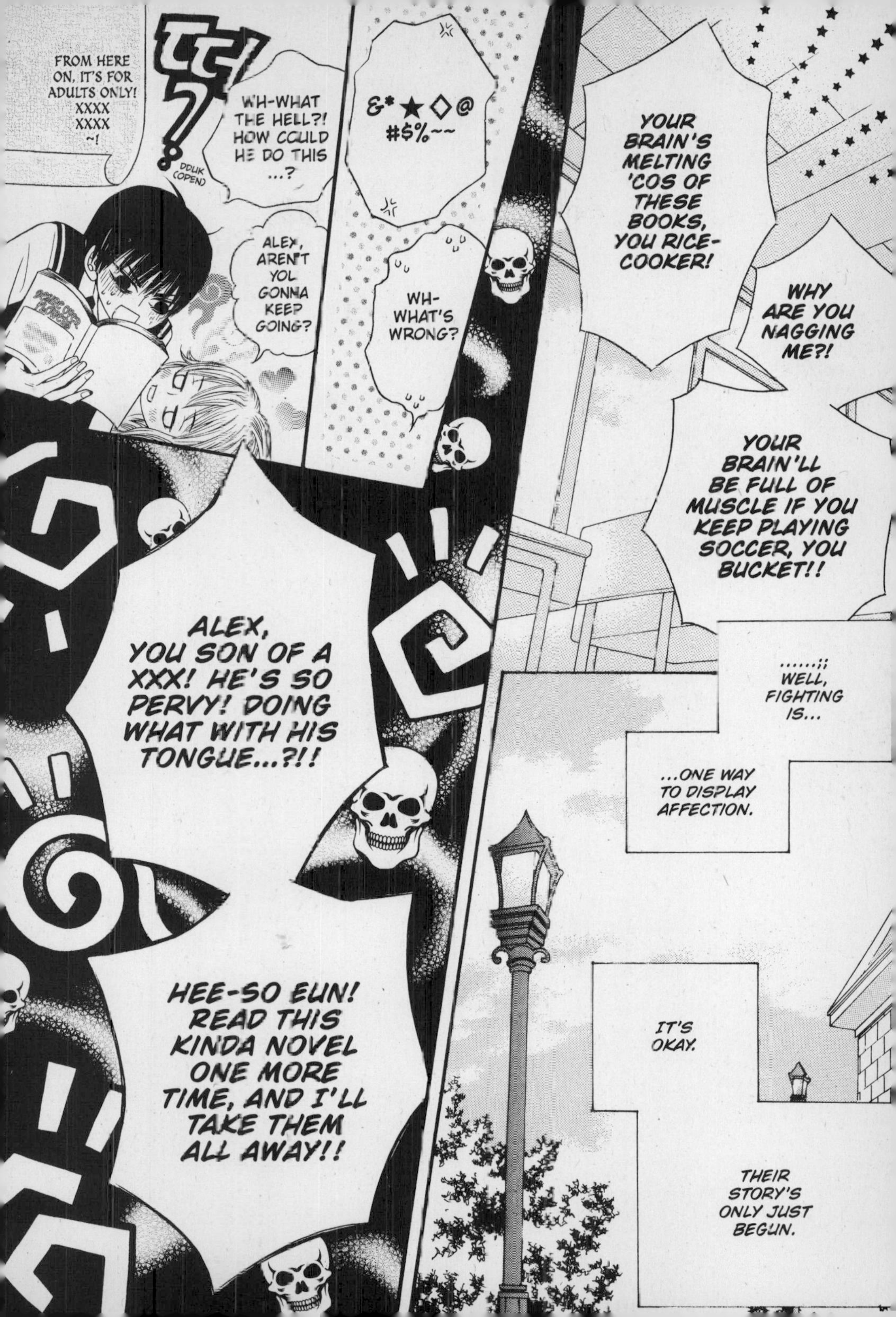
FROM HERE ON, IT'S FOR ADULTS ONLY! XXXX XXXX ~!
DDUK (OPEN)
WH-WHAT THE HELL?! HOW COULD HE DO THIS ...?
ALEX, AREN'T YOU GONNA KEEP GOING?
&*★◇@ #$%~~
WH-WHAT'S WRONG?
ALEX, YOU SON OF A XXX! HE'S SO PERVY! DOING WHAT WITH HIS TONGUE...?!!
HEE-SO EUN! READ THIS KINDA NOVEL ONE MORE TIME, AND I'LL TAKE THEM ALL AWAY!!
YOUR BRAIN'S MELTING 'COS OF THESE BOOKS, YOU RICE-COOKER!
WHY ARE YOU NAGGING ME?!
YOUR BRAIN'LL BE FULL OF MUSCLE IF YOU KEEP PLAYING SOCCER, YOU BUCKET!!
......;; WELL, FIGHTING IS...
...ONE WAY TO DISPLAY AFFECTION.
IT'S OKAY.
THEIR STORY'S ONLY JUST BEGUN.

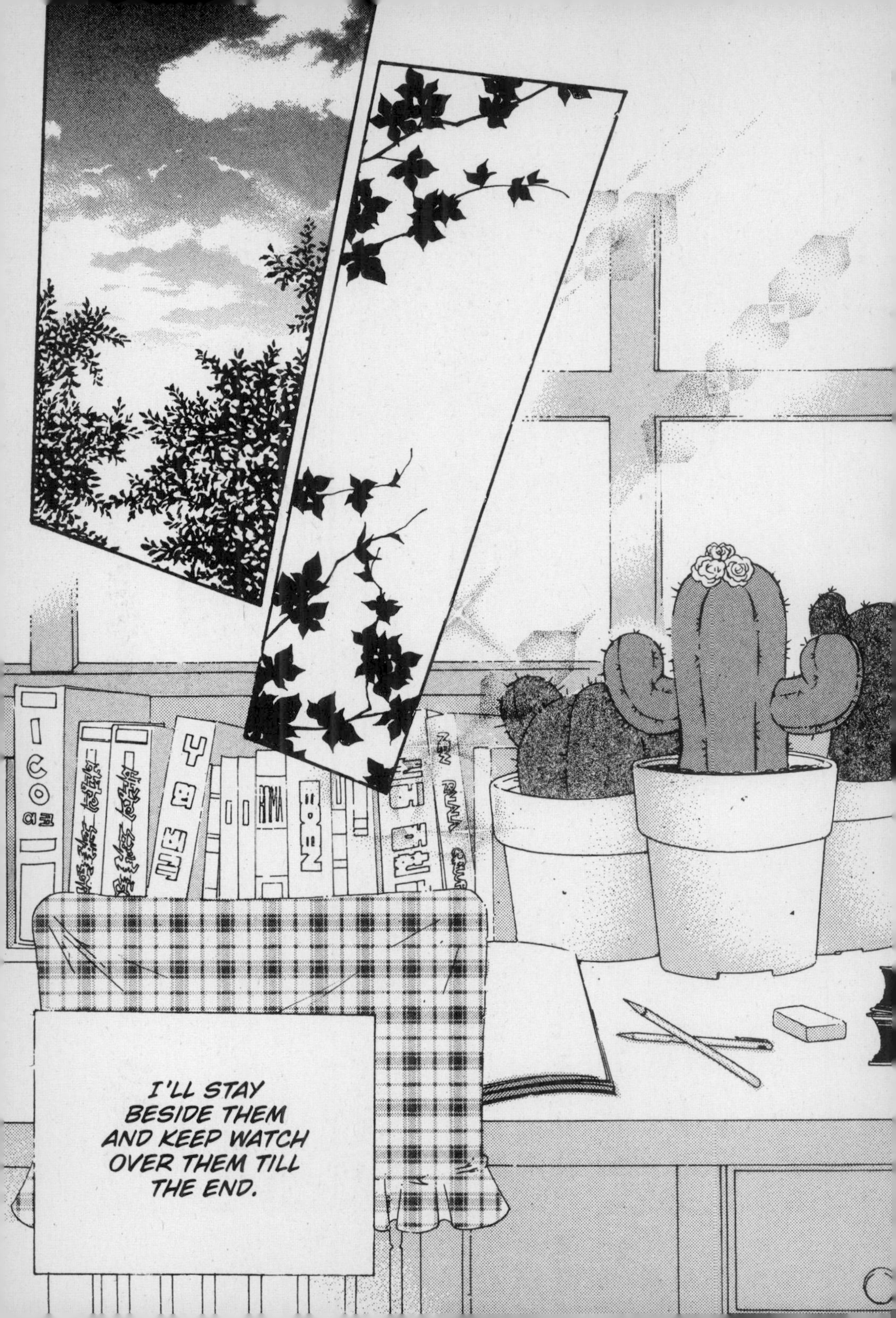
I'LL STAY BESIDE THEM AND KEEP WATCH OVER THEM TILL THE END.

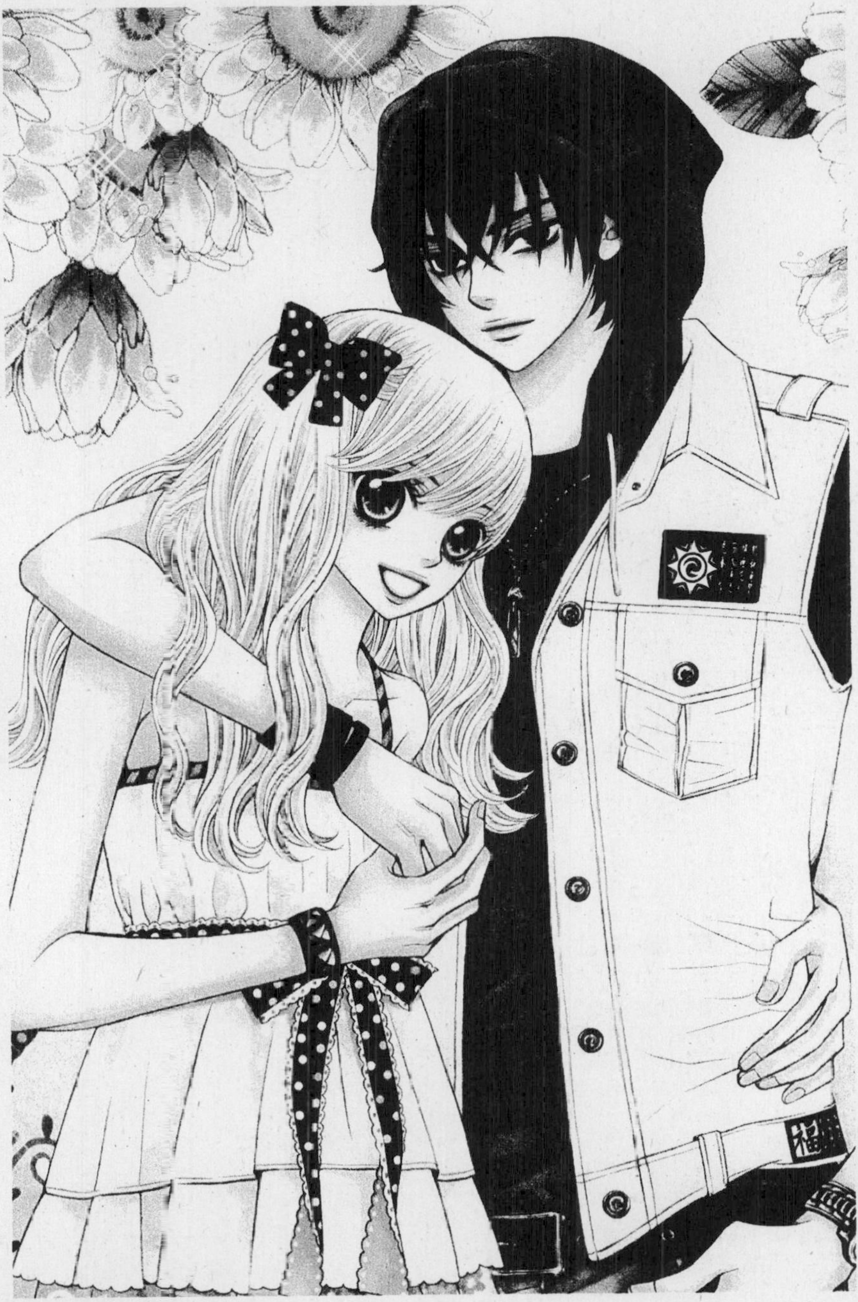

13th Boy

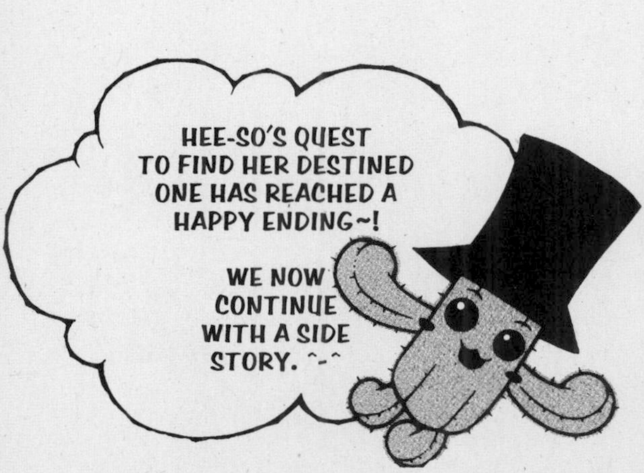
HEE-SO'S QUEST TO FIND HER DESTINED ONE HAS REACHED A HAPPY ENDING~!
WE NOW CONTINUE WITH A SIDE STORY. ^-^

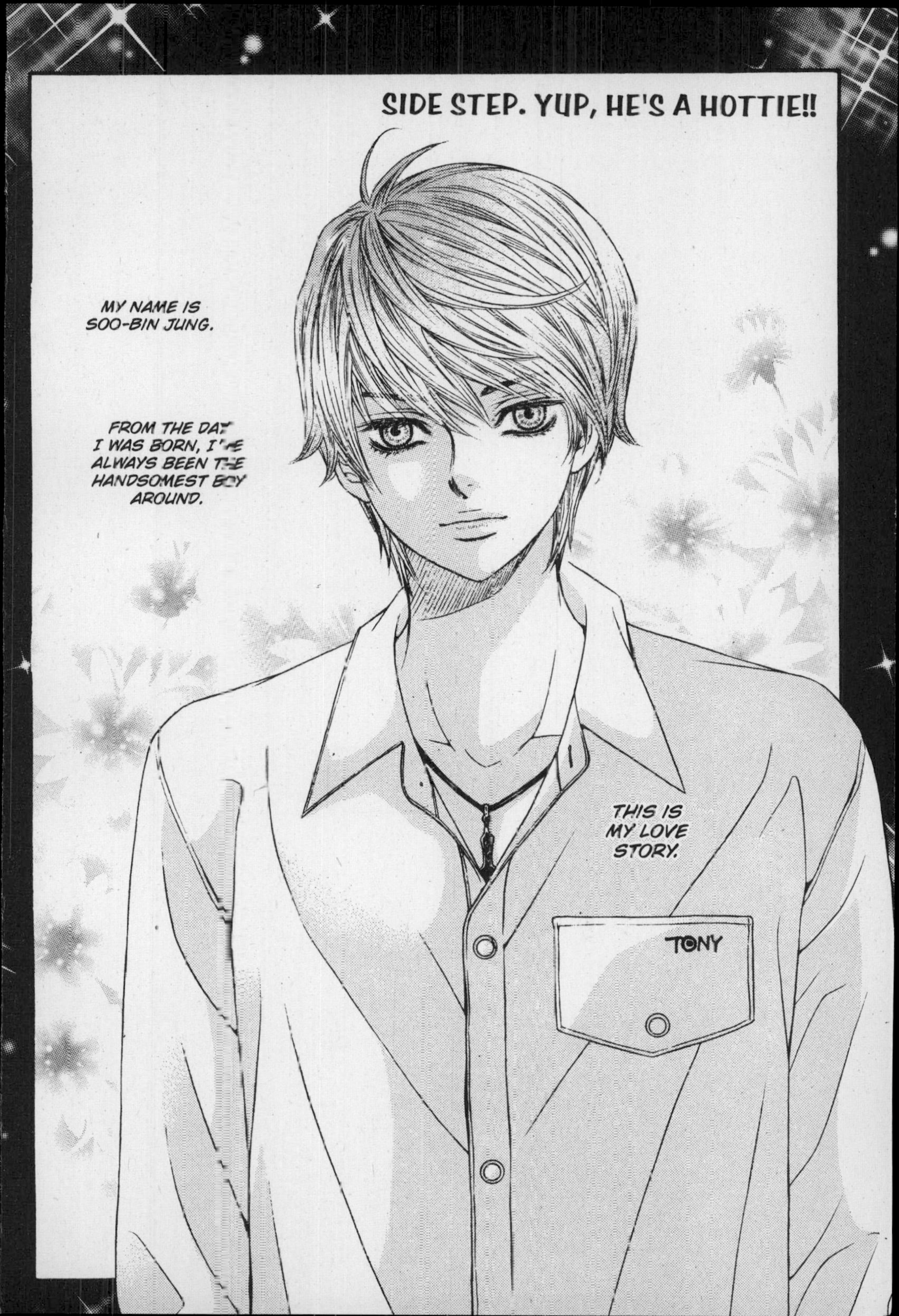
SIDE STEP. YUP, HE'S A HOTTIE!!
MY NAME IS SOO-BIN JUNG.
FROM THE DAY I WAS BORN, I'VE ALWAYS BEEN THE HANDSOMEST BOY AROUND.
THIS IS MY LOVE STORY.
TONY

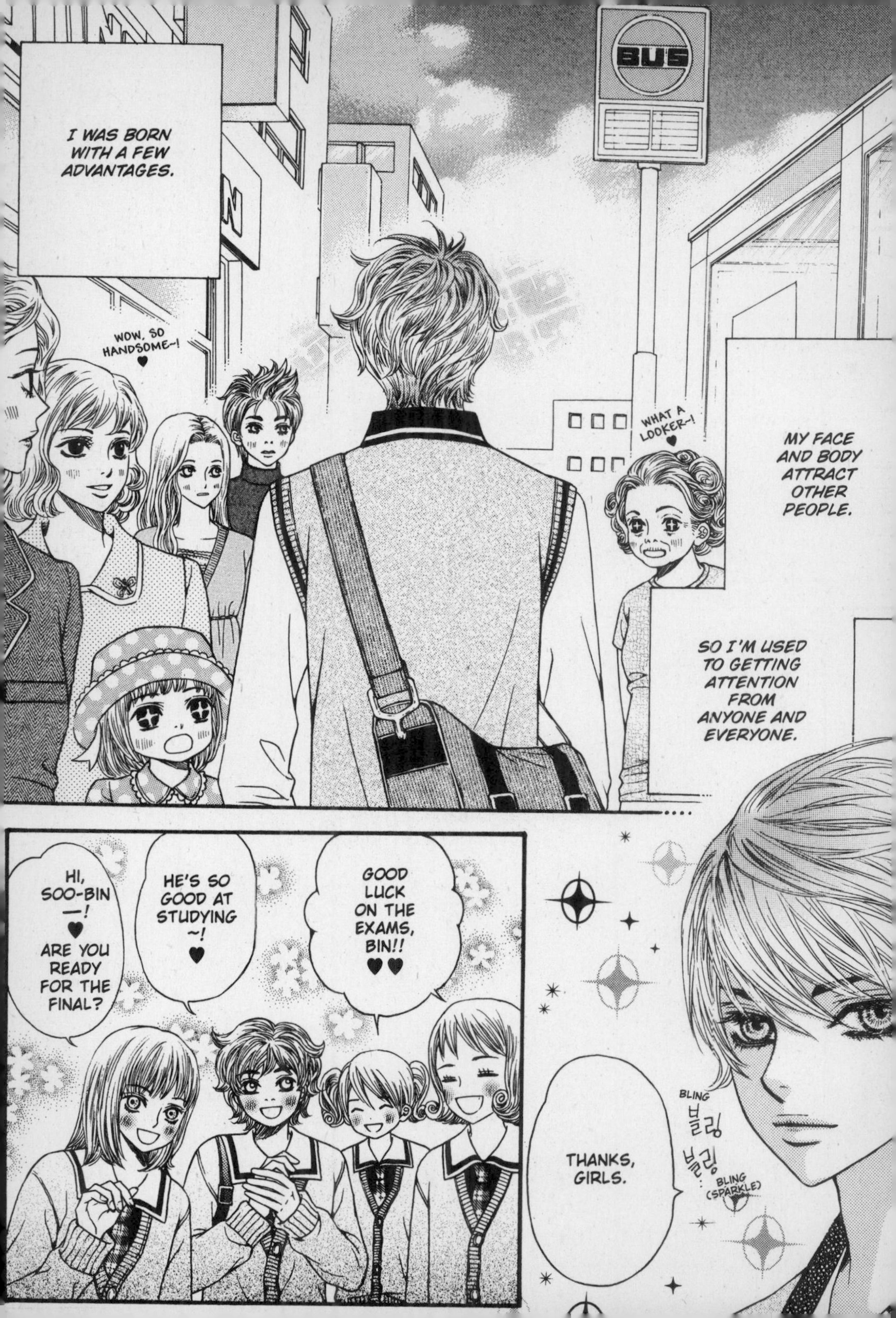

I WAS BORN WITH A FEW ADVANTAGES.
BUS
WOW, SO HANDSOME~! ♥
WHAT A LOOKER~! ♥
MY FACE AND BODY ATTRACT OTHER PEOPLE.
SO I'M USED TO GETTING ATTENTION FROM ANYONE AND EVERYONE.
HI, SOO-BIN—! ♥ ARE YOU READY FOR THE FINAL?
HE'S SO GOOD AT STUDYING~! ♥
GOOD LUCK ON THE EXAMS, BIN!! ♥♥
THANKS, GIRLS.
BLING
블링
블링
BLING (SPARKLE)

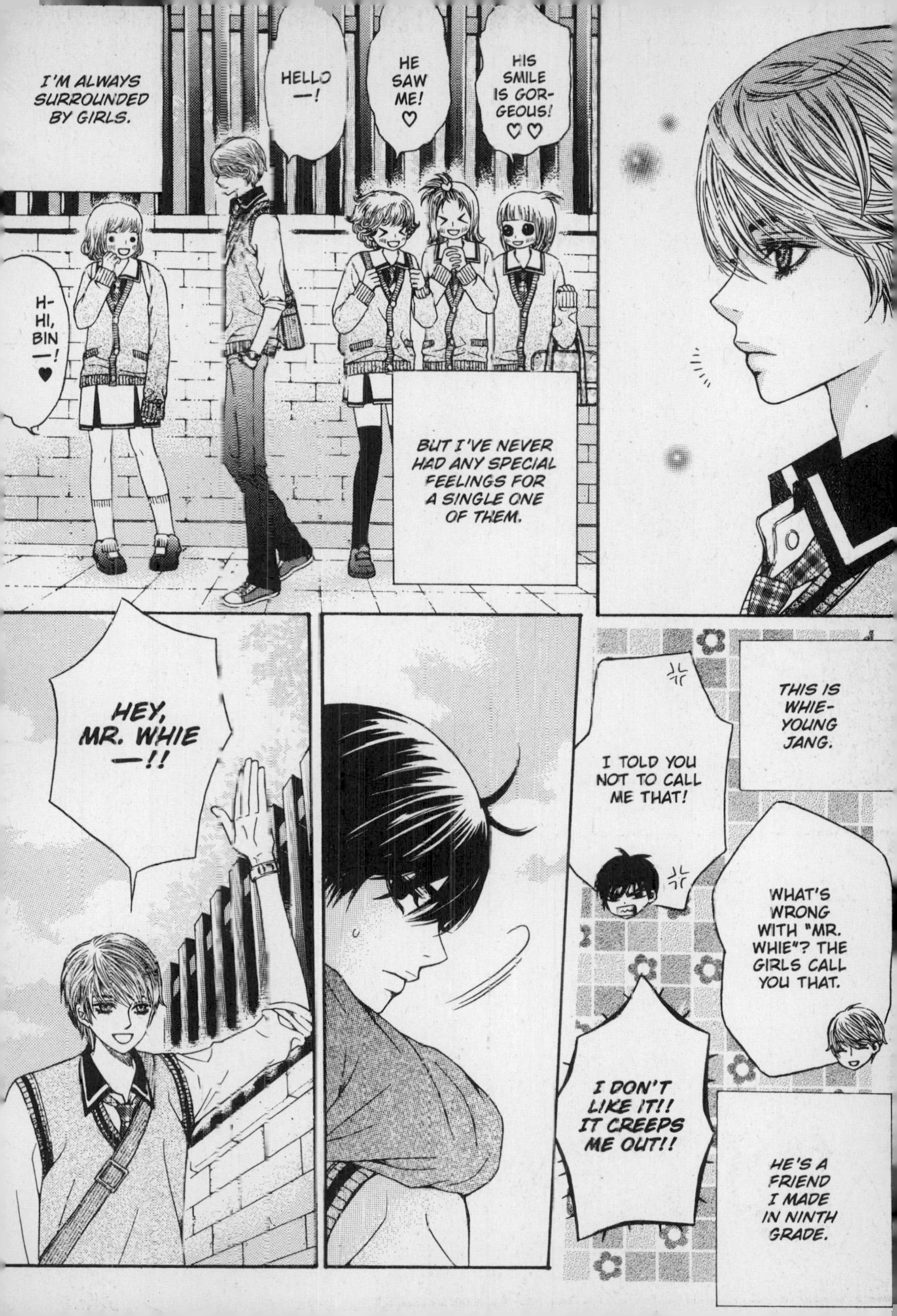
I'M ALWAYS SURROUNDED BY GIRLS.
HELLO—!
HE SAW ME! ♡
HIS SMILE IS GORGEOUS! ♡♡
H-HI, BIN—! ♥
BUT I'VE NEVER HAD ANY SPECIAL FEELINGS FOR A SINGLE ONE OF THEM.
HEY, MR. WHIE—!!
THIS IS WHIE-YOUNG JANG.
I TOLD YOU NOT TO CALL ME THAT!
WHAT'S WRONG WITH "MR. WHIE"? THE GIRLS CALL YOU THAT.
I DON'T LIKE IT!! IT CREEPS ME OUT!!
HE'S A FRIEND I MADE IN NINTH GRADE.

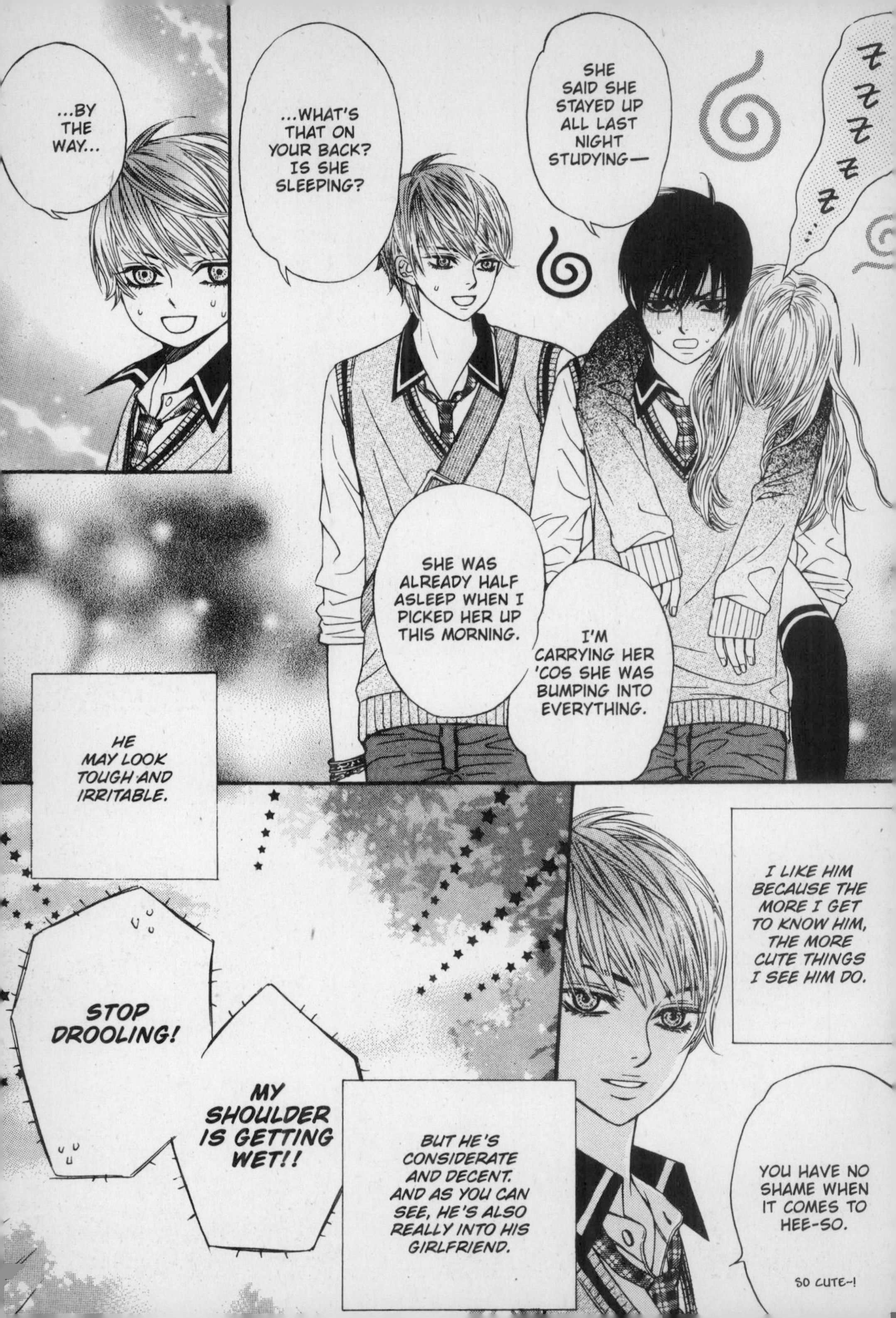
...BY THE WAY...
...WHAT'S THAT ON YOUR BACK? IS SHE SLEEPING?
SHE SAID SHE STAYED UP ALL LAST NIGHT STUDYING—
ZZZZZ...
SHE WAS ALREADY HALF ASLEEP WHEN I PICKED HER UP THIS MORNING.
I'M CARRYING HER 'COS SHE WAS BUMPING INTO EVERYTHING.
HE MAY LOOK TOUGH AND IRRITABLE.
STOP DROOLING!
MY SHOULDER IS GETTING WET!!
BUT HE'S CONSIDERATE AND DECENT. AND AS YOU CAN SEE, HE'S ALSO REALLY INTO HIS GIRLFRIEND.
I LIKE HIM BECAUSE THE MORE I GET TO KNOW HIM, THE MORE CUTE THINGS I SEE HIM DO.
YOU HAVE NO SHAME WHEN IT COMES TO HEE-SO.
SO CUTE~!

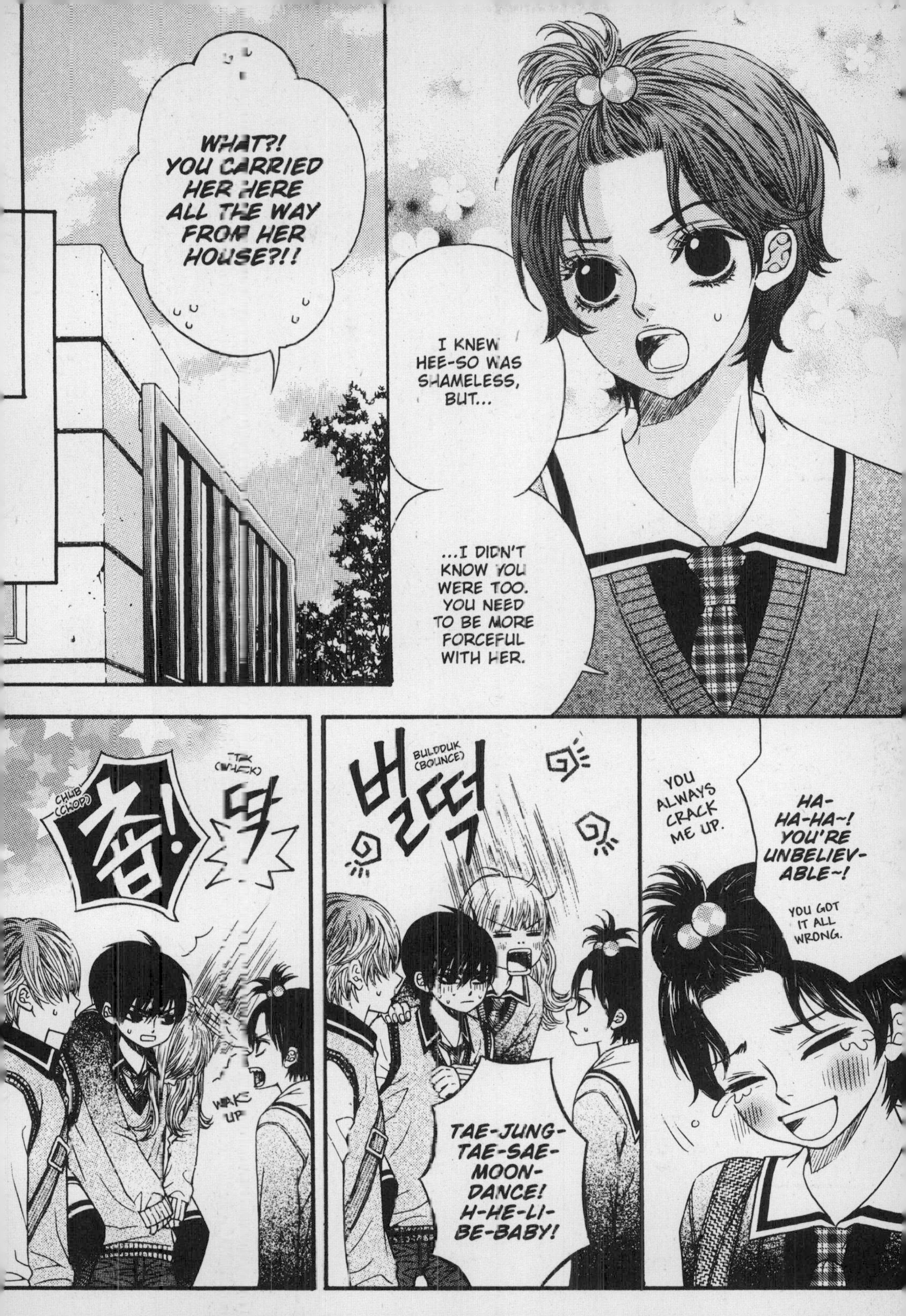
WHAT?! YOU CARRIED HER HERE ALL THE WAY FROM HER HOUSE?!!
I KNEW HEE-SO WAS SHAMELESS, BUT...
...I DIDN'T KNOW YOU WERE TOO. YOU NEED TO BE MORE FORCEFUL WITH HER.
CHUB (CHOP)
촙!
TTAK (WHACK)
딱
WAKE UP
BULDDUK (BOUNCE)
벌떡
TAE-JUNG-TAE-SAE-MOON-DANCE! H-HE-LI-BE-BABY!
YOU ALWAYS CRACK ME UP.
HA-HA-HA~! YOU'RE UNBELIEV-ABLE~!
YOU GOT IT ALL WRONG.

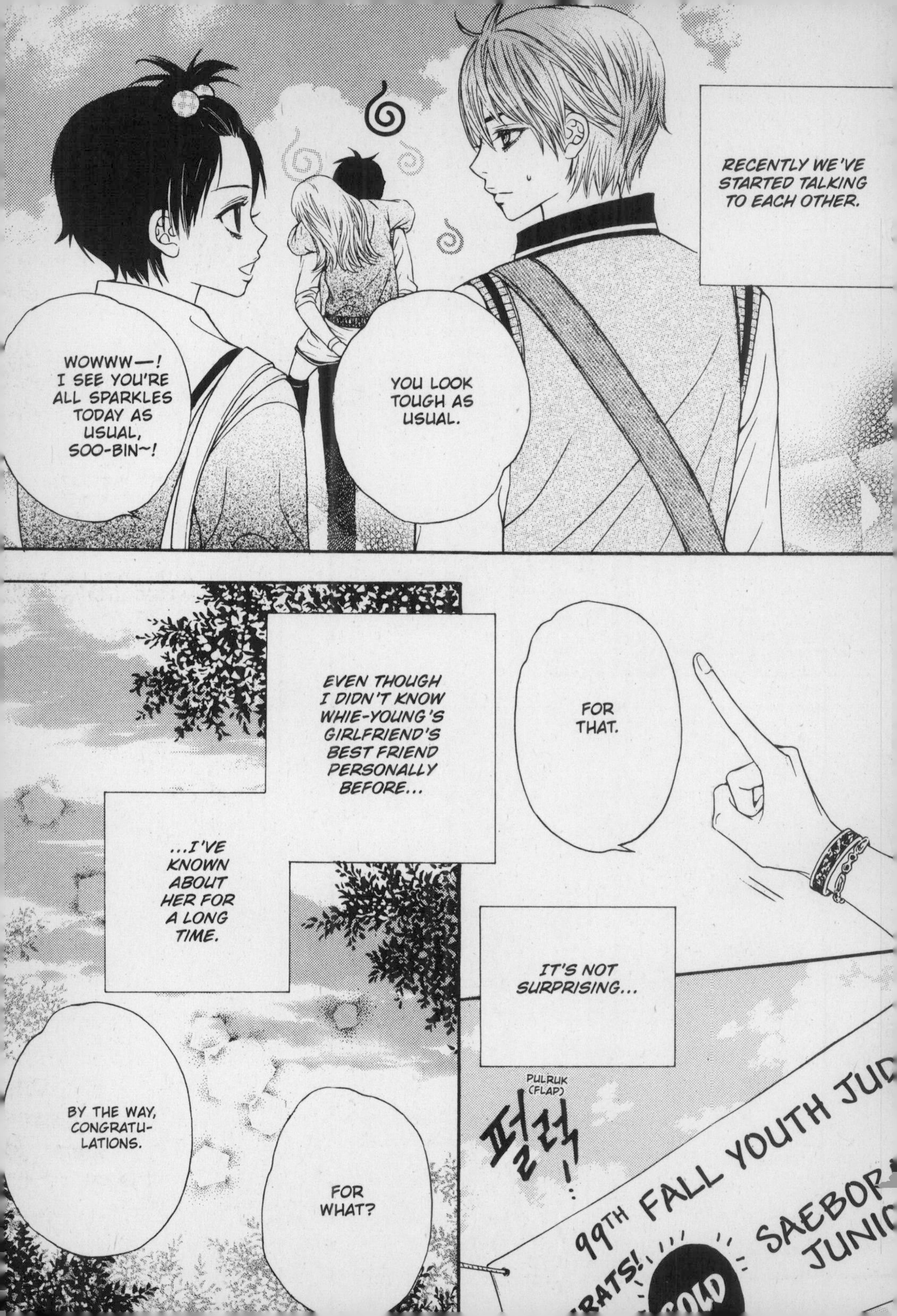
WOWWW—! I SEE YOU'RE ALL SPARKLES TODAY AS USUAL, SOO-BIN~!
YOU LOOK TOUGH AS USUAL.
RECENTLY WE'VE STARTED TALKING TO EACH OTHER.
EVEN THOUGH I DIDN'T KNOW WHIE-YOUNG'S GIRLFRIEND'S BEST FRIEND PERSONALLY BEFORE...
...I'VE KNOWN ABOUT HER FOR A LONG TIME.
BY THE WAY, CONGRATULATIONS.
FOR WHAT?
FOR THAT.
IT'S NOT SURPRISING...
PULRUK (FLAP)
99TH FALL YOUTH JUD
SAEBOR
JUNIO
RATS!
GOLD

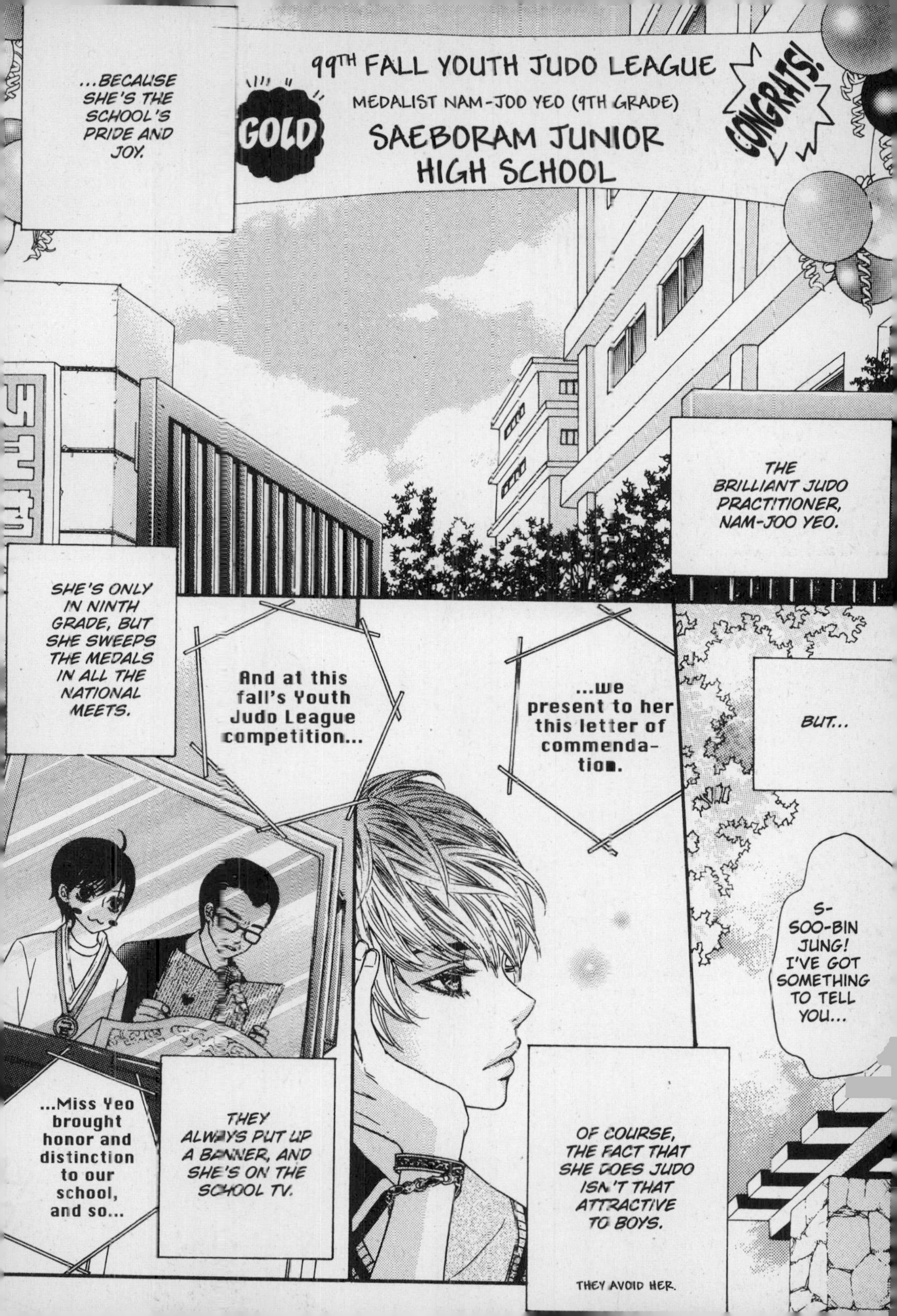
...BECAUSE SHE'S THE SCHOOL'S PRIDE AND JOY.
GOLD
99TH FALL YOUTH JUDO LEAGUE
MEDALIST NAM-JOO YEO (9TH GRADE)
SAEBORAM JUNIOR HIGH SCHOOL
CONGRATS!
THE BRILLIANT JUDO PRACTITIONER, NAM-JOO YEO.
SHE'S ONLY IN NINTH GRADE, BUT SHE SWEEPS THE MEDALS IN ALL THE NATIONAL MEETS.
And at this fall's Youth Judo League competition...
...we present to her this letter of commendation.
BUT...
S-SOO-BIN JUNG! I'VE GOT SOMETHING TO TELL YOU...
...Miss Yeo brought honor and distinction to our school, and so...
THEY ALWAYS PUT UP A BANNER, AND SHE'S ON THE SCHOOL TV.
OF COURSE, THE FACT THAT SHE DOES JUDO ISN'T THAT ATTRACTIVE TO BOYS.
THEY AVOID HER.

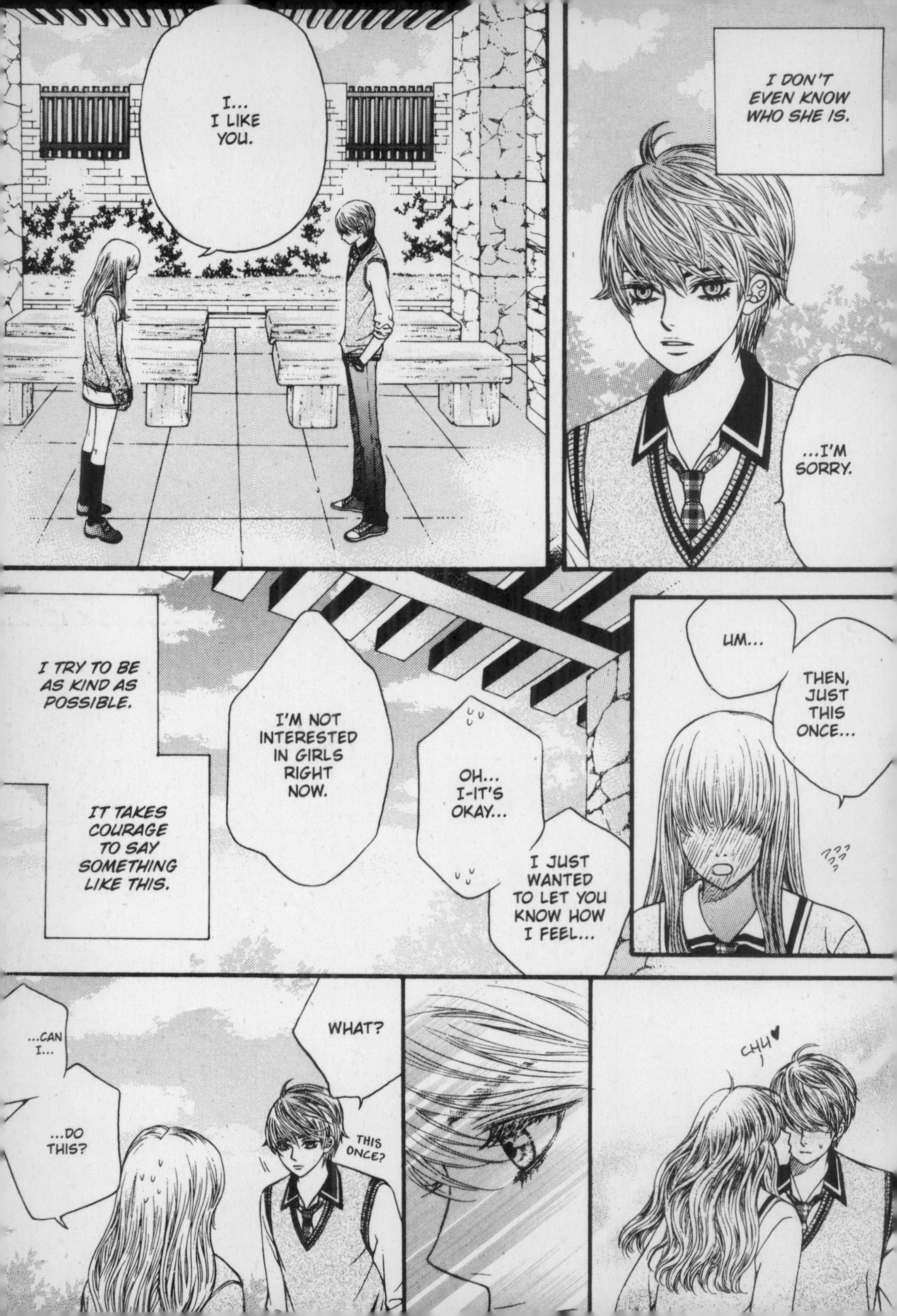
I...
I LIKE YOU.
I DON'T EVEN KNOW WHO SHE IS.
...I'M SORRY.
I TRY TO BE AS KIND AS POSSIBLE.
IT TAKES COURAGE TO SAY SOMETHING LIKE THIS.
I'M NOT INTERESTED IN GIRLS RIGHT NOW.
OH... I-IT'S OKAY...
I JUST WANTED TO LET YOU KNOW HOW I FEEL...
UM...
THEN, JUST THIS ONCE...
...CAN I...
...DO THIS?
WHAT?
THIS ONCE?
CHU♥

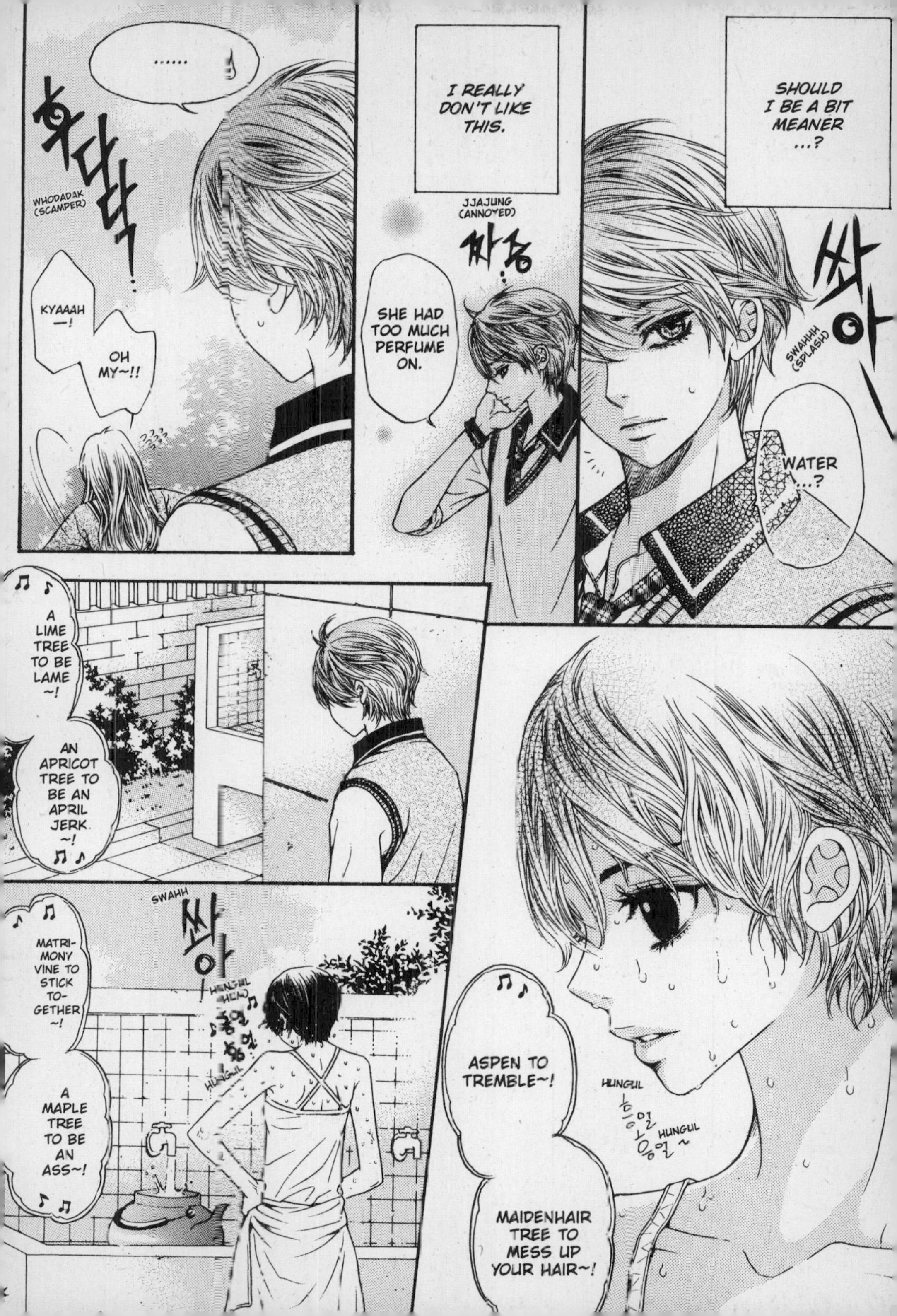
......
후다닥
WHODADAK (SCAMPER)
KYAAAH—!
OH MY~!!
I REALLY DON'T LIKE THIS.
JJAJUNG (ANNOYED)
짜증
SHE HAD TOO MUCH PERFUME ON.
SHOULD I BE A BIT MEANER ...?
쏴아
SWAHHH (SPLASH)
WATER ...?
A LIME TREE TO BE LAME ~!
AN APRICOT TREE TO BE AN APRIL JERK ~!
SWAHH
쏴아
MATRIMONY VINE TO STICK TOGETHER ~!
HUNGUL HUM
HUNGUL
A MAPLE TREE TO BE AN ASS~!
ASPEN TO TREMBLE~!
HUNGUL
HUNGUL ~
MAIDENHAIR TREE TO MESS UP YOUR HAIR~!

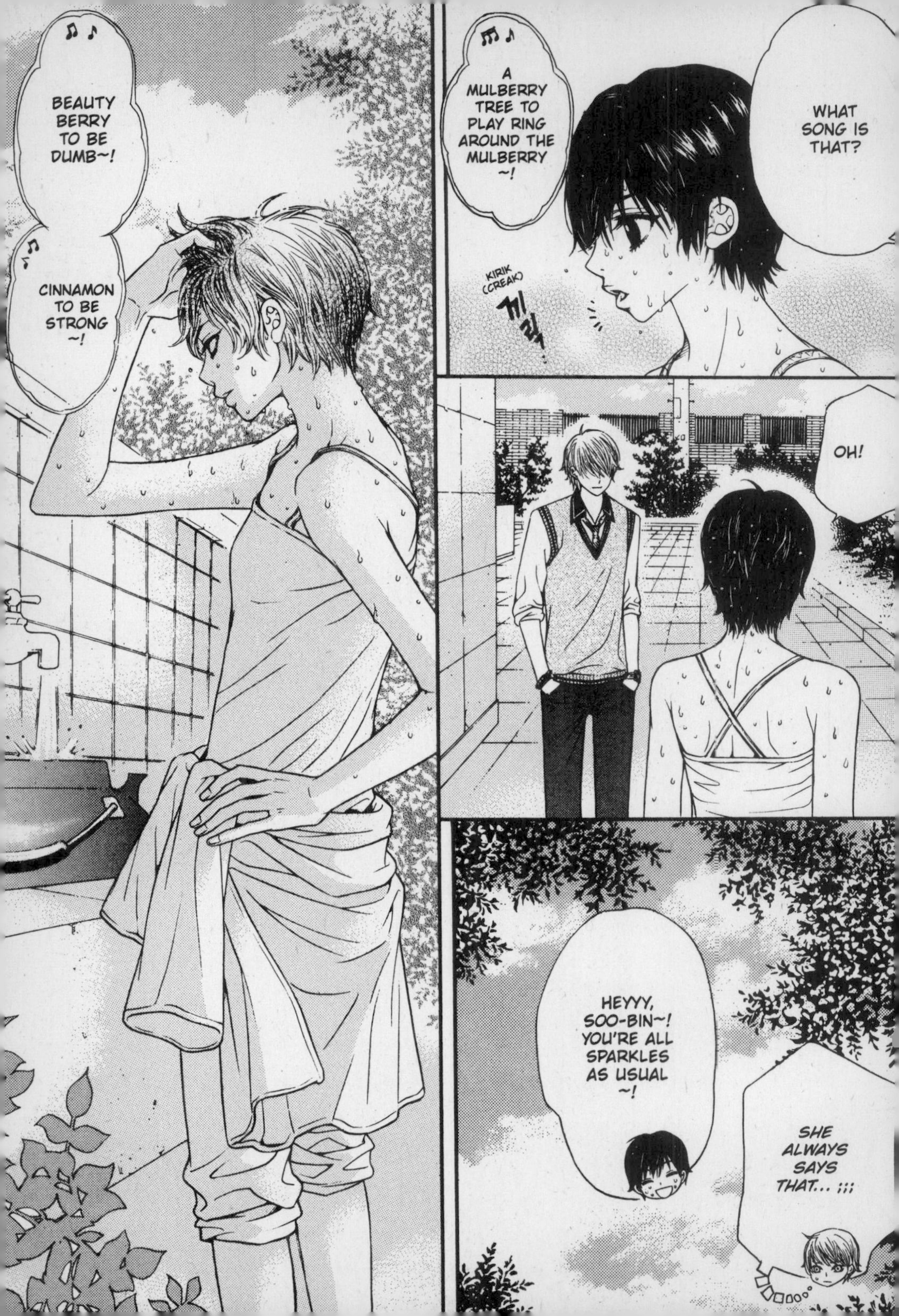
♫♪
BEAUTY BERRY TO BE DUMB~!
♪
CINNAMON TO BE STRONG ~!
♫♪
A MULBERRY TREE TO PLAY RING AROUND THE MULBERRY ~!
WHAT SONG IS THAT?
KIRIK (CREAK)
끼릭
OH!
HEYYY, SOO-BIN~! YOU'RE ALL SPARKLES AS USUAL ~!
SHE ALWAYS SAYS THAT... ;;;

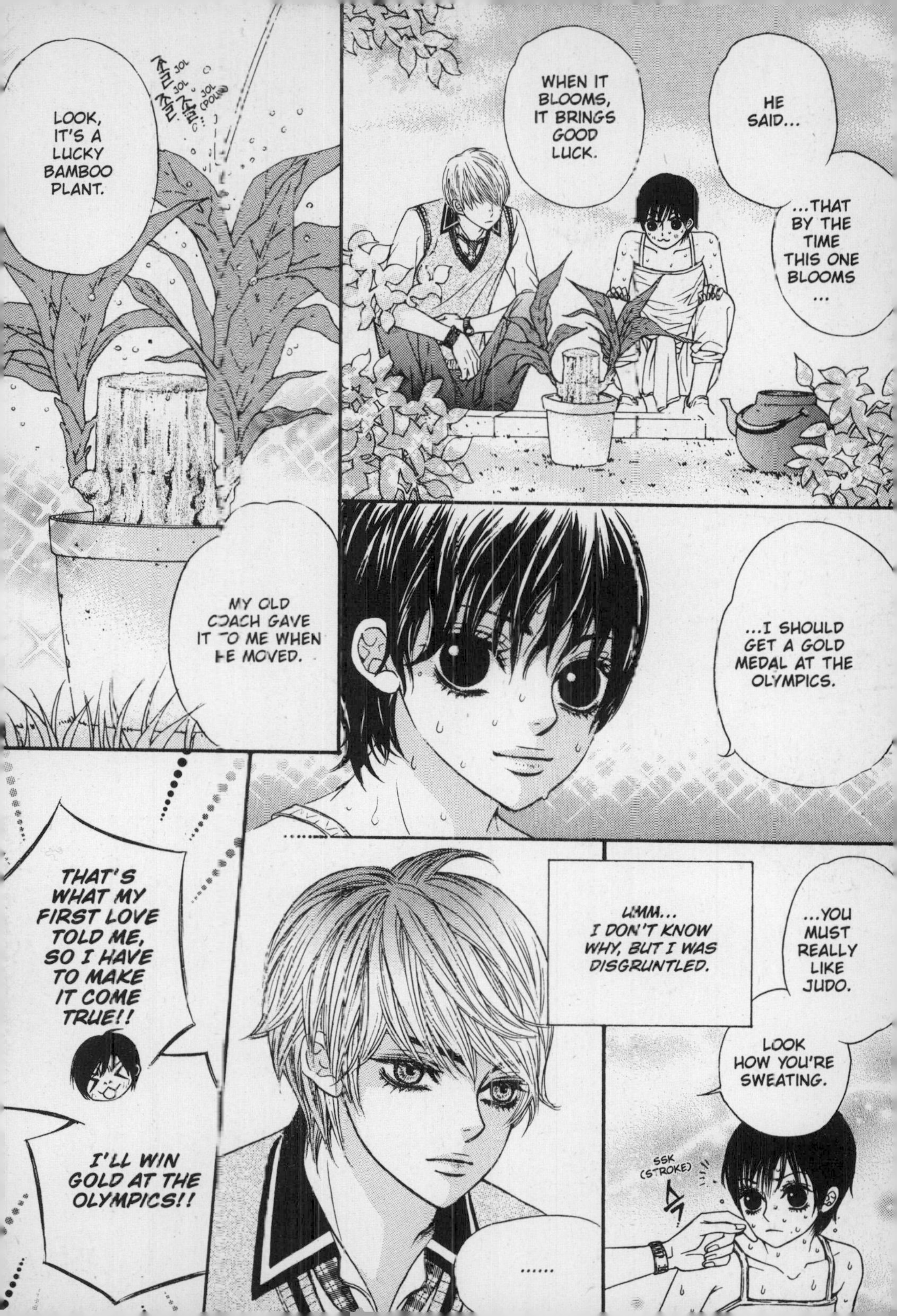

LOOK, IT'S A LUCKY BAMBOO PLANT.
JOL JOL JOL (POUR)
MY OLD COACH GAVE IT TO ME WHEN HE MOVED.
WHEN IT BLOOMS, IT BRINGS GOOD LUCK.
HE SAID...
...THAT BY THE TIME THIS ONE BLOOMS ...
...I SHOULD GET A GOLD MEDAL AT THE OLYMPICS.
THAT'S WHAT MY FIRST LOVE TOLD ME, SO I HAVE TO MAKE IT COME TRUE!!
I'LL WIN GOLD AT THE OLYMPICS!!
......
UMM... I DON'T KNOW WHY, BUT I WAS DISGRUNTLED.
...YOU MUST REALLY LIKE JUDO.
LOOK HOW YOU'RE SWEATING.
SSK (STROKE)

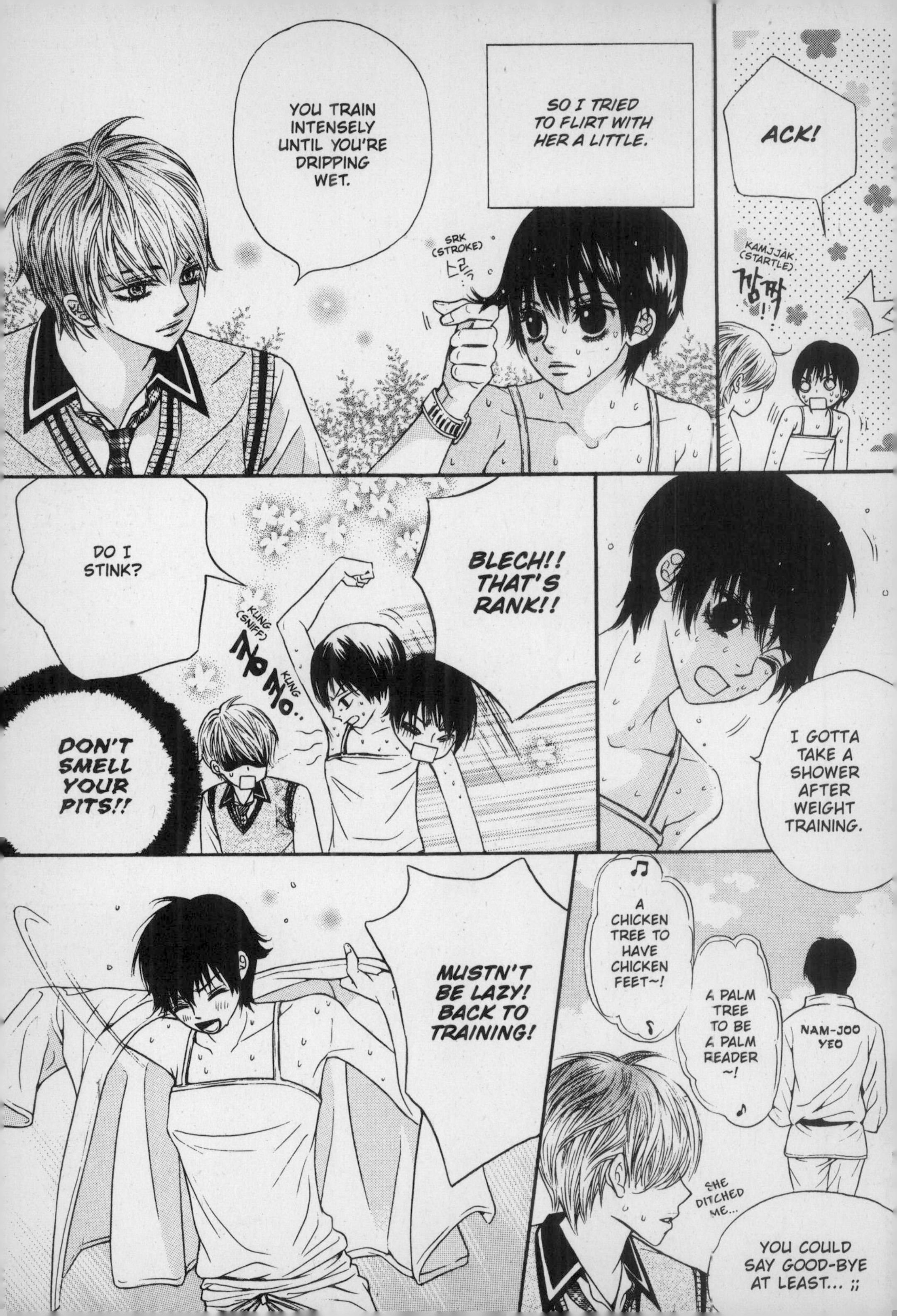
YOU TRAIN INTENSELY UNTIL YOU'RE DRIPPING WET.
SO I TRIED TO FLIRT WITH HER A LITTLE.
SRK (STROKE)
ACK!
KAMJJAK (STARTLE)
깜짝
DO I STINK?
KUNG (SNIFF)
KUNG
BLECH!! THAT'S RANK!!
DON'T SMELL YOUR PITS!!
I GOTTA TAKE A SHOWER AFTER WEIGHT TRAINING.
MUSTN'T BE LAZY! BACK TO TRAINING!
A CHICKEN TREE TO HAVE CHICKEN FEET~!
A PALM TREE TO BE A PALM READER ~!
NAM-JOO YEO
SHE DITCHED ME...
YOU COULD SAY GOOD-BYE AT LEAST... ;;

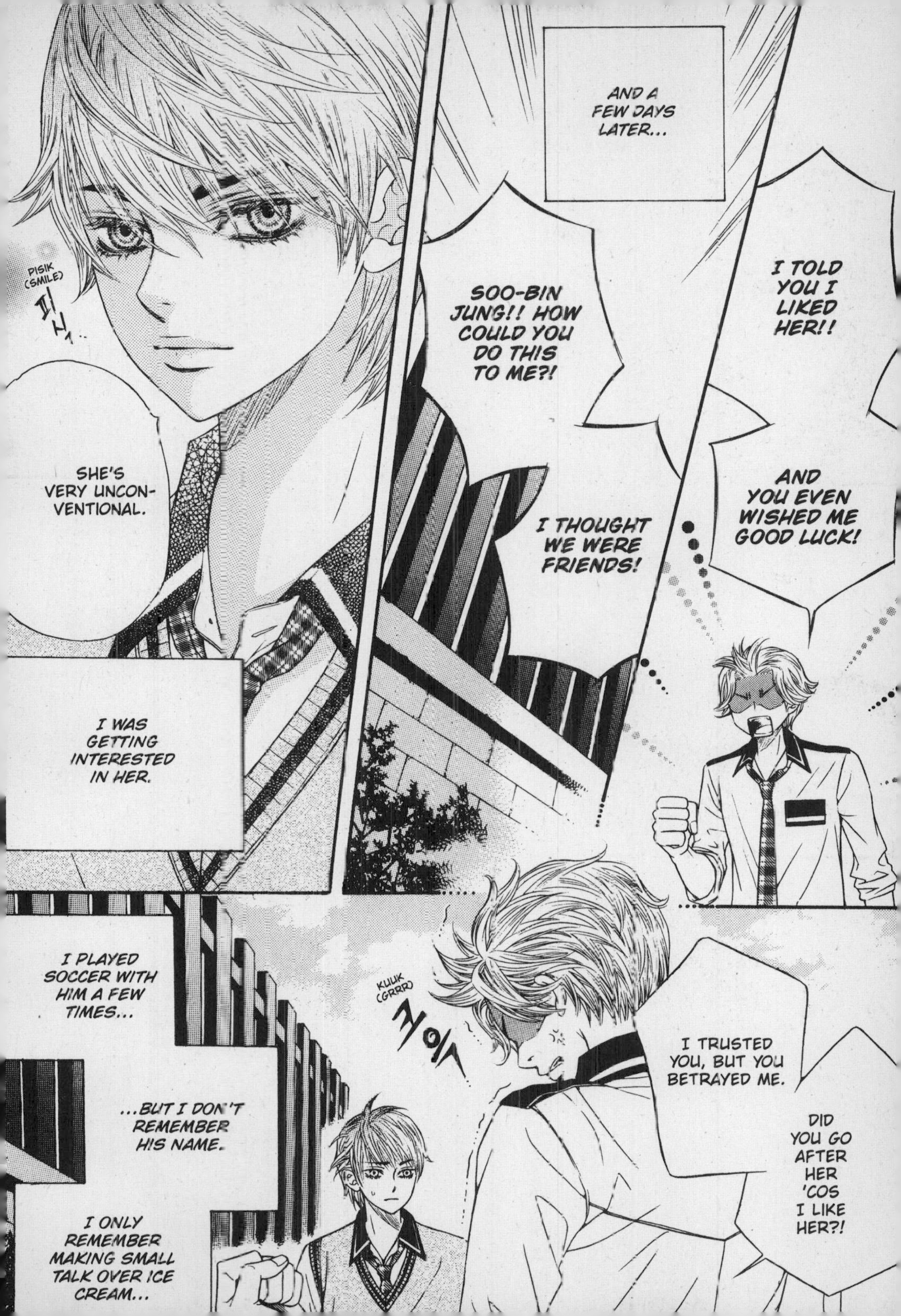
PISIK (SMILE)
SHE'S VERY UNCONVENTIONAL.
I WAS GETTING INTERESTED IN HER.
AND A FEW DAYS LATER...
SOO-BIN JUNG!! HOW COULD YOU DO THIS TO ME?!
I TOLD YOU I LIKED HER!!
I THOUGHT WE WERE FRIENDS!
AND YOU EVEN WISHED ME GOOD LUCK!
I PLAYED SOCCER WITH HIM A FEW TIMES...
...BUT I DON'T REMEMBER HIS NAME.
I ONLY REMEMBER MAKING SMALL TALK OVER ICE CREAM...
KUUK (GRRR)
I TRUSTED YOU, BUT YOU BETRAYED ME.
DID YOU GO AFTER HER 'COS I LIKE HER?!

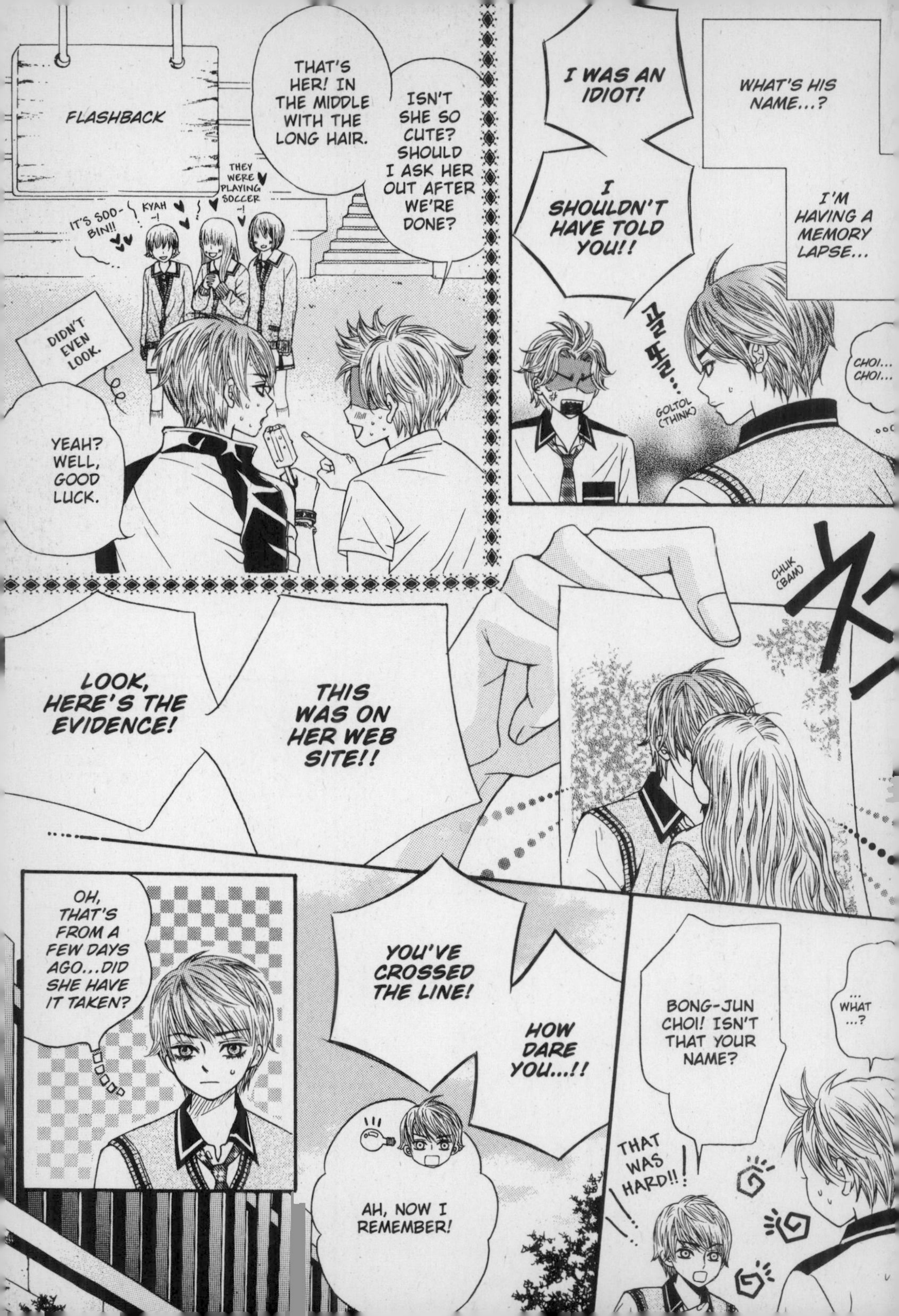
FLASHBACK
THAT'S HER! IN THE MIDDLE WITH THE LONG HAIR.
ISN'T SHE SO CUTE? SHOULD I ASK HER OUT AFTER WE'RE DONE?
THEY WERE PLAYING SOCCER ♥
IT'S SOO-BIN!!
KYAH ♥
DIDN'T EVEN LOOK.
YEAH? WELL, GOOD LUCK.
I WAS AN IDIOT!
I SHOULDN'T HAVE TOLD YOU!!
골똘...
GOLTOL (THINK)
WHAT'S HIS NAME...?
I'M HAVING A MEMORY LAPSE...
CHOI... CHOI...
...
LOOK, HERE'S THE EVIDENCE!
THIS WAS ON HER WEB SITE!!
CHUK (BAM)
OH, THAT'S FROM A FEW DAYS AGO...DID SHE HAVE IT TAKEN?
YOU'VE CROSSED THE LINE!
HOW DARE YOU...!!
AH, NOW I REMEMBER!
BONG-JUN CHOI! ISN'T THAT YOUR NAME?
...WHAT...?
THAT WAS HARD!!

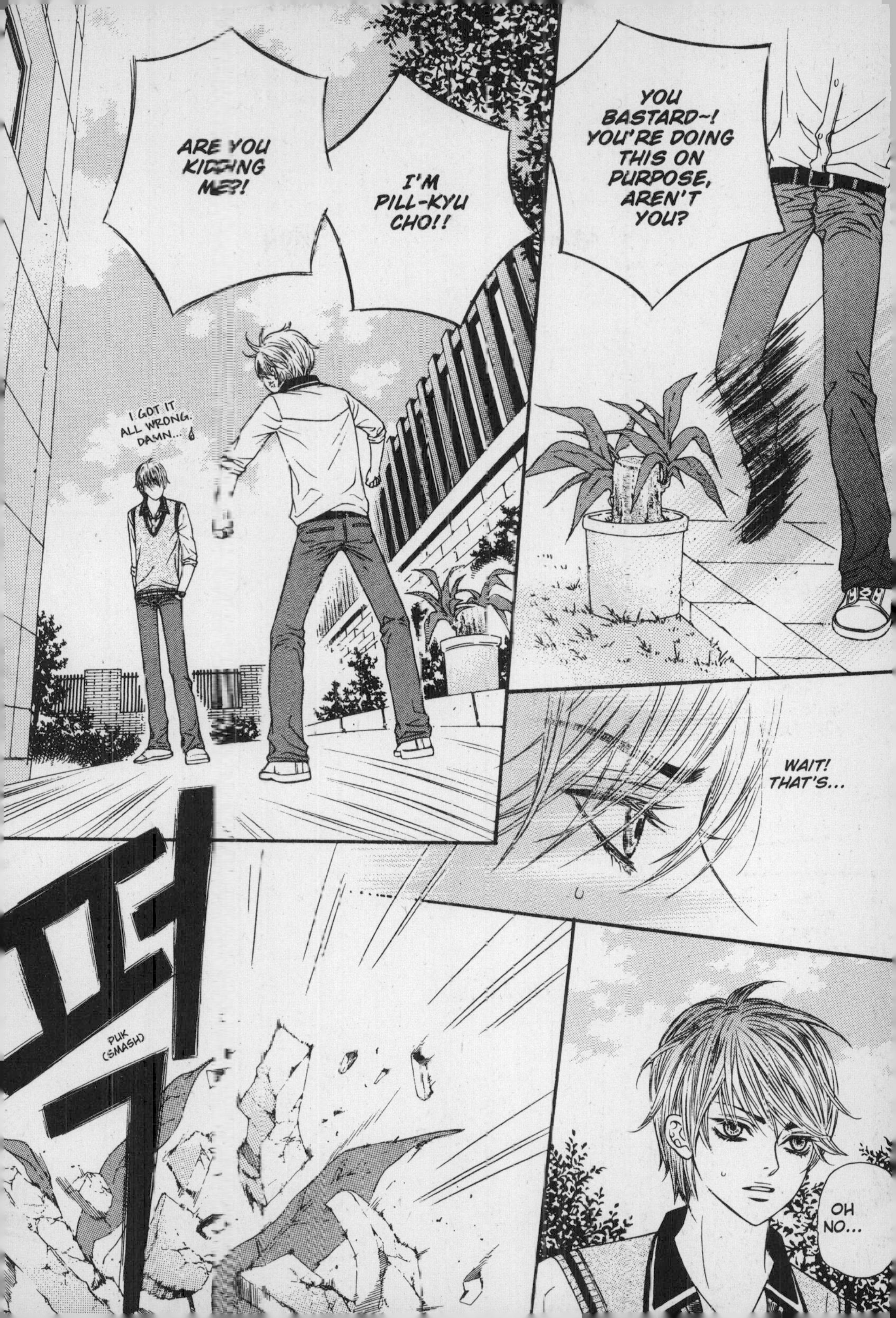
ARE YOU KIDDING ME?!
I'M PILL-KYU CHO!!
I GOT IT ALL WRONG. DAMN...
YOU BASTARD~! YOU'RE DOING THIS ON PURPOSE, AREN'T YOU?
WAIT! THAT'S...
PUK (SMASH)
OH NO...

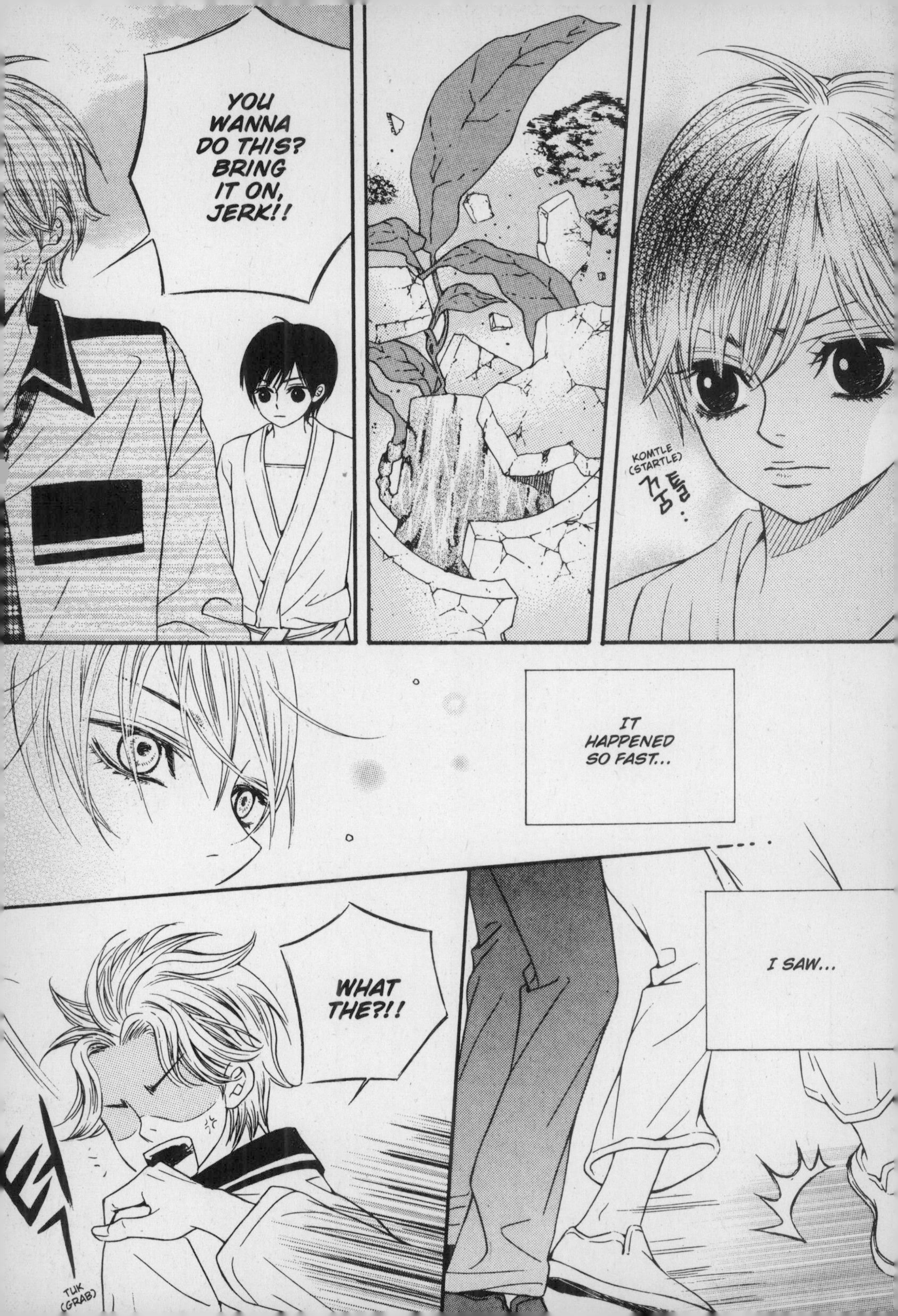
YOU WANNA DO THIS? BRING IT ON, JERK!!
KOMTLE (STARTLE)
껌틀...
IT HAPPENED SO FAST...
WHAT THE?!!
TUK (GRAB)
I SAW...

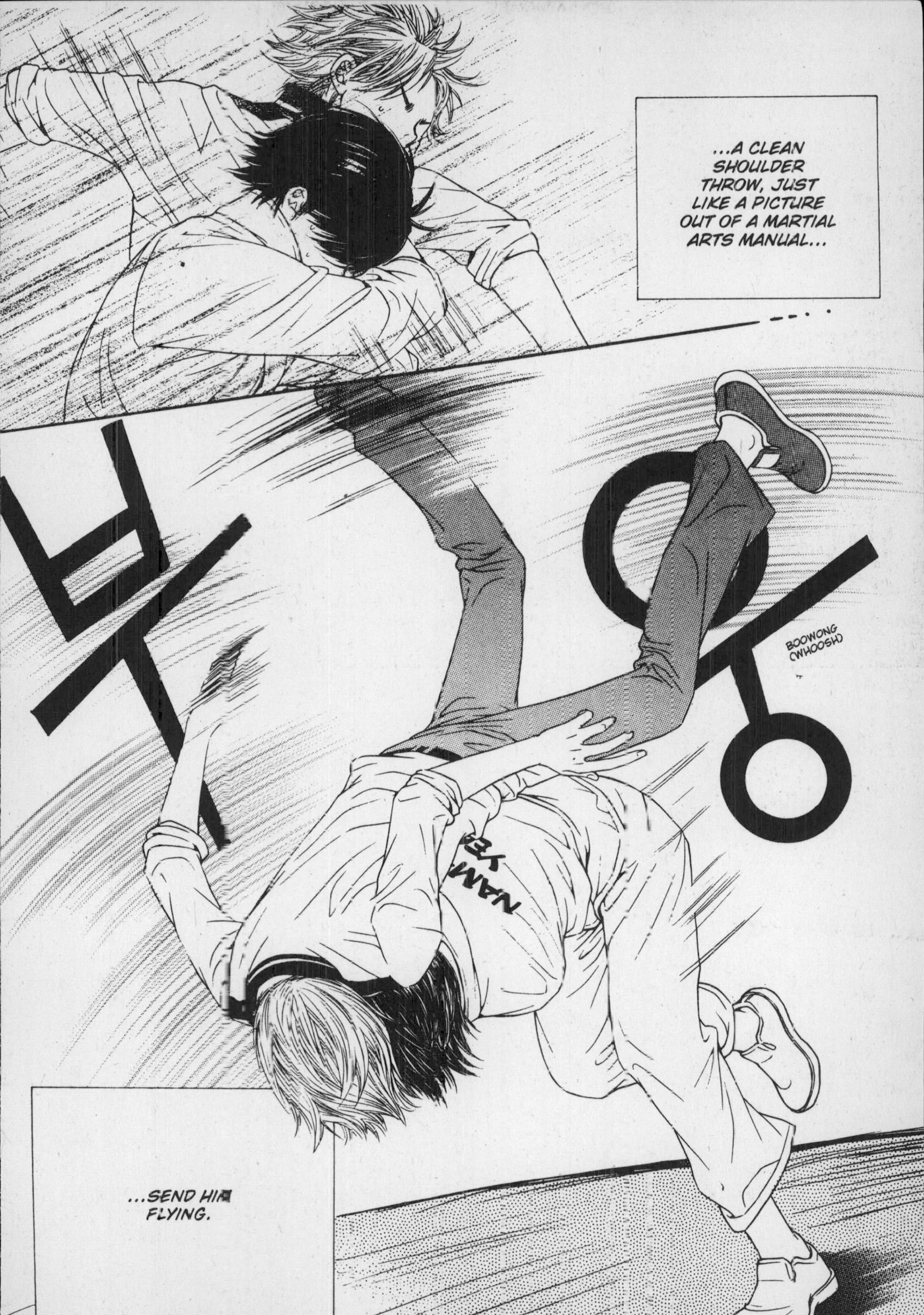
...A CLEAN SHOULDER THROW, JUST LIKE A PICTURE OUT OF A MARTIAL ARTS MANUAL...
BOOWONG (WHOOSH)
...SEND HIM FLYING.

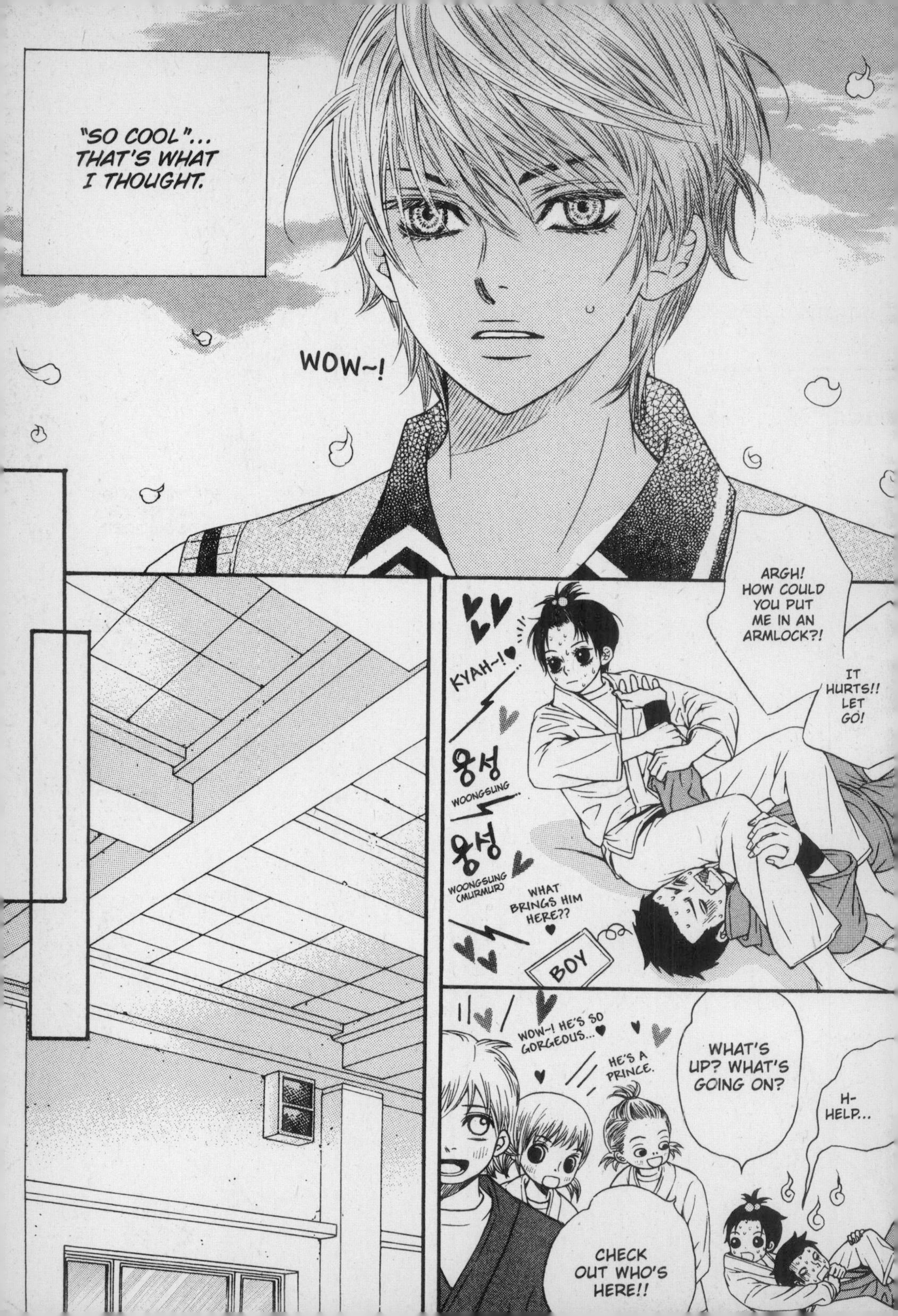
"SO COOL"... THAT'S WHAT I THOUGHT.
WOW~!
KYAH~!♥
웅성
WOONGSUNG
웅성
WOONGSUNG (MURMUR)
WHAT BRINGS HIM HERE??
BOY
ARGH! HOW COULD YOU PUT ME IN AN ARMLOCK?!
IT HURTS!! LET GO!
WOW~! HE'S SO GORGEOUS...♥
HE'S A PRINCE.
CHECK OUT WHO'S HERE!!
WHAT'S UP? WHAT'S GOING ON?
H-HELP...

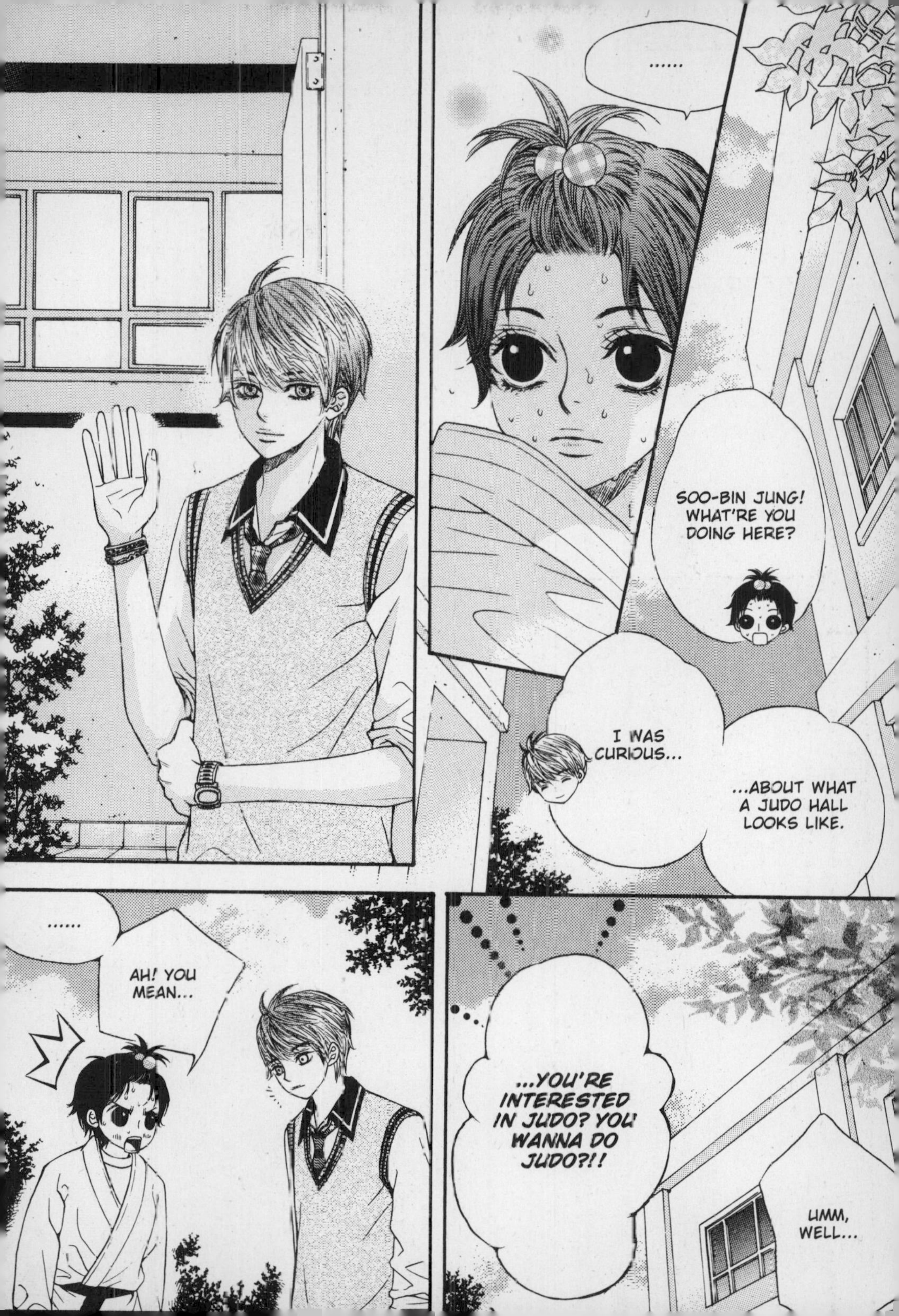
......
SOO-BIN JUNG! WHAT'RE YOU DOING HERE?
I WAS CURIOUS...
...ABOUT WHAT A JUDO HALL LOOKS LIKE.
......
AH! YOU MEAN...
...YOU'RE INTERESTED IN JUDO? YOU WANNA DO JUDO?!!
UMM, WELL...

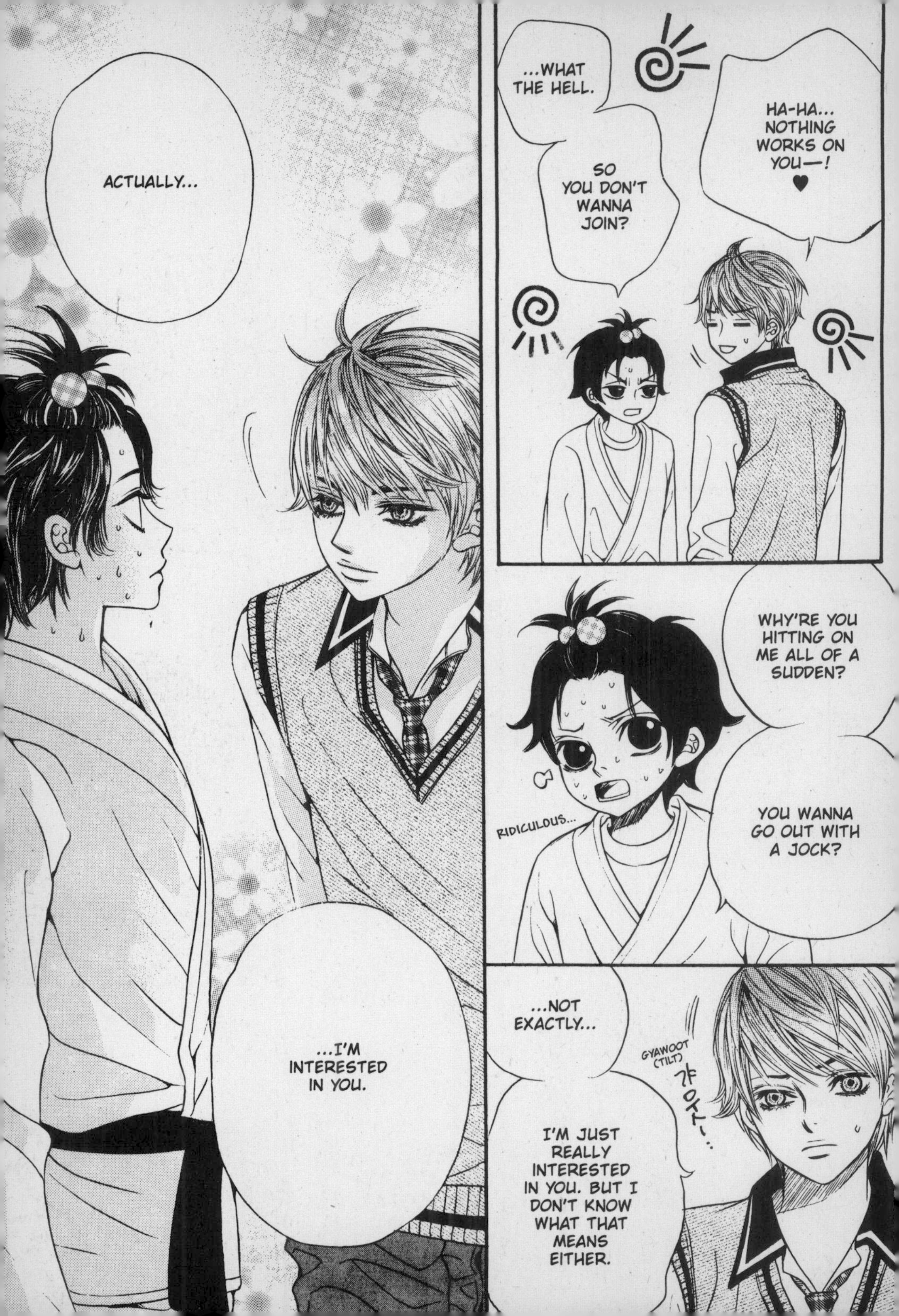
ACTUALLY...
...I'M INTERESTED IN YOU.
...WHAT THE HELL.
SO YOU DON'T WANNA JOIN?
HA-HA... NOTHING WORKS ON YOU—! ♥
WHY'RE YOU HITTING ON ME ALL OF A SUDDEN?
RIDICULOUS...
YOU WANNA GO OUT WITH A JOCK?
...NOT EXACTLY...
GYAWOOT (TILT)
I'M JUST REALLY INTERESTED IN YOU. BUT I DON'T KNOW WHAT THAT MEANS EITHER.

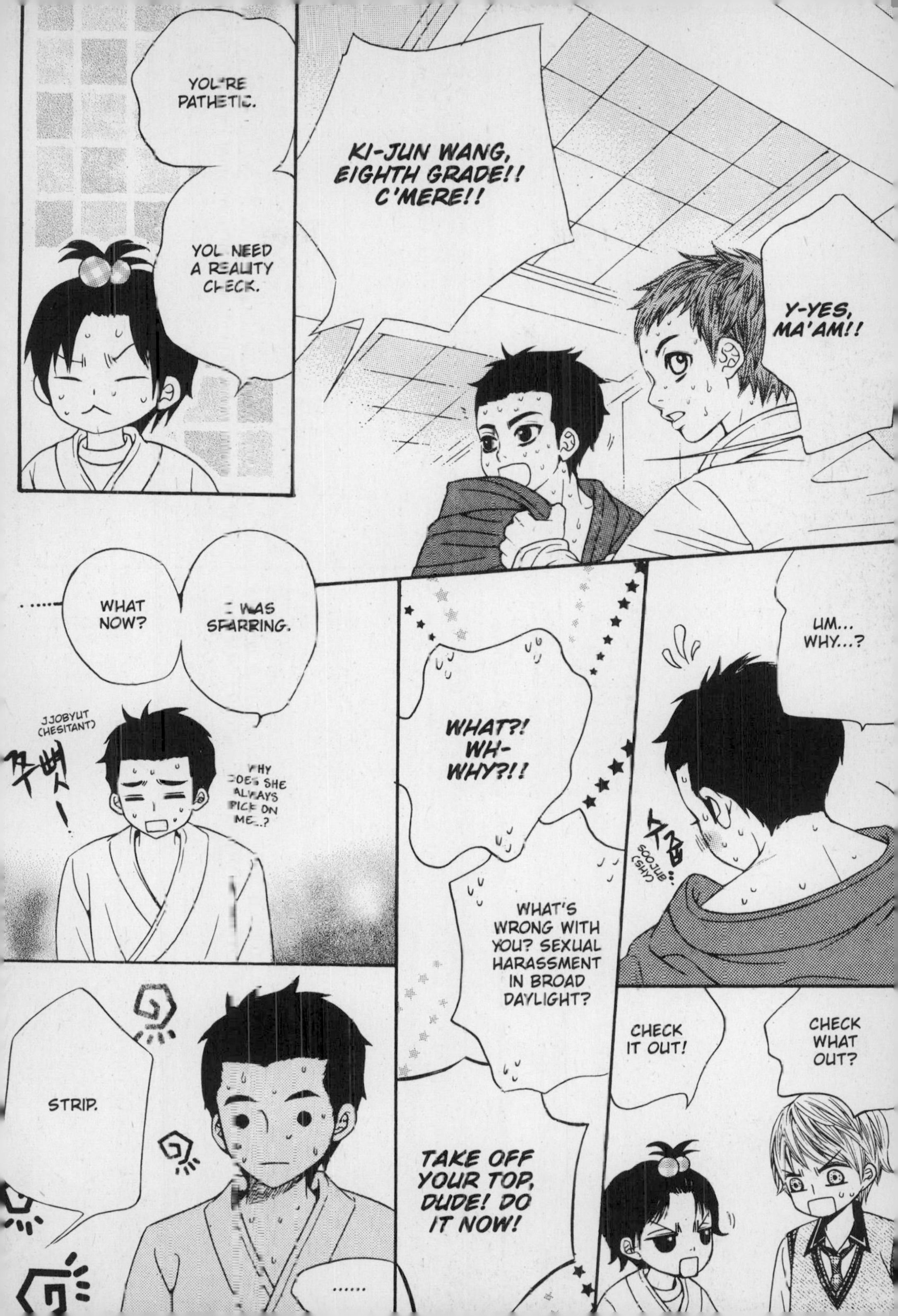
YOU'RE PATHETIC.
YOU NEED A REALITY CHECK.
KI-JUN WANG, EIGHTH GRADE!! C'MERE!!
Y-YES, MA'AM!!
......
WHAT NOW?
I WAS SPARRING.
JJOBYUT (HESITANT)
쭈뼛
WHY DOES SHE ALWAYS PICK ON ME...?
STRIP.
......
WHAT?! WH-WHY?!!
WHAT'S WRONG WITH YOU? SEXUAL HARASSMENT IN BROAD DAYLIGHT?
TAKE OFF YOUR TOP, DUDE! DO IT NOW!
UM... WHY...?
수줍
SOOJUB (SHY)
CHECK IT OUT!
CHECK WHAT OUT?

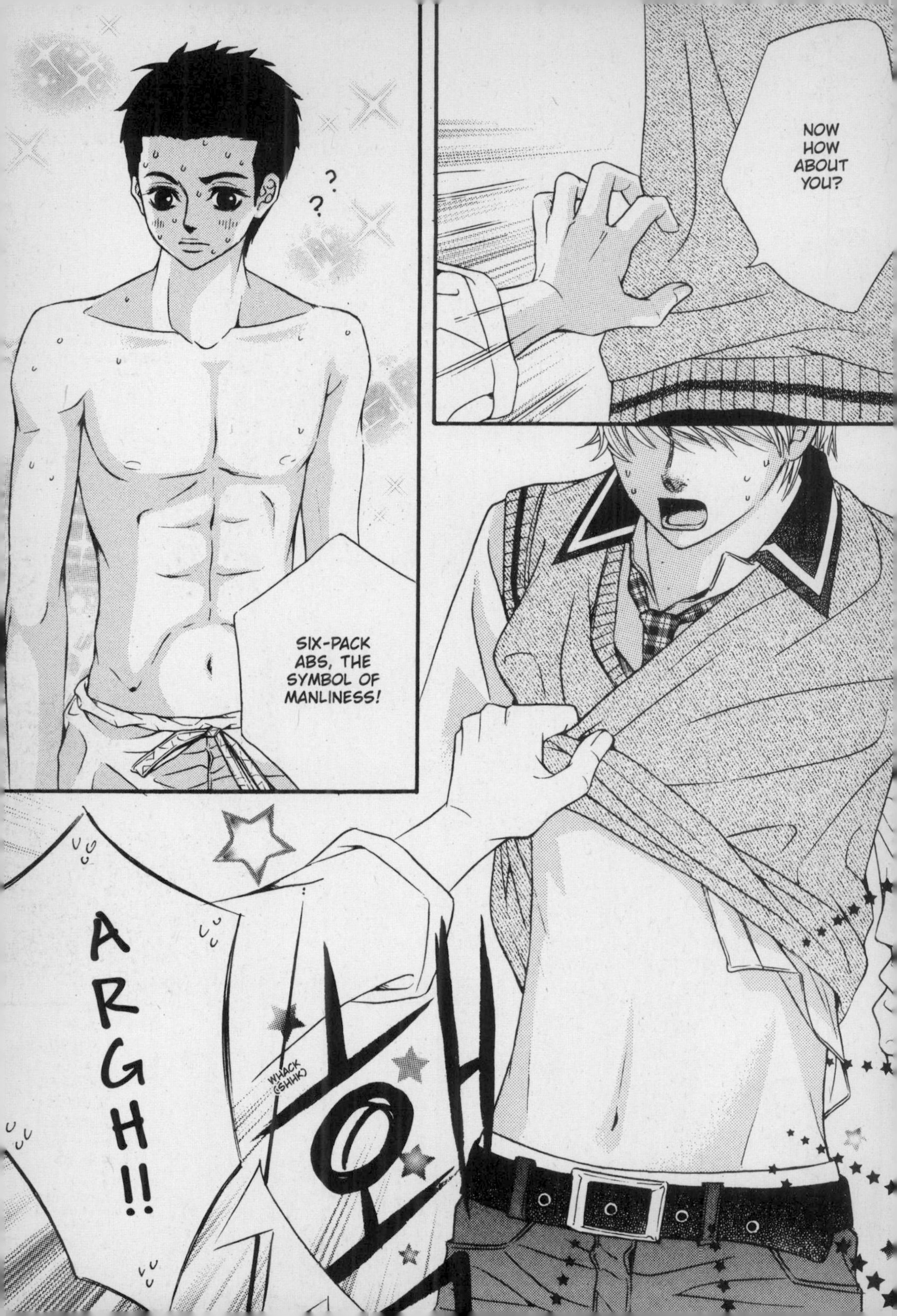

? ?
SIX-PACK ABS, THE SYMBOL OF MANLINESS!
NOW HOW ABOUT YOU?
ARGH!!
WHACK (SHHK)

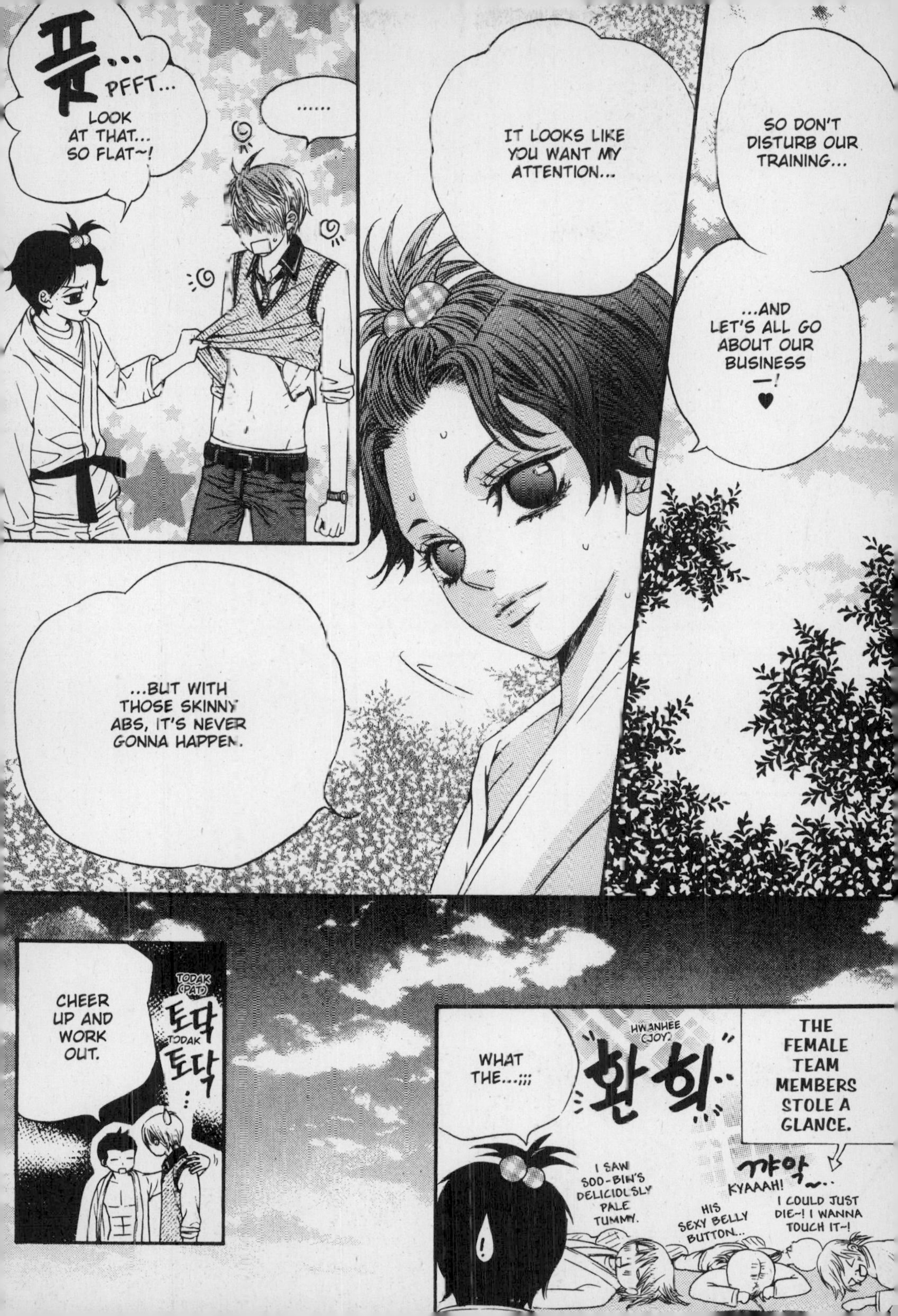

프...
PFFT...
LOOK AT THAT... SO FLAT~!
......
IT LOOKS LIKE YOU WANT MY ATTENTION...
SO DON'T DISTURB OUR TRAINING...
...AND LET'S ALL GO ABOUT OUR BUSINESS—! ♥
...BUT WITH THOSE SKINNY ABS, IT'S NEVER GONNA HAPPEN.
CHEER UP AND WORK OUT.
TODAK (PAT) TODAK
토닥 토닥
WHAT THE...;;;
HWANHEE (JOY)
환희
THE FEMALE TEAM MEMBERS STOLE A GLANCE.
I SAW SOO-BIN'S DELICIOLSLY PALE TUMMY.
까악~..
KYAAAH!
HIS SEXY BELLY BUTTON...
I COULD JUST DIE~! I WANNA TOUCH IT~!

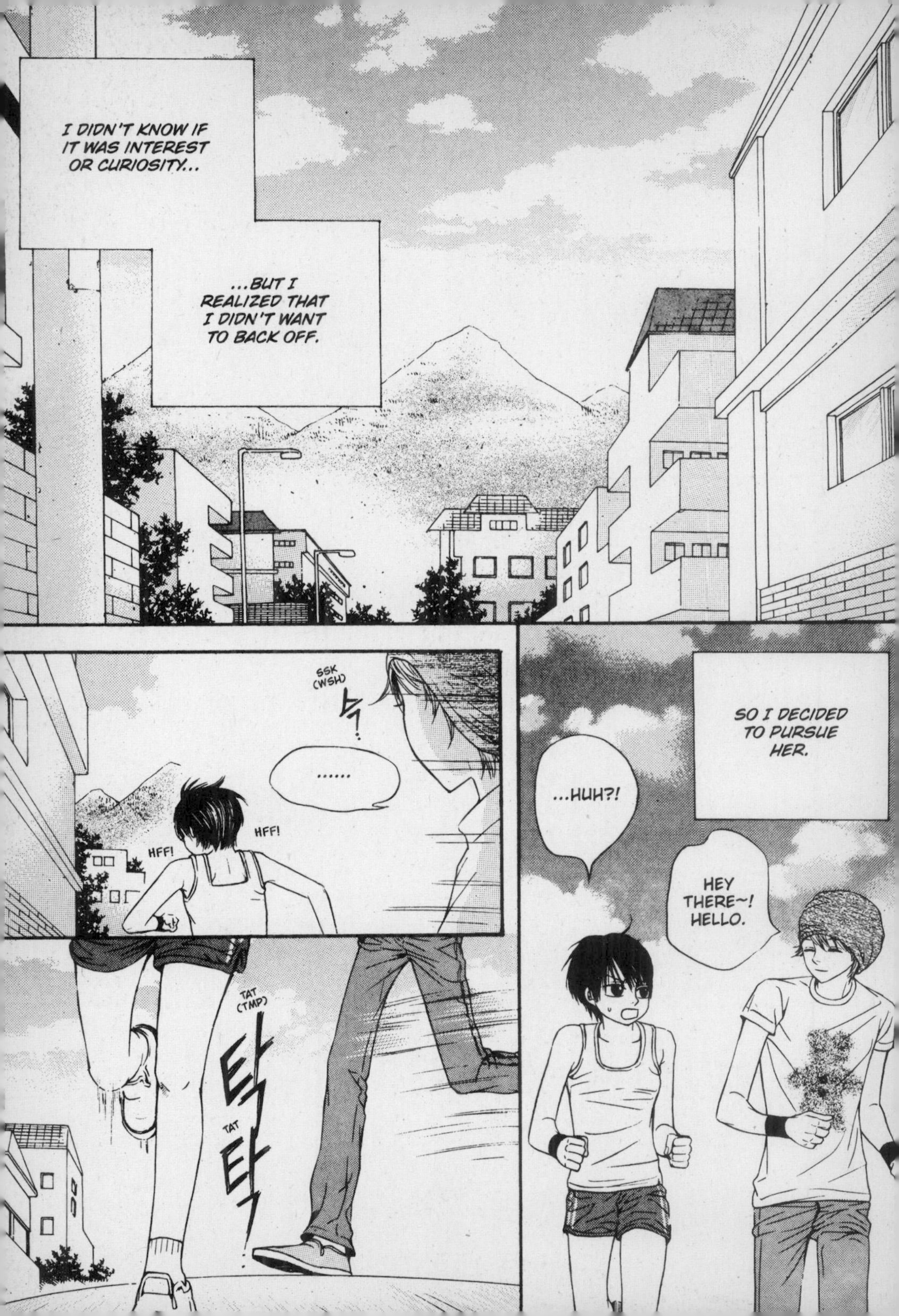
I DIDN'T KNOW IF IT WAS INTEREST OR CURIOSITY...
...BUT I REALIZED THAT I DIDN'T WANT TO BACK OFF.
SSK (WSH)
......
HFF!
HFF!
TAT (TMP)
탁
TAT
탁
SO I DECIDED TO PURSUE HER.
...HUH?!
HEY THERE~! HELLO.

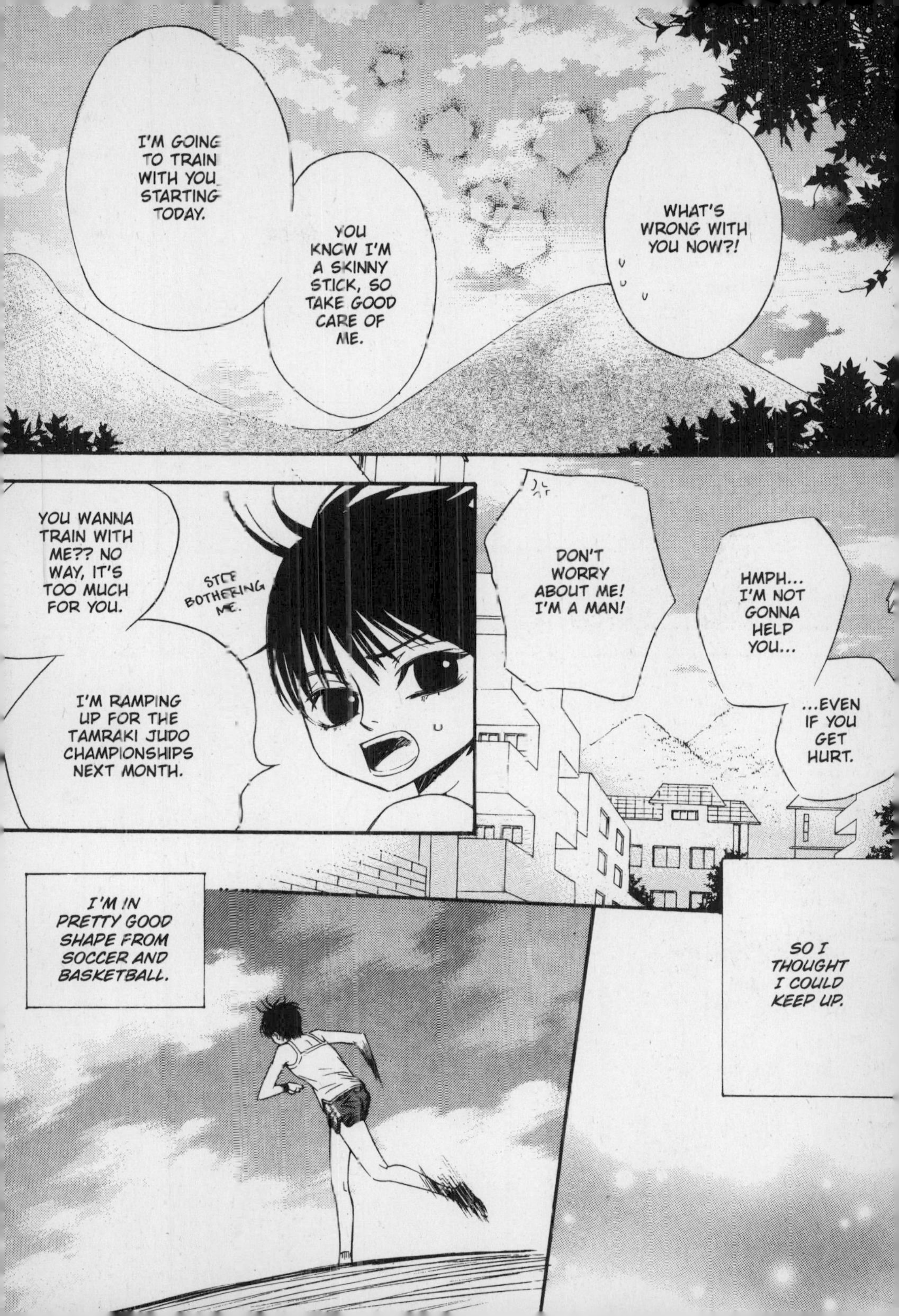
I'M GOING TO TRAIN WITH YOU STARTING TODAY.
YOU KNOW I'M A SKINNY STICK, SO TAKE GOOD CARE OF ME.
WHAT'S WRONG WITH YOU NOW?!
YOU WANNA TRAIN WITH ME?? NO WAY, IT'S TOO MUCH FOR YOU.
STOP BOTHERING ME.
I'M RAMPING UP FOR THE TAMRAKI JUDO CHAMPIONSHIPS NEXT MONTH.
DON'T WORRY ABOUT ME! I'M A MAN!
HMPH... I'M NOT GONNA HELP YOU...
...EVEN IF YOU GET HURT.
I'M IN PRETTY GOOD SHAPE FROM SOCCER AND BASKETBALL.
SO I THOUGHT I COULD KEEP UP.

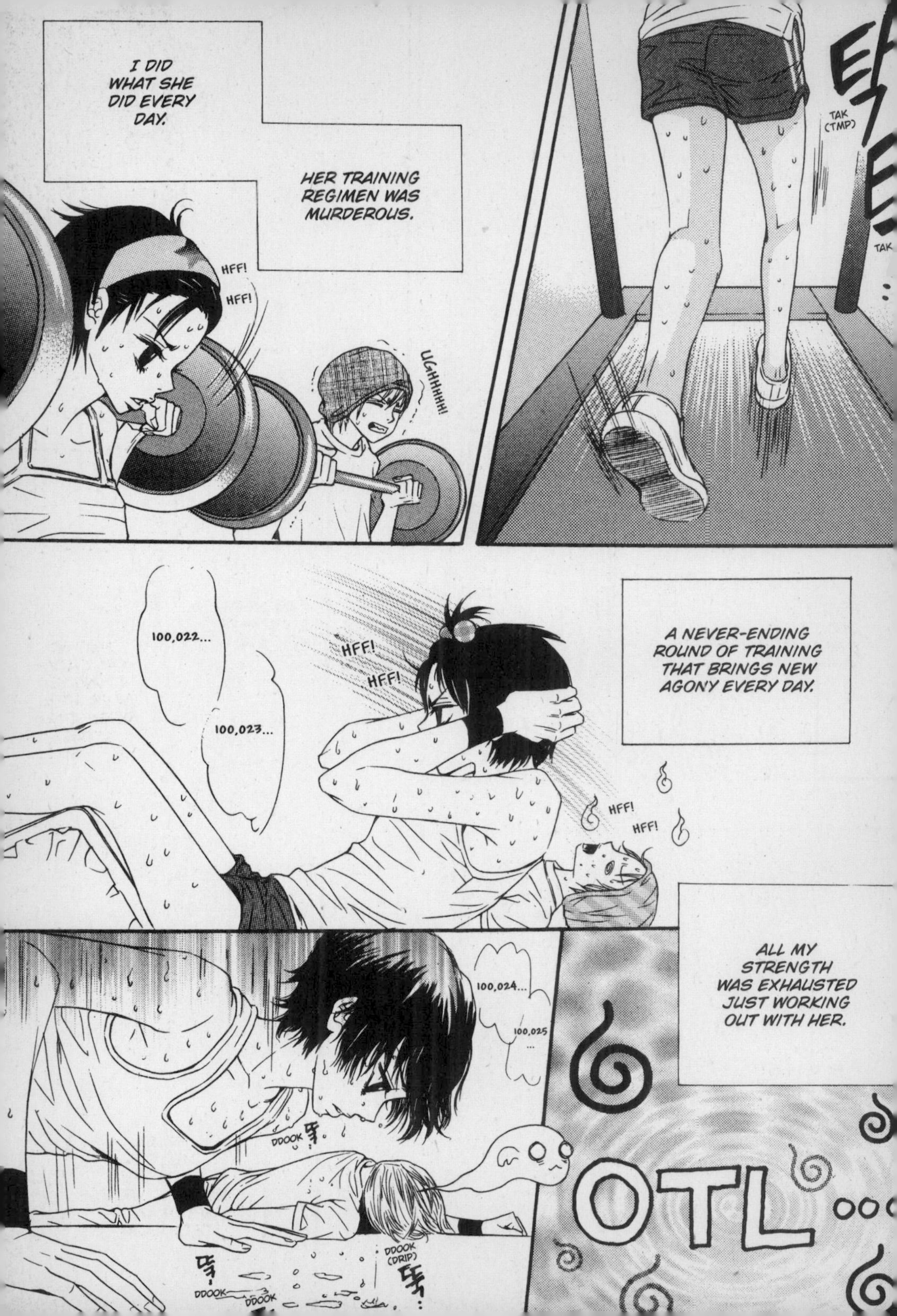
I DID WHAT SHE DID EVERY DAY.
HER TRAINING REGIMEN WAS MURDEROUS.
HFF!
HFF!
UGHHHHH!
TAK (TMP)
TAK
100,022...
HFF!
HFF!
100,023...
A NEVER-ENDING ROUND OF TRAINING THAT BRINGS NEW AGONY EVERY DAY.
HFF!
HFF!
100,024...
100,025...
DDOOK
ALL MY STRENGTH WAS EXHAUSTED JUST WORKING OUT WITH HER.
DDOOK (DRIP)
DDOOK
DDOOK
OTL...

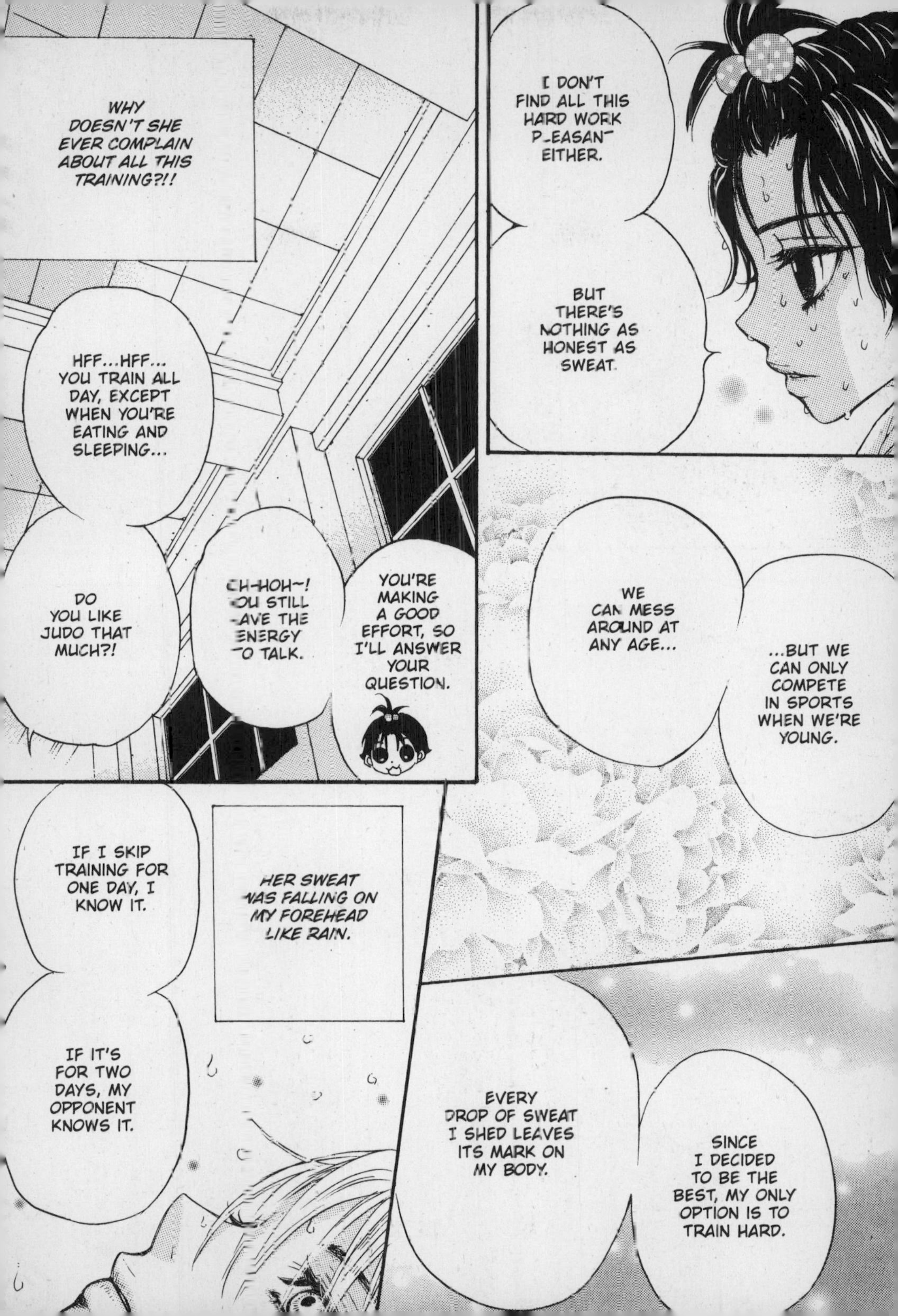
WHY DOESN'T SHE EVER COMPLAIN ABOUT ALL THIS TRAINING?!!
HFF...HFF... YOU TRAIN ALL DAY, EXCEPT WHEN YOU'RE EATING AND SLEEPING...
DO YOU LIKE JUDO THAT MUCH?!
OH-HOH~! YOU STILL HAVE THE ENERGY TO TALK.
YOU'RE MAKING A GOOD EFFORT, SO I'LL ANSWER YOUR QUESTION.
I DON'T FIND ALL THIS HARD WORK PLEASANT EITHER.
BUT THERE'S NOTHING AS HONEST AS SWEAT.
WE CAN MESS AROUND AT ANY AGE...
...BUT WE CAN ONLY COMPETE IN SPORTS WHEN WE'RE YOUNG.
IF I SKIP TRAINING FOR ONE DAY, I KNOW IT.
IF IT'S FOR TWO DAYS, MY OPPONENT KNOWS IT.
HER SWEAT WAS FALLING ON MY FOREHEAD LIKE RAIN.
EVERY DROP OF SWEAT I SHED LEAVES ITS MARK ON MY BODY.
SINCE I DECIDED TO BE THE BEST, MY ONLY OPTION IS TO TRAIN HARD.

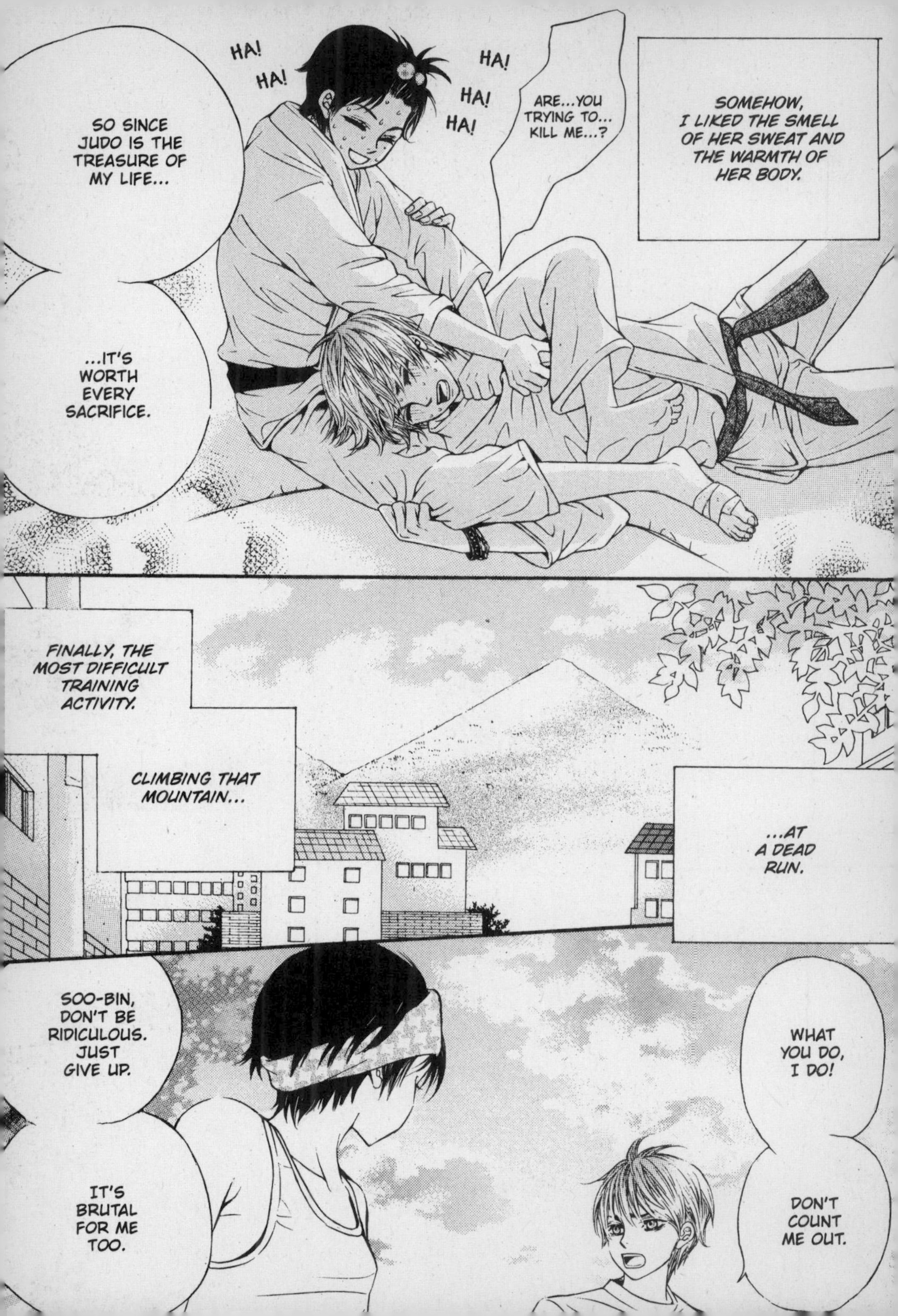
SO SINCE JUDO IS THE TREASURE OF MY LIFE...
...IT'S WORTH EVERY SACRIFICE.
HA! HA!
HA! HA! HA!
ARE...YOU TRYING TO... KILL ME...?
SOMEHOW, I LIKED THE SMELL OF HER SWEAT AND THE WARMTH OF HER BODY.
FINALLY, THE MOST DIFFICULT TRAINING ACTIVITY.
CLIMBING THAT MOUNTAIN...
...AT A DEAD RUN.
SOO-BIN, DON'T BE RIDICULOUS. JUST GIVE UP.
IT'S BRUTAL FOR ME TOO.
WHAT YOU DO, I DO!
DON'T COUNT ME OUT.

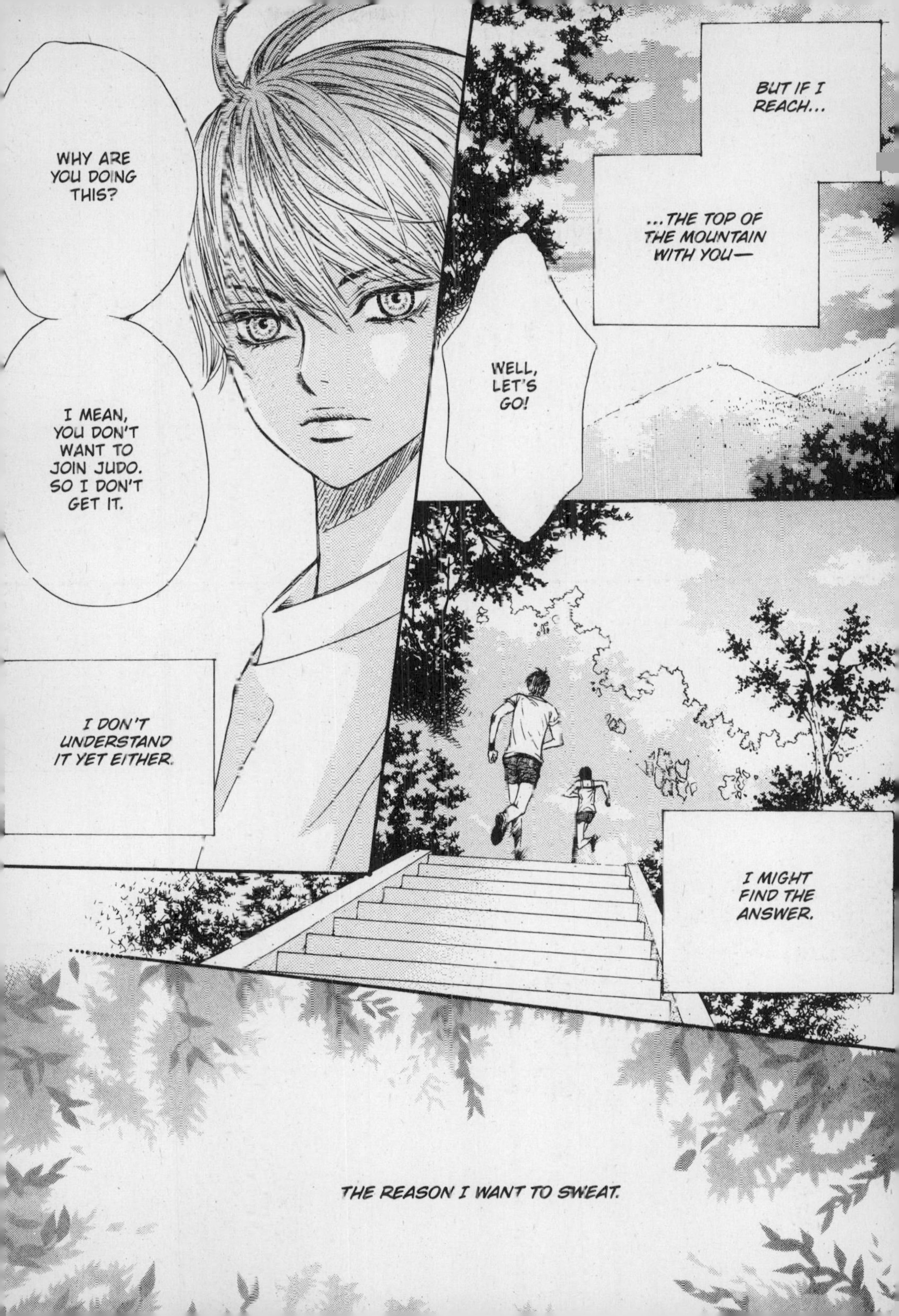

WHY ARE YOU DOING THIS?
I MEAN, YOU DON'T WANT TO JOIN JUDO. SO I DON'T GET IT.
I DON'T UNDERSTAND IT YET EITHER.
WELL, LET'S GO!
BUT IF I REACH...
...THE TOP OF THE MOUNTAIN WITH YOU—
I MIGHT FIND THE ANSWER.
THE REASON I WANT TO SWEAT.

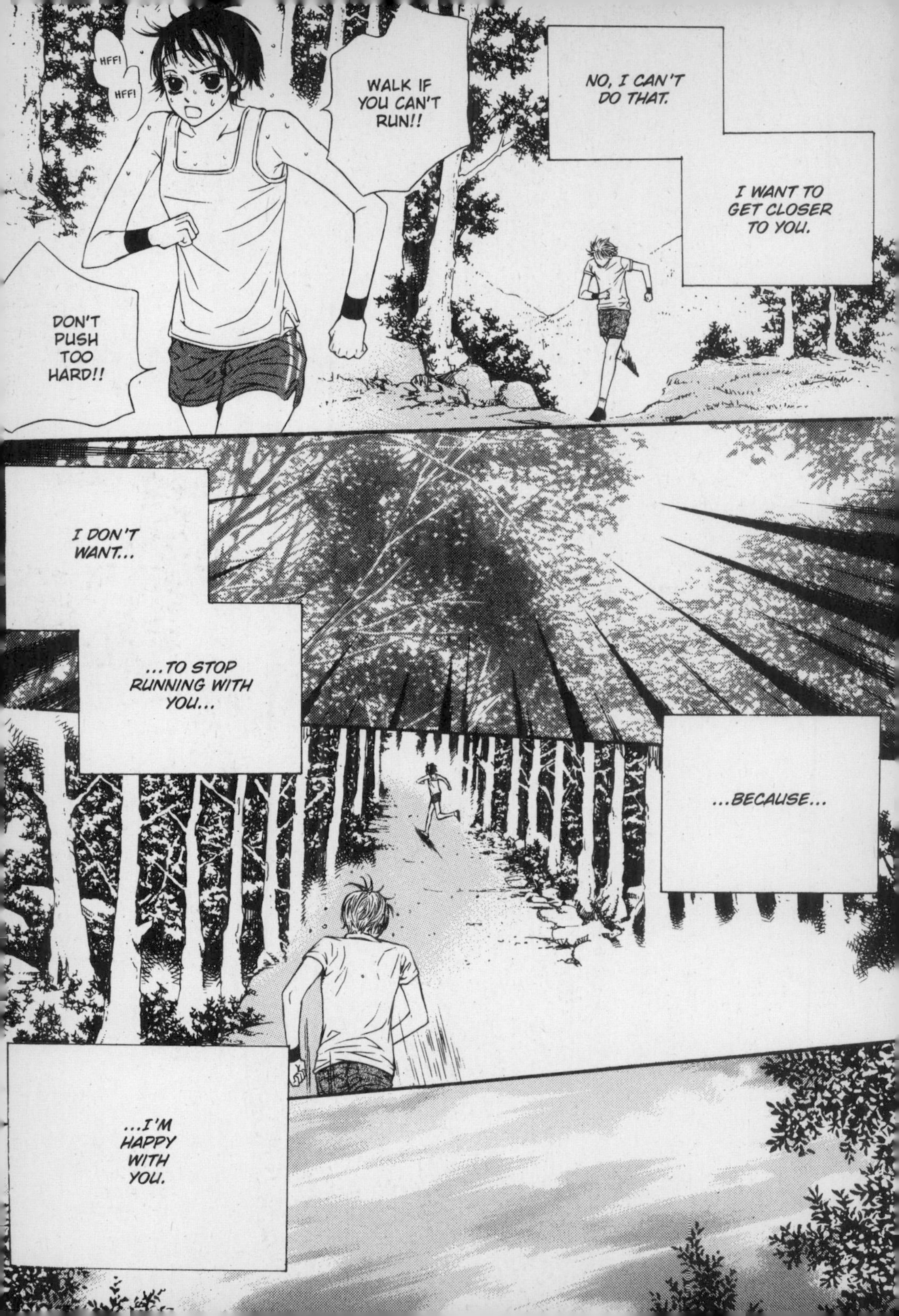
HFF!
HFF!
WALK IF YOU CAN'T RUN!!
DON'T PUSH TOO HARD!!
NO, I CAN'T DO THAT.
I WANT TO GET CLOSER TO YOU.
I DON'T WANT...
...TO STOP RUNNING WITH YOU...
...BECAUSE...
...I'M HAPPY WITH YOU.

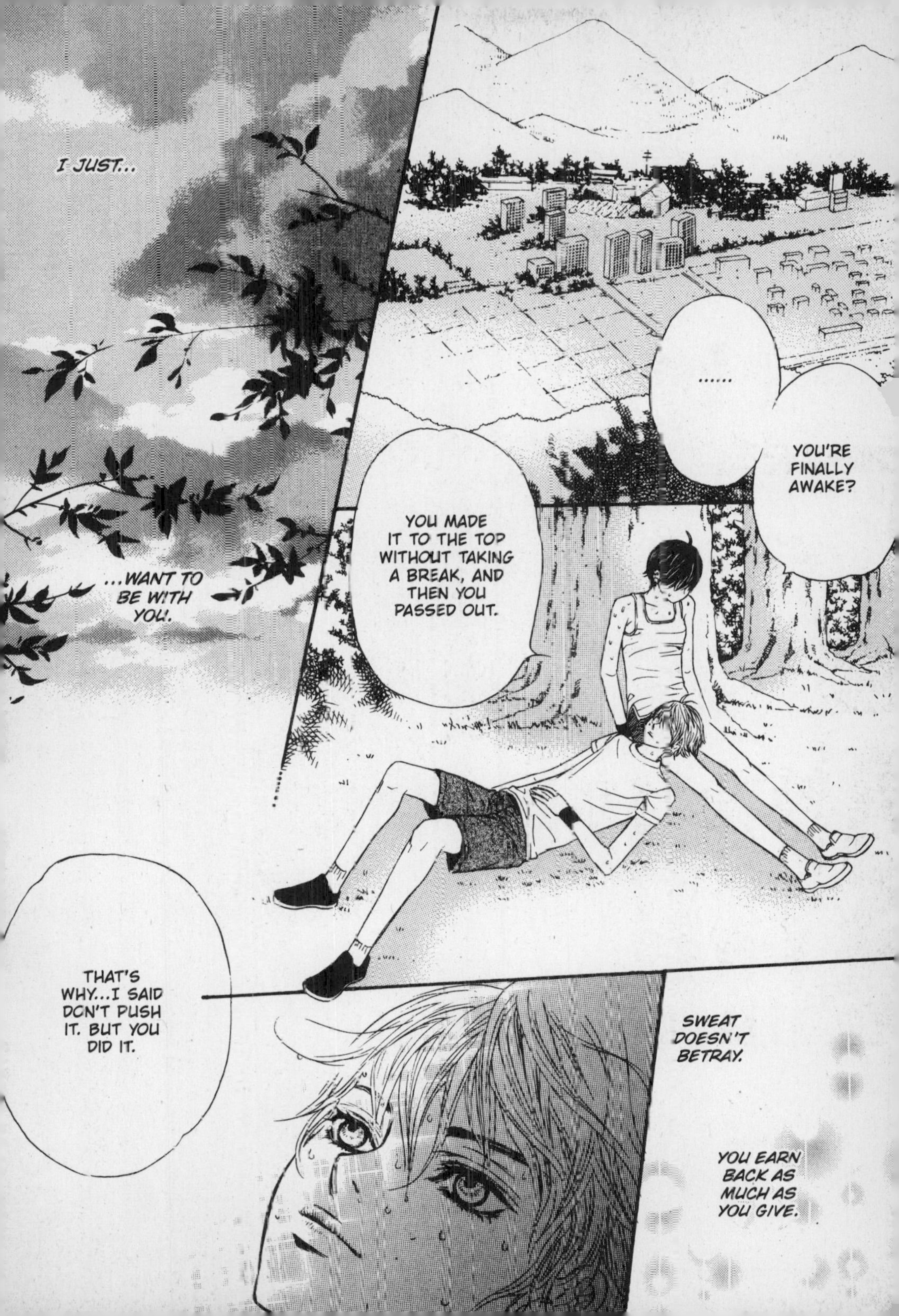
I JUST...
...WANT TO BE WITH YOU.
......
YOU'RE FINALLY AWAKE?
YOU MADE IT TO THE TOP WITHOUT TAKING A BREAK, AND THEN YOU PASSED OUT.
THAT'S WHY...I SAID DON'T PUSH IT. BUT YOU DID IT.
SWEAT DOESN'T BETRAY.
YOU EARN BACK AS MUCH AS YOU GIVE.

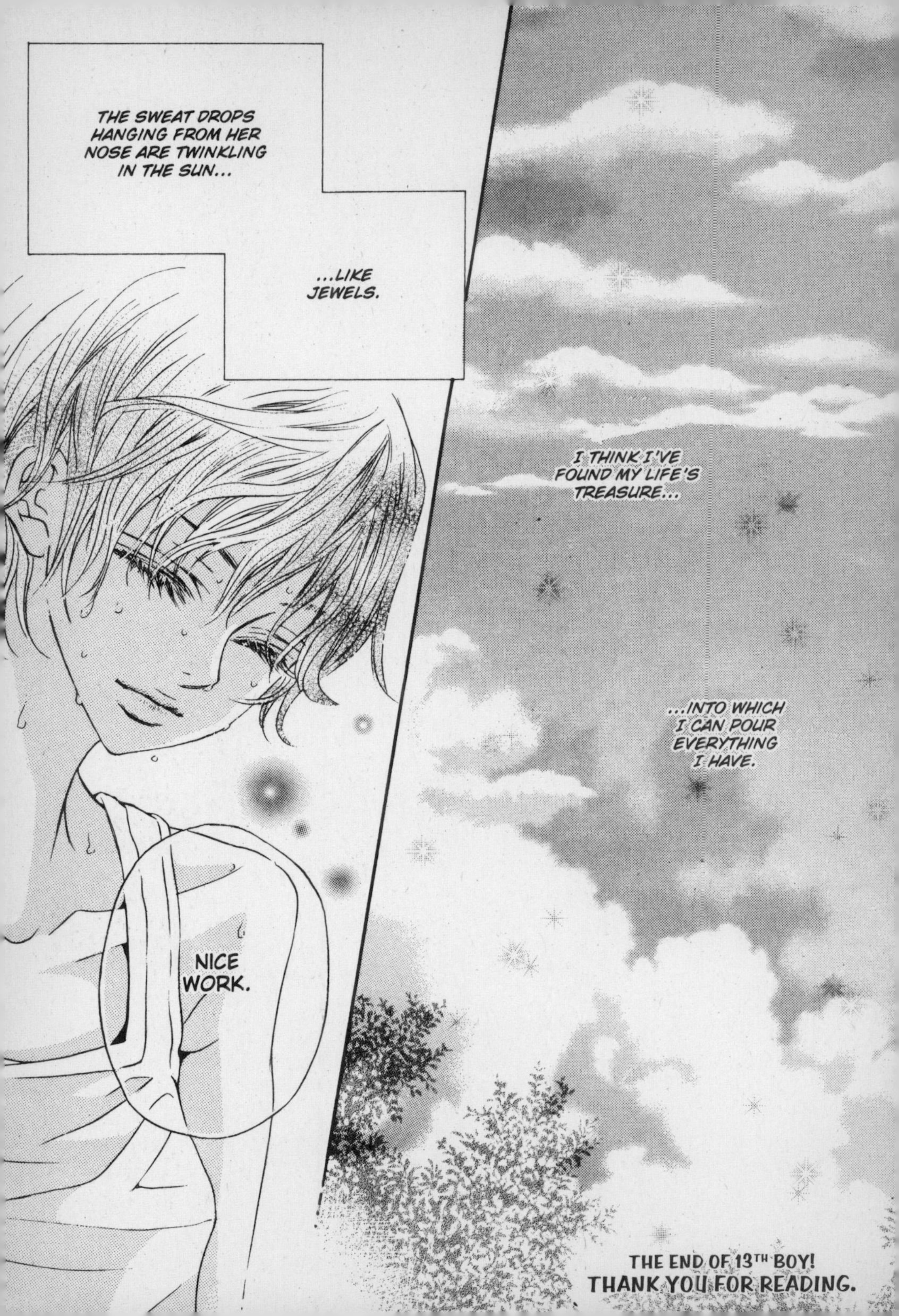
THE SWEAT DROPS HANGING FROM HER NOSE ARE TWINKLING IN THE SUN...
...LIKE JEWELS.
NICE WORK.
I THINK I'VE FOUND MY LIFE'S TREASURE...
...INTO WHICH I CAN POUR EVERYTHING I HAVE.
THE END OF 13TH BOY!
THANK YOU FOR READING.

13th Boy

Page 167
Tae-Jung-Tae-Sae-Moon-Dance! H-He-Li-Be-Baby!:
A mnemonic device in the form of a song commonly
used by students to memorize the names of the kings
from the Joseon Dynasty period of Korean history.

ENDING TALK

13TH BOY, WHICH SEEMED A LITTLE LIKE A FANTASY SOMETIMES, IS FINALLY FINISHED. =THUD= I WAS WORRIED THAT I'D NEVER MAKE IT THROUGH. BUT SOMEHOW IT'S DONE. ^ㅅ^

ALL THE PEOPLE WHO HELPED ME WITH THIS LAME COMIC ARE FLASHING THROUGH MY MIND. I ESPECIALLY WANT TO THANK MISS BABYVOX FOR HELPING ME FOR THE LAST EIGHT YEARS. ^ㅅ^ AND MANY THANKS TO MY EDITOR MISS SUNG-HEE TOO~~!

ALL OF YOU WHO READ THIS COMIC TO THE END WILL BE BLESSED~! ^ㅂ^

THE LESSON OF 13TH BOY IS "LET'S GROW CACTUS." PLEASE DO. (FOR THE RECORD, I HAVE THIRTEEN OF THEM.)

—JULY 2009,
SANG-EUN LEE

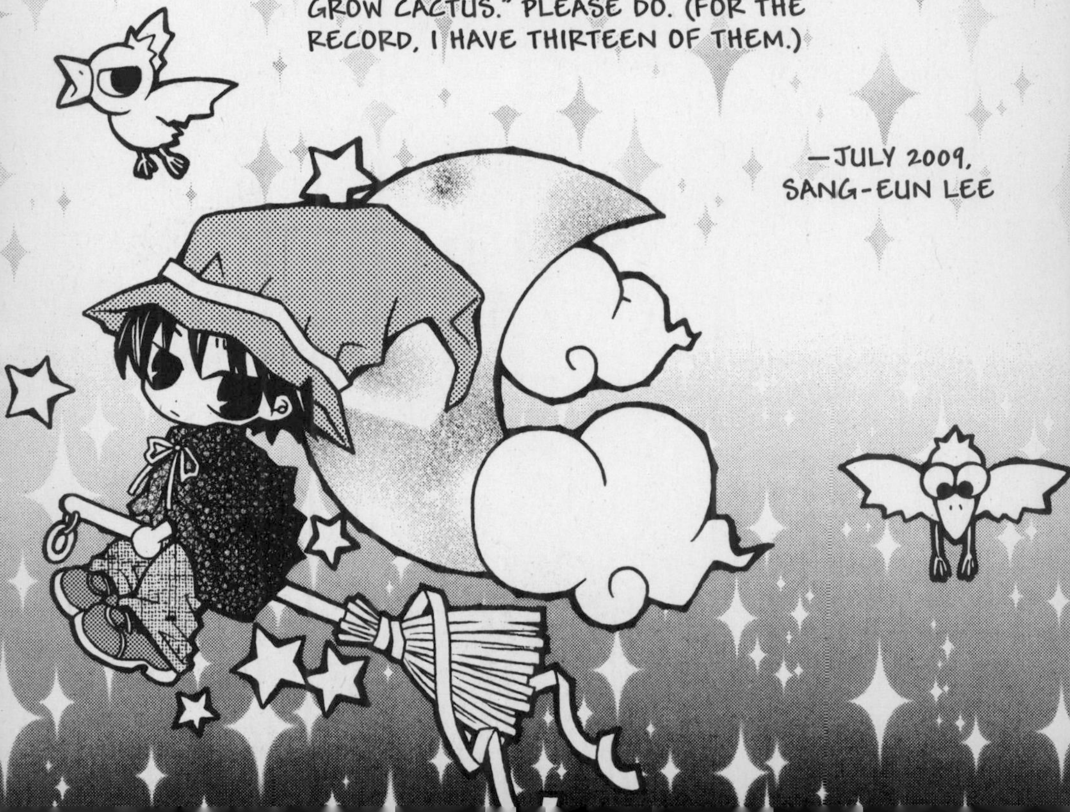

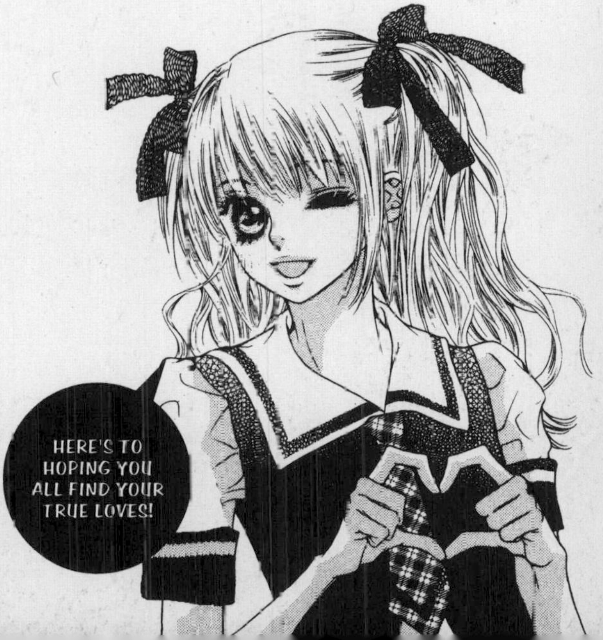
HERE'S TO HOPING YOU ALL FIND YOUR TRUE LOVES!

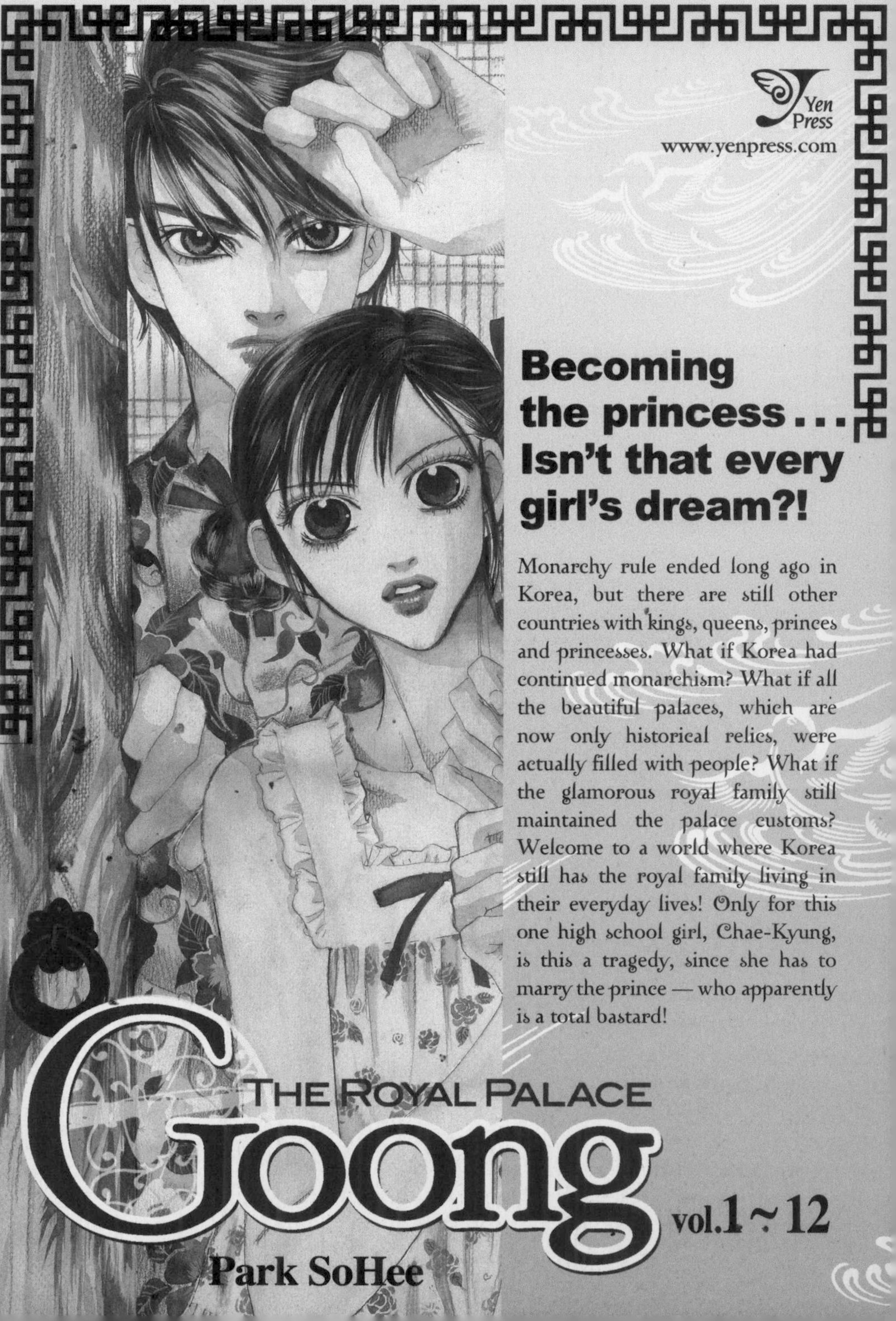
THE ROYAL PALACE
Goong
Park SoHee

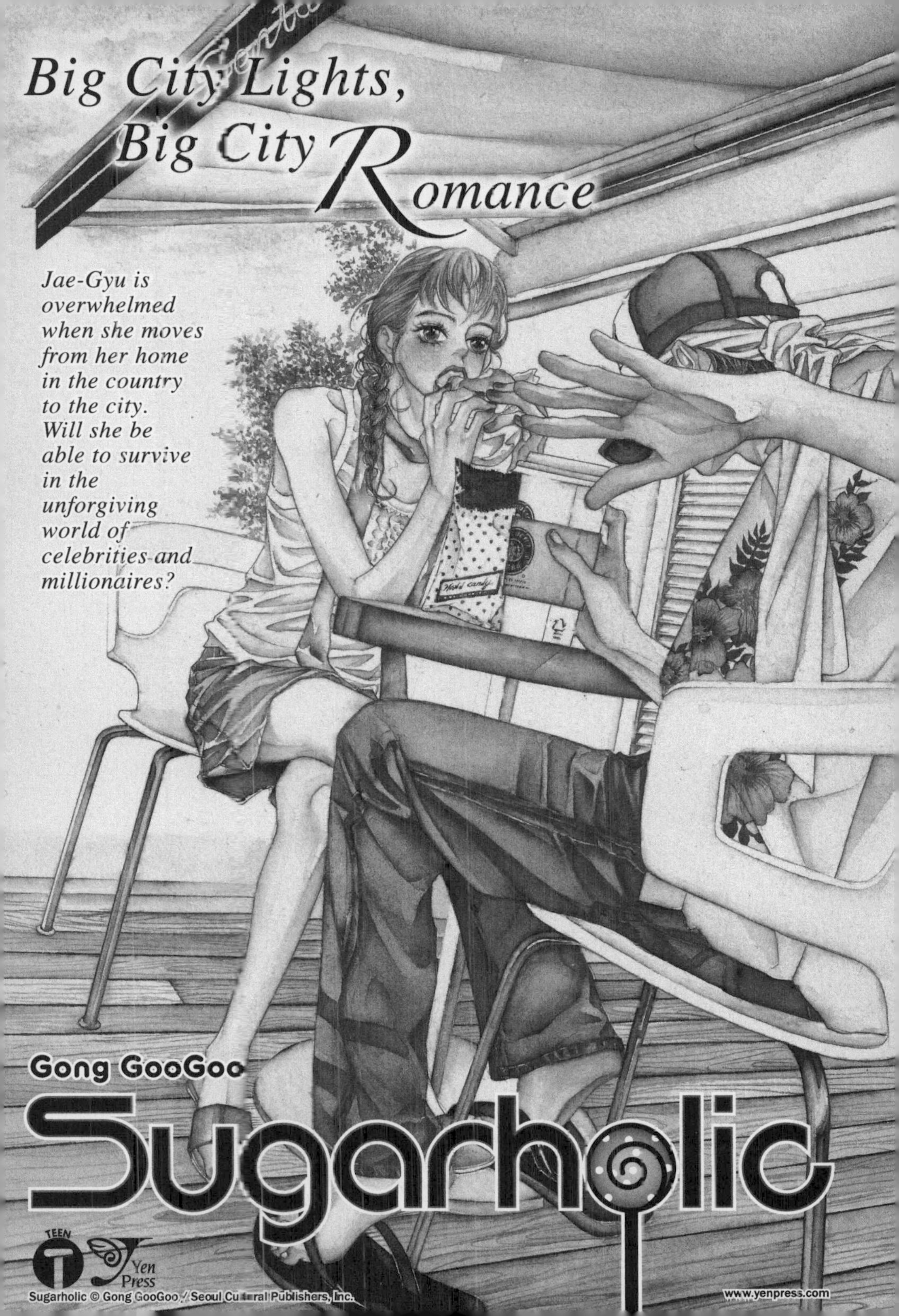
Big City Lights,
Big City Romance
Jae-Gyu is overwhelmed when she moves from her home in the country to the city. Will she be able to survive in the unforgiving world of celebrities and millionaires?
Gong GooGoo
Sugarholic
TEEN
Yen Press
Sugarholic © Gong GooGoo / Seoul Cultural Publishers, Inc.
www.yenpress.com

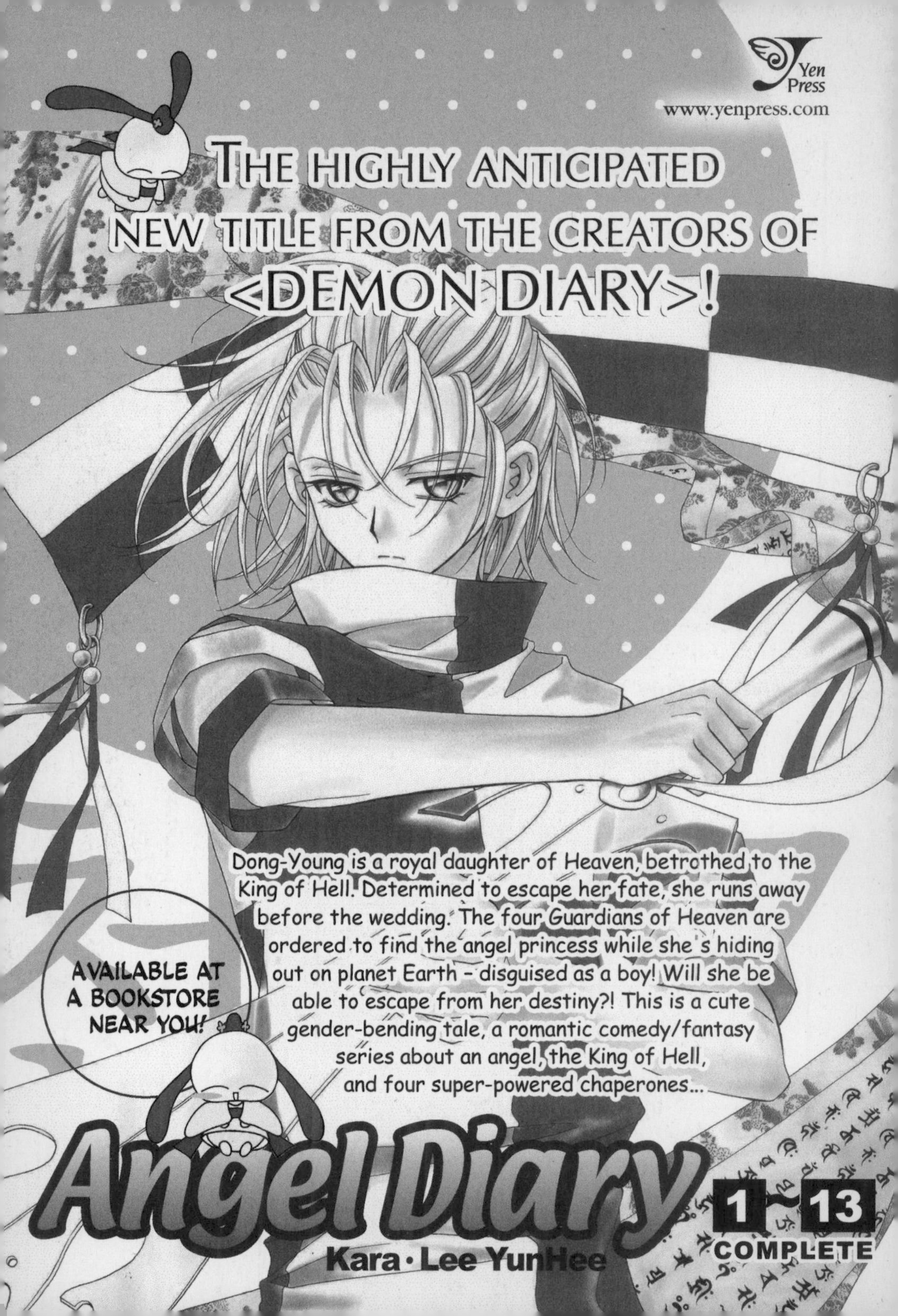
Yen Press
www.yenpress.com
THE HIGHLY ANTICIPATED
NEW TITLE FROM THE CREATORS OF
<DEMON DIARY>!
Dong-Young is a royal daughter of Heaven, betrothed to the King of Hell. Determined to escape her fate, she runs away before the wedding. The four Guardians of Heaven are ordered to find the angel princess while she's hiding out on planet Earth – disguised as a boy! Will she be able to escape from her destiny?! This is a cute gender-bending tale, a romantic comedy/fantasy series about an angel, the King of Hell, and four super-powered chaperones...
AVAILABLE AT A BOOKSTORE NEAR YOU!
Angel Diary
1~13
COMPLETE
Kara · Lee YunHee

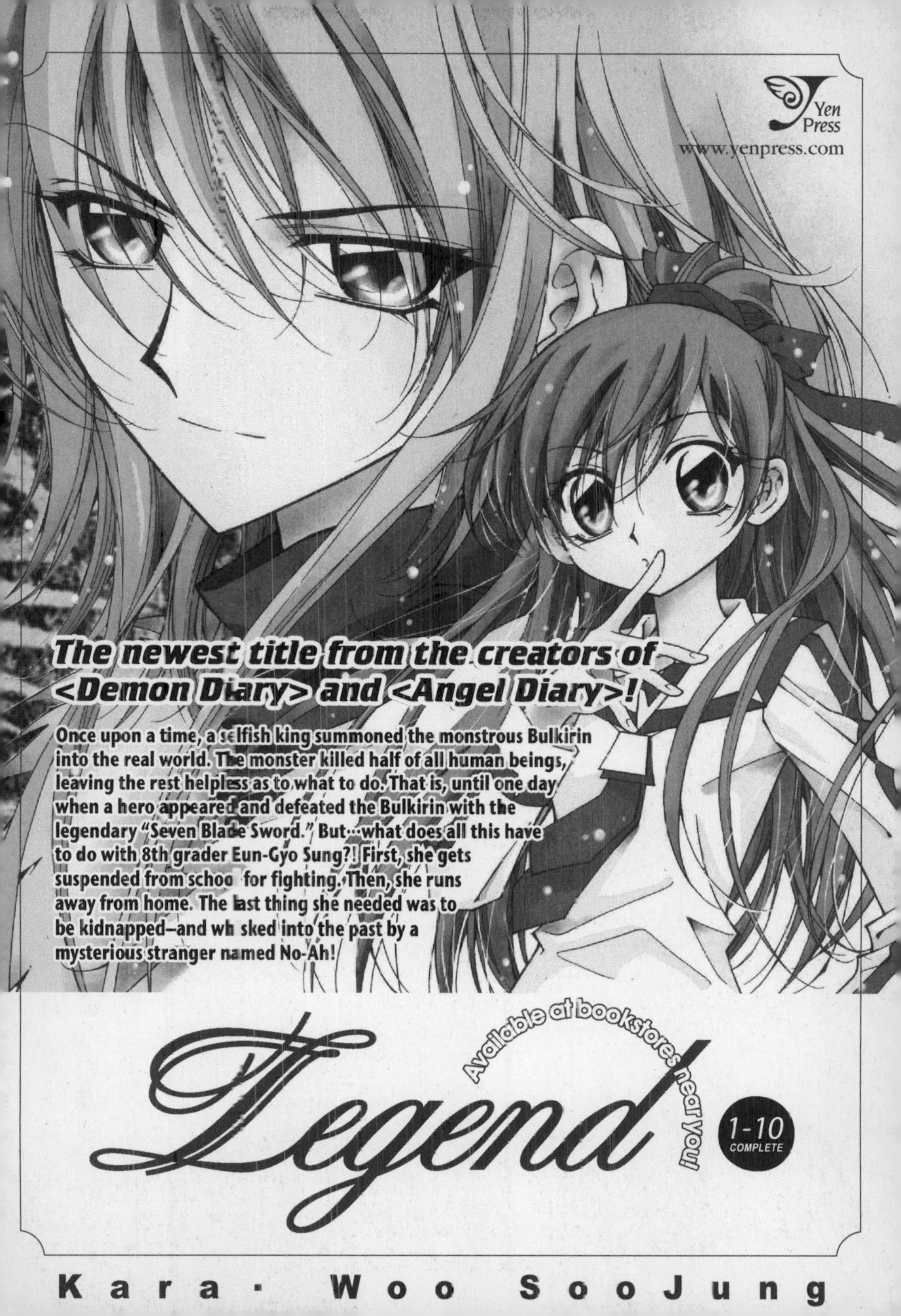
Yen Press
www.yenpress.com
The newest title from the creators of
<Demon Diary> and <Angel Diary>!
Once upon a time, a selfish king summoned the monstrous Bulkirin into the real world. The monster killed half of all human beings, leaving the rest helpless as to what to do. That is, until one day when a hero appeared and defeated the Bulkirin with the legendary "Seven Blade Sword." But…what does all this have to do with 8th grader Eun-Gyo Sung?! First, she gets suspended from school for fighting. Then, she runs away from home. The last thing she needed was to be kidnapped–and whisked into the past by a mysterious stranger named No-Ah!
Legend
Available at bookstores near you!
1-10
COMPLETE
Kara · Woo SooJung

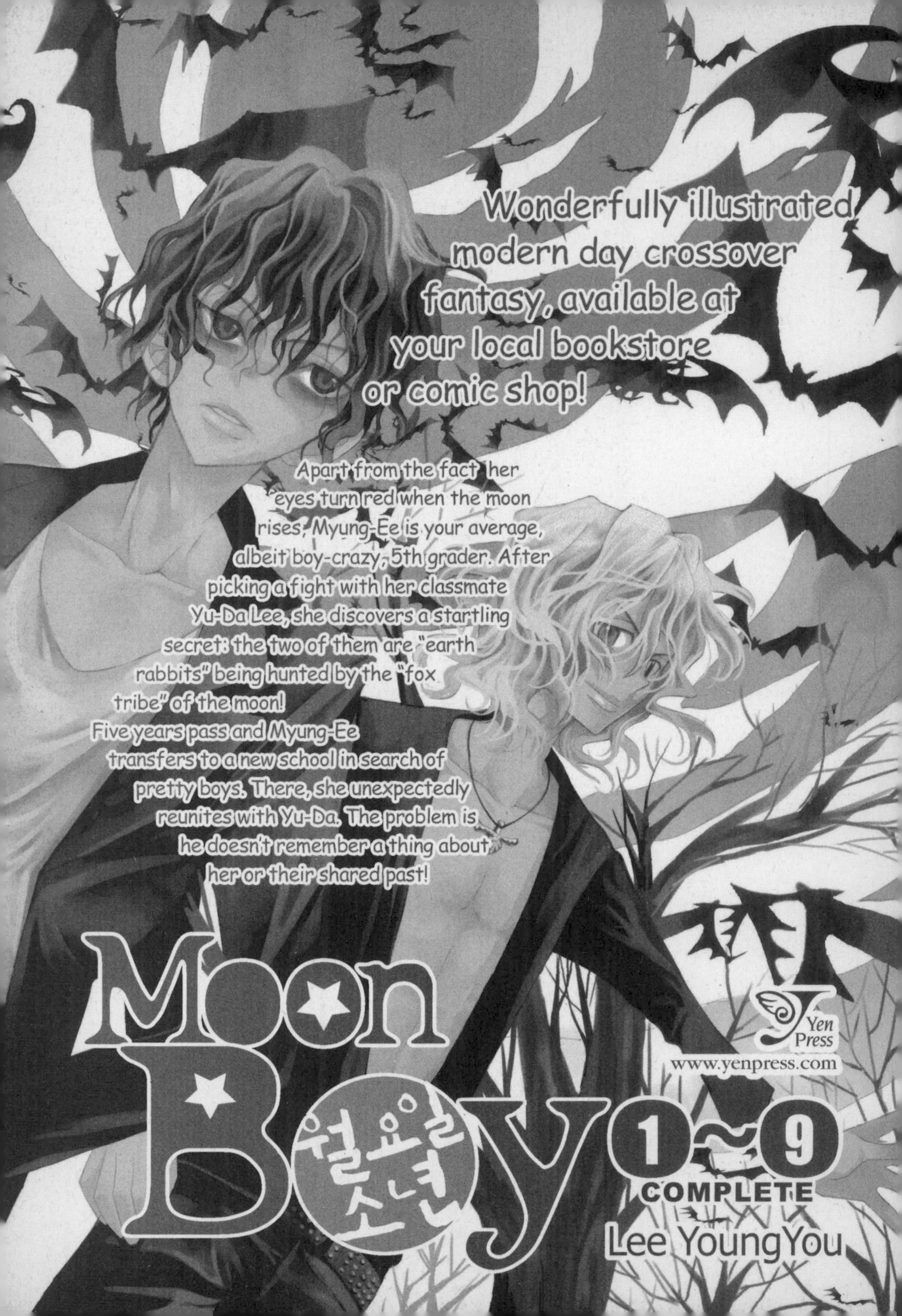
Wonderfully illustrated modern day crossover fantasy, available at your local bookstore or comic shop!
Apart from the fact her eyes turn red when the moon rises, Myung-Ee is your average, albeit boy-crazy, 5th grader. After picking a fight with her classmate Yu-Da Lee, she discovers a startling secret: the two of them are "earth rabbits" being hunted by the "fox tribe" of the moon! Five years pass and Myung-Ee transfers to a new school in search of pretty boys. There, she unexpectedly reunites with Yu-Da. The problem is he doesn't remember a thing about her or their shared past!
Moon Boy
월요일 소년
1~9
COMPLETE
Lee YoungYou
Yen Press
www.yenpress.com

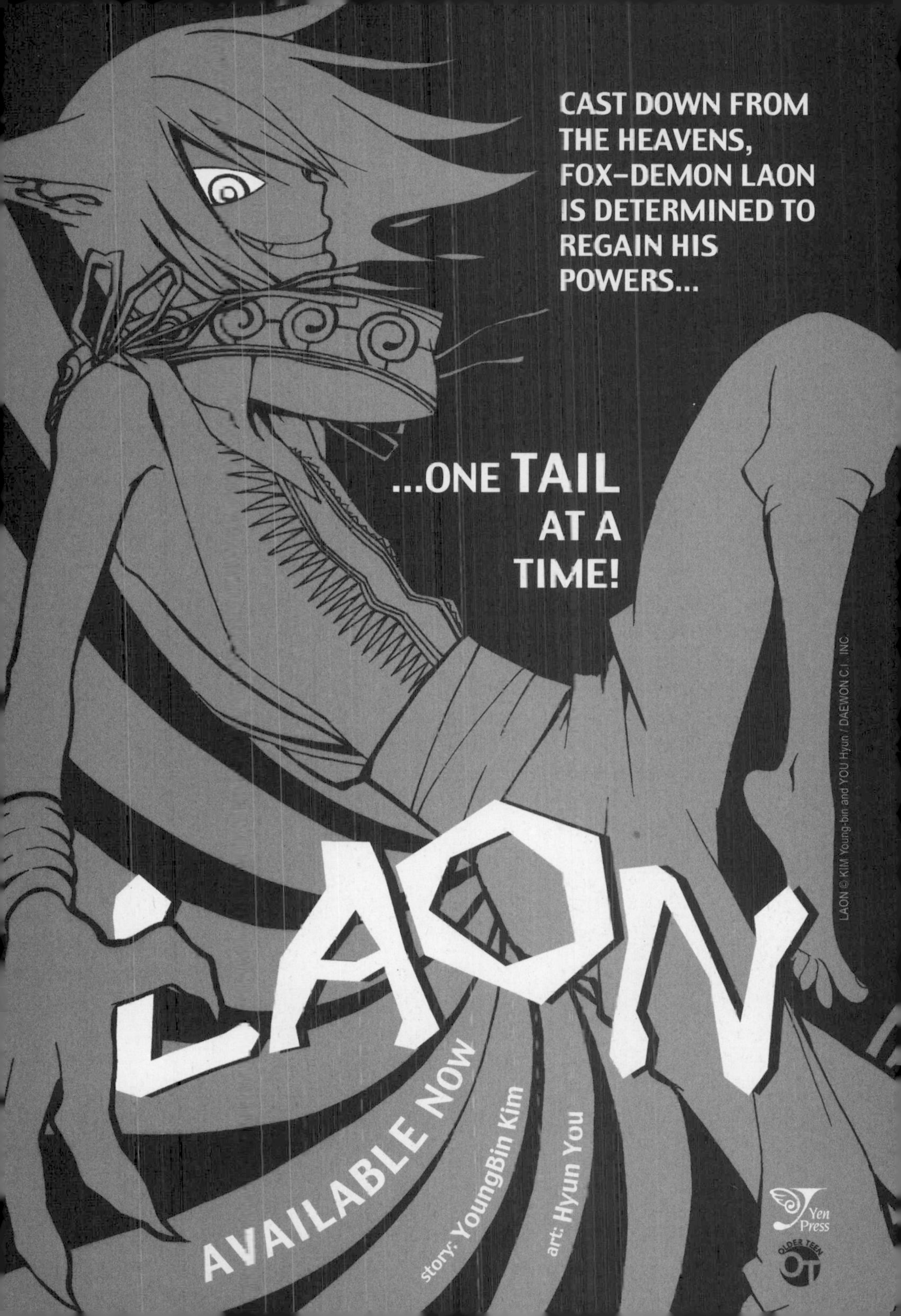
CAST DOWN FROM THE HEAVENS, FOX-DEMON LAON IS DETERMINED TO REGAIN HIS POWERS...
...ONE TAIL AT A TIME!
LAON
AVAILABLE NOW
story: YoungBin Kim
art: Hyun You
LAON © KIM Young-bin and YOU Hyun / DAEWON C.I. INC.
Yen Press
OLDER TEEN
OT

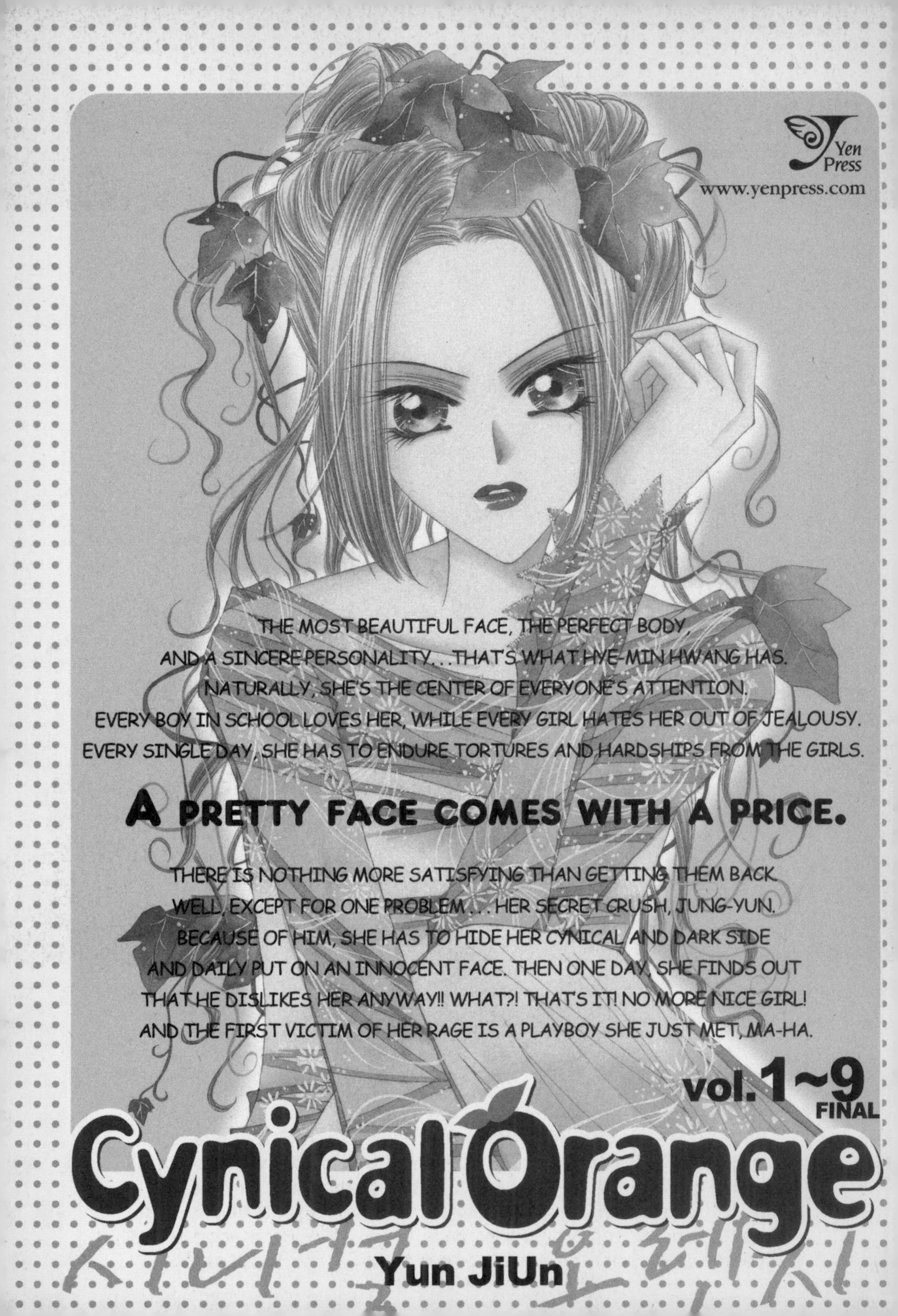
Yen Press
www.yenpress.com
THE MOST BEAUTIFUL FACE, THE PERFECT BODY,
AND A SINCERE PERSONALITY. . .THAT'S WHAT HYE-MIN HWANG HAS.
NATURALLY, SHE'S THE CENTER OF EVERYONE'S ATTENTION.
EVERY BOY IN SCHOOL LOVES HER, WHILE EVERY GIRL HATES HER OUT OF JEALOUSY.
EVERY SINGLE DAY, SHE HAS TO ENDURE TORTURES AND HARDSHIPS FROM THE GIRLS.
A PRETTY FACE COMES WITH A PRICE.
THERE IS NOTHING MORE SATISFYING THAN GETTING THEM BACK.
WELL, EXCEPT FOR ONE PROBLEM . . . HER SECRET CRUSH, JUNG-YUN.
BECAUSE OF HIM, SHE HAS TO HIDE HER CYNICAL AND DARK SIDE
AND DAILY PUT ON AN INNOCENT FACE. THEN ONE DAY, SHE FINDS OUT
THAT HE DISLIKES HER ANYWAY!! WHAT?! THAT'S IT! NO MORE NICE GIRL!
AND THE FIRST VICTIM OF HER RAGE IS A PLAYBOY SHE JUST MET, MA-HA.
vol.1~9
FINAL
Cynical Orange
Yun JiUn

The Antique Gift Shop

1~10
COMPLETE

Lee Eun

Available at bookstores near you!

Yen Press
www.yenpress.com

CAN YOU FEEL THE SOULS OF THE ANTIQUES? DO YOU BELIEVE?

Did you know that an antique possesses a soul of its own?
The Antique Gift Shop specializes in such items that charm and captivate the buyers they are destined to belong to. Guided by a mysterious and charismatic shopkeeper, the enchanted relics lead their new owners on a journey into an alternate cosmic universe to their true destinies.
Eerily bittersweet and dolefully melancholy, The Antique Gift Shop opens up a portal to a world where torn lovers unite, broken friendships are mended, and regrets are resolved. Can you feel the power of the antiques?

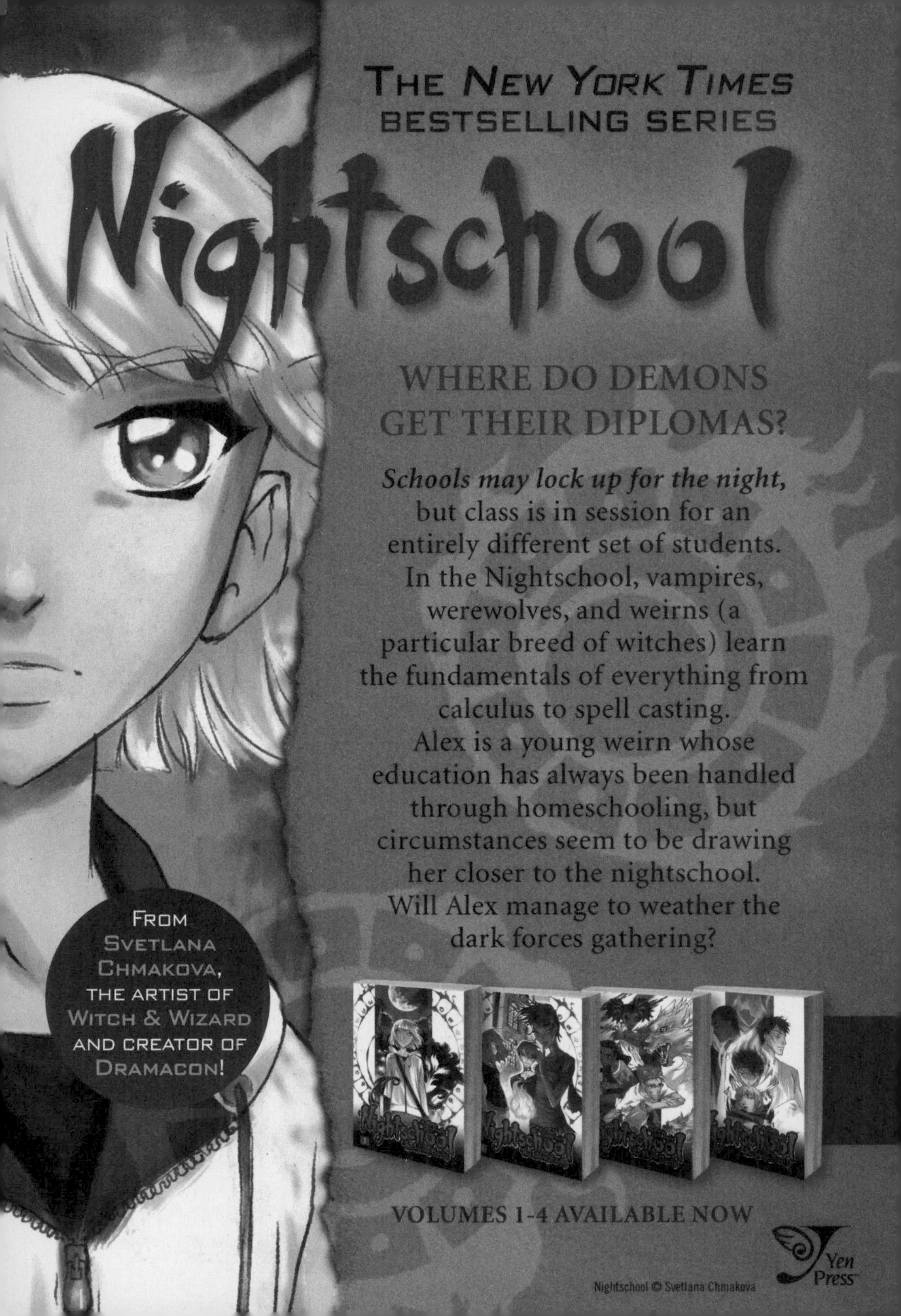

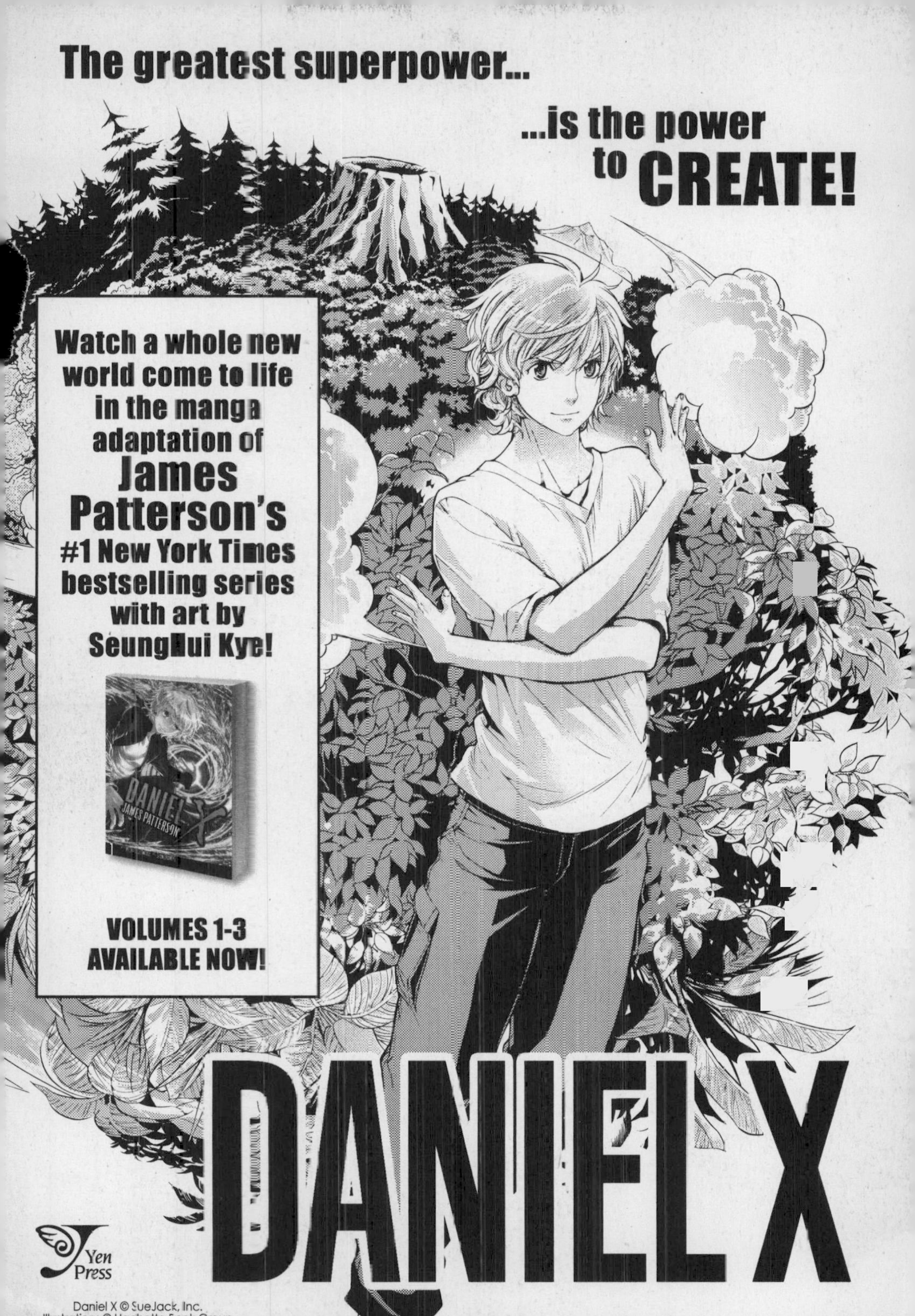
The greatest superpower...
...is the power to CREATE!
Watch a whole new world come to life in the manga adaptation of James Patterson's #1 New York Times bestselling series with art by SeungHui Kye!
DANIEL X
JAMES PATTERSON
VOLUMES 1-3 AVAILABLE NOW!
DANIEL X
Yen Press

13th BOY ⑫

SANGEUN LEE

Translation: JiEun Park
English Adaptation: Natalie Baan

Lettering: Terri Delgado

13th Boy, Vol. 12 © 2009 SangEun Lee. All rights reserved. First published in Korea in 2009 by Haksan Publishing Co., Ltd. English translation rights in U.S.A., Canada, UK, and Republic of Ireland arranged with Haksan Publishing Co., Ltd.

English translation © 2012 Hachette Book Group, Inc.

Yen Press
Hachette Book Group
237 Park Avenue, New York, NY 10017

www.HachetteBookGroup.com
www.YenPress.com

Yen Press is an imprint of Hachette Book Group, Inc.
The Yen Press name and logo are trademarks of Hachette Book Group, Inc.

First Yen Press Edition: July 2012

ISBN: 978-0-316-19083-1

10 9 8 7 6 5 4 3 2 1

BVG

Printed in the United States of America